Trail of Shadows

Trail of Shadows

*The Unsolved Murders
of Prohibition Agents
Dale Kearney and Ray Sutton*

Chuck Hornung *and*
B. Lee Charlton

McFarland & Company, Inc., Publishers
Jefferson, North Carolina

ALSO OF INTEREST
BY CHUCK HORNUNG
AND FROM MCFARLAND

*Wyatt Earp's Cow-boy Campaign: The Bloody Restoration
of Law and Order Along the Mexican Border, 1882* (2016)

Cipriano Baca, Frontier Lawman of New Mexico (2013)

*Fullerton's Rangers: A History of the New Mexico
Territorial Mounted Police* (2005; softcover 2011)

Some material in *Trail of Shadows* has been
previously published by Chuck Hornung or delivered by him as part
of his history conference papers, copyright 1971, 1991, and 2005.
Chuck Hornung has granted permission for this material to be
included in this work. No other use of this copyrighted material
is granted or implied by its inclusion in this book.

LIBRARY OF CONGRESS CATALOGUING-IN-PUBLICATION DATA

Names: Hornung, Chuck, 1943– author. | Charlton, B. Lee, 1934– author.
Title: Trail of shadows : the unsolved murders of prohibition agents
Dale Kearney and Ray Sutton / Chuck Hornung and B. Lee Charlton.
Description: Jefferson, North Carolina : McFarland & Company, Inc.,
2019 | Includes bibliographical references and index.
Identifiers: LCCN 2019017913 | ISBN 9781476677569
(paperback : acid free paper) ∞
Subjects: LCSH: Kearney, Dale, 1900–1930. | Sutton, Ray, 1873–1930. |
United States. Alcohol, Tobacco, and Firearms Division—Officials
and employees—Death. | Murder—Investigation—United States. |
United States—History—1919–1933. | Prohibition—United States.
Classification: LCC HV8144.B87 H67 2019 | DDC 364.152/30973—dc23
LC record available at https://lccn.loc.gov/2019017913

BRITISH LIBRARY CATALOGUING DATA ARE AVAILABLE

**ISBN (print) 978-1-4766-7756-9
ISBN (ebook) 978-1-4766-3588-0**

© 2019 Chuck Hornung and B. Lee Charlton. All rights reserved

*No part of this book may be reproduced or transmitted in any form
or by any means, electronic or mechanical, including photocopying
or recording, or by any information storage and retrieval system,
without permission in writing from the publisher.*

The front cover image is of storm clouds gathering over the northern
New Mexico mountains; also shown is a Prohibition agent's badge
(courtesy of the Bureau of Alcohol, Tobacco, Firearms and Explosives)

Printed in the United States of America

*McFarland & Company, Inc., Publishers
Box 611, Jefferson, North Carolina 28640
www.mcfarlandpub.com*

To the memory of those who have come before and persevered in their efforts to serve and protect while fighting against the crime and corruption confronting them. They were hired for a job and a vast majority performed in the highest tradition while blazing a trail for others to follow in the continuing search for truth and justice under the law. And to those many who chose to cross the line to the criminal side while in the service of their country, they missed the greatest rewards ever to be earned—honor, self-respect, and the law-abiding public's gratitude for a seemingly thankless job.

"My dream is of a place and time where America will once again be seen as the last best hope on earth."—Abraham Lincoln

Table of Contents

Acknowledgments ix
Preface 1
Introduction 2

Part I. The Gathering Storm

1. The Murders of Dale F. Kearney and Ray Sutton — 5
2. Prohibition: The Noble Experiment — 14
3. "Revenooers": America's New Enforcers with Limitations — 30
4. The Lawless Years — 36
5. Dale F. Kearney: Prohibition Agent, Badge 1422 — 42
6. Ray Sutton: Prohibition Agent, Badge 2400 — 50

Part II. Booze, Bootleggers, Blood and Seeking Justice

7. John F. Vivian, Ralph L. Carr and the Kearney Investigation Task Force — 62
8. The Buccaneers — 73
9. Family, Leads and Plans — 99
10. You Shall Know the Truth … — 107
11. The Forged Check—A Funeral—An Arrest — 121
12. The Jack Dionisio Matter — 144
13. Valentines—Gangster War—New Plans — 156
14. Star Power Visitors—Cornucopia—Vivian's Dismissal — 163

Part III. The Trail Markers Grow Dim

15. Reassignments	178
16. Conspiracy of Silence	188
17. The Final Trail Markers	200
Conclusion	207
Chapter Notes	213
Bibliography	222
Index	229

Acknowledgments

> Silent gratitude isn't much use to anyone.—Gladys Bertha Stern, novelist, critic

Of the many who have helped in the formation, editing, and creation of this book, first, I wish to thank my wife and family for quietly supporting my "play time" at the computer and visits to the libraries over the past several years. My appreciation extends to "D. Ray" Blakeley, former research director of the Union County Historical Society at Clayton, New Mexico, along with his associates for the giving of their time and efforts. A special thank you goes to Raymond Ellsworth Sutton (Ray Sutton's grandson) and family, who rediscovered the long-stored family treasures of information they willingly shared. Others include: the late Mike J. Pappas, "Flea In The Ear" columnist for *The Raton Range*, business owner, and author; William H. Darden, retired Deputy District Attorney, Colfax County, New Mexico; the staff at the New Mexico State Archives at Santa Fe (especially Al Regensberg, retired archivist) for their extended efforts; Larry B. Lambert, advisor, friend, and author of things that go bump in the night; and lastly, W. Peyton George and Robert S. Cavanaugh, The New Mexico Research Scholars at Santa Fe, New Mexico, for their support and friendship through the years.

—B. Lee Charlton

When I was a young man, I had the honor to have had Fred Lambert as a friend and mentor. At the time, Lambert was the last living ranger who had served with the New Mexico Territorial Mounted Police, and from him I heard many stories about these legendary frontier lawmen. During our many long discussions, while sitting around the kitchen table of his small home in Cimarron, New Mexico, he encouraged my desire to research the public and private lives of these territorial police and to record their stories for future generations. I owe a great debt to this man.

No person who undertakes to write a historical biography does so alone. I am grateful to many individuals, living and dead, from numerous libraries, historical societies, and government archives. I must acknowledge the late Katherine McMahan, Howard Bryan, and William A. Kelleher. These three individuals are greatly missed and fondly remembered for their gracious assistance in helping a young man develop his love for the history of the magnificent Land of Enchantment. Nancy Brown-Martinez,

Christopher Geherin and Jon Wheeler at the Center for Southwest Research and Special Collections at the University of New Mexico; Betty Lloyd at the Arthur H. Johnson Library at Raton; the staff at the county clerk's office in Clayton and Raton; J. Richard Salazar and the research staff at the New Mexico State Records and Archives in Santa Fe; and Dr. Myra Ellen Jenkins and Robert J. Torrez, who have both served as New Mexico's state historian, were very helpful. Also helpful have been friends and members of the Historical Society of New Mexico and the Wild West History Association. Thank you!

Among the many individuals who provided information shared in this account are Mrs. Nancy Robinson, Victor Grant, Mrs. Margaret Brooks Ward, Mrs. Virginia Stringfellow, Mrs. Mary Lail, John E. Southwell, Jim Money, C. E. Black, Sgt. Ron Taylor NMSP Ret., Joe Campanella, Joe Russo, George Stump, Lois Fornoff, Charles DiLisio, Joe Marchiondo. I also wish to thank former sheriffs J. Riley Hughes, J. B. McNeil and Ray Marty. A special thank you to editor Ed Murray and owner/publisher Gene Wisner of the *Raton Daily Range*, who first published my account of the death of Ray Sutton. James Perry Caldwell stands alone among first-generation participants in the Ray Sutton story; I am still amazed that he spoke with me.

The Good Lord gave me a loving wife and two sons who have supported me over the decades, as I searched government archives and newspaper files, conducted endless hours of interviews, and covered hundreds of miles of New Mexico backcountry seeking the truth about Ray Sutton's disappearance. Thank you to Pat Fuss—who has always welcomed us into her home—and her husband Ron who hosted the initial face-to-face between co-author Lee Charlton and myself at their home and, since that meeting, has provided many gentle and not-so-gentle comments about finishing the research and writing the book.

Yael, my little feline buddy, has kept me company while I, along with my co-author a thousand miles away, wrote and rewrote numerous manuscript drafts and spent hours on long-distance telephone calls. Yael has given her final approval to each page.

—Chuck Hornung

Preface

> Only by frankness concerning the truth that hurts can we secure a sustained respect for the truth that helps.—Glean Frank, president, University of Wisconsin, 1927

In 1841, Ralph Waldo Emerson wrote in his *Essay on Compensation* that "There is no such thing as concealment." The authors accept that philosophy, so via open records requests of the National Archives, we discovered a trove of aging, warehoused and long-forgotten documents related to the Kearney-Sutton case. These files contained incident reports, investigative memoranda, suspect interview notes, the dead agents' daily activity logs and their personnel files. These documents formed the first research leg used by the authors to reconstruct the assassination of Prohibition Agent Dale Kearney and the disappearance/murder of Prohibition Agent Ray Sutton. Building upon this massive federal archive base are the few remaining documents generated by state and local law enforcement officers; these are a second leg. The third leg of the research platform is the authors' data mining of private and public collections of contemporary newspaper files. The final leg that supports the first three legs are the interviews the authors conducted with surviving first- and second-generation principals and individuals associated with the events discussed in this treatise. Any misspellings of individual names appearing in quoted materials remain as presented in the source document.

> Once a thing is truly known, it can never be unknown.
> The difficulty lies in proving it is true.

Introduction

"Listen to the whispers and you won't have to hear the screams."
—Cherokee Indian proverb

This book is based on historic facts. Between July 1 and December 31, 1930, the United States Department of Justice honored the memory of five federal prohibition agents who died in the line of duty. Two of these five agents had been assigned to Region 10, an area encompassing the states of Utah, Wyoming, Colorado, Arizona and New Mexico. A small band of federal agents, local law enforcement officers, and prosecutors spent the waning years of National Prohibition seeking the killers; they experienced mixed results. The dark shadows of history soon embraced these events.

Our journey in writing this book began on different pathways during separate periods in our professional careers. We both became acquainted with Federal Prohibition Agent Zaccheus Raymond "Ray" Sutton for the first time in the 1960s. Decades after his disappearance, we learned about him through others who spoke for him in many formats: dusty crime reports; aged contemporary newspaper files; family bibliographies and photographs; and personal interviews with Sutton's friends, relatives and adversaries. We discovered details about Ray Sutton's public and private life and the efforts to kill him. And then, in 1968, a unique interview materialized with the last surviving murder suspect. This man had been Sutton's former lodge brother, alleged friend, and ultimate betrayer who "openly" admitted four decades later how he and others had conspired to kill Sutton and bury his remains.

Prohibition Agent Dale F. Kearney died in a hail of buckshot on a dark street in Aguilar, Colorado, a mere six weeks prior to Ray Sutton's disappearance. We surmised that both murders had certain interrelationships which could lead to the identities of suspects involved in both cases. We also learned of the dedicated perseverance of friends, families, and colleagues who doggedly sought to locate and prosecute the killers of both men.

Almost nine decades have passed since Prohibition Agents Kearney and Sutton reached the close of their final tour of duty. Officially, both investigations remain local "cold cases" in the Colorado and New Mexico counties in which they occurred. All the protagonists are now deceased as are most of the secondary figures in each case.

In 2013, the authors were drawn together by the mysterious web of secrecy surrounding the Kearney and Sutton murder cases. Our collaboration opened a new dialog that began through a reexamination of all known sources. This led us to pursue release of formerly classified government documents and to conduct an in-depth hunt for data held in private collections. These searches netted new information and a new blueprint emerged.

In this work we present a narrative of our investigative journey. We, as others before us, found answers and also discovered too many unanswered questions. The authors are the first investigative historians to determine how the Kearney and Sutton cases are interrelated. Secondly, we answer the question of why no one was ever charged or prosecuted for either of their deaths when the evidence we discovered clearly points directly to certain individuals. Join us as we travel down the Trail of Shadows and bring some light to the darkness.

Part I

The Gathering Storm

It may be that the trail of blood will seem to lie too thickly over the pages that I write. If I had to invent a tale I would fain lighten the crimson stain so that it would glow no deeper than a demure pink. But half a lifetime on the frontier attunes a man's hand to the six-shooter rather than the pen, and it is lucky that I am asked only for facts, for more than facts I could not give....

And so, I marshal my characters.—Wyatt Earp, "How Wyatt Earp Routed a Gang of Arizona Outlaws," *The Examiner* (San Francisco), Sunday, August 2, 1896

1

The Murders of Dale F. Kearney and Ray Sutton

> Down these mean streets a man must go who is not himself mean, who is neither tarnished nor afraid. The detective [agent] in this kind of story must be such a man. He is the hero....—Raymond Chandler, "The Simple Art of Murder," *The Atlantic Monthly,* November 1945

Dateline: Aguilar, Las Animas County, Colorado, Sunday, July 6, 1930

Exactly where Prohibition Agent Dale F. Kearney went on the Saturday evening of July 5, 1930, is unclear. The official investigation revealed that unidentified sources saw him heading out of Trinidad on the highway toward Aguilar around 11:00 p.m. He was apparently in pursuit of a bootlegger's load car. It is believed that Kearney had obtained information from someone, still unidentified, concerning a delivery being made to the mining town and that the load car had just departed. Dale may have hurried off thinking he might be able to make a delivery bust.

Subsequent investigative data indicated that someone had tampered with his vehicle's oil line while he had been working Trinidad nightspots on foot. The loss of engine oil to his 1928 Chevrolet sedan would have caused massive damage to the engine. A slow drip while the vehicle is sitting stationary becomes a bit more problematic in comparison to an engine running full bore for an extended time. The first indicator would be a lowering of engine oil pressure and a rise in the engine's temperature, indicating an insufficient or malfunctioning engine oil cooling system. Steam would begin to emit from the radiator area. Next, depending on the amount of oil loss, odors of burnt oil being blown on the hot engine body would find their way into the vehicle's passenger area. The engine would then begin shuddering and knocking, leading to a total engine freeze-up due to excessive heat and the absence of lubrication. What to do? If you turned off the ignition there was no guarantee the engine would restart. An alternate solution would be to slow your speed and put the transmission in neutral, allowing the car to coast for a distance without acceleration, then place it back in gear, accelerate for a short distance, and then repeat the coasting technique. Kearney may have used this methodology to reach his destination. If his car engine failed on the open highway, he would have been stranded in the open and easy prey for the occupants of any vehicles which may have been following him.

It was later reported to investigators by James G. Lile, the night mechanic and watchman at the all-night garage in Aguilar, that Kearney had reached town about 11:35 p.m. by slowly urging his vehicle forward. Kearney said he needed to telephone Charley's in Trinidad to come and tow the car back home for the needed repair. Lile said he had directed Kearney to the telephone at the Village Hall, situated a few blocks away. The Hall was a general meeting place for the community and commonly known to be the usual hangout for night marshal Henry Fawcett.

The mechanic also explained to the investigating officers that he had conducted a preliminary examination of Kearney's vehicle and found a loosened oil line connection that had caused an oil leak resulting in the vehicle throwing an engine rod. The engine broke down due to "hydrolocking," a term used to describe the cause of Kearney's misfortune. If an engine hydrolocks while at speed, mechanical failure is probable. Common damage modes include bent or broken connecting rods, a fractured crank, a fractured head, a cracked block, other crankcase damage, destroyed bearings, or any combination of these.

Saturday evening in Aguilar, a town that seemed to never sleep in its entirety, always had open "cafés" for the late-night travelers and local revelers. Every one of these establishments was known to serve bootleg booze. Kearney had been here before and was very familiar with such goings-on in this heavily ethnic mining community. Once his telephone call was complete, investigators surmised he returned to the nearby Alpine Rose Café where three or four cars were parked near the front entrance. According to witnesses, on entering, Kearney took a table near the front window, one that provided a view of the street.

The diner was not large but could accommodate a sizable crowd with its dozen or more tables and several booths. Across the room, at a corner table were four persons, two women and two men. The federal officer previously had arrested one of the men for liquor violations. As investigators would later learn, after Kearney finished his meal he walked over to the two couples occupying the corner table and picked up two of their glasses. They were empty but each had the lingering odor of whiskey. Looking at the man he knew as James "Jimmy the Jew" Merino, Kearney asked him for his "shot bottle" for inspection. Merino denied any knowledge of such a bottle and since Dale had not seen any alcohol consumed, it became a standoff. The two men quietly stared at each other before Kearney turned, walked to the front counter, paid his bill, and departed the café with a nod toward Merino as he exited the premises.

A short distance down the road he encountered John Frederico, the proprietor of the Eagle Café. They talked briefly before Kearney continued on past the Arcade Hotel, where he turned the corner and headed eastward. A few minutes later, he retraced his steps and began walking back toward his disabled car.

Later, crime scene investigators would deduce that as he walked along the narrow sidewalk that paralleled a boarded fence, the headlights from a slowly moving car to his rear switched on its bright headlamps, illuminating his entire figure—a normal thing a driver would do if he saw someone walking near the roadway at night. Five rapidly fired shotgun blasts tore through his upper torso from the direction of the wooden fence that bordered the sidewalk, terminating his life. The medical examiner believed he was dead before he hit the ground. Kearney's shattered wristwatch face displayed the hour as 12:20 a.m. mountain time.[1]

Minutes later, night marshal Fawcett walked into the Alpine Rose Café, an all-night short-order place, making his nightly rounds. Jimmy Merino asked the lawman if he had seen Kearney and mentioned that the officer had been in a few minutes earlier looking for the marshal. Fawcett had helped Kearney in the past on a few raids and suspected that Kearney might need him for something he had planned. With Kearney, he could never be certain since the agent enjoyed doing most of his work alone. Marshal Fawcett asked Merino which direction the agent had taken. He pointed down the street toward the hotel and said that everyone in the shop had heard cacophonous gunfire coming from that area not too long after Kearney had departed the diner.

Fawcett immediately headed in the direction indicated. And as he reached Mike Lazeroff's Green Light Café, the proprietor, who was standing in front of his place, told the lawman there had been shooting up the street about midway in the first block of Main Street. The marshal continued down the darkened street until he found Kearney's corpse on the sidewalk, lying limp in a pool of blood. Marshal Fawcett rushed to the Village Hall and telephoned the sheriff's office in Trinidad.[2]

Elijah J. Duling, Las Animas County sheriff, and undersheriff Williams arrived in Aguilar within the hour to take charge of the crime scene. Once they confirmed the deceased was Prohibition Agent Kearney, they notified the Bureau of Prohibition regional headquarters in Denver. The federal agency began activating their chain of command.[3]

"Dale Kearney Ambushed And Killed By Unknown Gunman," was the headline of the *Trinidad Chronicle-News* on Monday morning, July 8, 1930. The article reported that a short time after being assigned to the area, Kearney had conducted "a far reaching crusade at Walsenburg [a mining town a few miles north of Aguilar]. His action resulted in the arrest of a score or more of alleged violators of the dry laws and [seizures] of hundreds of bottles of bootleg liquor. This threw a new fear into Walsenburg's underworld and may have been the act that ultimately caused his death."

In a second article, "Dale Kearney Preferred To Be Lone Wolf," the newspaper noted a conversation Kearney had with a member of Sheriff Duling's office. The officer warned the federal agent to stop making those raids at night by himself. Kearney would merely laugh and intimate that he was able to take care of himself. Following criticism of his office by the media, Sheriff Duling declared that he and his deputies had never refused to accompany the slain agent when asked, but Kearney seldom asked for aid. "He played the part of a lone wolf and often spent the greater part of the night alone in Aguilar, Walsenburg and other camps."[4]

Dateline: Raton, Colfax County, New Mexico, Thursday, August 28, 1930

Prohibition Agent Zaccheus Raymond "Ray" Sutton, considered one of the best field agents in the New Mexico region, worked from his home in Clayton, New Mexico.

On Sunday, July 6, 1930, deputy regional administrator for New Mexico Charles H. Stearns instructed Sutton to join a newly formed investigative task force in Trinidad as soon as possible. Initially, Special Investigator John Richardson from the Denver office would head the new field team. Over the next seven weeks, Sutton would play a major role in this cross-border investigation.[5]

On Wednesday, August 20, 1930, Agent Sutton began implementing his task-force-approved operation to double down on the John Campanella's bootlegging cabal operating in northeastern New Mexico. Four weeks earlier on July 22, 1930, Campanella, the self-proclaimed "Al Capone of Colfax County," had been arrested by Sutton.

Sutton's plan involved the placement of misinformation in the hands of persons within law enforcement and with various social or business contacts in and around Raton, the gateway to southern Colorado and points north. He let it be known that he was seeking information on the location of two (nonexistent) stills near Dawson. Among those he told about his quest was his sometimes-informant James Perry Caldwell, an irascible, disgraced federal prohibition agent who had operated in concert with Campanella since at least 1925. The base for "Big John" Campanella's legal and illegal business operations was the village of Cimarron, located 42 miles southwest of Raton on the banks of the Cimarron River.[6]

On Thursday, August 28 Sutton received a midmorning telephone call in his hotel room, according to Seaberg Hotel telephone switchboard personnel. After lunching with his friend Joe Gilstrip in the hotel dining room, Grace McAlpin, the hotel desk clerk, observed Sutton leave the hotel dressed in his normal business attire: boots, khaki-colored pants, white shirt, leather buckskin-colored coat, and light-colored, wide-brimmed cowboy hat. No one saw him return. Hugo Seaberg's hotel served as Sutton's headquarters/home when he was working the Raton area.[7]

Colfax County Undersheriff George R. "Boots" Fletcher saw Sutton about 20 miles southwest of Raton, at about 1:50 p.m. standing near his parked government vehicle along the shoulder of the Dawson Road turnoff near Colfax. He appeared to be awaiting someone. The chief deputy saw Sutton acknowledge his wave as he turned north on the Raton-Cimarron road headed to the sheriff's office in Raton. Fletcher would be the last known person to see Ray Sutton alive. Both Sutton and his vehicle disappeared sometime after Fletcher departed the area.

Fifty-seven-year-old Ray Sutton, a vetted and experienced 20-year law enforcement professional, knew his job, the region's social and political structure, and the type of people who populated the region. He had been selected by senior regional management to serve on the blue-ribbon team of experienced field investigators initially assigned to handle the Kearney murder probe. Preliminary evidence suggested the Carlino brothers' Sicilian crime family as the assassins.

Federal agents in the Rocky Mountain region were cognizant that Colfax County, New Mexico's bootlegging operations provided product to their Colorado counterparts on a continuing basis. Proving these connections was Sutton's main responsibility and he had established an effective information network to assist him with that job. Following the killing of Agent Kearney, Sutton added an additional seek-and-find method to his successful variety of sting operations. Ray was not a pusillanimous man; he was determined to locate his friend's killers.[8]

Authors' Perspective: Federal prohibition field investigators were responsible for the enforcement of the National Prohibition Act. Although the federal law allowed for concurrent jurisdictional investigations by local, state, and federal authorities, by 1930 the law enforcement burden had fallen mostly upon the shoulders of the federal prohibition agents. Most cities and towns, and a majority of the state governments, had declined to fund local enforcement efforts due to the heavy fiscal burden required. A flummoxed Congress had created short-sighted legislation.

Federal field personnel overtly and covertly collected evidence of federal law violations dealing with illicit alcohol manufacture, distribution, and sales. The routine *modus operandi* of these officers was setting up "sting operations": an opportunity for violators to voluntarily involve themselves in an illegal operation that would lead to their arrest. The Sutton Plan was such a sting: the dissemination of misinformation concerning two nonexistent stills operating near Dawson. Contemporary reports indicate the plan was working.

APB: "Find Sutton!"

The task force team knew whom Sutton was using and meeting with regularly. He had reported these meetings to the team members, including his special plan for continuing to target the Campanella gang. Sutton had scheduled a meet with his part-time informant, James Perry Caldwell, just prior to his disappearance.[9]

Sutton's perspective on the use of informants was simple: he needed them and they needed him; he received information and they received payment for their service. It was a simple game of tit-for-tat; however, one never knew when a simple tip could turn major. A case in point: On Monday, August 25, 1930, Sutton and Colfax County Sheriff Al Davis raided a house located six miles south of Raton and arrested Sam Ullo and seized a small still. They learned of this operation from information gathered two weeks earlier in Trinidad, Colorado, when the Kearney investigation task force arrested four bootleggers, one of whom had direct affiliations with the Black Hand Society. The *Raton Evening Gazette* on Wednesday, August 15, 1930, reported on the Trinidad raid and published the names of those men arrested by federal agents. Two of these possessed the Dionisio surname.[10]

Formed in the early 1900s in New York City, *La Mano Nera* (Italian: Black Hand) became a part of the criminal underworld of America's Italian-Sicilian immigrants. As the decades passed, the society followed the ethnic groups west. In his book, *The Black Hand*, historian Stephan Talty wrote, the "infamous crime organization [...] engaged in extortion, assassination, child kidnapping, and bombings on a grand scale. [...] Only the Ku Klux Klan would surpass the Black Hand for the production of mass terror in the early part of the [20th] century."[11]

Whether the Raton raid registered on Sutton's psyche or not, his follow-up piece of detective work suggested a secondary link between the two geographic areas and the workings of the bootlegging organizations in southern Colorado and northeastern New Mexico. Preceding the Trinidad raid in August 1930, the local Black Hand Society had long ago become a subject of interest to certain local and federal law enforcement—and now the Kearney Task Force. During the initial interview of Mrs. Frances Kearney following the murder of her husband, she told the investigators about a Mr. Dionisio and his men paying undue attention to them while they were having a romantic dinner in a Trinidad restaurant on July 4, 1930, a mere 30 hours or less before Dale Kearney was killed. This incident is discussed at length in later chapters.

Few law enforcement officers had the capabilities to deal with the growing explosion in Italian-Sicilian crime stemming from national prohibition. Most state and federal agencies had neither intelligence networks inside these ethnic communities nor understanding of the culture and language spoken. Those that did understand were of the same ethnic heritage, generally.

In other areas, certain legal issues hampered the government's enforcement efforts whenever arrests were made of these known ethnic criminal subjects; witnesses would not dare testify against the criminals who directly threatened them or their family members—no witnesses, no prosecutable case. The Black Hand Society code of silence, "*omertà*," ruled the streets in ethnic America.

In Colorado, the society flourished and its control over bootlegging and the rackets was widely acknowledged. In northeastern New Mexico, the Italian-Sicilian population had their influences and viability, but not as obviously profound as their counterparts in Colorado. The media in Colfax County rarely took note of any local gang activities or ethnicities and relied on Colorado Associated Press dispatches to report and publish such stories.

Published research on the Hispanic Black Hand Society operations in northcentral New Mexico is relatively nonexistent. One of the best of these projects was undertaken by Dr. Robert J. Torrez, retired New Mexico State Historian, and in his report, he indicates thus:

> The [Hispanic] *mano negra* is a little known and poorly understood phenomenon that has been kept alive in northern New Mexico by a strong oral tradition [...] by numerous stories told by *viejitos* and old timers over the past four generations. I hoped to determine what the organization was, who was involved with its activities, what they actually did and what they hoped to accomplish. Three decades of diligent research has uncovered precious little about the organization and the men associated with its activities. A more recent study by [another researcher] reveals a tenuous association with prohibition era bootlegging and other criminal activity in northern New Mexico.[12]

Dr. Torrez did, however, discover the historical presence of the "black hand" (*la mano negra*) and their activities during his search for documentation of the organization near Tierra Amarillo in Rio Arriba County, New Mexico. He was searching for written notations, minutes of meetings, and/or membership rolls that could substantiate his thesis. He found no such documentation, but he did determine an isolated presence in the form of a Hispanic ethnic entity by the name of *la mano negra*. He was unable to clearly delineate any specific Italian-Sicilian involvement in northcentral New Mexico along the Rio Grande corridor.[13]

In retracing Ray Sutton's last journey driving his government-issued 1929 Pontiac four-door sedan, federal investigators surmised he traveled southbound on the Raton to Cimarron road until he reached the Dawson turnoff just north of the village of Colfax, a dying railroad shipping point with a general store and a few houses. Sutton took the turnoff headed to Dawson. A short distance up the road he executed a U-turn and pulled onto the wide southside shoulder and parked. From this vantage point he could see vehicle traffic coming and going along the Raton-Cimarron road while awaiting the arrival of his informant.

The old Raton-Cimarron two-lane gravel divided roadway, with its 15-foot-wide desert grass median, was being replaced by a new concrete, two-lane, single-strip, all-weather road and bridge/culvert system. Piles of road gravel, bridge timbers, and steel culverts were strategically placed alongside the roadway in preparation for the work crews moving north from Cimarron toward Raton. Another crew was working on the Raton Pass highway southbound to Las Vegas and Santa Fe; this old "scenic route" was created by convict labor in the late 1890s and is the foundation for present-day Interstate Highway 25.

Hiding site for Ray Sutton's missing car. Staged photo, demonstrating how the car was partially concealed by brush, for future legal proceedings (courtesy the Raymond Ellsworth Sutton Family Archives).

The two major roadways in Colfax County were being repaved and modernized, including adding of the new Zia-in-a-circle state road marker, assigning a number to the roadway placed in the center of the symbol, as part of the new state highway improvement program. In early April 1930, Congress appropriated over $300 million in federal aid to the states for new rural road construction, and New Mexico qualified for funding to be used in Colfax County.[14]

The Dawson coal mining complex had been named for the landowner who discovered coal on his property. The thriving coal mining town sat five miles into the hills north of the Raton-Cimarron highway. It was an active and thriving coal mining community of company-owned facilities that included worker and family housing for its 6,000 residents, a theater, a bank, a general store or two, two schools with an enrollment of 1,200 students, a park, and a sports field. At least seven mines were actively operating at the Dawson site, two of which were still being worked even though they were sadly listed among the major disasters in the history of American coal mining.[15]

In mid–September 1903 three men died in a fire in Mine No. 2. A decade later on October 22, 1913, an underground explosion killed 263 men. Fred Lambert headed a squad of State Mounted Police to maintain order at the site as mine officials conducted the recovery of the dead. A third disaster struck ten years later, as an additional 122 men were killed in a similar explosion on February 8, 1923.

Following the state investigations of the 1913 and 1923 disasters, mining experts attributed the explosions to dense enclaves of coal dust collected too near a dynamite blast, thus causing a chain reaction of explosions resulting in excessive deaths. Three hundred eighty-five grave markers remain today as simple, silent memorials to the lives and works of the immigrant miners who had been lost. The iron crosses and headstones still stand in the Dawson Cemetery, a fenced-in, brown, dry, windblown plot of sunbaked land outside the ghost town's southern limits.[16]

Ray Sutton knew the Dawson area well from his enforcement efforts over the last seven years. He claimed a number of arrests and seizures from local distributors who serviced the thirsty mine workers with liquor. Dawson was familiar ground to the federal officer.

It was mid-afternoon on August 28, 1930, when George R. "Boots" Fletcher, Colfax County's undersheriff, saw Agent Sutton parked alongside the Dawson road. He waved as he continued on toward Raton. Fletcher had been a longtime friend and colleague from earlier days when Ray served as Union County sheriff. At that time, Fletcher, a former range foreman for the CS ranch, was new to law enforcement. Since then he had been relatively successful in staying on the force by being picked up every two years whenever the sheriff was reelected or a new man won the office. For all intents and purposes, the former ranch manager turned lawman was now an experienced deputy, the "go-to guy" in the sheriff's office. He and Sheriff Al Davis worked closely with Agent Sutton in their joint raids on Colfax County bootlegger operations. In 1935, Fletcher, then Colfax County sheriff, was elected the first president of the newly organized New Mexico Sheriffs' and Police Association and served two terms in that office. J. Riley Hughes, Union County sheriff, followed Fletcher for two terms as the association's president.[17]

Authors' Perspective: Following his disappearance, a review of Sutton's files suggested that he may have been led into a bootlegger's trap in the hills surrounding the Dawson mining camp. In actuality, Sutton the manhunter had become Sutton the hunted—an unwitting victim of a well-planned double-cross by his informant in accordance with a plan orchestrated by John Campanella's bootlegger cabal.

In retrospect, if Agent Sutton was indeed awaiting the arrival of his informant and then went to confirm his "new information" in the presence of the informant, it appears that Sutton may have violated his long-established rule concerning data from informants. The rule was simple: Trust but verify. Never just accept the veracity of an informant's information or take action on the tip until the intelligence has been independently verified apart from the informant.

In the matters of the Kearney and Sutton inquiries, the Bureau of Prohibition elected to conduct parallel investigations in concert with the local jurisdictions. The agency was cognizant of the manpower, training, and budgetary limitations of Colorado and New Mexico officers concerning any protracted field investigations. It is important to remember that in 1930 the murder of a government agent was a state crime. It would be another five years before the president signed congressional legislation making killing a federal agent a national crime and authorizing the Federal Bureau of Investigation as the lead agency in investigating all such incidents.

There is no statute of limitations on murder and the investigation remains an open case until resolved by arrest and prosecution or other administrative means, based on the feasibility that all potential antagonists are deceased.

2

Prohibition
The Noble Experiment

"One of the great mistakes is to judge policies and programs by their intentions rather than their results."—Milton Friedman, American Nobel Prize economist

The violent deaths of Prohibition Agents Dale F. Kearney and Ray Sutton had never been contemplated specifically by the politicians and prohibitionists who proposed and implemented national prohibition in the United States. These political advocates were too busy with their thoughts of a new and peaceful transitional journey to Utopia, a state of mind that has never been achieved over the millennia of human history.

A new experiment in social revolution was born. The possibility of an improved social, economic, and religious society blotted out the reality espoused by Lincoln. Naiveté on the part of the "do-gooders" was boundless and pervaded the consciousness of the new majority in America. The leaders of America's Sicilian-Italian organized crime families saw the opportunity to take advantage of this national naiveté and develop a new "customer service" business created via this "experimental social program" called national prohibition. This new criminal enterprise would focus on the manufacture, sale, and distribution of the "forbidden fruit" of alcoholic spirits.[1]

Will Rogers, America's humorist, caught the mood of the nation when he said, "Prohibition is better than no liquor at all." The manufacture of "spirits" has been called the world's second oldest profession and the consumption of alcoholic beverages has played an unheralded role, for good or evil, in humankind's march to civilize our world. Religion, commerce, social and sexual customs, health practices, and communal governance have each contributed to the plethora of myths, legends and the reality of the effects alcohol has had upon human history.

Hindsight would suggest that any thoughts concerning the potential loss of local, state and federal tax revenues due to prohibition fell to the wayside during this wave of moral righteousness. It has been estimated that during the 14 years of National Prohibition over $1 billion in tax funding was lost, i.e., not collected. This amount doesn't include the cost of implementation and enforcement of the National Prohibition Act.[2]

To better understand the societal impact of National Prohibition, a brief review of the events and legislation that culminated in this noble experiment is necessary. In

Colonial America, alcoholic beverages were an accepted fact of life and their use was strictly governed by social custom. On February 22, 1777, the Continental Congress passed a resolution denouncing the distilling of liquor because it used vital food resources needed to prosecute the War for Independence. This request was mostly complied with until peace was restored to the new nation. The old morals of the pre-war era quickly returned as settlers moved westward from the eastern coastal regions and made new homes in the hill country and on into the Appalachian Mountains and the lands beyond the Mississippi River. Farmers grew cash crops of wheat, rye, corn and potatoes, but due to the lack of a developed series of roadways and few transport vehicles on the frontier, the transport of their agriculture products to lucrative eastern markets became moot. Thus, American entrepreneurial ingenuity conceived of "liquid crops" that could easily be transported via mules to market, and this segment of the new American distillery industry was born. It also paved the way for the new government to impose a means of taxation on various alcohol products.[3]

Government Regulations

During the first session of the new Federal Congress, a bill was introduced on July 4, 1789, to generate needed revenue to reduce the nation's war debt. This measure placed an excise tax on all alcoholic beverages produced in the United States and established a tariff on all imported liquors. Following a lengthy congressional debate, the Whiskey Act of March 1791 was passed and continued in effect until repealed on June 30, 1802. Treasury Secretary Alexander Hamilton had privately claimed the act was to serve "more as a measure of social discipline than as a source of revenue." The law, however, proved to be a substantial revenue-generating measure, while also functioning as a modest move toward a program of national temperance.

Within a year of the Whiskey Act's implementation, there were pockets of resistance. In these regions, whiskey served as a medium of fiscal exchange. Western Pennsylvanian farmers led the rebellion against the taxation law. Many of the Pennsylvania resisters were war veterans who believed that they were fighting for the tenet of "no taxation without representation" principle of the American Revolution. They seem to have overlooked the fact their region had a representative in Congress. The federal government maintained that the law was the legal expression of the taxation powers of Congress. These Keystone State citizens refused to comply with the tax and organized an "army" to defy federal tax collectors. In May 1792, President George Washington, acting as commander-in-chief of the United States military, led a 15,000-man expedition into Western Pennsylvania on a three-part mission: eliminate any potential localized violence, put down an armed insurrection against the constitutional authority of the new federal government, while also establishing the supreme authority of federal law over state law or local tradition.[4]

Successive "dry" forces of the republic continued to work to further ban the manufacture and sale of "spirits" over the ensuing decades. One of the earliest national prohibition movements dated back to the 1850s when Neal Dow, a Quaker businessman from the state of Maine, launched his campaign to ban the sale and consumption of alcohol. He was joined by the Sons of Temperance who, in 1856, demanded a constitutional amendment establishing national prohibition. As the national election of 1860 loomed, 13 of the 32 states had adopted some sort of statewide or local option prohibition law.

The movement was gaining popular support just prior to the War Between the States and Abraham Lincoln made a profound observation on the subject: "Prohibition will work great injury to the cause of temperance. It is a species of intemperance within itself, for it goes beyond the bounds of reason in that it attempts to control a man's appetite by legislation and makes a crime out of things that are not crimes. A prohibition law strikes a blow at the very principles upon which our government was founded." The temperance movement lost their fight for a constitutional amendment in the wake of the struggle to preserve the federal union.

The government as a rule depended upon voluntary compliance by producers to pay required taxes between 1791 and 1862, but the demand for liquor during the War Between the States created a massive liquor tax evasion movement. In response to this epidemic, Congress authorized the Secretary of the Department of the Treasury to create an Internal Revenue Service (IRS) to handle the growth of liquor tax collection duties. Within a year of its creation, organized alcohol criminals had become so pervasive that the IRS formed a three-man detective team dedicated to investigate and prosecute such alcohol-tax evaders. This unit was the first of its kind and gave birth to a coordinated federal effort of tax collection and law enforcement. The IRS and its "police force" continued to operate after the war ended. In later years, the small agency of the early 1860s grew into a behemoth with tentacles reaching into all facets of the nation's social and business fiber.[5]

Birth of the Prohibition Movement

In 1876, New Hampshire Congressman Henry Blair became the first person to introduce a constitutional amendment for national prohibition, but this resolution died at birth. As a senator in 1885, Blair introduced a second resolution with co-sponsor Senator Preston Plum of Kansas. The Senate Committee on Education recommended the measure for vote by the Senate in 1886; however, senate leadership never found the opportunity to bring the prohibition amendment before the upper house for debate or a vote. The prohibition fight continued in the states and territories with measured success. On February 19, 1881, Kansas became the first state to prohibit the sale of liquor within the confines of the state, and four days later President Rutherford B. Hayes forbade the sale of alcoholic beverages at all military posts in the nation.

Another small step toward national prohibition was accomplished in August 1890 when Congress passed the Wilson Original Package Act and President Benjamin Harrison signed it into law. The new federal statute stipulated that all intoxicating beverages manufactured in a "wet" region and shipped to another region via interstate commerce would become subject to the laws of the destination state or territory upon its arrival. However, the lack of any prescribed mechanism for enforcement of the law proved to be a major defect.[6]

The nation's small force of United States Marshals were directed to enforce a law that contained no penalty for violation. It would take Congress 23 years to address this enforcement's shortcoming. It should be noted that at the time there were two or more congressional persuasions existing pertaining to alcohol prohibition consisting of the "Drys" and the "Wets." The failure of the Drys' policies to pass the legislation without a means to enforce it illustrates the success of the Wets to derail any alcohol prohibition efforts nationally.[7]

In February 1869, New Mexico's United States Marshal John Pratt and his deputy raided Daniel Miller's brew site in San Miguel County because he had not paid his federal tax on the still's operation. A month later, Marshal Pratt sold Miller's "two copper stills and distilling apparatus" at the courthouse in Las Vegas to pay the overdue tax bill.[8]

By the time the New Mexico Territory began its reach for statehood, the Women's Christian Temperance Union (WCTU), founded in 1874, and the Anti-Saloon League, founded in 1893, had been active in territorial New Mexico for decades. In 1910, these lobbying groups mounted a massive campaign pressuring delegates to the territory's State Constitutional Convention to draft an article prohibiting the commercial sale and manufacture of alcoholic beverages in the new state. The measure gained little traction with the convention delegates. The WCTU and the League did not give up, they just strengthened their resolve.[9]

Authors' Perspective: In one of those "mouse in the corner" history moments one might ask what could have been heard discussed in the Estancia home of John and Louisa Collier? She was an officer of New Mexico Territory's WCTU chapter while her husband was the second in command of the Territorial Mounted Police. This small force of rangers would become responsible for the enforcement of any statewide alcoholic beverage ban upon the granting of statehood. John Collier and

Woman's Christian Temperance Union Pledge Card.

Fred Fornoff, captain of the territorial police, were both renowned for their love of a good smoke and a stiff drink—or two or three. Under new leadership, the New Mexico State Mounted Police enforced state prohibition in the Land of Enchantment between May 1918 until February 1921 when the ranger force was abolished.[10]

More Federal Laws

One of President William H. Taft's last acts in office was to sign the Webb-Kenyon Act, enacted by Congress on March 1, 1913. This piece of legislation was intended to reinforce the 1890 Original Package Act by advancing the violation of federal law concerning the interstate shipment of intoxicating beverages with the intent that it be used or sold in any manner in violation of the laws of the destination state. Once again, the federal lawmakers neglected, or intentionally omitted, a specified methodology for enforcement; thus, it became virtually as meaningless as the parent law.

Four years later in 1917, with war fervor growing across the nation, Congress passed an amendment to the Webb-Kenyon Act providing a fine of $1,000 for transporting liquor into a dry state. The federal government still depended upon U.S. Marshals, and local officers in the states, to voluntarily enforce the national prohibition laws. None of these federal acts discussed thus far had success in curbing the flow of liquor into purportedly dry regions.

The publication of investigative journalist Upton Sinclair's 1906 novel, *The Jungle*, focused on the Progressive movement in the United States. It told of a journey through the life of the main character, Jurgis Rudkus, who came to America from Lithuania in search of the American Dream to find freedom and fortune. As a result of Sinclair's written revelations concerning the unhealthy food supply system in the United States, the public uttered an outcry for corrective national action.

In 1906, Congress authorized, and President Theodore Roosevelt signed into law, two bills which would have long-range effects upon the health of the nation's citizens. The first law, the Meat Inspection Act, established standards for sanitary meatpacking through a system of inspections and penalties for violations. The second law, the Pure Food and Drug Act, specified a similar system of enforcement. Both laws barred "adulterated or misbranded or poisonous or deleterious foods, drugs, medicines, and liquor" from interstate commerce. Congress also provided the necessary enforcement powers coupled with established penalties to be applied against persons who did not obey the nation's alcohol beverage laws.[11]

Also, in 1906, Congress authorized the Commissioner of Indian Affairs (under the direction of the Secretary of the Department of the Interior) to establish a select federal force of Special Officers for the Suppression of Liquor Traffic on Indian Lands. When the Special Officer force was first created, the officers had been given the powers of Indian agents which included the authority to seize and destroy contraband. The federal Appropriation Act of 1913 conferred upon Special Officers the status of United States Marshals, including the right to carry weapons, and the same enforcement authority as the sheriff of the jurisdiction in which they were working. These federal agents were the nation's first police force to specifically enforce the prohibition of alcoholic beverage consumption on Indian reservations. The Legislative Assembly of the Territory of New Mexico in 1876 had enacted a law prohibiting the sale of alcoholic beverages to any Native Americans residing in the territory, living on or off a reservation. The 1876 law was updated and expanded in 1897, 1903 and 1907.[12]

German Militant Action Against the United States

Rising militant nationalism in Europe had begun a quickstep march toward destiny. In the summer of 1914, these dynastic empires—now grouped into two major national alliances—reached the point of no return. The Central Powers was composed of the German Empire, the Austria-Hungary Empire, and the Turkish Ottoman Empire and they opposed the Allied Powers which consisted of the emporium of Great Britain, France, Russia and Italy. During the first week of August 1914, the flashpoint occurred when Germany fired the shot that ignited a conflict which would ultimately encompass the globe and involve 166 countries by the end of hostilities in 1918. Initially, President Woodrow Wilson's government declared the United States would remain neutral in this European dispute saying, "We must be impartial in thought and action." However, other events would alter this point of view.[13]

Special Officer Badge, U.S. Indian Service, Department of the Interior (courtesy Chuck and V.J. Hornung Western History Collection).

In May 1915, a German submarine sank a passenger liner off the coast of neutral Ireland with the loss of 120 American lives. Imperial Germany apologized to the United States and restructured their naval attacks so as not to further provoke American action, and President Wilson promised to maintain America's neutrality.

On Thursday, March 9, 1916, a Mexican paramilitary band attacked the town and army post at Columbus, New Mexico, a few miles north of the United States-Mexico border, without warning. The raiders were led by Doroteo Arango Arámbula, who is better known as Francisco "Pancho" Villa, a bandit-general active in the then six-year-old Mexican Revolution. Villa served as commander of the Division Del Norte (Division of the North) of Mexico's Constitutionalist Army. In 1915, his forces were defeated twice in battles against the opposition and he went on "the run" seeking to rearm his faithful troops. Rumor reported that Villa's mission at Columbus entailed the retrieval of a cache of arms he had previously paid for but had not received from a group of gunrunners with whom he had contracted. On March 9, 1916, once he learned that he and his army had been defrauded by the "gringos," Villa attacked. Armament smuggling along the entire United States-Mexico border was big business and became one of the largest positive economic factors in the illegal market of weapon sales for a number of U.S.–based gun smuggling organizations.

The Mexican raiders killed 17 American civilians and soldiers in the attack on Columbus. In response, President Wilson dispatched 6,000 troops into northern Mexico, seeking Villa in a hide-and-seek game that continued for nearly a year before the president recalled the expeditionary force commanded by General John J. Pershing. Villa was never captured by United States forces. On Friday, July 20, 1923, he was murdered by seven riflemen, representatives of his former Mexican opponents, at his hacienda in Parral, Chihuahua, Mexico. He was 45 years old.[14]

In February 1917, British intelligence officers intercepted a telegram from the German Foreign Minister Arthur Zimmerman, in Berlin, to the Imperial German Minister to Mexico at the German Embassy in Mexico City. This diplomatic cable offered Mexican President Venustiano Carranza an alliance with the Central Powers in the event the United States joined the Allied Powers in the conflict in Europe. Germany guaranteed Mexico financial assistance to "reconquer" their former territories of what is now New Mexico, Texas and Arizona. The British government provided a copy of the Zimmerman cable to President Wilson and he released the message to American newspapers. This inflammatory attempt by Germany to cause additional trouble between the United States and Mexico occurred simultaneously with Germany's ill-advised decision to resume unrestricted naval warfare against transatlantic commerce. President Wilson called Germany's action a "war against mankind."[15]

On Monday, April 2, 1917, before a joint session of Congress, President Wilson submitted a resolution asking Congress for a declaration of war against Imperial Germany by demanding "the world must be made safe for democracy." Two days later, the Senate passed the war act by a vote of 82 to 6. The House concurred on Good Friday, April 6, by passing the war resolution with a vote of 373 to 50. Easter Sunday was a day of prayer across the nation.[16]

The United States of America entered the Great War in Europe, but it had no army or Navy for such a massive undertaking on a continent over 4,000 miles across the Atlantic Ocean. America's total military complement consisted of 127,588 officers and men in the regular force and 80,446 National Guard troops. The country needed a minimum of one million men as front-line troops to be considered a viable active fighting force. National Guard units across America were federalized and placed on active duty. Volunteer military recruitment stations were opened in every section of the nation, while draft boards were established in every county in every state. The first American units into the conflict were Navy antisubmarine units.

On Tuesday, June 13, 1917, five months after being recalled from his Pancho Villa duty in Mexico, General Pershing and the first elements of his command staff (a field artillery unit and three infantry regiments) formed one of the first American Expeditionary Forces to sail from Hoboken, New Jersey, bound for France. They arrived in the port of Saint-Nazaire on June 26, 1917, to a cheering multitude. The morale of the Allied forces soared as month after month more Yanks arrived in France. Following few months of training, on Tuesday, October 23, 1917, men of Battery C, 6th Field Artillery, fired the first American shots in the Great War. Over 116,000 Americans died, including 53,000 on the battlefield, in the nation's third-bloodiest war.[17]

The New Mexico Mounted Police in the Great War and State Prohibition

New Mexico's National Guard was ordered into federal service in May 1916 to replace the U.S. Army contingent stationed at Columbus protecting the Mexican border. With the army and the state's National Guard units removed from the border, Governor William E. Lindsey commissioned 274 residents of New Mexico's three southern counties bordering Mexico into a six-month period of service, without pay from the state, as special rangers of the Mounted Police, to serve as needed to protect the safety and security of the state's southern region. New special commissions were issued in 1917 and continued in force until a regular State Mounted Police company was organized under Captain Herbert McGrath in May 1918. The term of service for these paid state rangers would expire on December 31, 1918, unless the new governor recommissioned the force.

McGrath's Mounted Police company was composed of 14 rangers or privates, two sergeants, and a captain. During their eight months of service these 17 men made 452 arrests, plus conducted numerous other investigations not resulting in an arrest. This compilation included a number of prohibition enforcement activities.

In January 1919, Octaviano A. Larrazolo, the new governor, appointed Apolonio A. Sena as the Mounted Police captain. The state legislature authorized Captain Sena to have four sergeants and 17 rangers in his Mounted Police company. During the next two years this uniformed force of state rangers made 264 arrests: 96 in 1919 and 168 during 1920. In the fall of 1920, Sena resigned and was replaced by Lorenzo Delgado, a former San Miguel County sheriff, who led the New Mexico Mounted Police until they were abolished by legislative action in February 1921.

In New Mexico, prohibition enforcement became a function of the New Mexico Mounted Police as a result of a November 6, 1917, amendment to the state constitution. New Mexico voters had ratified Article 23 which approved statewide prohibition by a 3 to 1 vote. A large portion of the state's voters believed that all grain grown was needed for the war effort and not for the making of spirits for social drinking. There were some elements within communities and counties that disagreed. Voters in Taos and Rio Arriba Counties voted against the referendum. State prohibition in New Mexico took effect on October 1, 1918, and national prohibition on January 16, 1920.[18]

In 1921, Bronson M. Cutting, a Republican lawyer, land baron, and editor of the *Santa Fe New Mexican*, wrote a stinging editorial condemning the lax enforcement of the prohibition law in New Mexico, but especially in the capital city. Ironically, Cutting was an anti-prohibitionist and owned one of the largest and finest private wine cellars in the

New Mexico Mounted Police Badge, circa 1918 (courtesy Chuck and V.J. Hornung Western History Collection).

Southwest. In January 1928, he was appointed to fill New Mexico's vacant seat (due to death) in the United States Senate where he served until his death in a May 1935 airplane crash.[19]

The Colorado Rangers

In April 1921, two months after New Mexico abolished their state rangers, the Colorado legislature enacted House Bill 110 reorganizing the ineffective five-year-old State Department of Safety constabulary into a new statewide police force called the Colorado Rangers. The new force consisted of 39 uniformed rangers and 11 officers and headquarters staff. The rangers were under the direct management of the governor, with a captain handling the day-to-day field operations. The superintendent's administrative staff was located in Denver, but the field operations facility was headquartered in Walsenburg, 35 miles northwest of Trinidad on the road to Denver.

All of the new state rangers had seen overseas military service during the Great War. Many of the rangers came from Colorado's professional sector and held respectable positions in the state's social circles. The governor often used his police force as union strike suppressors, but their main legislative functions were to handle livestock theft investigations, fight the state's growing organized crime problem, mediate the continuing sheep-cattle range wars, and act as state prohibition enforcement agents.

During the decade of the "Roaring '20s" the Colorado Rangers were very active in prohibition enforcement in the southeastern section of the state, working closely with federal prohibition officers. Many myths of misconduct arose against the rangers' actions, like the one claiming they were part of the force that murdered miners and their families at the Ludlow Massacre in 1914—eight years before the rangers' formation. The guilty organization consisted of strike breakers in Colorado National Guard uniforms. Fiscal restraint measures in later years by the Colorado General Assembly resulted in termination of the ranger force in April 1927.[20]

Colorado Rangers Badge (courtesy Chuck and V.J. Hornung Western History Collection).

Impact of the Great War on Federal Revenues

The first effect of the outbreak of the war in Europe was a decrease in the revenue from import duties. This made necessary increased revenue from internal taxes and resulted in the act of October 22, 1914, which practically reenacted all of the Spanish-American War taxes including the luxury tax on telephone use. In December 1914, Congress approved the Harrison Act regulating the domestic use of opium and coca leaves and their derivatives. Although the act had nothing to do with the war, it represented the apex of a movement started years before to cut domestic and international trade in opium and other narcotic drugs. On its face, this act was a revenue measure, although the Supreme Court of the United States made the assumption that it had "a moral end in view."

Because of the Supreme Court's ruling, enforcement of these laws was placed in the hands of Commissioner of Internal Revenue Daniel Calhoun Roper (1917–1920), Democrat from South Carolina. John F. Kramer, an Ohio Democrat, would serve as the first appointed Prohibition Unit Commissioner (1919–1920). Thereafter, the Office of Deputy Commissioner in Charge of the Narcotics Division assumed the national narcotics mantle as part of the Bureau of Prohibition incidental to the subsequent 1927 reorganization. Interestingly, when the neophyte Prohibition Unit was first established in 1919, the Internal Revenue narcotics component became one of its branches. Many of the first assigned field investigators of the Prohibition Unit were on loan from the Narcotics Division of the Internal Revenue Service.[21]

If Congress had been slow in perceiving alcohol consumption as a national health issue, the two legislative bodies were even slower in assuming any role in the regulation of alcohol consumption. It took the nation's involvement in the terrible world war before the soon-to-be-called "Noble Social Experiment" became a reality in the United States. The war mobilization effort gave the national prohibition cause new ammunition. Government propaganda depicted brewers and licensed retailers as treacherously backstabbing American soldiers by diverting raw materials and labor from the war effort to an industry which debilitated the nation's capacity to defend itself. The central governmental message was that wartime prohibition would stop the waste of grain and molasses and would remove a handicap on mobilization efficiency.

In May 1917, Congress passed and President Wilson signed a law prohibiting the sale of liquor to all military personnel. Three months later, Congress enacted the National Food Control Act which made it illegal to manufacture distilled spirits from any form of foodstuff needed in the war effort; this edict closed the nation's distilleries. On September 2, 1917, a presidential executive order was issued transferring to the Bureau of Internal Revenue total control over the production of distilled spirits. A proclamation was issued on December 8, 1917, and directed that no food material should be used in the manufacture of malt

IRS Prohibition Agent Badge. Prohibition law enforcement officers of the U.S. Internal Revenue Service of the Department of the Treasury wore this style badge from 1920 until 1926 under the authority of the National Prohibition Act of 1919 (Bureau of Alcohol, Tobacco, Firearms and Explosives; ATF.com).

liquor except by license from the Commissioner of Internal Revenue. This pronouncement also restricted the amount of food material to be used for malt liquor and that it must not contain more than 2.75 percent alcohol by weight. A second proclamation was issued one year later that declared no food materials should be used for this purpose after December 1, 1918, regardless of whether or not such liquor was intoxicating.

In September 1918, President Woodrow Wilson asked Congress to enact the National Agriculture Act which established a wartime prohibition by making the manufacture of commercial intoxicants illegal after May 1, 1919, and the sale of any intoxicants after June 30, 1919, became illegal until the nation was removed from its war mobilization status. Medical and sacramental alcohol remained legal and could be produced and sold to federally licensed dealers.[22]

The Eighteenth Amendment

On Tuesday, December 18, 1917, members of the 65th Congress took a huge leap forward in pursuit of total alcohol prohibition for the nation. The lawmakers voted to send to the 48 states, for their ratification, a constitutional amendment establishing permanent prohibition on the manufacture and sales of alcoholic beverages within the United States. On Tuesday, January 8, 1918, Mississippi became the first state to ratify the new amendment and it was quickly followed by the Commonwealths of Virginia and Kentucky. The ball was rolling now and 394 days later, on Thursday, January 16, 1919, Wyoming became the 36th state to accept the measure. This vote resulted in the final approval of the Eighteenth Amendment to the Constitution.

The Colorado legislature had approved the measure on January 15, 1919, and on January 20, 1919, New Mexico became the 39th state to ratify the new law. Rhode Island was the only state to reject the proposal in its entirety. On January 29, 1919, the United States Secretary of State issued a proclamation stating that since 36 states had ratified the amendment, it had become part of the Constitution with the effective implementation date of January 16, 1920.

The Prohibition amendment implementation legislation plainly stated that the 48 states and the federal territories would hold "concurrent powers to enforce" the prohibition laws within their state or territories with the central government in Washington, but only a few states, and none of the territories, provided the legislation or the funding needed to implement that provision. Congress would not provide funding for any enforcement efforts or penalty provisions until the following year. State governments had the choice to assume or reject such funding within their own operational budgets. It became an issue of "states' rights" from their points of view. They maintained that if the federal government ordered the legislation to be a shared responsibility, the federal government should provide to the states the necessary financial support. The federal government failed to include state funding within the law leading the majority of the states unable to implement enforcement of the national alcohol prohibition law; thus, the final responsibility of enforcement fell on the shoulders of the federal government. There were exceptions to this course of action, however. The federal courts and prosecutions assumed final prosecutorial and hearing authority.[23]

National Prohibition Enforcement

The federal code designed to implement the prohibition amendment was the National Prohibition Act of 1919 as introduced into the House of Representatives by Andrew John Volstead of Minnesota; it became known alternatively as the Volstead Act. This legislation defined intoxicating beverages as containing "zero point five (0.5)" percent alcohol, delineated fines and prison terms for violation of the law, and authorized the Department of the Treasury, Internal Revenue Service, to enforce the provisions of the act in conjunction with state and local authorities. Without congressional approval, the tax collection service established an internal administrative Prohibition Unit to handle their new law enforcement duties.

Congress initially passed the Volstead Act, but President Woodrow Wilson objected to the measure. The chief executive reminded Congress that the Great War had not ended with an armistice on November 11, 1918, but with the signing of the Treaty of Versailles on June 29, 1919. President Wilson's point was simple: with the end of the war, the United States was no longer in a state of national emergency to justify limiting the civil liberty of the nation's citizens. Congress disagreed with the president and passed the Volstead Act over Wilson's objection on October 28, 1919. The celebrants of the occasion were concentrated in the Anti-Saloon League and Women's Christian Temperance Union, which vocally claimed that their consummate skill at pressure politics had maneuvered Congress into the "Noble Social Experiment."[24]

It was the new administration of President Warren G. Harding that ushered in National Prohibition as established under the Eighteenth Amendment to the Constitution in March 1921. Both Harding and his Airedale terrier, Laddie Boy, were very popular with the public. Laddie Boy even gave an "interview" to the *Washington Star* complaining that the White House security guard dogs were overworked and deserved shorter work days. The First Dog also addressed concern over National Prohibition since the master of the White House enjoyed an evening nightcap. Where would he get his liquor?[25]

In 1920, Herbert Hoover (at the time director of the American Relief Administration's effort to aid in the economic and social recovery of Europe following the end of the Great War) made an ominous assessment as the United States stood on the edge of an abyss: "Our country has deliberately undertaken a great social and economic experiment, noble in motive and far reaching in purpose." In later years this "noble experiment" slogan would gain momentum. As the nation jumped into the abyss, no one could imagine the depth they would fall.

In 1952, former President Herbert Hoover recalled the frustration his administration experienced with the enforcement of National Prohibition. In his *Memories* he wrote,

> Prohibition cast a cloud over all our problems of law enforcement and was generally a constant worry. I should have been glad to have humanity forget all about strong alcoholic drinks. They are moral, physical, and economic curses to the race. But in the present stage of human progress, this vehicle of joy could not be generally suppressed by Federal law.
>
> The first hard practical fault was in the concept of enforcement. The Federal law assumed that state and local officials would look after violations within the state, and that Federal government would simply stop interstate traffic. During nine years of the law prior to my administration, the officials of the states most clamorous for national prohibition, including Iowa, Kansas, Ohio, Indi-

ana, Alabama, and Georgia, steadily abandoned their responsibilities and loaded them upon the Federal government. Practically nowhere in the country did the local police force even take notice of violations, except as a basis of graft. The Federal government could not have come anywhere near enforcement with a police force of fewer than 250,000 men. In the meantime, the bootleg business had grown to such dimensions as to be able to corrupt or mislead the Federal enforcement officers all over the country.

However, under my oath of office, the very core of the Presidency was enforcement of the law. I therefore gave prohibition enforcement the utmost organization that the Federal government could summon. We secured legislative authority to reorganize, consolidate, and greatly expand the Federal agencies. [...] During my four years [as President] we increased the number of bootlegging citizens resident in Federal jails, or on parole, from an average of about 22,000 to about 53,000. These did not include the vast number of cases resulting in fines, padlockings, confiscations, and other suppression devices. The number of prohibition convictions rose to about 80,000 in 1932, and *finally demonstrated the futility of the whole business.* [Emphasis added by the authors.][26]

To say that the Department of the Treasury was ill-prepared to undertake the enforcement duties of nationwide prohibition of alcoholic beverages within the United States would be a vast understatement of facts. It would take the secretary of the Department of the Treasury an extended period of time to establish lines of coordination between the Prohibition Unit, the United States Customs Service, and the United States Coast Guard concerning each group's responsibility for enforcement and countering illicit manufacture, smuggling, and distribution activities incidental to the provisions of the Volstead Act of 1919.

One ironic incident in the national prohibition fight occurred during the 1922 general election when Andrew J. Volstead, the author of prohibition's Volstead Act, lost his congressional seat after a decade of public service. Considered to be an influential Republican legislator and lawyer by the voters and his peers, he was not unemployed for long. He became chief legal counsel to the head of the prohibition enforcement body, holding that position until Prohibition was repealed in December 1933. This one appointment serves as an example of the massive Republican political system that dominated the early operation of the prohibition unit. With the 1932 national election of Franklin Delano Roosevelt as president, a Democrat administration replaced the 14-year reign of the Republican Party in the executive branch of the federal government.

According to Laurence F. Schmeckebier's study of the Bureau of Prohibition's operation for the Brookings Institute in 1929, a bill was introduced in the 1924 House of Representatives making the Prohibition Unit a separate bureau within the Treasury Department and renaming it the Bureau of Alcohol Prohibition. The Prohibition Unit had never been officially established by law

Bureau of Prohibition Agent's Badge. When federal law created a separate law enforcement Bureau of Prohibition within the Department of the Treasury the reassigned agents carried this style of badge between 1927 and 1930 (courtesy the Bureau of Alcohol, Tobacco, Firearms and Explosives; ATF.com).

as a bona fide federal agency; all its powers were specifically vested in the Commissioner of Internal Revenue. The 1924 House bill called for the appointment of field agents only after civil service examinations and served as a medium to legitimize the unit's authority. This bill failed to come to a vote in the Senate.

The proposed legislation and the investigation behind the bill came to the attention of the newly appointed Assistant Secretary of the Treasury, General Lincoln C. Andrews, United States Army (Ret.). He adopted part of this bill in his 1925 plan of reorganization as a means to rid the unit of nonperforming corruptive political hacks and ward heelers.[27]

Unfortunately, Andrews served only two years (1925–1927) before the Washington "political tiger" devoured him via a series of political compromises and tradeoffs proposed by various congressional committee members and White House politicos. Andrews' last action before leaving office involved the successful congressional support of the reintroduced House bill in essentially the same form as that of the earlier offering. The Sixty-Ninth Congress passed the reorganization bill on March 3, 1927, to become effective on April 1, 1927, the same date General Andrews' resignation was accepted. The tiger got its flesh and blood, but the Department of the Treasury received its new bureau and civil service status for its employees.

Contrary to public law it took years before the new Bureau met all the conditions set by the Civil Service Commission's guidelines. The Commission required background reinvestigations of candidates and special testing following a two-week retraining course for all investigative personnel who remained in the ranks of the bureau. Several dismissals occurred involving certain undesirable traits and a lack of performance under the new standards. A number of selected personnel who had failed to pass the written tests were eventually "grandfathered" into the new organization with protected status. Politics continued to influence the careers of the politically astute.

On Monday, June 30, 1930, six months following civil service recognition, the Bureau of Prohibition was officially transferred from the Department of the Treasury to the Department of Justice as a totally separate and complete bureau within that bureaucratic body. The Justice Department also restructured its operation to coincide with a new regional concept. Of the previous 27 enforcement districts created by General Lincoln C. Andrews in 1925, this statute was consolidated into 12 districts closely following the boundaries of the ten federal circuit court districts.

Under the 1930 bureau transfer, the Department of Justice now contained three investigative bureaus under its enforcement umbrella: the Bureau of Investigation which handled 55 designated federal crimes (none of which involved the national prohibition laws) under the directorship of John Edgar Hoover; the Office of the United States Marshal directed by a chief marshal whose primary concern included the location and arrests of federal fugitives and all transportation of federal prisoners; and the Bureau of Prohibition which served as the primary enforcement arm of national prohibition.[28]

The Old Frontier West

People that study the world of phobias known that metathesiophobia is the fear of change and tropophobia is the extreme dislike of relocation or moving. These two phobias struck some of the remaining corrupt employees of the federal prohibition law enforcement staff like a lightning bolt on June 30, 1930. Others looked forward to the pending changes. The new realignment affected both the command structure and the ground forces of Prohibition Region 18. First, the old three-state area (Wyoming, Colorado, and New Mexico) had its designator changed to Region 10. Secondly, the new structure now also included the States of Utah and Arizona. Denver remained the headquarters city of the new five-state region. Some field agents were reassigned and the command structure changed minimally.[29]

According to Golden's *Colorado Transcript* dated July 3, 1930, John F. Vivian, a resident of Golden, Jefferson County, Colorado, and serving as the Region 18 Administrator, would assume duties as the new administrator of the expanded Region 10. Isaac S.T. Gregg, another resident of Jefferson County, Colorado, and political colleague of Vivian, was appointed as the new assistant prohibition administrator. In making the reorganization plan public, the Justice Department press notice said: "While all assignments of administrators and deputy administrators are temporary, most of them will be made permanent. A few changes and readjustments are likely to occur within the next three months, however."[30]

The May 1930 issue of the *Literary Digest*, the nation's leading periodical, reported that the majority of those they polled favored the repeal of National Prohibition. By the summer, the health of the United States economy also caught the attention of Americans as the nation begin a downhill slide into what historians have dubbed the Great Depression. The economic crisis had been triggered by the collapse of the nation's stock market on "Black Thursday" in late October 1929. The stock market was unable to recover from the two-day trading loss of over $30 billion. Banks failed across the nation and the ripple effect was speedy as workers lost their jobs and unemployment was felt in almost every family in the country.[31]

One troubadour ballad, author unknown, of the "Speak-Easy Era" caught the saga of Prohibition. At its height of popularity, the underground folksong became very popular at "social" events across all levels of American society:

> Sister's in the pantry bottling the suds;
> Father's in the cellar mixing up some hops;
> Junior's big V-8 is roaring at the gate;
> Ole Blue's on the front porch watching for the cops.
> Mother makes brandy from cherries;
> Grandpa distills whiskey and gin;
> Grandma sells wine from grapes on our vine;
> Good grief how the money's rolling in!

The nation's comedians found Prohibition a "gold mine" for joke material; "She was only a whiskey-maker, but we loved her still."[32]

Authors' Perspective: Oil had first been discovered in New Mexico in 1922 on the Navajo Indian Reservation in the northwestern corner of the state, west of Farmington. Five years later, on the flatlands near Hobbs in southeastern New Mexico, another large discovery was made and the Land of Enchantment became the nation's third-largest oil and natural gas producer. During the 1930s, New Mexico's 423,317 residents were among the nation's hardest hit people when the Great Depression took hold of the country's economy. Even bootleggers felt the worsening circulation of money, thus the decrease of customers and increase in competition.

In the midst of all the gloom and doom, Clyde W. Tombaugh, a professor at New Mexico's agricultural and mechanical university at Las Cruces, discovered a new planet in our universe. He called the heavenly body Pluto. Over the decades the power and clarity of telescopes improved and by 1978 astronomers discovered the true nature of Pluto and its moon, so in 2006 the scientific community reclassified Pluto as a "dwarf planet" and the search for new planets continues.[33]

3

"Revenooers"

America's New Enforcers with Limitations

"This law will be obeyed in cities, large and small, and in villages, and where it is not obeyed it will be enforced. [...] The law says that liquor to be used as a beverage must not be manufactured. We shall see that it is not manufactured. Nor sold, nor given away, nor hauled in anything on the surface of the earth or under the earth or in the air."—John F. Kramer, democrat, First Federal Prohibition Commissioner, 1919–1920

Dateline:
Monday, June 30, 1919–Tuesday, December 5, 1933

In the three months prior to the implementation of National Prohibition, the federal government got a taste of what was to come from those who opposed the measure. Liquor worth half a million dollars was stolen from federal government warehouses. It didn't take long for police administrators across the nation to realize that the enforcement of prohibition was going to be a Herculean task. According to Commissioner John F. Kramer, "The line of demarcation is no longer between those who favor prohibition and those who do not favor it, but the line is between those who are in favor of obedience to the law and those who are not." In simple facts, the Volstead Act of 1919 required that federal agents patrol a nation covering 3,500,000 square miles of territory, while requiring total abstinence of a population reaching over 122 million people who were accustomed to freely consuming over two million gallons of alcoholic beverages annually. Kramer fully recognized the problems that were yet to surface.[1]

The new federal officers were responsible for supervising the proper use of the 170 million gallons of legal industrial alcohol annually produced, the 11 million legal alcohol medical prescriptions issued by the nation's medical community, and the wine used by the religious community of churches.[2]

"On May 28, 1929, I announced the appointment of a commission to investigate and recommended action upon the whole crime and prohibition question," wrote former President Herbert Hoover in his *Memoirs.* Congress passed the Deficiency Act for the Fiscal Year ending June 30, 1929, to fund a national "blue ribbon" commission, with subpoena power, to study law enforcement efforts in the United States. The commission was extended into fiscal year 1930 by the Second Deficiency Act. President Hoover appointed former Attorney General George W. Wickersham to chair an 11-member body which was formally named the National Commission on Law Obedience and Enforcement. President Hoover addressed the committee meeting at the opening session, saying, "It is my hope that the Commission shall secure an accurate determination of fact and cause, following them with constructive, courageous conclusions." The commissioners quickly discovered what lawmen in the field already knew: "It is impossible to divorce the problems of law enforcement from that of enforceability."[3]

The Volstead Act took effect at 12:01 a.m. on Friday morning, January 16, 1920, and on Sunday, June 13, 1920, William D. Dorsey became the first federal agent to die enforcing National Prohibition. The last national dry agent to be killed, number 114, was Paul A. Reed on Wednesday, July 12, 1933.

The Simple Facts

Statistics compiled routinely by the Internal Revenue Service demonstrated the failure of National Prohibition as the increasing volume of the bootleg trade grew over the 1920s and beyond. For comparison purposes, note that in 1921, an estimated 95,933 illicit distilleries, stills and fermenters were seized by federal agents while in 1925 these same categories jumped to 172,537 seizures reaching 282,122 in 1930. The number of persons arrested in 1921 incidental to these removals totaled 34,175. By 1925, the number had risen to 62,747 and increased to a high in 1928 of 75,307. Concurrently, in federal courts convictions for prohibition-related offenses rose from 35,000 in 1923 to 61,383 in 1932. Estimates of the number of illegal speakeasies in the United States ranged from 200,000 to 500,000 over the same period.

Federal lawmakers had provided a number of ways for clever entrepreneurs to continue supplying the various publics' drinking habits. For example, the basic prohibition law provided that wine used for sacramental purposes by places of worship could be acquired from government warehouses by permits. During the federal fiscal year 1922, legal wine amounting to 2,139,000 gallons, in rounded figures, was sold nationwide, while in the fiscal year 1924 this consumption figure reached 2,944,700 gallons. The government no longer maintained this data after that fiscal year, so there is no way of knowing what the consumption level of fermented sacramental wine reached. However, it is clear that the legitimate demand would not increase 800,000 gallons in two years.

Section 29 of the Volstead Act legalized the home production of fermented fruit juices. Although the section was allegedly inserted to save the vinegar industry and the hard cider of America's farmers, California grape growers used this provision to legally produce a type of grape jelly that became available nationwide. This grape jelly, suggestively called "Vine-go," could morph into a strong wine by adding water and letting the mixture ferment for two months. America became blessed with new "believers" and grape jelly lovers.

The often-forgotten duty of the prohibition agents involved inspecting the legal manufacture of industrial alcohol, legal alcoholic medical prescriptions issued by physicians and pharmacists, and the issues of sacramental wines for religious ceremonies. The American Medical Association (AMA) reported "medicinal" alcohol prescriptions quickly became a million-dollar business for pharmacies and doctors. During the first six months of National Prohibition, 15,000 physicians and 57,000 druggists and drug manufacturers applied for federal licenses to prescribe and sell liquor to patients. By 1928, according to AMA member estimates, the nation's physicians were earning $40 million annually by writing individual "medical prescriptions" for the use of whiskey for "medicinal purpose." The federal government spent $15 million in support of the prohibition enforcement program in FY 1929.[4]

Success—Failures

On September 17, 1927, the *New York World* discussed the darker side of corrupt prohibition agents. "We have in the federal service a prohibition force which is recruited to a large extent from the very class of criminals which it is supposed to hunt down," warned the report. "Yet this highly dangerous class of men is loosed upon us, knowing quite well from the record cited above that it may kill with impunity, since the chance is almost negligible that it will suffer any punishment." The newspaper went on to cite the Bureau of Prohibition's own statistics for the period January 1 through September 1927, noting that of the 113 suspects killed by special agents, only 57 cases resulted in state or local authorities bringing murder prosecutions against the dry officers—56 of this number were either not convicted or found to have been justifiable in the actions taken.

Twenty-two of these state prosecutions were removed from the state's jurisdiction by the federal court with the federal prosecuting attorney acting as counsel for the accused. Of the 22 cases, 13 cases resulted in acquittals, one in a conviction, one in a plea of guilty, and seven were still pending as of the newspaper's published report.[5]

Who Is the Commissioner?

The original appointee, John F. Kramer (Democrat of Mansfield, Ohio), served from November 17, 1919, to June 11, 1921. His successor, Roy Asa Haynes, served until May 20, 1927, but due to an agency-wide reorganization, the latter's authority was curtailed on November 1, 1925, following the appointment of Assistant Secretary of the Treasury Andrews who appointed an assistant commissioner of Prohibition with equal authority, who also served until May 20, 1927. On that date, the two positions were reconsolidated back into a single function and a new commissioner, Dr. James M. Doran, was appointed and served until July 1, 1930. On that date, the law enforcement duties of the Bureau of Prohibition were transferred from the Department of the Treasury to the Department of Justice.

With respect to the position of the Assistant Secretary of the Treasury, five persons had held the office between January 1920 and April 1925. For eight months prior to the new appointment, the office remained vacant. During this vacancy, no one appears to have been especially charged with the supervision of the prohibition forces or its coordination with the other responsible services. On April 1, 1925, Congress confirmed the appointment of Lincoln C. Andrews, United States Army (Ret.) as Assistant Secretary of the Treasury. Secretary of the Treasury Andrew W. Mellon personally proposed his nomination and authorized Andrews to revamp the national prohibition effort. As an expert in the "principles of scientific management," as taught by the eminent Frederick Winslow Taylor, General Andrews was given "carte blanche" authority to bring operational efficiency to the Prohibition Unit and its sister forces. Within the first year, he had called for the dismissal of all field investigators nationwide; the "great cleansing" effort to weed out non-performers, corrupted appointees, and political hacks had begun.[6]

Many things contributed to this situation according to the Wickersham Commission Report in 1930. The special investigation team named them thus:

a. The Eighteenth Amendment was submitted and ratified during a great war. The National Prohibition Act was passed immediately thereafter. During a period of war, the people readily yielded questions of personal right to the strengthening of government and the increase of its powers.
b. In the second place, the magnitude of the task was not appreciated. It seems to have been anticipated that the fact of the constitutional amendment and federal statute having put the federal government behind national prohibition would of itself operate largely to make the law effective. For a time, there appeared some warrant for this belief. [...] But soon after 1921 a marked change took place. It became increasingly evident that violation was much easier and enforcement much more difficult than had been supposed. The means of enforcement provided proved increasingly inadequate. No thorough-going survey of the difficulties and consideration of how to meet them was undertaken, however, until violations had made such headway as to create a strong and growing public feeling of the futility of the law.
c. A third cause was lack of experience of federal enforcement of a law of this sort. The subjects of federal penal legislation had been relatively few and either dealt with along well settled common law lines, or narrowly specialized. There was no federal police power and the use of federal powers for police purposes became important only in the present century. The existing federal machinery of law enforcement had not been set up for any such tasks and was ill adapted to those imposed upon it by the National Prohibition Act. But it was sought to adapt that machinery, or to let it find out how to adapt itself, without much prevision of the difficulties. Inadequate organization and equipment have resulted.
d. A fourth cause which had serious incidental effects was the attempt to enforce the National Prohibition Act as something on another plane from the law generally; an assumption that it was of paramount importance and that constitutional guarantees and legal limitations on agencies of law enforcement and on administration must yield to the exigencies or convenience of enforcing it."[7]

General Andrews discovered the mechanics of the former Prohibition Unit's enforcement efforts fell short in three principal ways. Firstly, the Prohibition Unit and its sister agencies' organizational lines of coordination, the varied functions of the personnel involved, and little to no law enforcement training of the agents along with insufficient managerial guidelines and expertise further compounded the situation. Secondly, the federal prosecuting organizations and the structures of the federal courts were not in place to handle the corresponding increases in prohibition arrests, trials, and sentencing matters. Thirdly, the means to ensure that the concurrent enforcement action of the states were funded and in place were neglected.[8]

Dr. James M. Doran, the last Commissioner of Prohibition in the Department of the Treasury, told *Time* magazine on January 21, 1929, that it would take $300 million annually to do Prohibition enforcement properly. When Congress initially had failed to provide funding to the states to implement its portions of this national program, it was assumed that the states would voluntarily undertake their own program to assist the federal government financially. This would not prove to be the case. In June 1929, Wisconsin joined Maryland, Nevada, Montana, and New York as the only states that did not enforce the federal prohibition laws.

In May 1923, New York State repealed its State Prohibition Enforcement Act. Many historians view this action as the beginning of the end of national prohibition. The governor and first lady of New York, Franklin Delano and Eleanor Roosevelt, were openly supportive of the efforts of Mrs. Pauline Joy Morton Sabin's Women's Organization for National Prohibition Reform. The heiress to the Morton Salt Company fortune and her high society friends helped lead the way back to normalcy by establishing one of the largest and most effective movements in the nation. The organization disbanded following the ratification of the Twenty-First Amendment that repealed the Eighteenth Amendment in December 1933, thus ending National Prohibition, an era that began with high hopes and ended in the midst of the Great Depression.

Early on, the problems of prohibition enforcement efforts were first highlighted in 1921 when Mrs. Mabel Walker Willebrandt, the Department of Justice's assistant attorney general, reviewed the difficulty the Department of the Treasury had in enforcing prohibition. She wrote: "[Hundreds] of prohibition agents had been appointed through political pull, and were as devoid of honesty and integrity as the bootlegging fraternity. I found that there were scores of prohibition agents no more fit to be trusted with a commission to enforce the laws of the United States and to carry a gun than the notorious bandit Jesse James."[9]

Mrs. Willebrandt would not be the last voice to claim these misgivings. According to the government's internal audits, between January 17, 1920, and June 30, 1930, the federal prohibition enforcement effort employed 17,972 field agents, but during the same time frame the bureau fired or dismissed 13,586 of the same agents. Many officers had been found to have been corrupted by bribes. In 1929, the newly formed National Commission on Law Observation and Law Enforcement determined that prior to 1927, in many of the 27 prohibition enforcement districts, the average length of a field agent's service was less than six months. Roy Haynes, one of the commissioners, noted "few men in any line or calling are subject to the temptations which beset the prohibition enforcement agent at almost every turn."[10]

Authors' Perspective: In 1928, the Bureau of Prohibition inaugurated a training program conducted by the senior staff of the 27 regional field offices in conjunction with the Civil Service Commission. Members of the reorganized bureau—exclusive of field personnel, clerks and Washington headquarters staff who were already serving under regulations of the Civil Service Act of 1923—were required to undertake and pass a written questionnaire of 40 multiple-choice questions on criminal investigation and constitutional law. Nationally, 59 percent of the test-takers failed the initial exam. Some were allowed second chances. In the end, a select number of capable, experienced, and trusted field personnel who had completed favorable background investigations but remained unable to pass the examinations would be "grandfathered in" the new organization with the approval of regional and headquarters management.

One of the prohibition agents who flunked the Civil Service test in New Mexico and had been dismissed from the service was seven-year veteran Jose G. Lovato. In October 1930, Lovato, now the Republican candidate for sheriff of Rio Arriba County, New Mexico, was arrested by Special Officers of the U.S. Indian Service at the San Juan Pueblo and charged with introducing and transporting whiskey onto an Indian reservation and the destruction of evidence. Lovato's public service career ended.

In early 1923, New Mexico lawmakers were unable to agree on a method for the state to enforce alcohol prohibition, but they did enact legislation prohibiting the sale, cultivation or importation of *cannabis indicia*, commonly called marijuana. The law did not expressly forbid mere possession of the drug, but lawmen presumed that anyone they found in possession of the weed had imported it illegally.

The *Santa Fe New Mexican* had drawn attention to the marijuana problem in 1922 during a report on the state penitentiary board's investigation into questionable operations at the state's main correctional facility. A convict had testified he could buy marijuana cigarettes anytime he had a dollar. A century later, very little has changed in the New Mexico prison system.

4.

The Lawless Years

> "Prohibition has made nothing but trouble.
> When I sell liquor, it's called bootlegging;
> when my patrons serve it on [Chicago's]
> Lake Shore Drive, it's called hospitality."
> —Alphonse "Scarface Al" Capone, Prohibition Era racketeer

The common denominator among bootleggers was the means of product delivery from the manufacturing site to the distribution location. Ordinary-looking automobiles with high performance engines and stripped-down interiors were the favorites even though circumstances sometimes dictated the use of the more sophisticated vehicles. These could range from chauffeured limousines to hearses to the more mundane farm truck. Methods changed based on the success of the government's agents and the number of loads lost due to seizures.

Product seizures—the confiscated booze from load vehicles, warehouses, or still sites—were considered to be part of the bootlegger's costs of doing business. Not only did the "boots" keep track of their losses, but the prohibition field agents and local officers normally kept their own seizure records. This documentation included the quantity of booze captured; the "retail" value of the product seized; the location, date, and time of the seizure; and the form of packaging used. These raid details could also include tracking of how and where the bootlegger acquired the various ingredients, should the violators have had records at the seizure site indicating their purchases. Each seizure provided a slightly different clue that aided in an analysis of the bootlegger's overall *modus operandi*.

The Grasslands Raid

On Saturday, August 3, 1929, Union County Sheriff A.W. Tanner and his deputy, V.A. Garcia, joined forces with Cimarron County Sheriff H.W. Barrick of Boise City, Oklahoma, and a civilian deputy named Butler. They seized not one, but two 200-gallon stills at a single remote location operating about a half-mile inside New Mexico. The site proved to be a remote line shack on private property within the Kiowa National Grasslands reserve. Kiowa Creek provided a natural source of water. The brew site was further identified as the area located northeast of Clayton off the highway to Boise City, present day U.S. Highway 56 and 64. This isolated roadway provided an easy access to interconnecting maintained highways in three states: Texas, Oklahoma and New Mexico.[1]

Sheriff Barrick had developed the information leading to the seizure. Only one of the stills was in operation when the site was raided. Even so, this was a big score for the two county sheriffs' departments. According to the August 5, 1929, issue of Clayton's *Union County Leader*, 81 barrels of finished whiskey and mash including 420 gallons of the pure stuff ready for market were found. This raid was the largest seizure in New Mexico since the inception of Prohibition. Circumstances would suggest that the owners/operators of the stills had been warned of the raid since no arrests were made on site.

The county officers dumped the mash and piled up the empty barrels, setting fire to the whole works, including the whiskey that was ready to be transported to the public. Even after a decade of Prohibition enforcement activities, federal and state law enforcement agencies were not prepared to remove and store large quantities of evidence. In most cases, they followed the general operating procedure for remote locations and torched the site. This action prevented any further use of the equipment or supplies and provided a negative journal entry in the bad guys' financial ledger.[2]

By the summer of 1930, no one had yet made a connection between the style of operation conducted at the Kiowa Grasslands site and the Aguilar ranch location raided in Colorado by Agent Kearney. In fact, some officers suspected that the New Mexico site may have been owned by an Oklahoma investor. The similarities of the two sites

Brewing equipment and supplies captured at a moonshine still site by federal agents in New Mexico. This was a remote brewing site so the agents rendered the still equipment useless and burned the supplies after taking photographs and conducting an inventory (courtesy New Mexico State University Special Collections and Archives Howard S. Beacham Papers #0349).

each having 200-gallon stills in operation tended to validate earlier intelligence reports on Colorado's Carlino crime family's suspected expansionary influences. Hindsight suggests these two sites were the beginnings of a new trend, a change in brewing operations. The bootleggers were seemingly in the process of replacing the 20-, 50-, and 100-gallon capacity stills that had been the norm in earlier years. Prohibition Agent Sutton did not have an opportunity to view the Union County site or its contents prior to the destruction. The absence of any federal participation, if they were available, to join in this raid may suggest that the local officials desired the credit for the raid to impress local voters.[3]

The larger the still capacity, the higher the profit and returns to the boots. Unfortunately, this new scenario also meant that larger facilities had climbing operational expenses and a need to increase security for the still operations. The one thing that was constant in Prohibition enforcement and bootlegging was "change," and the criminals were winning the war. Occasionally, law enforcement officers got lucky, like the seizure in Union County and on another occasion when Agent Kearney stopped the old Ford flatbed truck up near Walsenburg. Again, he didn't catch any key leader, but he did arrest the truck driver, confiscate the vehicle, and seize the load. The driver refused to talk about the truck's contents, its site of origination, the delivery destination, or anything else for that matter.

It was one of Kearney's best. Three 40-gallon barrels of finished whiskey and another hundred gallons of bottled whiskey in quart containers wrapped in straw sleeves were found hidden in a special flatbed compartment beneath several bales of hay. Total estimated wholesale loss to the crime family: perhaps $10,000 before further adulteration and repackaging to pint bottles. The value of the load equated to over four times the annual salary that Kearney earned as a federal agent. The seizure had a definite impact on the bootlegger's bottom line and warranted their attention.

Once the spirits were cut a few times and bottled into pint quantities, the value would exceed $60,000 in retail sales. Skilled cookers could produce 200 gallons of liquor per day, seven days a week, provided their brew supply lines and cooking operations remained intact. It would be reasonable to conclude that circumstances limited the Aguilar ranch operation to two or three cooks per week. Even at this rate of production, the rural operation must have provided a hefty return on investment.

While searching the Aguilar ranch buildings, agents discovered more than two-dozen oak barrels aligned in two rows, three barrels high. Sacks of grain and sugar were neatly stored in an adjacent area under a heavy canvas tarpaulin. Additional empty oak barrels were housed in an attached storeroom. Ten mash vats were found situated in a separate large room concealed by a series of false walls in proximity to the operational still itself. Heat for the still appeared to be supplied by an underground gas-fed fuel line that originated from an adjoining nearby storage shed camouflaged as a large tack shed contiguous to the unused corral. No domesticated animals were discovered on the property.

Authors' Perspective: There were known criminal contacts between the Colorado crime families and those in the eastern United States. That fact alone may be a clue as to the identity of the organization responsible for the Aguilar ranch site. Perhaps the crime families were importing their cooks from other regions of the country. They were known to import gunmen for special services when needed, why not apply the same rationale to still operators?

Colorado had always been a vacationing "Mecca" for the eastern states' gangsters, including those based in Chicago, Detroit, St. Louis, Boston, and New York City. The infamous Alphonse Capone was a known visitor to Colorado, some say he even visited Trinidad and purchased some real estate under an assumed name. Federal agents from across the nation believed they would eventually learn the details of the specific bootlegging group running specific operations in the different states. This remained an ongoing quest for federal officers.[4]

The Carlino group was infamous throughout the Rocky Mountain region by virtue of their past decade of violence, intimidation, murder, and strong-arm management techniques. In their own way, the brothers had streamlined the bootlegging industry along the corridor between Trinidad and Pueblo. Their influences were well known among federal prohibition agents.

"*Caveat emptor*–buyer beware"

Local residents were aware that Sam and Pete Carlino operated the Pueblo Olive Oil Company housed on the second floor of the small family grocery store located in Pueblo's Italian section. Grocery store customers never suspected that the business upstairs was the headquarters for this southern Colorado mob. There was nothing noteworthy or stylish in the furnishings or fixtures. The oil company office consisted of a desk, a telephone, a large round card table and chairs, a couple of leather couches, two floor lamps and a radio.

Sam Carlino, the younger brother by five years of the two crime boss siblings, was 36 years old, with straight, pomaded black hair, olive complexion, and cold black eyes. By looks, he favored the popular 1920s movie star Rudolph Valentino. Since Sam had returned to Pueblo from his self-imposed California vacation in late 1929, the brothers had made some very important business arrangements and plans, some of which would revolutionize the "business" in Colorado.

In 1928, the New York-based Mafioso leaders, Charles "Lucky" Luciano and four of his closest associates: Benjamin "Bugsy" Siegel, Morris Barney "Moe" Dalitz, Meyer "The Accountant" Lansky, and Frank "The Prime Minister" Costello, founded a secret national organized crime structure. The plan allowed for the reorganization of all bootlegging, gambling, prostitution, and associated operations in the principal eastern territories in order to economically capitalize the "business" profits. Wholesale and retail prices were set, and controlled territorial boundaries were established among the five major New York crime families.[5]

The increasing impact of the non-aligned "independent bootleggers" had been causing a negative financial drain on the established distributorships' bottom lines. It had become a national problem. This, in turn, impacted other "business" operations throughout the country. The new arrangement allowed for setting up a "Commission" to direct overall national operations involving those families who agreed to combine their interests. Any family head who controlled a large geographic area could become a member of the Commission. The two Carlino Brothers of southern Colorado had their eyes on becoming a part of that Commission.

Those few families who declined to participate were found to be of the "old Sicilian school" of the "Mustache Petes" and preferred to follow the time-tested doctrine established in the old country. The new operation would eventually "cull the problems" of the old model and become part of a lasting national empire that operated across several future decades. Young Lansky, an accountant, was the brains behind the new reorganization efforts. In the underworld, news of these new structures traveled quickly all the way to the Pacific coast where Pete Carlino learned of this "thing" while in California. The plan appeared to be amazingly simple and something that the Carlino brothers could support. After all, they were a part of this era where new ideas and new methods would replace the old to make way for the younger leaders. The brothers saw this movement as their destiny to solidify their control of all of Colorado's bootlegging and rackets which would elevate their personal statures nationally with the major families in New York, Chicago, and Detroit. After all, they had won the war against the rival Danna brothers. Who else would have the guts to challenge them?

Following a little fire insurance scam in San Bernardino, California, in late 1929 that netted him $5,200, Pete Carlino thought it would be in his best interests to return home a little earlier than anticipated. Since the arson cops in San Bernardino wanted to discuss the issue that arson was not an acceptable method to make a few bucks, Pete left rather hurriedly.

By late November 1929, Pete Carlino had relocated his family to their new residence on Federal Boulevard in Denver, the home base of crime boss Joe Roma. Sam followed with his family a short time later. Their operations in Pueblo and Trinidad had remained intact and continued under Sam's control in Pete's absence. Maybe now they could develop a few inroads into the Denver territories in the interim while lining up the families before going statewide. One of these men was Joe Roma who had once worked for them.

The Carlino brothers clearly saw themselves as the future "big bosses of Colorado." Unfortunately, a newly created self-congratulatory mantra tended to cloud their thinking. *"E'il nostro destino. L'intero stato chiama. E'nostra per la presa.* [It is our destiny. The entire state beckons. It is ours for the taking.]" The brothers didn't truly understand the principles of cause and effect in relation to short-sighted planning. They saw only their visions of boundless success. A great deal of higher-level reasoning on their part would have been to their advantage and definitely would be required in the immediate future to convince the other established families and the acknowledged independent bootleggers to fall in line. Such reasoning abilities had not been a major part of their gene pool, however. Ultimately, they determined that the help of out-of-state "supporters" would be necessary if they were to successfully unseat Roma from his high command perch.[6]

Authors' Perspective: In light of the local Italian/Sicilian mobs' well-known mission to control the manufacture and distribution of illegal liquor in Colorado, it is interesting to consider comments made concerning the Ku Klux Klan's covert operations in the state during this same timeframe. Ray Marty served as Las Animas County's

4. The Lawless Years

sheriff from 1937 through 1944 having succeeded Elijah Duling. In his golden years, Marty told Chuck Hornung that most of Colorado's dry agents had been members of the "Secret Empire" in the 1920s. He also said that the Exalted Cyclops, the Klan leader, came from Trinidad and that the Klan members especially volunteered as "posse" members to assist the feds conducting raids on the brew stills and supply depots owned by Italian Catholic, Jewish, and/or black bootleggers. The veteran sheriff also claimed that the Klansmen were compensated for their assistance with the booty captured during the raid. Since documentation is slim, the authors are not certain how factual this information may be.

The authors note that Robert Alan Goldberg, in his *Hooded Empire: The Ku Klux Klan in Colorado*, claims the Klan did exercise powerful economic and political influence within the Centennial State and a number of other states during the 1920s and 1930s. Goldberg explains in detail the problematic enforcement efforts of Klan members in law enforcement as well as the identity of the number and locations of the Klaxons (KKK chapters) throughout the state. He points out that Trinidad did boast of a large Klan affiliation membership during this era.[7]

5

Dale F. Kearney
Prohibition Agent, Badge 1422

"I never knew him. My mother's father died in the line of duty, a hero in my eyes."—Bob Lukens, Dale F. Kearney's grandson, March 5, 2013

Dale Francis Kearney was born at home in the farming community of Bode, Delana Township, Humboldt County, in northcentral Iowa on Monday, January 22, 1900. The community was first settled in 1881 as a shipping point on the newly constructed Burlington, Cedar Rapids and Northern Railroad. The Twelfth United States Census (1900) listed Bode with 409 people in 1900. A few years later, the Kearney clan was settled in Boulder County, Colorado. Dale's wife, Frances Elizabeth Brown, was born in the agriculture community of Longmont in the St. Vrain Creek Valley of Boulder County on Sunday, February 25, 1900. The federal headcount that year gave Longmont, Colorado, 2,201 residents.[1]

Kearney finished his public school education when he graduated from the 12th grade. On Saturday, April 13, 1918, he was sworn into the United States Army and after basic training he was assigned to the 402nd Telegraph Battalion in the Signal Corps. The Great War in Europe to "make the world safe for democracy and to end all wars" concluded with an armistice at 11:00 a.m. on Monday morning November 11, 1918. Kearney returned home and was discharged from his military duties on Monday, July 7, 1919. On July 7, 1930, following the report of his death, the *Niagara Falls Gazette*, published in New York State, took note of Dale Kearney's wartime service saying that he "was decorated for bravery under fire."[2]

It appears that one of Dale Kearney's first actions after returning home to St. Vrain Creek Valley was to find Fran Brown. It is unknown when Kearney married Miss Brown, but the *Longmont Ledger*, July 21, 1922, announced the birth of the couple's first child, a daughter they named after her mother. In August 1925 the couple's three-year-old daughter Francis died and was buried in the Brown family plot in Longmont's Mountain View Cemetery. A decade after Dale had returned stateside, he was living at 1028 Lawrence Street in West Denver with Fran and their daughters Kathleen and Caroline.

On Monday, July 1, 1929, Dale Francis Kearney took the oath of office as a prohibition agent, with a salary of $2,300 per year, and was assigned to the Denver office. Eight and a half months later, on March 15, 1930, having completed a period of on-the-job probationary training, Dale was reassigned as the resident agent for Las Animas and Baca Counties in the southeastern section of Colorado. He would live in Trinidad, regarded by the Prohibition Bureau as one of the most corrupt towns in the Centennial State with a well-established criminal component. The area was the southernmost center of operations for the Carlino brothers and the Black Hand Society. The 1930 United States Census for Las Animas County, Colorado, recorded 11,732 people living in Trinidad, the county seat.[3]

The area's old timers still recalled the Baca and Jaffa families as early community leaders. They also remembered W.B. "Bat" Masterson as the town's marshal in 1882 and that his brother James had been a deputy sheriff along with New Mexico gunfighter Mason Bowman. During the same era, dentist John H. "Doc" Holliday had been a frequent patron of the town gambling parlors. In the second half of the 1880s, former peace officer Wyatt Earp and his wife would visit Trinidad when they were traveling on the annual circuit of Western-slope gamblers.[4]

Official photograph of Prohibition Agent Dale F. Kearney (courtesy the Bureau of Alcohol, Tobacco, Firearms and Explosives; ATF.com).

Area Recon Mission

The records of the Colorado Highway Department contain information about the state's road building history. In 1919, the Centennial State was one of four states to become the first to enact a gasoline sales tax to fund highway construction; the tax was one cent per gallon that first year. The Colorado Highway Advisory Board voted on December 1, 1917, to accept a 50/50 partnership with the federal government to fund construction of a 16-foot-wide concrete highway between Pueblo and Trinidad at a cost of $267,199.91. In 1918, this road was dubbed the National Old Trail Road and had road signs marked "NOT" with black letters on a white square; later the road extended into New Mexico via Raton Pass as U.S. 40 and today is known as I-25. The road leading northeast from Trinidad to La Junta followed the Santa Fe Trail and was so called in 1930. From Trinidad, eastward into Baca County a traveler would have used the Plains-Mountain Highway system of graded country roads.[5]

Prohibition Agent Kearney familiarized himself with the main roads of southeastern Colorado's Los Animas and Baca Counties and was able to recite from memory the various turnouts and blind curves, especially those along the NOT Road that led northward toward Pueblo, whether he was driving during the day or at night. Whenever he partnered up with vetted Trinidad police officer Oscar Vandenberg, they would patrol these roadways looking for suspicious bootlegging vehicles speeding to their delivery sites. The two men also worked the highway south toward Raton Pass and the state line with New Mexico. The Colorado officers, working with Agent Ray Sutton in New Mexico, would set up road barriers at key locations, places where the officers had unobstructed two-way views of oncoming highway traffic, and just wait for the loaded cars to attempt a speed-by without stopping. This procedure had a high success rate for a short while until the bad guys became aware of these techniques.[6]

Resident Agent Kearney

A short time after arriving in Trinidad, Kearney led a raid that shut down a 200-gallon still at one of the old ranches outside of the mining camp at Aguilar. He learned from his training and experience that the only way to convict a "bootlegger" of a crime was to catch them in the act of making, selling or transporting their illegal products. On this raid, he seized one of the larger cooking sites then operating in remote southeastern Colorado. The Bureau of Prohibition headquarters in Denver reported similar, but usually smaller, site seizures in New Mexico's Colfax and Union Counties. The shutdown of the lucrative Aguilar production site may have been the basis behind the organized criminals' plan to rid Las Animas County of an honest and too active prohibition agent. Unknown to Kearney, he had been given the kiss of death.[7]

National Administrative Changes

The *Raton Evening Gazette*, June 22, 1930, carried the headline "Hoover Plans Decisive Test of Prohibition" and told readers how President Herbert Clark Hoover was enacting measures to fulfill the pledge he made during his inaugural address on March 4, 1929. In his interview, the president promised that within days there was going to be a new Prohibition enforcement agency director, new administrative and personnel structure, and a change in the methodology of enforcing the national alcohol prohibition law.

The *Washington Post,* among other capital area newspapers, broke the news on Tuesday, June 24 that Amos Waller Wright Woodcock had been appointed by President Herbert Hoover as the new head of the Prohibition Bureau. He was a decorated army officer in the late war, an attorney general for the state of Maryland, a current National Guard officer, and was currently the highly successful nine-year veteran United States attorney of Maryland. The *New York Times* felt that Woodcock's appointment was ironic since Maryland was the only state in the union that had not enacted a state law to enforce national prohibition. Thus the state earned the nickname "Sopping Maryland," while its largest city Baltimore became known for being "wringing wet." A residents' poll taken in Woodcock's hometown of Salisbury showed strong support of repealing the Eighteenth Amendment. The *New York Times* concluded that Woodcock was undertaking "the most difficult job under the government."[8]

5. *Dale F. Kearney* 45

Journalist H.L. Mencken described Woodcock as a "small, neat, smooth-shaven, baldheaded fellow" who had "the most august and puissant post in the government." The new dry chief was called "vigorous and fearless" in prosecution of an offender by a *Baltimore Sun* reporter, who was recalling that while Woodcock was the federal attorney he had prosecuted over 11,000 prohibition cases and won on over 9,000 of them. A reporter for the *Washington Post* said Woodcock had a "friendly smile, but hardly a trace of humor" with a winning personality "so persuasive, so manifestly honest and honorable" as to be much like Abraham Lincoln, but he was also "the most naïve and unsuspecting official at the Capital." This man was a workaholic to the point the *Literary Digest* joked, "His hobby seems to be work." Few doubted that the Prohibition Bureau finally had a real leader.[9]

Over a half a continent away, Woodcock's new job was received with mixed emotions. Everyone in Colorado knew that this leadership change in the nation's capital would upset the status quo in the Centennial State. Las Animas County's seat of government was considered second of two main centers of Southern Colorado's organized crime operations. The city of Pueblo, located 85 miles to the north, was covered by a

Amos W.W. Woodcock being sworn in as director of the Bureau of Prohibition. Appearing from left to right, Charles B. Sornborger, appointment clerk at the Department of Justice, Woodcock, United States Attorney General William DeWitt Mitchell and G. Aaron Youngquist, the Assistant Attorney General (courtesy the Chuck and V.J. Hornung Western History Collection).

four-man team that included Prohibition Agent William E. Nance. Nance ranked first in the region based on recent Civil Service Commission tests of field agents. Denver wore the crown as crime central for the region. The common link shared by the Pueblo and Trinidad federal Prohibition enforcement offices was simple; both areas were controlled by the Carlino Brothers.[10]

The *Colorado Transcript* was the community newspaper for Golden, Colorado, longtime home of the Coors Brewing Company prior to the advent of national prohibition. This suburban Denver newspaper headlined a story on July 3, 1930: "Vivian To Head Enlarged 'Dry Law' District." John F. Vivian was well known in Colorado political circles, whose membership understood that Amos W.W. Woodcock had a "true" mission supporter in the expanded Rocky Mountain region in the person of Vivian.[11]

On Friday evening August 4, 1930, Director Woodcock spoke to the nation during a 15-minute address carried by the National Broadcast System's radio network. In his talk he promised to enforce the National Prohibition Law "fairly, honestly, earnestly, and lawfully" with an emphasis being placed on citizens' voluntary compliance in obeying the "no commercial for sale" of alcohol. He outlined a plan to recruit and train highly qualified agents to work with local and state officers to decrease alcohol consumption. Woodcock said that if citizens didn't like the law they should work to force Congress to alter certain provisions or to totally abolish the law. But until Congress acted, federal efforts would reach a new level of "vigorous enforcement." Within a short time, the Department of Justice published *The Value of Law Observance*, a small booklet written by Woodcock to lend support for his mission and to expand on information from his recent radio broadcast message.[12]

Nearly a year later on Tuesday evening, July 7, 1931, Director Woodcock gave the nation his report concerning the accomplishments of his first year in office. The Columbia Broadcasting System's radio network carried the 15-minute address. Woodcock reported that his new team had prosecuted 58,173 cases in the federal district courts resulting in 50,334 convictions. His agents had destroyed 21,321 illegal stills and caused the collection of $5,497,566.40 in fines. New agents were being selected based upon "intelligence and character" with an emphasis on "brains and not brawn." These men were being trained in investigation techniques and the laws of evidence. The dry chief reiterated the Bureau's continuing focus on the "commercial violator" and stated that it was his intent to "leave the purely private violator to his own conscience." Woodcock understood that private consumption of spirits was prohibited by the Constitution and federal and state laws, but he had compromised with his Methodist social beliefs and his views of an individual's right to privacy. He and most of the people in the United States believed that the nation's "noble social experiment" was dying a slow but certain death.[13]

The Prohibition Bureau had three distinct classifications of field agents: prohibition agent, prohibition investigator, and the prohibition special agent. The "Special Agent" title was reserved for a separate unit who functioned as intelligence officers who were the eyes and ears of the bureau chief in each of the regional offices. Their mission was to locate corruption within the bureau and conduct major investigations within the region, as assigned. Those enforcement personnel who held management or other specialty classifications slots were also agents, but they were professionally identified by the position they filled, e.g., regional administrator, deputy regional administrator, prohibition inspector, et al. The exception to the general agent classifications were the contracted "Special Employees" who, in fact, were paid informants, hired on an as-needed, per diem basis.

The new Bureau reorganization meant nothing to the men and women who did not respect the prohibition laws or its enforcers, for they had many names for the law's enforcement agents. The shortened term "prohis" had been used by the media for brevity and derogatorily by the criminals from the beginning to describe the legions of politically appointed unskilled civilian personnel chosen to become prohibition law enforcement officers. Over a decade later, the bootleggers gave these men a more affectionate reference: "assholes," a term denoting the more deprecatory and fitting frame of referenced disrespect.[14]

Regional Conference

Tuesday, July 1, 1930, marked the end of Kearney's first year as a prohibition agent. Dale was attending a special three-day meeting in the Denver federal building conference room for all the dry agents from the new five-state region. More than 60 investigators were gathered together to complete the bureau's interdepartmental transfer from the Treasury Department to the Department of Justice. The bureau had completed all the mandates required by the Civil Service Commission to bring its personnel up to established standards to become civil service employees with all rights and benefits of this status. This "new beginning" was the fourth reorganization in the Prohibition Bureau's ten-year history.[15]

The assembled agents learned that Director Woodcock planned to establish a training school for agents based upon the concepts used by General John J. Pershing in France for training his officers. He would establish a promotion system based upon the structure used by the United States Army. Agents were encouraged to seek higher education levels because new agents would be recruited from the nation's colleges and graduate schools. The director was going to create a new style of "military organization" with a strong *esprit de corps* in the ranks.

Agents would be required to keep a daily action log and also maintain numerous avenues of statistical data that would be forwarded to the national headquarters so that the director had a daily record of the success and failures of the new enforcement effort. Woodcock also planned to make a fact-finding tour of each Prohibition Region to visit agents and citizens so as to acquire a better understanding of the enforcement challenges each region faced. Some journalist joked about Woodcock's plans to reform prohibition enforcement, but he was not deterred in his mission.[16]

During the regional conference, Kearney found time to have a casual visit with his former mentor John Richardson who now served the Denver office as the senior Prohibition investigator for field operations. Within a few months he would be named the temporary deputy regional director for field operations. Richardson had been instrumental in the selection of Kearney for his first field assignment following a review of his performance working out of the Denver office. Agent Nance of the Pueblo office also had input in Dale's selection based on his experiences with the same criminal families encountered in the Pueblo region.[17]

All of the federal officers who attended the Denver conference returned home with a new badge and a new photo identification and authority card issued by the Department of Justice. The new badge was a gold shield surmounted by a wing-spreading eagle. The center of the three-inch shield contained an embossed seal of the Department of Justice. The blue ribbon above the seal contained the name "Bureau of Prohibition" in gold letters, while the larger, bottom blue ribbon had gold letters bearing the identifier "Prohibition Agent." On the reverse of the new badge was a machine-stamped number. The eagle-topped gold shield replaced the blue enamel elongated shield used from 1927–1930 when the Bureau was in the Department of the Treasury.[18]

Back to Work

During this era, most home telephones were on multi-party lines and a telephone operator was required to place long distance calls for their subscribers. Whenever Kearney was away on assignment, Fran had the task of recording telephone call messages. On the evening of his return home from the Denver conference, Dale focused on two recent entries in the home logbook. Each was listed as a hang-up with no message, but Fran had noted that she could hear the caller's heavy breathing that sounded like a man's and some background noise like that of a railroad train station. It was not uncommon for a caller to ring a wrong number and hang up without speaking, but not twice in the same week and on the same day with the same background noise. The first call had come in on Tuesday around 1:00 p.m. with the second at 2:30 p.m. On the same evening of his return, Dale received a threatening phone call and noted its contents in his telephone logbook.

The new ID folder and badge issued to Prohibition Agents in 1930. A new commission folder and badge was issued to agents when the Bureau of Prohibition was transferred from the Department of the Treasury to the Department of Justice in 1930 (Bureau of Alcohol, Tobacco, Firearms and Explosives).

All day Thursday and part of Friday, July 3–4, Kearney worked on his information filing system and unfinished case reports using the new reporting format required by the Department of Justice. He also mentally planned his next week's travel, following a review of the mail which had accumulated while he was in Denver. The mail always brought something new, usually notices from the Pueblo or Denver Office advising of suspicious criminal activities to be checked out. Occasionally, Denver forwarded a few letters from local townspeople or community leaders in his territory accusing someone of unlawful alcohol sales or consumption. Most of the accusations were unworkable allegations, but Kearney had been trained to handle each diplomatically with a personal visit as time permitted.

On the Fourth, after an early dinner for the girls, the Kearney family walked around the neighborhood watching their neighbors fire off assorted fireworks in the declining hour of daylight just before the evening darkness engulfed the area. It was after dark when the Kearneys returned home and the babysitter soon arrived. Dale and Fran were going out for a "dinner date."

Mrs. Kearney would later tell investigators that she had learned that the brothers Scarino, Dan and Joe operated the Saddle Rock Café, one of the nicest Italian restaurants in town. Dan had the duty in the day time with Joe covering the evening hours. Unknown to Fran, the two men would occasionally help her husband with tidbits of information that they had overheard during their shifts. While dining that evening, Dale quietly alerted his wife not to look up immediately but to casually notice the several different suspicious men who had entered the restaurant during their stay. One of them appeared to be "spotting" him: identifying him one to the other. Kearney knew one of these men as a Dionisio family member, a noted Sicilian hood rumored to have Black Hand Society connections. The others in the group were unknown to Dale. When the man noticed Fran observing him, he seemed to become upset and agitated. Nothing occurred but Fran Kearney had become a bit more informed on some of the shady individuals who "peopled" her husband's world. Some of these men were no longer random faceless names, she now knew how a few appeared and acted while in public view. This new knowledge made her apprehensive.

Saturday, July 5, 1930, was Dale F. Kearney's last day as a terrestrial being. The morning came and went with Kearney doing some needed yardwork around his house and reading his new training information provided at the Denver conference. Around noon, Dale drove his car down to Charley's Chevrolet Garage to have his vehicle serviced, another reason he had taken a train to Denver. Once the car servicing was complete, he returned home to prepare for his usual evening field investigation activities. Around 7:00 p.m. Dale departed on his routine local "lone wolf search and destroy mission." He told Fran that he would return sometime between 11:00 p.m. and midnight. It was long after sunup Sunday morning when Mrs. Kearney heard a car drive up to the house.[19]

6

Ray Sutton
Prohibition Agent, Badge 2400

> "What you leave behind is not what is engraved on stone monuments, but what is woven into the lives of others."—Pericles, Greek general, orator and statesman, 400 BCE

Zaccheus Raymond "Ray" Sutton was born Saturday, November 15, 1873, at Plattsville, Taylor County, Iowa, into a family of nine. According to the 1870 federal census the county was home to 6,989 people and today remains one of the least populated counties in the state. Taylor County sat adjacent to the state line with Missouri along its southern border. The county was named in 1847 for General Zachary Taylor who would be elected the nation's 12th president a year later. On August 15, 1874, the future Mrs. Ray Sutton, Maggie Mae Walton, was born a few hundred miles east in Cedar County, Iowa—the same year Herbert Clark Hoover was born in Cedar County. He would become President of the United States in 1929.[1]

Also, the firebrand slave abolitionist John Brown and two of his raiders had lived in Cedar County when they planned their infamous 1859 attack on the United States Army Arsenal at Harpers Ferry in the current state of West Virginia. In a strange twist of fate, John Brown's distant niece, Martha Letitia Brown, would become the mother of James Perry Caldwell, a major player in the mystery profiled in this work.[2]

In 1889, both the Zaccheus N. Sutton and George E. Walton, Sr., families relocated to different regions along the Kansas-Oklahoma line in anticipation of the opening of the Oklahoma Territory for White Settlement. The two families were unknown to each other before they homesteaded in the western half of the original Cherokee Outlet. Both Sutton and Walton claimed their homestead lands as Union veterans of the War Between the States and became honored heroes in their new settlement. Ray Sutton's father died a decade after settling in Oklahoma and was buried in the evergreen-tree-lined Fairmont Cemetery at Fargo in the Spring of 1909.[3]

On Saturday, March 2, 1889, President Benjamin Harrison signed congressional legislation authorizing almost three million acres lying in the heart of original Creek and Seminole Indian reservation lands for non–Native American homesteading. The land rush began at noon on Monday, April 22, 1889, and each male adult who participated qualified to file for a 160-acre homestead. Ray Sutton was 16 years old at the time his family first took part in this run, and they made a second run a few years later—two of the most dramatized episodes in the western settlement saga.

The Sutton family established their first Oklahoma Territory homestead near the centrally located settlement of Mulhall. Z.N. Sutton planned to work his new land in anticipation of more acreage being opened up further west in the Cherokee Indian lands. He did so for six years. Ray Sutton was 20 years old when the Cherokee Outlet run took place on September 16, 1893.

One of the new settlements, Woodward, became the newly established county seat of "N" County which the new residents later voted to also name Woodward. The land was not really suited for farming, but the rolling open plains and lush grass made it ideal for cattle raising. The Sutton families homesteaded several hundred acres, based on the number of family filings at 160 acres allotted per person, just a few miles north of the Cheyenne and Arapahoe country along the Northern Canadian River in the Oleta Township. Like the other land-run families, the Sutton clan filed their homestead claims as individuals to form a contiguous body of land.[4]

Ray Sutton Family, circa 1899. Maggie Mae and Ray Sutton with their baby, Nello (courtesy the Raymond Ellsworth Sutton Family Archives).

Ray came of age in this rugged land along with his sisters and younger brother Hiram and lived like most farm/ranch youth during the decades prior to the turn of the 20th century. Hiram Sutton's second wife was Bertha A. Walton, the younger sister of Ray's wife.[5]

On March 13, 1894, the town of Woodward became the locale for an army payroll robbery by the bandit team of Bill Doolin and Bill Dalton. The early Tuesday morning holdup of the Santa Fe messenger netted the robbers $6,540; the two outlaws escaped.

Sutton was also a contemporary of Woodward resident Temple Houston, the renowned gunfighter/lawyer son of Sam Houston. On August 21, 1894, the *Guthrie Daily Leader* called Houston, "the silver-tongued orator of Oklahoma." Houston killed fellow attorney Ed Jennings on October 8, 1895, in a saloon fight at Woodward, resulting from an earlier courtroom confrontation between the two men. A year later, also in

Woodward, Houston shot another man. The lawyer and a farmer had a disagreement in front of the Cattle King Hotel and both men went for their revolvers. Houston was quicker and hit the man twice. He paid a misdemeanor fine for "unlawful shooting" of his weapon. He practiced law in Woodward until his death at age 41 in 1905.

Sutton would have had to have known Chris Madsen, a deputy United States Marshal, who served the Woodward area for the federal court at Guthrie. Two other community leaders would have included Will E. "Billy" Bolton, who was the secretary of the Oklahoma Territory Live Stock Association and editor of the *Live Stock Inspector,* and John E. "Jack" Love, the six-foot four-inch first sheriff of Woodward County. The *Woodward News,* June 8, 1894, described Love as "well informed on the laws and [he] fearlessly executes all orders of the court."

Born in Denmark, Chris Madsen became a law enforcement legend as one of the "Three Guardsmen" of Oklahoma along with Bill Tilghman and Heck Thomas. These deputy United States Marshals brought law to a hostile frontier in what became the 46th state.[6]

Sutton had been interested in both law enforcement and livestock raising as a means of making a living. He had become acquainted with Maggie Mae Walton via her older brother George. At the age of 22, while employed as a deputy sheriff and a brand inspector for the local livestock association, Ray would propose marriage to 18-year-old Maggie Walton. The couple were married by Shannon McCray, a magistrate, on Tuesday, August 4, 1896, at Woodward. They settled a small homestead in the far western part of the county near the community of Shattuck, which was built along the Southern Kansas Railroad, later a part of the Santa Fe railway system. The area was great country for raising wheat, cotton and broomcorn. The Sutton's would have three children: a daughter, Nello, born in 1899; a son, Raymond, born in 1901; and a second daughter, Hazel Ann, born in 1905.

In 1890, Congress joined the Indian Territory and Oklahoma Territory into a single joint territory and in 1907 it became the 46th state, called Oklahoma. The first state legislature created some new counties to help govern the growing western region and among these was Ellis County created out of part of Wood-

The Sutton Family Children, Hazel, Nello and Raymond George "Bud," circa 1915. This picture was taken in Des Moines, New Mexico (courtesy the Raymond Ellsworth Sutton Family Archives).

ward County along the Texas boundary. Governor Charles N. Haskell appointed 37-year-old Ray Sutton as the first sheriff of Ellis County and the Sutton family moved to the new county seat at Arnett. The sheriff's office was in the small wooden courthouse. In 1908, the Oklahoma state legislature voted statewide prohibition and Sheriff Sutton had his first experience enforcing such a law.[7]

The memory of hard men like Bill Doolin, Bill Dalton and Temple Houston had a profound effect upon Sutton. The new sheriff took a friendly and less confrontational approach to law enforcement. It worked. Two years later, Ray was elected Ellis County sheriff by a sizable vote and he was re-elected in November 1914. Most people liked Sutton the public servant and Sutton the businessman. Ray believed in the future of the new county. He and his brother-in-law George Walton owned stock in banks at Shattuck and Gage.[8]

The Move to New Mexico

In April 1915, the *Clayton News* and the *Des Moines Swastika* newspapers reported that a group of Oklahoma business associates of Sutton were exploring Union County for economic development opportunities. On June 7, 1915, Ray Sutton resigned his sheriff's commission and began his family's relocation to Des Moines, New Mexico, an area situated 80 miles west of Clayton. Besides business opportunities, he had a second reason for relocating to New Mexico. He was searching for a healthier climate for his wife who suffered from asthma. Just a short time after her arrival in New Mexico, she was hospitalized for her condition in the Clayton community hospital. The *Clayton Citizen* of December 14, 1916, reported that Mrs. Sutton had recovered from a severe three-month-long asthmatic attack.[9]

The Des Moines townsite was first laid out in 1887 as a railroad junction along the Colorado and Southern Railroad. W.G. Sears (Sutton's Ellis County, Oklahoma, friend) bought the original townsite deed and began development of a new residential addition to the town. Sutton bought a town lot and also filed a homestead for his Open A Ranch headquarters. He ran cattle on the open range north of Des Moines. Sutton used the same brand in Oklahoma and he had a practice of carrying two 20-dollar gold pieces inscribed with the "A" on the faces of the coins. The inscriptions resembled the Greek letter "lambda."

There were persons who believed the marked coins were gifts by his masonic brethren to honor his "raising" to the third-degree master mason position followed shortly thereafter with his elevation to the "thirty-second degree" walk in the burning sands of the higher mysteries of masonic teachings. A masonic open "A" symbolizes the "square" used in Blue Lodge rites that indicated he, as a master mason, was always "on the square"—fair and honest—in his dealings with others in life.[10] Perhaps, the coins held a double meaning for Ray Sutton.[11]

In the early 1970s during the early stage in the research for this work, C.E. Black, one of Sutton's rangeland neighbors, was interviewed about the Sutton family. "I remember very well the first time I saw Ray Sutton," recalled Black. "The range was all open from my father's ranch house over to Des Moines. Sutton and N.E. Nance had brought a herd of cattle from Texas to New Mexico and were grazing them on the open range. Like most any young fellow, with a good cow pony and saddle, I had to go out and see who they were."

The Sutton family lived in a house Ray had built in the new addition to the original Des Moines townsite. Black remembered the Sutton family as "tops as friends, and neighbors." He recalled, "My girlfriend, who became my wife, and I went to many a party at Ray's house; as we were good friends of Raymond and Nello; there was a younger daughter, too, but have forgotten her name." Thirteen-year-old Hazel Ann Sutton died of a heart problem on July 7, 1919, the possible victim of undiagnosed heart disease mostly inherited from her father's side of the family. She is buried in the Sutton family plot in the Clayton Cemetery.[12]

The *Union County Marriage Record Book Three* records that marriage license #1604 was executed by the wedding vows of Raymond W. Means and Nello M. Sutton on Sunday afternoon, June 2, 1918. They were married in her parent's home at 405 Oak Street in Clayton. The young couple settled in Portales. Later, Ray Means relocated his dental practice to Tucumcari.

Ray Sutton, New Mexico Businessman

Ray Sutton and J.L. Pryor, another former Oklahoman and Ellis County banker with whom Sutton had been affiliated, incorporated the State Bank of Des Moines, the community's first bank. The town of Des Moines' furniture dealer, S.R. Witcher, and the druggist, Elza Davis, were also from Ellis County. The Des Moines newspaper, *The Swastika*, used the Indian nickname for the Cimarron and Northwestern Railroad that made the community a cattle shipping point. The old newspaper's masthead reads, "Official Paper of Union County, New Mexico."[13]

After Sutton's arrival in Union County in early 1915, he accepted an appointment as a cattle brand inspector. This position gave him the basic introductory tool to allow him the opportunity to meet and greet the area's ranch owners, a necessary task if one desired to run for Union County sheriff. He did. Cattle and horse ranching were the two activities that served as the linchpins in holding the key to winning the votes of the large-property owners. Ranching in New Mexico had long been the path followed by previous victorious candidates for office.

In the summer of 1916, the Union County Commissioners appointed Sutton the county's delegate to the "National Good Roads Convention" to be held at Raton in August. The gathering was chaired by Oklahoma showman Col. Gordon "Pawnee Bill" Lillie. This national gathering gave Sutton a platform to become acquainted with other New Mexicans who became friends and later helped him with his federal officer duties.[14]

Ray Sutton, County Sheriff

Eighteen months after his arrival in northeastern New Mexico, Ray Sutton won the Republican nomination for sheriff in heavily Democrat-leaning Union County. On

November 7, 1916, he defeated J.E. Skelton by 118 votes. The *Clayton Citizen* said that Sutton "is just a natural born sheriff." Two years later, he won reelection against a Democrat and a Socialist, compiling 77 more votes than his opponents combined. The *Clayton News*, a Democrat newspaper, questioned how Sutton was so successful, saying,

> It's strange, but true. This is the second time that Sheriff Ray Sutton, running on the Republican ticket, has been elected in this Democratic county. Of course, he is elected with Democratic votes, but that is not strange—many men are elected with Democratic votes. The strange part of it is: How does Mr. Sutton harmonize the so widely divergent elements of his support? Why is it that the ministers of the gospel—preachers of the doctrines of the Goodly Nazarene—the teachers, the gamblers, the bootleggers, and the scum, all seemingly devoutly believe their salvation depends upon Sutton? What is "The Tie That Binds?"

The *News* editor seems to have answered his own question. People liked and trusted Sutton.[15]

Sutton's ability to reach across political affiliations was exemplified in 1917 when Andy H. Hudspeth, a Democrat leader and New Mexico's United States Marshal, appointed Sutton as a special deputy U.S. Marshal and authorized the Union County jail as a holding facility for federal prisoners. A year later, Washington E. Lindsey, a Republican and New Mexico's new governor, appointed Sutton as a non-salaried New Mexico Mounted Police officer with authority to name assistants, if needed, to conduct state police business in the northeastern section of the state.

When Ray Sutton was first elected sheriff, he kept his rangeland and cattle herd, but he sold his Des Moines house and Lot 19 in the new addition to B.F. and Mattie Abernathy for $383.86 and moved his family into Clayton. In the county seat, Sutton bought lots 12 and 14 in Block 1247, 405 Oak Street. The Open A ranch operation was left in the charge of a trusted black cowhand. Ray Sutton continued his work as a freemason, while Margaret was active in the Eastern Star. She had been serving as Worthy Matron of the Clayton lodge the year her husband was killed. Sutton also became a member of the Clayton Rotary Club where his friends nicknamed him "Buffalo Bill." He was a brother in the International Order of Odd Fellows and a founder of the Union County Historical Society.[16]

On May 18, 1917, President Woodrow Wilson signed the National Selective Service Act authorizing registration of all men between the ages of 21 to 31 years of age for military service as part of the nation's war effort. The act also established local draft boards to implement the law. Sutton, as sheriff, was appointed chairman of the Union County Draft Board. These citizens drew the names of fellow citizens to fight with the American Expeditionary Forces in France.

As a senior citizen, C.E. Black discussed his experience with the draft board. "When I was called for army duty in World War I, Raymond [Sutton] was on the induction board in Clayton. Just before I was called in, the whistles blew and bells rang, and the wires reported the war was over. When I went in for my exam, Raymond said: 'We'll go ahead and examine all day just in case the information is incorrect.' But thank goodness it was the end of the war." Ray Sutton had been a Union County delegate to the "Win the War for Peace Convention" held in Albuquerque during September 1918.

Another wartime position held by Sheriff Sutton was that of chairman for the Union County Council of Defense. He had been appointed by the leadership of the state council of defense. This 11-man county committee was charged with overseeing the war effort in Union County and making sure that all citizens did their civic duty by supporting war bond drives, Red Cross campaigns, draft procedures, and food and supplies rationing regulations. The committee also kept local aliens under surveillance as proscribed by provisions of the war acts.[17]

In the early years of President Woodrow Wilson's administration, his cabinet secretaries were examining ways to keep America white, Anglo-Saxon and Protestant. Wilson, a Progressive Democrat, banned interracial marriages in the District of Columbia, segregated government office buildings after over 50 years of a desegregated clerk and support staff and encouraged increased segregation of the nation's military forces. Demographics were being examined by government agencies to redefine the nation's ethnic, racial, and religious beliefs. A zenith in this effort was reached on November 12, 1914, when President Wilson told William Monroe Trotter, publisher of Boston's *The Guardian* newspaper, and other black leaders who were visiting the White House that "segregation is not a humiliation [to black people] but a benefit and ought to be so regarded by you gentlemen." Days later mass protests spread across America. The racial divide championed by Progressive Democrats bloomed into a staggering social and economic issue that grew rapidly after World War I into the Civil Rights movement that continues today.[18]

One summer night in 1918, Sheriff Sutton and two of his deputies broke up a Clayton lynch mob led by two Hispanics, whom the lawmen arrested for assault and rioting. The mob had attacked an Irish immigrant they felt was an anti-war, radical, draft-dodging slacker. Ireland was engaged in a war for independence from the British Empire and thus would not join the Allied Forces fighting Germany in France. A large percentage of Union County Hispanic families had sons serving in the military and patriotic fervor ran high in the county. Sutton had seen almost every type of injustice committed by man but incidents like this caused him to think that humans were nothing more than animals at times and damned by their insatiable craving for self-gratification and violence. One didn't have to live in the big cities to see this type of unacceptable behavior.[19]

In northern New Mexico many young men of Mexican heritage and Roman Catholic faith have been members of the Brotherhood of Light or the *Penitentes*. This highly religious sect observed the literal word of the Gospel narrative, including self-flagellation for sins and crucifixion of members during Holy Week celebrations. Sheriff Sutton, as other sheriffs in his region, faced difficulty obtaining criminal evidence from one member against another. The courts often found jury members were reluctant to convict a brother devotee even when they knew him to be guilty. Sutton understood the religious devotion, but not the defiance of the law.[20]

As 1918 dawned, the world was entering the fifth year of a global conflict that claimed multiple millions of lives, and now a deadly influenza pandemic joined in the carnage. The great pandemic infected and killed millions worldwide making it one of the deadliest natural disasters in human history. Most of the victims were predominantly healthy young adults. On July 7, 1919, Hazel Ann Sutton died, and her mother always believed the teenager's death was due in part to this disease because it may have worsened her heart condition. Since New Mexico had no statewide health agency in 1919, health records relating to Hazel's death were not found.²¹

One of the most difficult things to experience and fathom as a parent is the death of one of your own children. In the cycle of life, it is believed that the parents are supposed to be the ones to die first, but sometimes life doesn't follow the supposed-to-be logic of mankind. During the war years, Ray Sutton had frequently complained of slight chest pains but put it off to "indigestion" and failed to seek any medical examination. Maggie wasn't so sure that indigestion was an accurate diagnosis. What impact, if any, his medical concerns had on Ray's decision to not seek re-election as sheriff in 1920 are unknown.²²

Even as he was leaving the sheriff's office, Sutton's adversaries took a parting swipe at him in October 1920. He was charged in the Federal District Court at Santa Fe with "attempting to influence" a witness. However, upon completion of a case review, Federal Judge Colin Neblett found no credibility to the allegation and dismissed the charge against Sutton.²³

The former sheriff now took more interest in his business investments as the board of directors for the state-chartered Bank of Des Moines began negotiating the institution's sale to a larger banking enterprise, the Farmers and Stockmen Bank of Clayton. The sale was completed in 1920 and Sutton accepted the position of vice president and member of the board of directors with the Clayton bank. The next year, he accepted a position as vice president of the newly established Union Title and Loan Company of Clayton.²⁴

Sheriff Ray Sutton, daughter Hazel and wife Maggie Mae. When this photo was taken in Clayton, New Mexico, circa 1919, Raymond George was in the military and Nello was married (courtesy the Raymond Ellsworth Sutton Family Archives).

His prior ownership interest in the Bank of Des Moines and his ranch had served as Ray's "investments in community" evidence needed to meet the economic investment provision, as required by state law, for a candidate to seek public office. Before statehood, it was a common practice for "fly-by-night" politicians to try to win elections from honest property owners who had dedicated themselves to clean government. When outsiders came in, criminal violence often followed. Lawmakers at the Capitol enacted the investment in community law to assure that candidates intended to remain in the community over a continued period rather than for a short-term period of personal gain.

Following Hazel Sutton's untimely death in 1919, Maggie and Ray Sutton decided to honor her memory in the form of giving something back to the community. With help from their druggist friend Elza Davis, the couple established three drug stores in Union County that were strategically located so as to service the rural populations. The drug store managers were instructed to provide free medicines to those who had no money. Local financial recovery from the impact of the national influenza epidemic and war ration restrictions had been hard for some families.[25]

Ray Sutton, Federal Prohibition Agent

Ray Sutton was a successful businessman and a dedicated law enforcement officer who found meaning in his federal job. In 1923, he was recruited as a federal prohibition agent in New Mexico. His background as a range detective and sheriff provided Sutton law enforcement and management experience, plus a wide assortment of contacts. These attributes had attracted the attention of the Prohibition enforcement officials in Albuquerque and they wanted to hire him as a field supervisor. A top field agent earned a federal government salary of $1,800 per year. To provide a reference for this salary level consider that the 1929 New Mexico Legislature established a new salary schedule for county sheriffs. In 1930 a Class A County like Bernalillo (Albuquerque) was to pay their sheriff $3,500. For the blue-collar workers of the period, 25 cents an hour was considered top wages for a working man.[26]

By the time Sutton's federal employment paperwork was completed and approved, the supervisor position had been eliminated without the regional management's knowledge. Ray was offered and accepted a reduced starting position and salary with the promise he would be promoted as soon as budget allocations permitted. That minor road-bump didn't preclude regional management from using him as a field troubleshooter, however. Sutton's official personnel file documents his assignment to at least five different New Mexico posts within a two-year period (1923–1925) absenting him from his Clayton home base for short-term undertakings ranging from two to seven months in length.

As one of only ten federal Prohibition agents to cover the entire state of New Mexico, the territory Sutton was assigned encompassed the northeastern portion of the state from the Colorado-Kansas-Oklahoma borders west to include Taos County to the Rio Grande, then southward toward the region around San Miguel County, and on southeastward toward Portales in Roosevelt County—a big area to be covered by one man.[27]

Sutton transferred his masonic memberships from Oklahoma on June 23, 1919, but stopped paying his dues to the Shriner's Temple in Santa Fe by early 1923. He may have also gone inactive with his Blue Lodge membership at the same time. His reasons were private but may have related to his new employment with the federal government. An ethical conflict between his official capacity and his professional and social memberships may have been at issue. Most social clubs had established some form of "members only" private drinking "salons" since the beginning of Prohibition during the Great War, where they could and did consume their pre-Prohibition legal, or post-prohibition illegal, caches of libations. As long as liquor was not sold by the drink, the members' supplies remained the common property of the dues-paying membership. Sutton was always the cautious man in deflecting the appearance of any conflict of interest in matters such as these.[28]

The period of 1923–1925 had been formative years in Prohibition Region 18 that included the hiring or replacement of a number of investigative and management personnel. Besides employing Sutton, the Bureau hired a new Regional Administrator (John F. Vivian) in 1923 and a Deputy Regional Administrator for New Mexico (Charles H. Stearns) in 1925.

Sutton survived the Bureau of Prohibition reorganization in 1927 and the transfer of oversight between cabinet departments in 1930. Prohibition Agent Ray Sutton's official personnel file indicates he also did not pass the multiple-choice examinations required under the federal civil service regulations in 1930. However, the Prohibition leadership in New Mexico requested that Sutton be granted a waiver from the new civil service policy and be retained because his services were invaluable to the success of future operations. Sutton had proven himself through his dedication to duty, his honesty and loyalty, his extensive law enforcement record, and his wide-ranging network of informants. These views concerning Sutton's performance qualities were further con-

Official photograph of the New Mexico Agents, Bureau of Prohibition, Department of the Treasury, circa 1928. Seated (L-R): Ray Sutton, Walter L. Hill, Regional Administrator John F. Vivian, Deputy Administrator (New Mexico) Charles E. Stearns, Howard Beacham. Standing (L-R): Joseph W. McBroom, Melvin K. Clark, Clarence U. Finley, Robert L. Neal, and Harold S. Dew (courtesy New Mexico State University Special Collections and Archives, Howard S. Beacham Papers #0349).

firmed by regional management at Denver. The new management in Washington, D.C., concurred with field managers and Ray Sutton was retained as a federal officer.[29]

Sutton's daily logbook, for the six months prior to his death in August 1930, notes that he drove 8,858 miles, interviewed 297 people, appeared in court 37 times, made 20 arrests, conducted 17 liquor raids, and took a total of five days off from his official duties. His supervisor called him "one of the most capable men in the service."[30]

PART II

Booze, Bootleggers, Blood and Seeking Justice

"Crime is increasing. Confidence in speedy justice is decreasing. [... W]e must critically consider the entire Federal machinery of justice. [...] There would be little traffic in illegal liquor if only criminals patronized it. We must awake to the fact that this patronage from large numbers of law-abiding citizens are supplying the rewards and stimulating crime. [...] If citizens do not like a law, their duty as honest men and women is to discourage it as a violation; their right is openly to work for its repeal."—President Herbert Clark Hoover, Inaugural Address given at Washington, D.C., March 4, 1929

"The problem of law enforcement is not alone a function or business of government. If law can be upheld only by enforcement officers, then our scheme of government is at an end. Every citizen has a personal duty in it. The duty to order his own actions, to so weigh the effect of his example, that his conduct shall be a positive force in his community with respect to the law."—President Herbert Clark Hoover, address to the American Newspaper Publishers' Association, April 22, 1929

7

John F. Vivian, Ralph L. Carr and the Kearney Investigation Task Force

"Organized crime is a better business than any we know of at this writing."—"The Law Is Challenged" (editorial), Trinidad (CO) *Chronicle-News*, July 8, 1930.

Dateline: Denver, Colorado, Sunday, July 6, 1930

John F. Vivian, Administrator, Region 10, Bureau of Prohibition

Investigative reports indicate that on Sunday, July 6, 1930, Vivian had been awakened by an early morning phone call from the Denver office duty agent reporting the murder of the first federal prohibition agent in Colorado since National Prohibition began. Vivian was told that Agent Dale F. Kearney had been shot at Aguilar. Vivian requested that the duty agent notify all senior staff of an emergency meeting to be held that morning. He also asked for John C. Richardson's home phone number. Richardson was the region's senior investigator and would lead the federal murder investigation team. Vivian ordered him and a team of Pueblo first responders to Aguilar. After setting his team in motion, Vivian next notified both the Denver-based United States Attorney, Ralph L. Carr, and the Office of Director Woodcock at the Bureau of Prohibition in Washington of the murder of Agent Kearney.[1]

Vivian resided in the affluent enclave of Court House Hill, a neighborhood within Golden, Colorado, 15 miles distant from his Denver office. He was a soft-spoken man with years of practice with a politician's ready smile; his constituents frequently commented how his physical features reminded them of Old St. Nick. Although John Vivian received only the basic eighth-grade public school education of his era, he continued his "private education" through a wide range of state and federal personal contacts and involvement in the Republican Party's political machines that ran the Centennial State.[2]

Lawrence Cowle Phipps, his principal mentor, had been Colorado's United States Senator since 1919. He was a millionaire and had retired from Carnegie Steel as a senior executive. It was rumored that Phipps had been a major financier of the Colorado Ku

Klux Klan during the early to mid–1920s. His financial support to candidates for local and state offices consisted of large donations and the votes of a majority of Klan members.³

The Vivian family's rise in Colorado politics began shortly after 1905 at the local level and continued to grow to become legendary. His son, John Charles Vivian, followed in his father's political footsteps and in 1930 served as the attorney for Jefferson County, Colorado. The Republican administration in power in Washington publicly recognized and appreciated his family's years of service and party allegiance.

During the last week in June 1930, William Dewitt Mitchell, President Hoover's attorney general, designated Amos Waller Wright Woodcock, a former military officer in the Great War and Maryland's attorney general, to be the new director of the Prohibition Bureau. This directorship made him Vivian's new boss. George W. Wickersham, William H. Taft's attorney general (1909–1913) had personally recommended Woodcock to President Hoover as the right man to lead the Bureau of Prohibition.⁴

In the early 1900s, any sixth-grade student who had read his *McGuffey's Reader* or a Dime Novel adventure tale knew that a "sycophant" was a toady or unflattering parasite type of personage, while a "snollygoster" was an ambitious, boastful, talkative, unprincipled sort of fellow. The person was not a good role model but was a good candidate to be the villain in any story.

Enter John F. Vivian who had a zeal for the prohibition cause. In 1914, he played a leading role in drafting the first strict statewide prohibition legislation while serving as a secretary to Governor George Alfred Carlson. The bill prohibited any aspect of the manufacture or selling of alcohol and became the state law in 1916—four years before national prohibition legalities. Vivian's political record included service as a precinct committeeman and party chairman for Jefferson County, a stint as a Republican national committeeman and a three-time state chairman of the party. His history included three terms as mayor of Golden, Colorado, in the early 1900s where he enforced the communities' existing temperance sentiments to keep saloons in the area closed on Sundays.

Vivian established his priorities as a practicing politician, a forum that served him well, and was especially pleased with his role when "doing the Lord's work," as he told his many friends and supporters. This attitude found a favorable reception with the Women's Christian Temperance Union, the Anti-Saloon League, and other church and Prohibition advocate groups. It became difficult for any questioner to separate Vivian's view of politics from an otherwise implied religious intent. His image helped solidify the impression that the City of Golden and all of Jefferson County was indeed "the Vivian family's county." There were many people within the county courthouse and state capitol who concurred with that assessment.

When the position as prohibition administrator for Prohibition Region 18 first became available in 1921, Vivian expressed interest in the job and became the obvious political appointee based upon his active Republican political career and his role in developing the state's prohibition laws; he had neither prior law enforcement experience nor prosecution experience in his background. Vivian lost the appointment to E.H. McClenahan. Little known attributes about Vivian were his qualities as a mountebank and an expert at mendacity. Within the year, Regional Director McClenahan, along with four of his subordinates, were discharged without prejudice for filing false reimbursement claims for the use of their personal vehicles while on official duty. A false rumor quickly spread around town that the five officers had been caught operating a brewing still and selling its product. Vivian refiled his application for the vacated post and was appointed to the vacancy in 1923.[5]

John Vivian was always seeking advancement and increased political power. While still serving as regional administrator, Vivian joined two other men in the 1926 Republican Party primary for nomination as candidate for Colorado governor. He came in second in a three-way race. At the time, no federal or state laws precluded such double political activity by federal employees.

> **Authors' Perspective:** In 1939, Carl Hatch, the senior senator from New Mexico and an Old Guard Democrat in opposition to President Roosevelt's Progressive Democrat's attempt to establish complete control over party patronage, joined Republicans in introducing *An Act to Prevent Pernicious Political Activities* in Congress. The bill was seen as a means to limit certain political activities by federal employees, as well as by some state and local government employees who work in connection with federally funded programs, from engaging in partisan political activities. The legislation, commonly called the Hatch Act, set forth restrictions to ensure that federal programs are administered in a nonpartisan fashion, to protect federal employees from political coercion in the workplace by the party in power and to make certain that federal employees are advanced based on merit and not based on political affiliation. The act was last updated in 2012.

Regional Administrator Vivian, a Chameleon

As the region's prohibition administrator, Vivian soon learned that criminal investigations could be run just like a political campaign; in neither did you leave anything to chance. He had adapted this bit from former Assistant Secretary of the Treasury Lincoln C. Andrews during the latter's tenure as the federal government's manager of the entire national prohibition enforcement programs. It was rumored that Amos W.W. Woodcock, the new director, would follow along the same style of administration initiated by Andrews since both men had military backgrounds.[6]

John Vivian, the absolute sycophant/snollygoster, had done his homework. He knew that Woodcock's primary political claim to fame was that he did not create any dissent within the Grand Old Party. He himself had followed a similar pathway to his present position, except he had no prior military experience. Like the young John Edgar Hoover—who for the previous six years had led the "fact-finding" Bureau of Investigation—Woodcock, a confirmed bachelor, lived alone during the week. Hoover lived at home with his mother. Both of these lawyer/bachelor administrators were known to be dedicated completely to their mothers. Woodcock also had two sisters who were living at home and the women all spoiled and doted over him as a loving son and big brother.

Under General Andrews' hiring guidelines, Vivian remained in place as one of five out of 27 regional administrators General Andrews had inherited when he first assumed office. How he survived the major cleansing of field personnel is unknown, but Vivian had powerful political contacts and he was in the throes of campaigning for state governor in 1925. Andrews continued his program for change and his new policies dictated that the field should focus primarily on the principal sources of illicit alcohol production, sales, and distribution as carried out by organized crime families. He limited targeting individual or independent violators, or the small mom-and-pop home-manufacturing operations as practiced by much of the public at large. He believed these individual issues could be addressed later.

In the final analysis, Andrews' program for a total cleansing of the Prohibition Unit did not prevail. Andrews eventually succumbed to growing political pressures resulting from the Hoover Administration's bowing to congressional pressures. He resigned within two years of his appointment; however, his successful restructuring of the nation's enforcement operations would be retained and improved upon—lasting through the end of National Prohibition and well into future decades. In the end, Andrews had become the principal victim of the same political tiger he had tried to destroy, one that remained alive after his departure in all its shadowy constructs within the deep state of national government.

John Vivian's ability to survive the initial cleansing centered on his skill to adapt to change; he found little fault in implementing the new Andrews focus on prohibition crime. Later, he chose to implement his own version of the new course of hardline enforcement. His focus centered on the destruction of leading organized crime families in the region. Both New Mexico and Colorado were being eaten away socially and politically by these entrenched forces of darkness and violence. Vivian didn't know exactly how to accomplish this but his experienced managers in the field would have known and they became his eyes and ears.

Vivian's field teams made rapid adjustments to this new investigative format and they were doing extremely well in their drives to identify the criminal leaderships even though the arrests and convictions of upper echelon levels had stalled. Most recent office statistics revealed increasing numbers of arrests of nonaligned independent bootleggers coupled with reports of declining street prices for bottled spirits. This appeared to be a signal of change, one his field managers saw as a precursor to increased criminal warfare.

The national economic picture had been showing a continued decline in corporate and operational growth within most of the states. Unemployment suggested new and expanding opportunities in many of the regions of the country—one that involved the illicit manufacture of alcohol. Statistical analysis gave evidence that the floodgates were opening and the rise of the newly unemployed public saw bootlegging as a way out of unemployment by making inroads into the underground marketplace and driving down the profits of the established organized gangs. Such setbacks did not stand well with the bootleggers, for they, too, were businessmen and understood the economics of the bottom line as evidenced by the recent formation of the New York crime families' consortium.

Authors' Perspectives: Regional Administrator Vivian knew the game and he was not immune to playing the political card by redirecting blame and changing team members whenever his programs or efforts appeared to falter. Few had the manipulative skills he possessed. His friendly demeanor belied his true character. He may have recognized the Kearney murder as his opportunity to document his personal perspectives on the case for probable future political career enhancement.

One can visualize John Vivian sitting at his desk, documenting recent events in his personal journal. His thinking may have been: *I must maintain a personal record to illustrate my acute awareness of the importance and urgency of this matter. Thus, documenting my leadership and firm actions to manage this critical investigation surrounding the unfortunate and untimely death of one of my own young agents is necessary.*

Ralph Lawrence Carr, United States Attorney for the State of Colorado

Ralph Lawrence Carr had been awakened from a deep sleep by Administrator Vivian's telephone call to advise him of the Kearney murder and its circumstances. As the chief federal law enforcement officer over Region 10, he grasped the potential of the case. The killing of a federal officer would bring the national media to his very doorstep. Carr's experience told him what the stakes were on cases such as these. His experience told him that it all comes down to how one handles such situations. He also recognized that both he and Vivian were cut from the same political cloth. Circumstances always shaped the politician's future. The way one responded to events such as these became the measure of the true leader. The degree of flexibility one had in being able to manipulate a solution to a particular problem could determine the outcome for all.

Carr pledged both his and the United States Attorney General's full support to the Bureau of Prohibition and the Las Animas County Sheriff's Office. Investigation would later determine that at the end of the conversation, Carr sat quietly for a moment, his mind rapidly planning a similar but separate course of action, one that he didn't discuss with Vivian. Carr dialed the private phone number of a special acquaintance. When the party answered, Carr scheduled a meeting in Denver for later that evening.

Carr had a background in the newspaper business before he studied law and opened a practice in various small communities near Trinidad. And like Vivian, the political bug bit him and he decided to enter politics full time. In 1929, he was appointed to his current position by President Herbert Hoover's Department of Justice and that fact lay his loyalty. But Carr had his eyes on a bigger office down the road.

Both Vivian and Carr were cunning in their own way, neither being more transparent than the other. It was a given that each would be watching the other and measuring the other's response to the murder investigation. Following a full day of meetings with the Bureau of Prohibition senior management and a series of news conferences, Carr had one more task to complete after he left the office. The time was 7:00 p.m. exactly when he met with his confidential source, an undercover federal agent—the one he had placed deep within the southern Colorado mob.

Authors' Perspectives: The authors are familiar with clandestine meetings between law enforcement officers and their confidential sources of information. So too, United States Attorney Ralph Carr, the principal federal law enforcement officer in the state, having a meeting with an undercover agent would not be considered an unusual situation by other federal prosecutors, rather it would be viewed more as an "intelligence gathering" move on his part. Within the U.S. Attorneys' offices across the country, appointments of temporary "special agents" from the ranks of private investigators, former law enforcement officers, or others with the "necessary skills or access" was not an uncommon practice. It depended on the needs of the service and the availability of trusted investigators to conduct undercover activities. The existence of Ralph Carr's undercover agent and work assignment would not be revealed until months later, following the attempted murder by organized crime of the agent on the streets of Denver.

The Investigation Starts Gathering Steam

On Monday, July 7, 1930, before receiving and forwarding his field updates on the Kearney murder, Regional Administrator John F. Vivian dictated a telegram to the personal attention of his new boss in Washington: "Amos W.W. Woodcock, Director of Prohibition, Department of Justice, Washington, D.C., I regret to advise that Agent Dale F. Kearney was shot and instantly killed yesterday morning at Aguilar, Colorado. Letter follows. Vivian."[7]

That same morning in Trinidad, the newly created Kearney Investigation Task Force membership had begun to slowly file into the Harvey House dining room. A copy of the morning's *Chronicle-News* bore the headlines, "Dale Kearney Ambushed And Killed By Unknown Gunmen, Trinidad Prohibition Agent Brutally Murdered As He

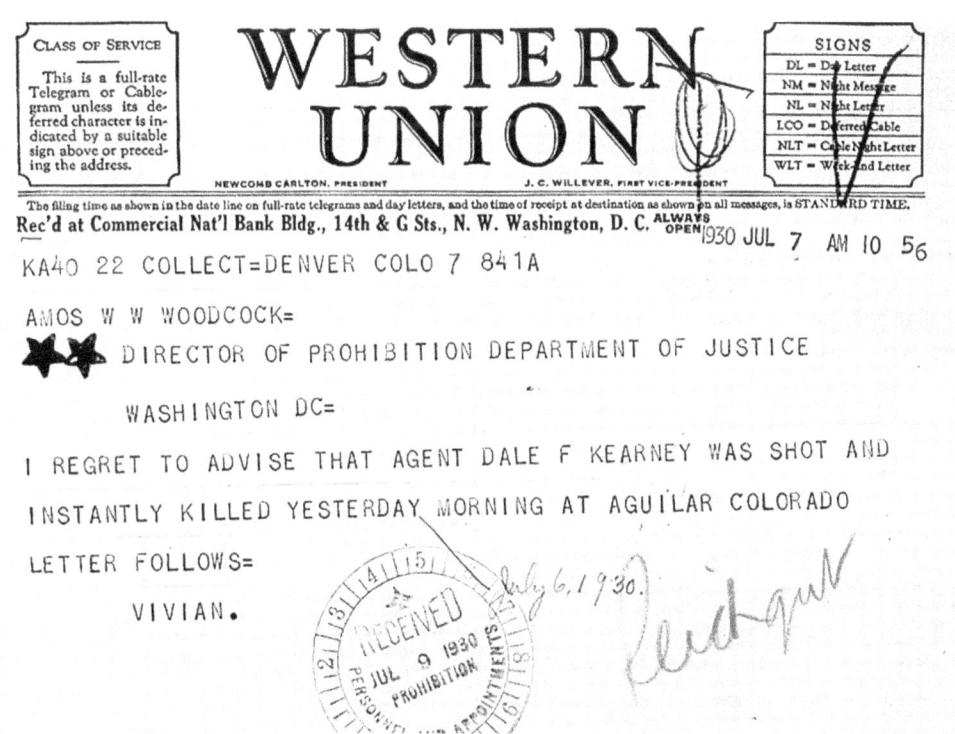

Telegram notifying Director Woodcock of Agent Kearney's Murder (Dale Kearney's Official Personnel File).

Walked Down Main Street of Aguilar Sunday Morning–Federal And County Officers Launch Thorough Probe."

The newspaper's storyline echoed the information discussed with Administrator Vivian and Sheriff Duling except for a new perspective put forth by the sheriff. He had opined that possibly two cars were involved in the shooting with one of them coming up behind Kearney as he walked on the street, keeping him silhouetted in the headlights, while the shooters opened fire from behind the fence. Did Duling have new information not yet included in his earlier reports? Or was it all mere speculation on his part? Nance would have to caution him about future pronouncements of unproven and incomplete investigative data to the media.

The team subsequently selected the Trinidad Masonic Hall as their interim central base of operations. The site could be secured from outsiders and would be available at midday in time for Richardson's arrival. The Masonic Hall is located off Trinidad's main boulevard near the center of town. Seldom was the facility used during the day and that made it a relatively secure place for the investigators to meet and prevent any "eavesdroppers" from listening to any task force discussions. The meeting room used by the team was located at the bottom of the first-floor stairwell in the converted basement, with only one door affording access. Lighting came from four table lamps placed atop a grouping of mismatched tables provided by the Lodge.

Monday afternoon Senior Investigator John Richardson, recent arrival from Denver, stood before the assembled group of seven federal agents in the basement briefing room. The States of Colorado and New Mexico were to be the team's center of attention. The team knew that bootlegging activities in the state had historically involved cross-border distribution routes impacting multiple states nationwide including the Canadian and Mexican borders. Richardson's information had been collected by Administrator Vivian's special regional field intelligence program to gather and correlate such data.

The leading and controlling organized families in each area of the states were identified: Denver, Pueblo, Trinidad, Walsenburg, and others in Colorado along with Raton, Clayton, Taos, Las Vegas, Portales, Albuquerque, and elsewhere in New Mexico. The main transportation routes were also tagged: the Mexico border leading to Denver and back again. In the Kearney case, the initial focus eliminated Mexico and most of southern New Mexico from the investigation. Only Colorado and northeastern New Mexico affiliations were suspect. This view was subject to change, if required. It never changed.

Following his briefing on the contents of the Las Animas County Sheriff's Office reports and the coroner's report, Agent Nance advised the team that the pending coroner's inquest regarding Kearney had been scheduled for Saturday, July 12. Richardson and Nance were to attend and accompany Mrs. Frances Kearney. The young widow had told Nance that a local newspaper reporter had come to her home for a statement on her husband's death and "she lit in to them with a vengeance while pledging to open up a whole can of worms on corruption and a few other things at the inquest." Nance had subsequently cautioned her about talking to the media further regarding any aspect of the investigation since it could hurt the team's efforts. She agreed to not speak with the press again.

The Denver Associated Press outlet reported on the status of the Kearney case on Tuesday, July 8: "Murder Of Kearney Is Being Probed, Shooting of Prohibition Officer

Accepted As Challenge To U.S. Law." The public wanted more news and the newspapers wanted more sales, so the reporters hounded the federal officers for more information. Two days later a news conference was held at the federal building in Denver.

On Thursday, July 10, 1930, Regional Administrator John F. Vivian and United States Attorney Ralph L. Carr held their second joint news conference on the government's investigation of the Kearney ambush. Carr's statement was the major presentation:

> Today [...] the federal government in Washington D.C. began its quest to find the slayers of Prohibition Agent Dale F. Kearney, who was ambushed and killed in Aguilar this past Sunday. The Attorney General, William D. Mitchell, has dispatched federal operatives to Colorado to take up the hunt for the killers and to help crush the defiant liquor racketeers of southern Colorado.
>
> He has further announced that he has approved giving full cooperation of the Department of Justice to local authorities in their drive to rout the liquor gangs responsible for the death. We will neither identify the number of operatives that will be arriving in Colorado or reveal their identity.
>
> We wish to further advise you that a dozen or more federal agents are presently investigating the Kearney murder and liquor activities and met with District Administrator John Vivian yesterday. Plans for an offensive against the criminal violators responsible for the Kearney slaying were discussed. We can give you no further information and we will accept no questions at this time.[8]

The beast had been fed and the media madness was now in full swing.

Dateline: Aguilar, Colorado, the Kearney Murder Crime Scene, July 6, 1930

The eastern mountain slopes of the Sangre de Cristo Mountain Range cast ominous dark shadows over the rolling countryside leading to Aguilar. Situated within the foothills adjacent to the range, the town was known for its illicit bootlegging, ethnic culture and mining union activities since before the beginning of National Prohibition.

William E. Nance, a five-year prohibition agent in the Pueblo, Colorado, office had served three years as a Pueblo City police officer prior to entering federal service. His past experience included investigations with local Aguilar officers who had discovered that the old mining tunnels running under and around the camp had been used to cache bootlegged liquor. Nance knew nothing had changed since the earlier times. Now, with the Kearney murder, he knew that once more the old records would have to be pulled and reviewed for any leads that could be of value in support of the new murder investigation.[9]

Nance and his fellow crew of agents arrived in Aguilar about 7:00 a.m. They had made the trip from Pueblo in record time. Sheriff Elijah A. Duling, his Undersheriff L.W. Williams and Deputy Sheriff Charles Juliano were at the scene awaiting the arrival of the federal agents.[10] Duling was a man of medium stature, middle aged, with a cattleman's weathered face. He wore the general uniform of his station: a wide-brim cowboy hat, lumber-style canvas jacket, dark trousers and cowboy boots. He was a rancher by profession and a sheriff by choice and election, with only a little over six months on the job.

Some of his friends saw him as one of a new breed of police officials and a public servant who was ready to make some profound changes in their communities. He was part of a growing number of lawmen who fought to remove the vestiges of corruption and crime that had over the past three decades become entrenched in the older mining communities within the county. The disdain for the law was especially profound in towns influenced by the ever-present Italian or Sicilian crime families who had their fingers in all levels of these ethnic communities.

The federal agents who accompanied Nance were Willard E. Lukens, P.D. Smith, and Henry Dierks, a "Special Employee" (undercover informant) with some modicum of criminal investigation. Other federal agents would join the investigation team later. Sheriff Duling advised the federal agents that they had no clues as to who the slayers were and surmised his fear that they were seeing the beginning of a new gang war like the one between the Danna and Carlino factions that occurred in the early to mid–1920s. He pledged to give the federal agents his full support and welcomed their assistance. Both the sheriff and his men had worked with Kearney occasionally and liked the man. Duling remarked that the deceased had his own way of working and that his deputies had cautioned Kearney on several occasions not to go running around these towns by himself at night. Kearney, however, sometimes maintained that cocksure attitude way of ignoring good advice. The sheriff sympathized about the loss of an associate.

Dr. Ben Bashoar, the acting Las Animas County Coroner, had arrived a few hours earlier from his Trinidad office and had completed his preliminary field investigation. Photographs and basic sketches of the crime scene had been taken and completed. Dr. Bashoar was preparing to have the body removed just as the federal officers arrived.

He uncovered the upper portion of the decedent's body. Nance verified the body to be that of Kearney. Coroner Bashoar postulated that Kearney was hit by at least five shotgun blasts from one or more shooters and the cause of death—multiple rounds in the upper torso and portions of the upper right arm. Bashoar believed Kearney died instantly. The agent's pistol was still in place in its shoulder holster under his left arm. Time of death was approximately 12:20 a.m. based on comments received from the town marshal and Kearney's broken watch. Five empty shotgun shells had been collected from alongside the fence enclosing a nearby empty lot. A detailed autopsy would be conducted and a report would become available later that afternoon.

The sheriff indicated that there had been six people inside the café at the time of the shooting: a cook, a waitress, and four customers. All maintained they hadn't seen anything regarding the actual shooting. It appeared that Kearney came in the café around 11:30 p.m. ate a meal, and then left heading down the street. They also stated that about ten or 15 minutes later they heard a series of shots—five or six. They stated that one of them had gone over to the café's front window but didn't see anything. They may have heard a car driving away, but they could determine nothing further.

Sheriff Duling indicated that one of the men may have been the former owner of the café. More information would become available for the federal agents once Duling's deputies completed their written reports. He added that a neighbor who lived near the garage down the street, Charles Cozzi, said that he had heard the gunshots and a car drive away at a fast rate of speed but he didn't see anything when he looked out his upstairs window. James Lile, the garage watchman said he had talked briefly with Kearney when he first arrived in his disabled car. One additional matter, a garage man from

Trinidad named "Charley something," arrived in his truck shortly after the shooting and stated that he had been called by Kearney to come pick him up and tow the car back to Trinidad. He was standing by pending release of Kearney's vehicle.

The lead federal agent would have requested a list of all of persons interviewed and their addresses along with the names of all the law enforcement and coroner personnel at the crime scene. He would have also explained to the local authorities his immediate role as the designated agent in charge of the investigation, subject to change by the Prohibition Regional Administrator in Denver.

According to established investigative procedures Agent Nance recommended that a parallel federal investigation be undertaken in support of the county sheriff's investigation. Both officers knew that the primary jurisdiction rested with the county authorities, but as the case would probably require assistance beyond the county or state areas, the federal government would provide such help. Nance requested that his agents conduct the death notification to the Kearney family of the death and Sheriff Duling concurred. Nance and Lukens subsequently departed the crime scene en route to Trinidad and the Kearney home.

Once the notification was complete and Fran Kearney had regained her composure, Regional Administrator John F. Vivian received a telephonic update from Nance on Kearney's death based upon his discussions with the local authorities. In turn, Vivian advised Nance that United States Attorney Ralph L. Carr had received the pledged full support of the United States Attorney General with additional funding and personnel to be forthcoming. Vivian also noted that Agent Ray Sutton of Clayton, New Mexico, had been assigned to the investigation and would meet Nance at the Harvey House in downtown Trinidad before noon Sunday.

The Formation of the Kearney Investigation Task Force

Ray Sutton first learned of the murder of Prohibition Agent Dale F. Kearney early on Sunday morning, July 6, via a telephone call from Deputy Regional Administrator (New Mexico) Charles H. Stearns in Albuquerque.[11] Stearns gave Sutton his new assignment: Proceed directly to Trinidad and meet with Agent William E. Nance who was currently leading the foundling Kearney investigation task force. Stearns had further informed Sutton that Prohibition Agent Clarence Ulysses Finley—formerly working out of Albuquerque office but now temporarily working in Alamosa, Colorado, on special assignment for Administrator Vivian—would also be joining the task force. Finley was one of the top ten investigators in the region.

Authors' Perspective: Sutton had known Kearney briefly having met the Colorado agent in connection with the trans-border bootlegging investigations they were both working in early 1930. Based on his local and federal experience in the field, Sutton was familiar with the areas and people in northeastern New Mexico, southern Colorado, and Oklahoma.

In 1930, Alamosa, Colorado, was a key railroad junction on the western side of Colorado's section of the Sangre de Cristo Mountains. The community served as the county seat of Alamosa County and shares a common border with Taos County, New

Mexico. This region is rumored by some to be the ancestral home to the Italian Black Hand Society and the Hispanic White Caps gang, yet Trinidad continued to serve as the center of the Sicilian Black Hand Society in southern Colorado with direct ties to the old country. These Sicilians, however, were not of the Mustache Pete consortium. These gentlemen had modified their operations to fit within the Carlino Brothers' proposed restructuring strategies.[12]

8

The Buccaneers

"The Constitution only guarantees the American people the right to pursue happiness. You have to catch it yourself."—Benjamin Franklin

Aguilar, Colorado: "The Gateway to the Spanish Peaks"

The Apishapa River waters a beautiful valley on the eastern slope of the Colorado Rockies. The area was first home to the Ute Indians and they shared the valley with French-Canadian trappers before the American adventurers found the lush green valley and brought their sheep to graze the river-fed meadows. The Mexicans also found this high country suitable farming and ranching. A small trading post was established in 1861 and a settlement took root around it as the site was midway between the towns of Walsenburg and Trinidad. Soon the Catholic Church built an adobe mission and people began called their new home San Antonio Plaza. The village grew quickly after the Walsenburg-Trinidad stage line established a relay station and corrals along the river near the plaza. A hotel, mercantile store, feed store, blacksmith shop, a bakery and restaurant, and a couple of saloons were built.

The first culture change arrived in the valley in 1878 when a railroad depot and livestock shipping corrals were constructed in the village. More businesses were established as the village grew into a town. Even a bordello saw a steady stream of customers. A decade later coal was discovered in the nearby hills and mountain ridges. Now the plaza settlement became a shipping point for coal and a real townsite was platted on land owned by Jose Ramon Aguilar, and people referred to their community as Aguilar. It was incorporated as a city in 1894 and the 1900 Federal Census recorded 698 people living in the town.

The second change started in the early 1900s when the Italian miners struggled to organize labor unions to deal with working conditions in the coal mine and "decent compensation" for mine laborers. The Colorado Mine Labor War was felt in Aguilar and the community was split over the conflict. The Hasting Mine exploded in 1917 and killed 121 miners. This event caused a downward death spiral for the coal mining industry in Las Animas County. The 1920 Federal Census said 1,236 people called Aguilar home.

The legends told about Aguilar during the Roaring '20s deal with an underground tunnel system used by bootleggers to store their product. One tale has a tunnel running from Aguilar to Walsenburg big enough to drive a Model T through it. The town was nicknamed "Little Chicago" because many infamous gangsters were rumored to hide out in the area to "cool off" from their criminal activities while back East. Another tale claims that when Aguilar received a federal WPA project to construct a water and sewer system, the work destroyed the bootlegger's tunnel system. One tale is true, Aguilar circa 1930 was not known to be a friendly place for outsiders, especially federal law enforcement officers.

The demand for coal declined in the late 1940s and by the early 1950s area mining camps began to close. The mining company owned camp buildings, and housing units were bulldozed to avoid property taxes. Today, the mountains and hills of the Apishapa River Valley around Aguilar are littered with foundations and cemeteries that serve as ghost town makers on the landscape. Aguilar today is home to less than 500 people.[1]

Raton, New Mexico: "The Gate City to the Land of Enchantment"

In 1930, the community of Raton, New Mexico, was a town celebrating its 50th birthday. The town fathers were open to opportunities for the more astute and enterprising of its community members. In fact, some people saw the locale as an "open town" whose 7,000-plus population provided cover for most of the questionable activities of the local business leaders and political bosses who shared common visions of the American Dream, the gathering of profits, and a thirst for alcohol.

Turn back the sands of time to the late 1870s and we find the original Raton townsite, situated along the old Santa Fe Trail at the base of Raton Pass. The area had been homesteaded by Thomas Boggs, a friend of mountain man and explorer Kit Carson, and called Willow Springs Ranch. In the fall of 1880, the little settlement of Willow Springs became the northern New Mexico headquarters for the advancing Atchison, Topeka and Santa Fe Railroad as the system moved over Raton Pass and entered the New Mexico Territory. The newly developing community renamed itself Raton, meaning rodent or rat that abundantly infested the piñon pine trees that covered the local mountainous hills.

On July 23, 1881, Gus Hornung, a new resident to the tent/boxcar village, wrote one of his many letters to his brother back in Kentucky, working the family farm. Gus, the manager of the Raton Coal and Coke Company and a business leader in the village, told him about his new home, saying, "The community name is Spanish for rat, and we have a few [rats] living here."

There was a time when the railroad camp became so wild the "good citizens" organized a "vigilance committee" to assist their part-time deputy sheriff maintaining order. One night a few local men drank too much, formed a lynch mob and hanged a "tinhorn" gambler. By 1884, disorder reigned rampant to the point that a search committee asked gambler/lawman Wyatt Earp to become the county's undersheriff to restore law and

8. The Buccaneers

BIRD'S EYE VIEW, RATON, NEW MEXICO. POPULATION 7,000, ALTITUDE 6,666 FEET

RESOURCES, COAL MINING, RAILWAY SHOPS, CATTLE RAISING AND GOOD FARMING SECTION

Raton, New Mexico, circa 1930. This photo was taken from Goat Hill behind the Colfax County courthouse, the square and round towers are visible at the bottom of the picture. The railroad yards, shops, roundhouse, and the consolidated railroad station are in the middle of the picture. The Raton Mountains are in the background (courtesy Chuck and V.J. Hornung Western History Collection).

order, while the newly elected sheriff recovered from wounds received in a shootout in a Raton graveyard with outlaws. Earp's wife told him to decline the offer after the couple toured the county. Raton was a coal mining boomtown on "the make" and she did not wish to live in another Tombstone drama.

Colfax County today remains a home to cattle, sheep and horse ranching; farming; timber logging; railroad economies; snow skiing on Angel Fire Mountain; summer water sports on Eagle Nest Lake; and, of late, an expanding big-game hunting and fishing paradise for the rich and famous. The county is also the home of Philmont Scout Ranch, the Boy Scouts of America's 140,177-acre national youth camp and adult leadership training center at Cimarron, as well as the National Rifle Association's national hunting and shooter training programs at the Whittington Center near Raton.

Raton nicknamed itself "The Gate City" since the community controlled the connecting mountain pass between Colorado and New Mexico. During the early decades of the 20th century, the populations of Colfax County, New Mexico, and its Colorado sister counties to the north shared a similar composition. Multi-ethnic emigrants abounded as ranch hands, cattlemen, cowboys, farmers, fieldworkers, railroad depot workers, store owners, clerks, and workers in the ever-present mining companies. Local financial agents controlled the flow of needed capital, some of which was most likely illegal. National prohibition and the ever-increasing worldwide fiscal depression added to the area's troubles.[2]

The Rise of the Buccaneers

Northeastern New Mexico replicates Colorado's southern terrain where the Great Plains meet the smaller foothills before they reach the stark outcroppings of the Rocky Mountains. Here, one can witness extended portions of the Sangre de Cristo Mountain Range as it moves ever southward from central Colorado through Colfax County and on toward the southeastern portions of the Santa Fe basin. These mountains store within their bowels untold quantities of coal and mineral treasures like gold and molybdenum, as suggested by the many active and abandoned mine shafts that pepper the slopes of the nearby mountain ridges.

The miners toiled in cramped underground crawl spaces with only the light of a headlamp to illuminate the darkest of work areas—frequently working in unsafe environments where maltreatment and indifference on the part of the company occurred daily. These men came to the mines from more than 27 different countries in search of work, opportunity, and the opportunity to realize the American Dream. Mining had existed in the region since the mid–17th century, a time long before the land had been ceded to the United States to become part of the New Mexico Territory at the close of war with the Mexican Republic.

The Coal Mining Camp

Some 29 miles southwest of Raton is a lovely canyon valley that once served as the home of the coal mining town of Dawson. A railroad freight line was constructed between Dawson and Tucumcari in 1901 to connect with railroad points in the East. In 1906, the Phelps-Dodge Corporation subsequently purchased the townsite and coal fields from W.B. Dawson and created a company-owned community. By 1930, this mining operation increased with the development of several contiguous onsite mines and housed over 7,000 inhabitants. Today nothing remains of the town except ruins of the mining operation and the well-populated cemetery.[3]

There were other active coal and logging camps in Colfax County located around Raton in a horseshoe pattern. These coal camps of Sugarite (522 people in 1930) and Yankee (178) were founded northeast of Raton; Brilliant-Swastika-Blossburg (606) and Gardiner (314) were developed and situated due west with Koehler-Van Houton (704) and Dawson to the southwest. Catskill was a small, fun-loving logging camp on the Vermejo River with its own mercantile/bar/bordello and a newspaper called the *Catskill Sawdust*. These settlements are all ghost towns today.

At most mining or logging sites, both in New Mexico and Colorado, miners and loggers were paid in "scrip" rather than cash. Scrip, paper or metal token, was a form of localized legal tender that could only be spent at the establishments operated by the issuing agency. The scrip payment practice evolved because it was often impractical for companies to maintain large amounts of cash at their insecure and unprotected remote mining locations.[4]

A second factor favored the company. Viewing the system from an economic standpoint, scrip payment limited an employee's ability to choose how they spent their earnings. In company towns, scrip was usable not only for the purchase of goods at the company store, but for rent, medical treatment, tools, food, and entertainment. The mining company stores faced little or no competition due to their remote location and the miner's inability to travel easily. Prices for goods and services at company-owned enterprises were set artificially high to cover their "cost of doing business."

In Dawson, the Phelps Dodge Corporation operated a commodious mercantile store. It was a forerunner to the modern department story, and the management gladly accepted miner's scrip so they could buy material from payday to payday. This style of company-owned business received significant advantages in using scrip. Private issue or trade money reduced the outflow of capital, strengthened the company's cashflow, and reduced payroll theft, thereby lowering the cost of security for the mine operation.[5]

Edward "Lalo" Zavala told a *Santa Fe New Mexican* reporter what he recalled about how his parents used scrip when he was a child growing up in Dawson. The mine company paid workers in "miners scrip so they could buy material from payday to payday, and then when payday came around, they collected what they owed them and sometimes the miners were left with nothing." Miners and loggers who received pay envelopes marked with a curly line across them called this symbol the "bobtail check" or the "snake." It meant no wages were due to the employee because of their outstanding credit debt to the company store.[6]

The scrip payment system was widely criticized by labor unions as exploitive, due to the company's monopolistic pricing programs at company stores. Once issued as currency, the scrip becomes undervalued at less than 90 cents on the dollar in the camps due to the purposeful markup of prices. Unions also claimed the system created problems for workers who needed to support overseas relatives, since scrip had no value outside the camp. Company scrip was discounted when converted to cash to be mailed or wired overseas.[7]

Investment Opportunities

Company mining towns or logging camps were a prime market for financial entrepreneurs or "money changers" who exchanged scrip to cash. Some even arranged, for a small fee, to deliver funds overseas via their family or business connections. During the Prohibition Era these same investors offered their support to bootleggers who in turn supplied the needs of miners and loggers.

Enter the entrepreneur. These "backers" or "financiers" of illicit activities are frequently individuals, male or female, with considerable means and are often prominent citizens within their community. Often, such backers will fund several operations simultaneously while maintaining a very low profile in connection with any attempt to conduct illicit activities, e.g., gambling, prostitution, and illegal beverage distribution.

These investors also provided a means to effectively redirect the flow of illegally acquired money into legitimate business ventures. In today's world, this style of financial exchange is called "money laundering" and is a federal crime.[8]

Giuseppe Tomas DiLisio

Private banker Giuseppe Tomas DiLisio, alias Joseph Thomas DiLisio, alias Joe DiLisio, offered miners a banking system they couldn't refuse at Gardner and later at Raton. He understood local and international banking; miners did not. He was bilingual in English and Italian; most miners were not. Joe had found his niche. He converted their company scrip into cash for a small fee and then remitted the cash sums to their designated overseas recipient through his private bank. People liked Joe DiLisio and his warm and friendly demeanor. He learned firsthand about employer-miner relationships and the conditions under which the miners labor and management operates. Joe DiLisio's deep understanding of human and business insights became the cornerstone of his Colfax County business empire.[9]

DiLisio emigrated from southern Italy in 1905. He first traveled to the mining areas north and west of Trinidad, Colorado. Within a few years, Joe moved from El Moro to the Gardiner coal camp in New Mexico Territory where new owners hired DiLisio to recruit Italian miners from Colorado to work its new coke oven sites. The area had originally been known as Blossburg in the 1880s. In the new camp DiLisio began a successful mercantile store and tavern on land he leased from the mining company. Most people found him to be a warm, kind, friendly, humble, smart and caring individual who loved to play in the band at camp dances.

Joe played the clarinet while Alex Valdez and Theodore Gardner played the guitars. Gardner, the camp policeman, had a deep singing voice for ballets and love songs. The Gardner band played at DiLisio's place each night, and certain nights the "telephone girls" at the Gardner switchboard would ring all the telephone party lines in Gardner, Koehler, Van Houton and Dawson and "broadcast" the music via the telephone hookup into the miners' homes so the women and children could enjoy the entertainment along with their fathers and older brothers at the DiLisio tavern. The facility was segregated with a partition setting aside a small area for Negro patrons to have their drinks and play their games. The rest of the building was open to all other ethnic groups. Evenings in DiLisio's tavern must have been exciting because when the building was torn down in the 1950s it had over a hundred bullet holes in the ceiling and walls. There are many unmarked graves in Gardner's Negro burial plot, yet no records have been found that any investigations were undertaken to determine causes of death.

In the early 1900s, Gardner had a church, a school, sometimes a hospital, and DiLisio's store and tavern. The tavern was the only public recreation spot in Gardner where men could play *numeri*, *bocce*, or darts and drink—then drink some more. No women or children were allowed in the tavern except during evenings when the establishment hosted public community dances.[10]

In 1912, at 26 years of age DiLisio was naturalized as a citizen of the United States of America. His future appeared to be secure, so he married, had his first child, and within several months, he relocated his new family to Ludlow, Colorado. He had further expanded his growing business enterprises. Neither he nor his mining camp neighbors could have prepared for the bloody event that still haunts Colorado labor unions.[11]

The Ludlow Massacre

Labor unions had long attempted to establish themselves in the Colorado mines. For the most part these attempts failed, but the unions were persistent. Early in 1913, a group of Colorado miners under the guidance of the United Mine Workers of America (UMWA) drew up a list of demands and presented them to the mine owners: (1) UMWA recognition by the coal companies as the mediator for all miners; (2) A raise in the hourly wage; (3) An eight-hour workday as Colorado state law provided; (4) Hourly pay for work done by a miner that didn't directly produce coal; (5) A miner-elected "check weigh-man," instead of a company-appointed man, to determine the true weights of coal mined by the individual miner; (6) The right to purchase goods from any store the miner chose; (7) The right to select non-company-owned housing; (8) The right to select their own medical doctor; (9) The fair enforcement of the Colorado mining laws by the state government; and lastly, (10) Ending the practice of management using company guards to "strong arm" miners into complying with arbitrary company policies.

A primary issue concerning hardworking miners was use of the company-controlled weigh-men who routinely shorted selected individual miners on their daily weight of coal-mined count. Weight mined determined the rate of pay earned by a miner. The union claimed that some miners were daily shorted as much as 400 or more pounds per ton mined. This was a loss for the miner and a gain/profit for the mining company. If this was not open robbery of labor, then it was surely indentured servitude. Both actions are a crime under state and/or federal laws.

The Colorado mine owners would neither acknowledge the union demands nor agree to any change. Mine owners, billionaire John D. Rockefeller, Jr., and his Colorado Fuel & Iron Company, wanted no part of any situation they felt would cause them to lose money. For years management had fought every attempt at union organization, using exceptionally blunt tactics. The mine guards, at the direction of the company owners, removed "troublesome" workers and their families from company housing and property. This action was often accomplished by violence against the targeted miners.

All attempts by the UMWA to persuade mining management to negotiate led to failure. And with this non-change of events, the mine workers answered the union "call out" for a labor strike. More than 12,000 miners walked off the job on September 23, 1913. All mine owners in the region were impacted, but the primary focus of the union efforts centered on the three largest companies: the Colorado Fuel & Iron Company (CF&I), the Rocky Mountain Fuel & Iron Company (RMFIC), and the Victor-American Fuel Company (VAFC).

Most prominent of the group was the CF&I with its regional headquarters in Pueblo employing 7,000 onsite employees. The company's board of directors, chaired by John D. Rockefeller, Jr., refused any form of recognition going to the UMWA. Rockefeller bluntly stated that he neither needed nor wanted any union representation at the CF&I sites. The company had considerable political power because they owned over 60 other mining operations in the three-state Rocky Mountain region that encompassed portions of Wyoming, Colorado, and New Mexico.

The mining companies retaliated against the walkout with a mass eviction of miners and their families from company housing. Among those evicted from Ludlow was the Joe DiLisio family. How or why they were caught up in the process is unclear. Perhaps it was because DiLisio provided miners assistance with his private banking services and merchandising activities or maybe it was a simple matter of his ethnic origin. Rockefeller was a known bigot.

Within days of the walkout, the struck companies began searching out and importing laborers from overseas to replace the strikers. Recruitment ads were sent to overseas countries boasting of the United States as a "land of milk and honey—where the streets are paved with golden opportunities." This same method had been used in 1903 during the last major recruitment effort when Irish emigrant miners went out on strike protesting the same issues. The Italian and Eastern Europe countries' workers had responded a decade earlier and replaced a majority of the Irish in the Colorado mines. What had worked before could surely work once more.

During the 1913 lockout, the UMWA used its strike funds to rent land east of the southern Colorado coal camps and near the main entrance to the mine properties. Union officials ordered tents, necessary household equipment and supplies while quietly establishing a series of "tent colonies on the plains." Thousands of miners set up housekeeping in the flimsy tented structures at each strike encampment. The miners were confident that the strike would be of short duration as they and their families settled into their outdoor life.

Meanwhile, the coal companies invested heavily in hiring more private guards and more rifles and ammunition. Pueblo's CF&I steel mills constructed a convertible style open-armored car for the company strikebreakers' use. The car was nicknamed the "Death Special" because it had thick bulletproof steel sides and machine guns mounted in the back compartment. The miners had given the car its name because the company-hired gunmen took perverse delight in spraying bullets through the miners' tents as they roared past the various colonies on their way to and from various mine companies' office sites. Miners eventually responded in kind.

The politically powerful mine owners had no trouble persuading Governor Elias M. Ammons to call out the Colorado National Guard on October 28, 1913. At first, the Guard's appearance in the strike zone calmed the situation, but the sympathies of the state militia leadership lay with mining company management and the situation changed quickly.

Colorado National Guard Adjutant-General John Chase, who had served during the violent Cripple Creek labor strike of 1903, imposed a harsh regime on the workers' campsites. The strikers maintained that both the National Guard and the mine company guards and private detectives indiscriminately fired into the workers' tent camps during the day and night, often killing or wounding strikers and their families. The killing of women and children could not and would not be condoned by the miners or the general population of the country. Union leaders issued a call to arms, urging its memberships to acquire "all the arms and ammunition legally available."

Shootings happened so often that the miners dug trenches beneath their tents to crawl into to avoid the flying bullets. Women and children would hide behind metal stoves or in the dug-out pits below the tent's flooring in an attempt to not be killed by the random fire. According to family stories, Joe DiLisio's wife, Christina, and their infant child experienced such occurrences when they had to hide behind their metal stove on one or more occasions.

8. The Buccaneers

A specific act by representatives of the mining companies set the course for widespread death and destruction. Unknown mining camp guards and militia men dressed in the uniforms of the Colorado National Guard set fire to the tent city at Ludlow during the evening hours following a long day of fighting. The discovery of the bodies of two women and 11 children were found huddled together, suffocated and burned, in one of the trenches beneath a burned-out tent. This singular event become known as the Ludlow Massacre of Monday, April 20, 1914.

Dozens of mines were attacked by the striking miners and their supporters over the ten-day period following the Ludlow Massacre. The battle raged along a 40-mile front from Walsenburg to Trinidad. There were also several skirmishes along the front with the Colorado National Guard. In Wyoming, 5,000 additional miners were reported to have armed themselves and were prepared to cross the Colorado State line and go to Ludlow in support of the impacted strikers and their families. Retaliation by both sides of the strike would continue for several additional months.

In the annals of union strife, the Rockefeller name would be forever tarnished with the blame for this anti-union atrocity. The fighting ended only after President Woodrow Wilson sent in federal troops, who reported directly to the Army's chief of staff. The military disarmed both the Colorado National Guard and the miners and disbanded and arrested the mining companies' private militias in the process. This action enforced a strained peace for a few weeks. The end of the strike came, however, when the UMWA ran out of money and the miners were forced to terminate their 15-month walkout on Thursday, December 10, 1914.

An estimate of the total number killed during the all-inclusive period of violence

Ruins of Ludlow, Colorado, after attack by mine guards and militia (Wikipedia Commons).

ranged between 69 and 199 lives—among the number were the two women and 11 children murdered at Ludlow. The statistics do not reflect the countless injured and wounded during the conflict. The Ludlow Massacre stands today as the deadliest labor strike incident by any management organization against organized labor in the United States. A massive monument, information panels, and a quiet rural family-friendly park marks the massacre site.[12]

Tony F. Marchiondo and Joe DiLisio

The Tony F. Marchiondo family moved to Raton from the nearby Gardiner coal camp in 1913 and opened "The Golden Rule and New York Stores," a dry goods and grocery business a few blocks north on First Street from Joe DiLisio's new Raton Mercantile Company. Marchiondo later operated stores in the railroad livestock shipping towns of French, Springer and Roy.

Marchiondo had a ready laugh and strong handshake. He spoke Italian and English and understood basic medical procedures, so he was the *"medico"* at Gardner after the mining company moved its hospital operation to Raton. Tony was the midwife to many *paisano* children in the camp. His store in Raton was the hub for quality cheeses, spaghetti, pepperoni, olives and other such items.[13]

Tony had first worked in the coke oven operations at Gardiner, but at what point he transitioned into the mercantile business is unknown. Joe DiLisio had worked in Gardiner immediately prior to his move to Ludlow. Could Marchiondo have taken over the Gardiner store site vacated by DiLisio? If so, could DiLisio have encouraged Marchiondo to join him in his relocation to Raton for both their families' safety? It seems more than coincidental that both made the move to Raton in the same year with their same style of stores on the same street.

During this period, Joe DiLisio also made investments in Raton saloons, especially those that catered to local miners, lumbermen, cattlemen, and railroad travelers. One such saloon was located on the street floor of the Haven Hotel, another South First Street establishment located directly across from the Santa Fe railroad terminal and workshops. The Coors Brewing Company of Golden, Colorado, built a regional storage facility in the building just south of and contiguous to the saloon and hotel. A total of four saloons were located along First Street within a three-block area during the early 1900s pre-Prohibition era.

Like the earlier German emigrants who had discovered a secret formula for success within the mercantile business, certain emigrated Italian families found the saloon business to be a very good way to move into the merchant class and to serve their communities. In some circles, the saloon served as a social club and a protective association as well as a bank. This philosophy coincided with that of Joe DiLisio, who soon realized the full potential of the combined financial benefits of each of these representative service activities. In the old country, the private bank provided avenues for short-term loans of a nature allowing the bankers to charge appropriate fees and various interest rates to any "approved" borrowers without any outside interferences.[14]

In 1918, the state of New Mexico chartered the International State Bank as an authorized state financial institution with headquarters in Raton. Joe DiLisio, Sr., served as president. His "image" as a prominent member of the business and social communities to which he catered was now firmly established. He bought out his mercantile store partner, Modesto Rauzi, in 1922 and relocated the mercantile store from its South First Street location to the corner of Clark and South Second Street, a few blocks distant from its original location. The move coincided with the state highway department's redesign of its roadways that led to Second Street becoming the main business street in Raton. The new store was renamed "DiLisio's."[15]

To his fellow emigrant countrymen, he never forgot his roots and from where he came. He owed a great deal to these people with whom he shared a common heritage. As long as the mining camps issued scrip, the DiLisio mercantile store and saloons accepted it as cash subject to the special discount. He or his employees would then exchange the accumulated paper at the camp stores for a variety of goods at face value and make them available for purchase at the Raton store. He, in effect, had succeeded in obtaining a brand of "discount pricing" from both the company stores and his customers. His saloons closed due to implementation of New Mexico's State Prohibition law in 1917.[16]

> **Authors' Perspective:** Joe DiLisio tended to downplay his bank presidency role in favor of his "merchant" status in operating one of the two major grocery stores and a general merchandising store in the county. He even used the descriptor "merchant" in lieu of "banker" in his response to the government census taker when the Department of Commerce conducted the Fifteenth Census of the United States in 1930. Why he would negate his bank presidency status in favor of the merchant label is unclear, unless he wished to minimize his influences in the New Mexico financial world. Since the catastrophic stock market crash of 1929, Congress had undertaken a comprehensive review of federal banking regulations. Perhaps DiLisio preferred a lower professional profile to shield his rumored underground financial operation.

Banking in New Mexico

In 1994, the Academic Press published a study by three economists entitled, "*Why Do Banks Fail? Evidence from the 1920s.*" The men reported the major reasons were: First, the post–World War agriculture price boom burst in the early 1920s and the farmer who just a year earlier was commanding top-dollar for his agriculture products could no longer repay his crop loans and went broke. This caused massive farmer loan defaults, weakening many farming country banks. Union County, New Mexico, also suffered a three-year drought that dried up the crops and baked the ground. However, beef and sheep commodities remained stable. Second, automobile sales in New Mexico's rural counties almost doubled from the decade of the 1910s, thus small-town residents could travel to larger communities for their family needs and this included their financial needs. Larger community banks were charging eight percent interest on the same loan for which smaller rural banks charged ten percent interest. This loss of loan fees affected small banks' cashflows and contributed to their inability to remain in operation.[17]

In 2014, the *Journal of Monetary Economics* published a study by two historian-economists called "Local Banking Panics of the 1920s: Identification and Determination," that added a third cause contributing to small-bank failures. The case was made that the banks had very little of the right style of oversight or regulations by states who granted state charters to small community facilities. National charted banks required stronger regulation compliance, while "private banks" operated with no governmental oversight.[18]

The bank executives of Union, Mora, Harding, Taos and Colfax Counties met in conference during the last full week in July 1929. These men gathered in Raton and held wide-ranging discussions concerning the financial solvency of the banks in their region. They devised a strategy for current and future business and personal loans. Over a year later the *Raton Evening Gazette* told readers that national banking leaders were talking about "a return of good times" and making "positive projections" for the future. These financiers missed the mark.[19]

At the end of the 1920s, New Mexico had seen most of its underfunded small community banks fold. By the time the nation's bank closing situation became a national financial crisis during the 1929–1932 period, New Mexico experienced only a 3 percent closures rate. The United States as a whole was stunned by a 10–20 percent state closure norm nationally.

In the spring of 1995, the Federal Reserve Bank of St. Louis published David C. Wheelock's "Regulation, Market Structure and the Bank Failures of the Great Depression" in their *Review* journal. This article explains this complex issue in simple terms. The National Bank Holiday of 1933 stopped the hemorrhaging of cash from local banks; the reopened banks were able to document their solvency to the banking public thus restoring confidence. Other national banking laws governed gold and silver trading and a standard monetary value for federal money, and more laws abolished local bank notes and scrip, required deposit insurance, and standardized loan requirements.[20]

The 1915 session of the New Mexico State Legislature enacted laws dealing with banking in the new state. These laws replaced the hodgepodge of territorial laws ranging back to 1850. The new law established the State Banking Department headed by a state bank examiner who administered New Mexico's banking laws and had supervision over all state-chartered banks. By 1940, the responsibilities of the department had grown to include monitoring state-charted building and loan associations and small loan companies as well as regulation of all speculative stock transactions. The department was now required to conduct two financial examinations of each state-chartered bank annually and one exam each for all other state-chartered financial concerns.[21]

As previously noted, Joe DiLisio received a New Mexico state charter for his international banking operation in 1918. The new bank was funded with $25,000 in capital and became the 72nd state financial institution licensed under the new state banking laws established in 1915. The *New Mexico Blue Book of 1919* contains a copy of the New Mexico Bank Commission's annual report ending November 1, 1919, showing that New Mexico's state-chartered banking institutions contained $20,779,020.47 in funding capital. Colfax County was home to five state banks: Dawson ($50,000), Springer ($50,000), Maxwell ($30,000), Blossburg ($15,000, the minimum capital allowed for a charter), and the new DiLisio bank at Raton. The county had three federally chartered banks: the First National Bank of Raton ($100,000), the National Bank of New Mexico of Raton ($50,000), and the First National Bank of Cimarron ($50,000). Within a generation, the state banks at Dawson, Springer, Maxwell and Blossburg failed as did the national bank at Cimarron. DiLisio's bank quickly provided for Cimarron's financial needs with a branch operation.[22]

Two years later, the World War was over and the city of Raton's 1920 population was 5,544 individuals, meaning that about a fourth of Colfax County's citizens now lived in the county seat. In 1930, Raton boasted of a 6,090 community population while the county had lost 3,393 residents due to fewer local employment opportunities in agriculture, ranching and mining. Ten years later, Raton had gained 1,517 more residents during the decade, while the county lost 439 individuals. Raton was now home to almost half of Colfax County's population in 1940. Census data shows that Raton reached a population zenith in 1980 at 8,225 and has experienced a steady decline to about its size of the 1930s. Today, Colfax County has half the population it had recorded in 1920.

The records of the State Banking Department (headed by state bank examiner Woodlan P. Saunders and located in the New Mexico State Records Center and Archives at Santa Fe) contain a September 15, 1942, stability review of Joe DiLisio's state-chartered bank. This report makes it clear that his financial institution had survived the nation's Great Depression in a sound fiscal situation in spite of the past two decades of national economic misfortune, drastic downward shifts in local employment opportunities, an almost 3,000-person local population decline, and now the monetary drain on the local economy caused by World War II.[23]

To the general populace, Joe DiLisio became known within the community as "Mr. Raton," and in later years he would be characterized as a leading member of the business, social, and political milieu. Indeed, as one of the founding capitalists in the county, he found much success in banking as well as with his merchandising store and earlier saloon businesses.

Financiers and Bootleggers

It was the joint responsibility of the bootlegger and his financial angel to assure the secrecy of their business arrangement, especially if the "money man" financed a coterie of reliable operators under the control of the boss bootlegger. Over a period of many years, this working relationship could yield very favorable financial results for all. In small towns, personal background and relationships are not too difficult to determine if one is in the banking business. Chances are that almost everyone in town has had or will have some business over time with a local banking concern. Financiers have to be very discriminating about their activities and choice of the men they back with great care placed on the man's technical skill, his known reputation for integrity and reliability, ethnic heritage, and his family history as it relates to "community (and banking) interests."

Some financiers have potent political connections that may be used quietly to protect their financed operations. To have someone in your corner with such connections is an added bonus to the bootlegger and the still operator. The "code of silence" is known and practiced both formally and informally within the Italian and Sicilian ethnic communities and extends to their activities as a part of the enduring culture. Silence is a most important friend in maintaining the inner workings of illegal financial ventures.

Before Colorado passed a state prohibition law in 1916, the illegal New Mexico booze manufacturers were organizing themselves to quench not only the thirst of their own local inhabitants but included those in neighboring Colorado as well. Due to the Colorado dry law, the bi-state, cross-border illicit marketplace began to flourish with new "underground" transportation networks and alcohol manufacturing alliances taking form.

New Mexico followed Colorado's lead in 1917 by banning all forms of alcohol consumption by the public. The governor gave the New Mexico Mounted Police the duty of enforcing the state ban on alcohol in 1918. This enforcement action almost upset the underground transportation network until the New Mexico legislature abolished the state ranger force in 1921. The lawmakers were convinced by "fiscal analysts" that the mounted police budget was too expensive for the new state's taxpayers base. The state's criminal element gave a party to celebrate the new "bootleg moonshine business" opportunities now made safe in the ten-year-old Sunshine State.[24]

These bootleg transportation networks soon became part of the larger alliance with separate and frequently shared routes to neighboring Colorado as well as to Mexico, Canada, Louisiana, Illinois, Michigan, California—just about everywhere in every direction.

John Campanella, Bootleg Mogul

John "Big John" Campanella of Cimarron was another Colfax County Sicilian-Italian entrepreneur. This 47-year-old opportunist was not a student of zymology, but he was a crafty bootlegger who had been brewing "moonshine" spirits since 1915. He was a master in the art of evading federal and state liquor tax enforcement officers. While the issue of state prohibition was being debated in Santa Fe in 1917, he quickly and quietly consolidated control over all the "private distilleries" in the northeastern section of New Mexico. Seemingly, every bootlegging operation: the still operators, the supply system, the clandestine distributors' routes, and "a security network" functioned under his management by the time prohibition became law.[25]

Campanella knew how to maintain a semi-quiet profile, masquerading in the shadows as a Cimarron-based mercantile business owner while his teenage sons Louis and Joe ran the store. Like all good citizens who operated a saloon prior to prohibition, John closed his Cimarron establishment in accordance with the new state law. Campanella's side business was an "open secret" even though he strived to remain out of the law enforcement spotlight as much as possible. Too much of the wrong publicity could damage his business and personal freedom.

As an extra precaution to guarantee a safe and discreet underground operation, Campanella used money to open and shut a lot of doors ... and mouths. He had located a few precinct constables who would look the other way for a small "donation" to their "campaign fund" while he conducted business in their township. He had learned early that it only takes one or two officers on the take to keep a lid on things in an area where almost everyone deals in some way with the local bootlegger: café owners, drug store operators, milkman, hack drivers, even candy store operators. Campanella used an intermediary named James Perry Caldwell to pay his "guardians."

Investigators learned that "Big John" never worked alone. Authorities were never able to get an exact count as to the total number of "associates" Campanella supervised at any given time. Supply and demand with an occasional bit of persuasion aimed at other established independent "boots" or troublesome "newcomers" served to keep his operations within northeastern New Mexico totally operational and profitable.

A new question should be asked: To what extent did community dry goods and grocery businesses contribute supplies to the bootlegging enterprise in rural counties? Historians may suggest that they were significant, if you consider the number of private citizens who engaged in their own manufacturing process and their requirements for sugar, grain, fruits, yeast, bottles, barrels or kegs, and malt. It should be remembered that federal law allowed for manufacturing of alcoholic beverages for personal or family consumption. Several bottling companies across the states existed to provide "home bottling and manufacturing supply kits" as well as furnish a variety of bottling needs for soft drinks, food products, pharmaceutical and other commercial needs.

The National Prohibition Act allowed for home manufacturing of wine, beer, whiskey, or any other consumable alcoholic product, provided such products were for home or individual use only and not sold to others. Statistics from the Prohibition Era seem to indicate that a large segment of the population did some quantity of home processing.

Sugar is one of the key ingredients of the alcohol distillation process. The large quantities used by the still operators would place them in the "preferred high demand" list of customers serviced by the sugar distributors. The general manufacturing formula varies, but the general rule for "moonshine" alcohol is one pound of sugar to grain per gallon of water of total volume. For a 50-gallon cook, you would need 50 pounds of sugar and 50 pounds of grain to ferment a resulting 50 gallons of mash.[26]

> **Authors' Perspective:** Prohibition Era data suggests principal illegal still operators produced unlimited quantities of alcohol product in their large 150-, 200-, 500-gallon, and, later, with their super 1,000-gallon stills. Usually three cooks (brew sessions) per week, per site, could produce a significant quantity of consumable alcohol assuming the availability of needed grains, yeast, sugar, and malt. At a cost of $20 per gallon for prime liquor as produced by John Campanella, the payout for 3,000 gallons per week would approximate $60,000 in 1930s-era dollars before diluting the contents by a factor of two to four times. A simple monetary conversion of 1930s era money value to the present day shows that $60,000 in Prohibition Era money would be worth about $880,000 in 2017 currency value-adjusted for inflation. This is "real" money in either economic time frame.
>
> There are many questions that need answers if the complete history of the Prohibition Era is to be told. Where could sugar and malt and the other ingredients in such large quantities be purchased? How much of each did the legitimate community use on a continuing basis? How large was the underground supply chain? What and to whom did these wholesalers provide supplies?

In 1932, Prohibition Investigator W.E. Lukens, working out of the Denver office, undertook a preliminary investigation of the two Zerobnick Bottle Works locations in Denver. The case involved the illegal sale and possession of property designed for the illegal manufacture of intoxicating liquor. The firm had been operating over the previous six years before it was raided by teams of federal agents and Denver police officers. One of the firm's owners claimed to have done $300,000 in sales in 1930 alone—an equivalent of $3.8 million in 2017 currency valuation. Sixteen workers were arrested along with the Zerobnick principals. Among the documents seized, were a series of customer records for a three-year period that included known or suspected "bootlegging clientele" from multiple cities and states. One name of interest to this narrative was that of "John Campanella." There were also other "clients" listed from northeastern New Mexico. Other organized crime figures included Joe Roma and three of the Smaldone brothers of Denver as well as activities carried on jointly and independently by the Carlino brothers of southern Colorado. The secreted journals included a limited selection listing the dates, itemized purchases, and the cost owed or paid per illicit client. Some 35 subjects and their interrelationships were noted.[27]

The whole supply system operated like a simple firefighter's bucket brigade. The farmers sold their raw produce to a crop brokers who sold the crop to a manufacturer who produced a commodity to be sold to a wholesaler who sold their supplies to a regional warehouse distribution company who in turn sold all the items that a local retail business stocked. This type of legitimate operation would be an ideal cover partner in the supply chain for a bootlegger.

James Perry Caldwell

In mid–1930, Zenas Ward, the 30-year-old foreman for the state highway district yard, had indicated to Perry Caldwell that an opening in the Cimarron roadway maintenance workforce could become available in a few weeks. The district office was waiting for the "go ahead" to begin the replacement of the hardpack Colfax County highways with a new concrete one; the roadcrews referred to this as "putting in a hard road."[28]

The area job market was in a distressed condition, mirroring the nation's sharp decline into economic depression. Caldwell relied on the part-time job that he didn't talk about outside his immediate circle. His "other job," the nighttime one he held for the past few years, only paid for services of a few hours each week. One duty involved checking the "safety of the roadways," for Campanella's bootleggers who needed confirmation that revenuers had not established any roadblocks that would interfere with their runs north.

For the larger part of his life, Perry Caldwell grew up in Colfax County, New Mexico, and had known John Campanella since the early 1900s. During his mid-teen years and early twenties Caldwell was "copping," local police service or mining guard work, in the region around Springer and Raton. Following the implementation of federal prohibition, Campanella began to comprehend the advantage of having a federal officer on his payroll. The possibilities of having a controlled operative within the federal enforcement body who could report on plans that might negatively impact his business activities caused Campanella to encourage Caldwell to seek appointment as a federal prohibition officer. The two men were not the first to corrupt the federal prohibition efforts in this fashion.

People who knew Caldwell had no doubt where his loyalties were before he entered on his ill-planned career as a federal prohibition officer. During his seven months of probationary employment, he moved freely throughout Colfax County strongly urging his "targeted clientele" to engage the services of John Campanella for deliveries of fine hooch to their local establishments: the speakeasies, the "blind tigers," and various private residential sales outlets operating in the area. The money was good for a few months until someone or perhaps many "someones" reported his conflicting behaviors to the Denver Regional Prohibition Unit Office.

By the end of August 1925, 36-year-old Caldwell was summarily terminated from government service. No exact cause for the dismissal is indicated in James Perry Caldwell's official personnel file. Dismissal in this instance is a term used for forced termination in lieu of criminal prosecution, a practice not uncommon to the Prohibition Unit of 1925. If asked, Perry Caldwell would explain his termination was due to a "government reorganization and downsizing"—an internal Prohibition Unit euphemism used in this instance to describe the government's process of eliminating its corrupt employees. It sounded better to be "downsized" rather than "fired." His dismissal became effective August 31, 1925. His departure came about simultaneous to, but separate from, the ongoing "great cleansing" reorganization action being implemented by General Lincoln C. Andrews, Assistant Secretary of the Treasury. Most people outside of government knew nothing of the developing Andrews Plan for the Prohibition forces during this period and accepted Caldwell's version of the termination.[29]

The Early Years of the James M. Caldwell Family

The James Caldwell family moved from Arkansas to New Mexico Territory in 1877. James Martin Caldwell and Martha Letitia Brown, a niece of the infamous Kansas segregationist John Brown, were newlyweds when they homesteaded some public land in Colfax County. Within months, lawlessness erupted over homestead issues between the new owners of the Maxwell Land Grant and homesteaders residing on the grant's lands. For their personal safety, the Caldwell family relocated to the Indian Territory (Oklahoma) where they remained for several years.[30]

Prior to 1870, Lucien B. Maxwell had consolidated, via inheritance and purchase, sole title of the Beaubien-Miranda Mexican Land Grant (now called the Maxwell Land Grant) that encompassed almost two million acres of northeastern New Mexico and portions of southern Colorado. Maxwell sold his grant interests to a consortium of local investors who later sold their interests to European bankers, who declined to accept homesteaders on the company's properties.

The battle raged on for a number of years before the legal disagreements were settled in the courts. In 1879, the railroad made its way southward over Raton Pass to a townsite five miles south of the Colorado-New Mexico border. Don Miguel A. Otero, Sr., a vice president of the Atchison, Topeka and Santa Fe Railroad, served as the town's namesake. The location was to be home for the railroad roundhouse and service center; however, the area lacked a main water source to fill its needs. Eventually, the railroad was forced to relocate its operations to Willow Springs, the watering stop along the Santa Fe Trail located at what is now Raton. This dependable water supply allowed the new townsite to develop into the principal railroad, mining, and ranching center for trade in northeastern New Mexico. Today it is the seat of government for Colfax County.[31]

James Perry Caldwell became the fifth son of six males born to the Caldwell family on January 26, 1889, in Tahlequah in the Cherokee Nation portion of the Indian Territory. In 1899, a much-enlarged Caldwell family became part of an entourage of 17 families traveling by covered wagon to the New Mexico Territory. The old Santa Fe Trail led them westward as it cut through the Oklahoma panhandle from Kansas and then branched off southwesterly through the prairie toward present day Clayton, New Mexico. That portion of the trail was known as the "dry trail" because of the lack of water along its route. Most travelers favored the northern trail toward Willow Springs where water was plentiful.

Once relocated, the elder James Caldwell purchased and operated a sawmill on the border of Colfax and Mora Counties. Later, the family established "J.M. Caldwell and Company," a ranch near Springer. Perry grew to manhood here, learning to hunt and ride while always watching his older brothers whom he emulated whenever possible.

If one sibling did something noteworthy, Perry would notice and waited to replicate or even surpass it. He had that deep-seated need to always be the better performer, no matter how long it took. He had been this way his whole life. Maybe this was another reason he entered the federal law enforcement service, to get back at his brothers who favored local law enforcement.

A particular case in point involved the 1909 killing of a big "brown she-bear" and her two half-grown cubs in the wilds of Colfax County near Black Lakes. The *Springer Banner* honored Perry's older brother, Count, with the title of "County Champion Bear Hunter" for killing three bears at one time. That title served as both a compliment to his courage and as an object of humorous derision between the brothers and among the family members.

Perry had waited 15 years before he was able to claim his own similar fame. In October 1924, a few months before being hired by the Treasury Department, Perry "killed a monster Silvertip bear in the Costilla Creek region" in the back country of Taos County. The bear allegedly charged him, and after taking quick aim, he shot the animal between the eyes using his .32/.20 caliber rifle. The bear reportedly stood over 36 inches high at the shoulders and measured 18 inches from tip of nose to the middle of the forehead and weighed more than 1,300 pounds. Once skinned, the pelt alone weighed over 200 pounds. Local hunters and ranchers who knew the area stated that the dead bear had a mate of equal size in the area. This event didn't equate to the drama of Count Caldwell's encounter, but it served to illustrate Perry's competitive nature.

At various intervals over the years, the majority of the Caldwell brothers embarked on part-time careers in local law enforcement. Berlin, as the third-oldest child, served on the town police force at Springer and periodically as a Colfax County deputy sheriff.

People characterized him as one who "feared neither man nor beast and always treated his prisoners with respect." After the county seat of government was relocated to Raton in 1897, the old courthouse served as the Springer municipal court and jail. It also became Berlin Caldwell's residence and his wife Matilda cooked for the city prisoners and they all ate at the family table before the inmates returned to their cells. In 1928, Berlin was nominated as a candidate for Colfax County sheriff but lost the general election.[32]

Lee Caldwell, Berlin's younger brother, also experienced some early public service in Colfax, Mora, and Luna Counties. Prior to 1918, Lee ventured south to work for the Deming City Police Department. In February 1918, Lee was appointed police chief and served in that capacity for two months before resigning and accepting a commission as a sergeant of the prestigious New Mexico Mounted Police. Lee served eight months as a state ranger before a new governor was elected and appointed his own men in the ranks of the mounted police. Lee returned to the Springer area to become a ranch owner and lumberman/logger.[33]

Walter was the youngest Caldwell brother and had fought his way up the ranks to become the New Mexico Middleweight Boxing Champion in the early 1920s. Perry, a large burly man with an imposing physique, competed with Walter's boxing friends who traveled to the area. Those challenged by Perry, as sparring opponents, included such fighters of the day as Jess Willard, the Pottawattamie Giant, who stood six feet, six inches, in height and weighed in at 245 pounds. Willard claimed the title of the heavyweight champion of the world in 1915 only to lose the crown to Jack Dempsey in 1919. Perry also claimed to have sparred a few rounds with Jack Dempsey.

Perry Caldwell joined the Masonic Lodge in Raton and later became a Noble (a thirty-second degree mason) on February 22, 1918, as a Life Member of the *Ballut Abyad* Shrine in Santa Fe. Records indicate that Perry was twice married: first at the age of 25 or 26 to Stephanie McIvar. The couple had one son. In March 1914, she took the infant, via the Santa Fe Railroad, to her parent's home in San Jose, California. She and the boy never returned to Springer and nothing more is known of this marriage or its termination.

His second marriage, date and location unknown, was to Agnes Jessica "Jessie" Blanchard, born in Socorro, New Mexico, in 1890. Jessie was of French descent on her father's side; he had been born in Canada. Her mother was born in Colorado. Between 1917 and 1920, three children were born to Perry and Jessie, two boys and one girl: Jimmy, Carl, and Dorothea. Jessie's sister, Catherine Blanchard, married Perry's brother Walter in 1923; they were divorced by 1926.[34]

Perry Caldwell and the Kearney Murder Case

On Friday, July 12, 1930, the findings of the Las Animas County, Colorado, coroner's inquest concerning Prohibition Agent Dale Kearney's murder appeared in the pages of the *Trinidad Chronicle-News*. The headlines summed up the coroner's findings: "Kearney Murder Still Remains Deep Mystery; Inquest Fails To Produce Any Information On Fatal Shooting; Agents Do Not Testify; Wife of Murdered Officer Also Declines To Take Stand."[35]

Four days later, another article posted from Walsenburg, Colorado, appeared noting the coming investigations by federal and local law enforcement: "Drive Planned On Gangs By Government; Federal Agents Will Make Thorough Search Of Southern Colorado; Will File Complaints To Make Every Effort To Apprehend Assassins Of Dale Kearney."[36]

On a day in late July 1930, Prohibition Agent Sutton arranged a meeting with Perry Caldwell. By now the two men had known each other nearly a decade. The two men first met in Springer where Perry's brother Berlin was the resident deputy sheriff. Perry happened by the office while Sutton was visiting with his brother. It was near the time that Sutton had been planning to leave his position as sheriff of Union County. They shared membership in the New Mexico Shriner's lodge in Santa Fe.

Sutton knew the reasons for Perry Caldwell's dismissal from federal service. He, in fact, had participated in the investigation that led to the man's termination. Sutton was duty bound to report on such matters especially when they affected his own associates. He didn't abide Perry's connections with Campanella then or later into the 1930s, but that doesn't preclude using the man in furthering his ongoing investigations whenever it was practical and necessary. The Kearney investigation was one such matter and top-tier priority.

Caldwell maintained his relationship with the bootleggers in the area and still worked as Campanella's pay-off man to some area constables. Whenever Sutton asked for specific information concerning local bootlegging matters, Perry would offer a lead or two for follow up. These usually led to the seizure of a small still and maybe the arrest of its operator if he was of the independent boots working outside the Campanella network. If and when Caldwell's information proved valid and operational, Sutton would see that a cash reward would make its way to him—more pocket money for his playtime at various speakeasies while away from home "on business" trips. Perry knew that any information he shared with Sutton would translate to a larger degree of protection for him, not Campanella. He played both sides.

> **Authors' Perspective:** Later evidence discovered by the authors suggests that for several years in the late 1920s, John Campanella had provided bribe money to Perry Caldwell to pass on to Ray Sutton. Caldwell knew that Sutton could not be bought, so he kept the money. Over the years, Perry covered this theft by becoming a part-time confidential government informant for Sutton. Had Campanella or any of his vast army of minions found out about Perry's double-dealing, Caldwell would have been unceremoniously dropped into a very deep hole.

John Campanella Arrested at Cimarron

Following his meeting with Perry, Sutton returned to the Seaberg Hotel in Raton to complete his two reports that would serve as the foundations of a search warrant on the Cimarron business and outbuildings belonging to John Campanella. Based on his stakeouts of the area and other local informant data, all indications were present that new shipments were being prepared for delivery to the Colorado side of the border.

Thus far in his investigation, Ray couldn't connect Campanella's mercantile store to his moonshine operations, but he knew that it had to be involved in the illicit business if for nothing more than supplies. Sutton always looked at the "pure facts" using simple cattleman logic: If something walks like a calf, sounds like a calf, smells like a calf, and looks like a calf, it had to be a calf.

Investigators learned that Sutton had set up a series of post office box drops in the various counties within his territories that could be used by his area informants to alert him about illicit activities in their areas while he was away. In Raton, for example, the post office was a large Roman-style structure with offices on the second floor and the general operating postal services on the ground floor. The customer mailbox wall was situated to the right of the main entrance as one entered the building. The wall contained specifically identified mail slots for "In Town," "Out of Town," "Packages," and "Overseas Mail." A fifth slot had no name, but people who used it knew its purpose: to pass information to Prohibition Agent Sutton. The postmaster transferred any envelopes found in the slot to Sutton's regular post office box. Sutton had a similar arrangement with Otto Jacobs, manager of Raton's Seaberg Hotel.[37]

After a seven-year absence from Cimarron, Fred Lambert and his family returned to the area in 1925. Lambert and his father-in-law, Abraham C. Hoover, purchased the 66-year-old adobe Swink Hall and adjoining property, located diagonally across the street from the St. James Hotel, and converted the old dance hall and former beer brewery into a full-service gas and automobile repair station. On the remainder of the property the two men, along with Manuel Cruz (Lambert's 18-year-old Santo Domingo Pueblo Indian ward) built a few tourist cabins and remodeled an old gambling parlor building into the Canyon Lunch Café, operated by Lambert's wife Katie. Coincidentally, the new tourist encampment was located directly across the street from the Russo family mercantile store and Campanella's warehouse.

Since returning to Colfax County, Fred Lambert had been serving as a special deputy sheriff stationed at Cimarron. In 1928, he was appointed a brand inspector for the New Mexico Cattle Sanitary Board. A short time later, the Sheep Sanitary Board gave him the same appointment for the northeastern part of the state. He established a network of deputy inspectors in New Mexico and at shipping points in Alamosa and Trinidad, Colorado, giving him a wide area of coverage. Nothing moved through the territory without his awareness. His men legally could, and did, move freely on the cattle, horse, and sheep ranches and at railroad and truck shipping points within their region. No one questioned the state inspector's authority or why he was working in the countryside. Lambert's network included tips of suspected illegal activities along with their inspection reports they submitted to him. Lambert assured Sutton that any applicable information concerning stills or bootlegging would find its way to him.

In his daily field reports, Sutton never specifically identified Lambert's level of cooperation or his network of associates. That was too dangerous for many reasons, one never knew who had access to the information once it hit the regional office in Denver. There were still those in the Bureau of Prohibition who were untrustworthy. Sutton got around this by invoking a cloak of invisibility to his "anonymous source of information."

The lead that led directly to the raid on John Campanella's Cimarron operation came from Maria Cleofas Gonzales, who had been the longtime housekeeper for the Lambert family ranch on the Cimarron River. When the Lamberts started their café, tourist cabin, and service station business they hired Mrs. Gonzales as their housekeeper for the cabins and as the part-time cook to help Katie in the café. One day Maria overheard some guests in one of the cabins discussing how they had finalized a pending moonshine delivery to John Campanella for the following week. Maria told Lambert, Lambert told Sutton, and Sutton arranged for an immediate meeting with Supervisor William E. Nance of the Kearney Investigation Task Force and Deputy Administrator Charles H. Stearns in Albuquerque. It was agreed that now was a propitious time to raid Campanella.[38]

It had been two weeks since the Kearney murder. Pressure from Denver to find Kearney's slayer required a quick strike on any and all suspected bootlegging activities associated with the southern Colorado and northeastern New Mexico network. Bureau of Prohibition management and the United States Attorney believed that the psychological impact of arrests could work wonders and maybe even offer up some information

Old Town Cimarron, NM, in the late 1930s, along South Collison Ave. This postcard view is oriented north toward the Cimarron River and New Town Cimarron. Fred and Katie Lambert's Canyon Lunch Café appears on the left along with rental overnight cabins, which sit on the southwest corner of South Collison Ave. (NM 21) and 17th Street. The adjoining Canyon Garage was owned and operated by Lambert's father-in-law. Across the street on the southeast corner of 17th Street is the Rosso Mercantile complex. John Campanella's storage barn was behind the Rosso buildings. The massive old St. James Hotel, renamed the Don Diego after the Lambert family sold the establishment, covers the land between 16th and 17th Streets. The Cimarron River is marked by the line of trees (courtesy Chuck and V.J. Hornung Western History Collection).

pertaining to the Kearney murder. If none were forthcoming, at least the arrests would slow down the bootleggers' normal operations and put them on notice that no one would be immune from intense investigative action.

Investigation revealed that Ray Sutton had prepared his proposal and justification for the Campanella take-down and entrusted the package to Agent C.U. Finley for a hand-carry delivery that same day to Deputy Administrator Stearns in Albuquerque. A second report with cover memorandum, addressed to John F. Vivian, the Regional Administrator, and Ralph L. Carr, the United States Attorney, was forwarded to Denver through Agent Nance at Trinidad. By Friday, July 18, they had their answers. Search warrants had been issued in record time.

On Tuesday, July 22, 1930, Sutton proceeded to Cimarron, with the warrant in hand, accompanied by a joint force of federal and Colfax County lawmen. Lambert's official livestock inspection reports revealed that at the time of the Campanella raid he and one of his deputy brand inspectors were north of Taos near the Colorado line arresting three horse thieves and recovering 118 horses. The two lawmen took the arrested men and animals north to Antonito, the nearest jail, and turned their catch over to the Conejos County sheriff's office for safekeeping until New Mexico officers could arrive to take charge of the case.[39]

The Russo family store compound was an "L" shaped structure situated on the northeast corner of 17th Street and South Collison Avenue (NM 21). The one-half block wide structure sat contiguous to a parcel of open land. Off to one side stood an old wooden barn Campanella leased from Russo and used for "supply storage" and junk. Big John was dumbfounded at the scope of the federal team's search. They seized his business and private records, vehicles, and all monies on hand, but they found only a few barrels of finished illegal liquor product. All of the structures on Campanella-owned and leased property were inspected, but the feds missed his main booze storage dump on the western slope of the Cimarron Mountain range.

Fortunately for "Big John" Campanella, he had wisely created a backup storage location in the northern portions of the Moreno Valley located at the end of the old Elizabethtown Road near the base of Baldy Mountain. The federal government didn't know about this new cache site at the time or there may have been a much larger quantity of illegal assets seized.[40]

The Moreno Valley compound had been created because Brownlow Wilson, owner-manager of the WS ranch, and Toke Harp, his new range foreman, had stumbled upon "Big John" Campanella's large brew site in Coal Canyon while seeking some missing cattle on the Van Bremmer pasture range. Wilson confronted Campanella and ordered him to dismantle his operation on WS lands. Strangely out of character, the bootlegger chief complied. Wilson later discovered that some of his cowboys and the range foreman he had recently fired for being incompetent had worked for Campanella. They had been transporting bootlegged product across the WS range, on WS pack horses, around the mountains and down into Dawson in exchange for a supply of liquor. This method of bypassing the use of highways into Dawson was the reason Sutton could never discover the delivery method used to bring illegal product into the coal camp.[41]

Campanella quickly discovered that this was no peccadillo action. The federal agents confiscated his New Town Cimarron business office and his Old Town outbuildings subject to government forfeiture proceedings. Needless to say, Campanella had nothing to discuss with the agents and remained silent during the search and seizure and his detention. He was, however, unable to hide the seething rage he held for Ray Sutton and his raider team.

The Kearney Task Force Continues Their Assignment

On Thursday, July 24, 1930, two days following the arrest of John Campanella, Agents Nance and Richardson scheduled a meeting with Sheriff Elijah A. Duling in Trinidad. The sheriff proved to be more than just cooperative; he became a fount of information on the local bootlegging operations as to who was running what, where, and with whom. He wouldn't say how he developed this information, chalking it up simply to his new reform policy and the support of his deputies and the general public. More than likely he provided the information for his own protection and that of his men. If the bootleggers were now killing federal agents, how long before they would begin eliminating local officers? He knew of the police officer killings in Pueblo and Denver earlier in the year. Nance and Richardson were in Sheriff Duling's office reviewing his case files and comparing them to the files that Denver had sent them on the names and people identified thus far in the investigation.

Both federal agents were aware of the information obtained in Aguilar (from the initial interviews of those present in the Alpine Rose Café) and elsewhere by both local and federal authorities. James "Jimmy the Jew" Merino, the former owner of the Alpine Rose Café, knew he and the others would be immediately suspected of being involved. He had told the other witnesses to speak freely about whatever was asked. Merino admitted his prior arrest by Kearney for selling liquor at the café. He also said that after Kearney had departed, he had had Charlie Jones go to the café's front window to observe where Kearney went. Jones stated that as Kearney started down the street, he stopped and spoke for a few minutes with John Frederico, the proprietor of the Eagle Café, a few doors down from the Alpine Rose. Kearney continued on, passing through an arc of light filtering through the windows of the Arcade Hotel on the next corner. That was as far as Jones could see him before Kearney turned the corner. The time then was around 12:15 a.m. A few minutes later the people in the Alpine Rose heard five or six shots fired in rapid succession. The shots came from the direction of the Arcade Hotel.[42]

Merino then indicated that Town Marshal Fawcett entered the café around 12:30 a.m. and Merino asked if he had seen Kearney, saying that Dale had been in a few minutes earlier looking for him. No mention was made to Fawcett that Kearney had eaten a meal and had approached the group in the café asking Merino for his shot bottle. The marshal asked Merino the way Kearney had gone and Merino told him the direction taken and that the group heard five or six shots shortly after Kearney had left. It was also learned that Charlie Jones recently had purchased the Alpine Rose Café. He confirmed the initial statements of Merino.

When interviewed, town Marshal Fawcett reported that he immediately left the café heading toward the Arcade Hotel. As he reached the Green Light Café, the proprietor, Mike Lazeroff, stopped him and told him about hearing gunshots coming from down the street. Fawcett found Kearney's body on the sidewalk lying in a pool of blood. Fawcett immediately went to the city hall and used the telephone to call the sheriff's office in Trinidad. Sheriff Duling's written report indicated that he promptly responded in good time and once onsite they took charge of the crime scene.

On July 24, 1930, Agent Nance summed up the latest information for Sheriff Duling. Records in the Bureau of Prohibition files in Denver revealed that Jones and Merino had some interesting local business friends, as well as a few in Pueblo and Denver. These people included members of the late Danna gang, who had lost their private war with a few of the more successful independents who were known to federal authorities. The agents' reports indicated that they intended to further interview Jones and Merino in greater detail. Interestingly, the two men lived some distance from Aguilar; Merino resided in Leadville, a mining town in the mountains 40 miles west of Denver, about 130 miles north of Aguilar. Jones lived in Canon City, home of the state prison, which was about 60 miles distant from Aguilar.

The federal agents had been authorized to arrest both men as material witnesses and remove them "for safekeeping in protective custody" to Trinidad and house them in the Las Animas County Jail under the protection of Sheriff Duling. They were to be kept from the possibility of any physical harm from any outside threats. Both law enforcement agencies would attempt to determine why the men and their women happened to be so far away from their homes on the night Prohibition Agent Kearney was murdered. The sheriff saw no problem in assisting the federal agents in this undertaking.

The continuing Kearney investigation resulted in a number of additional arrests in Aguilar, mainly the owners and operators of nearby local cafés in proximity to the Alpine Rose Café. Most of these subjects were known to the authorities. It's apparent from Kearney's earlier investigative reports and subsequent follow-up intelligence that the identities of some of those most recently arrested were well known to authorities. To what extent those subjects from the Alpine Rose Café cooperated by giving up any additional information remains unknown. The mere fact that they were held for several days "for their own protection" raises the question: from whom were they being protected?

On July 16, 1930, the wire service report of the Associated Press stringer in Trinidad provided the names and locations of the nine persons arrested during the federal task force's raids on four establishments in Aguilar. The pertinent part of the published bulletin read,

> Among those arrested were Martin Diulio, Dominic Nazaro, Lewis Nickoloff, Tony Christo, John Fetrico [Petrico], John Matelko, Jim Caputa, Mike Pacholl [Pacheel], and George Ferris. The entire group was scheduled for arraignment on charges of sale and possession of intoxicating liquor and maintaining a nuisance. The arrests were made at the Bluebird Café, the Arcade, the Eagle Café, and the Green Light Café [...]
>
> Unofficial information suggested that the roundup was based on information received from the four persons arrested previously: James Merino, Mr. and Mrs. Charles Jones and Marie Gouthro.

These arrests constitute the first direct advance against persons with possible connection to Kearney's slayers.[43]

The Conspiracy to Murder Sutton Takes Shape

Later, the investigation revealed that around July 24, 1930, Joe McAllister was informed by John Campanella that they, the Campanella organization of which McAllister was a part, were going to kill Sutton and that McAllister had no choice. It was then that he told McAllister of monies that had been given to Caldwell to bribe Sutton to keep him from taking action against the Campanella organization. Unexpectedly, Campanella offered McAllister $500 if he would take on the job to kill Sutton. He declined. Campanella then instructed McAllister to set up a meeting within the next week between the two men and Caldwell, to be held at the McAllister home. Subsequently, the meeting would occur on the following Friday. Joe had arranged for his wife and family to be at her sister's home for supper on that evening. The men could count on at least a couple of hours of conversation alone. The kidnapping and murder conspiracy had begun.

At the next meeting of the conspirators, Campanella stood firm in his belief that the group needed a foolproof plan, one that could be done quickly and safely for all concerned. He was talking of Sutton's death. Those present were now part of a conspiracy to commit murder. Caldwell and McAllister looked at each other. Campanella had just cast the dice for all of them and none had a way out and each one knew it. The group would meet again in a few weeks.[44]

In small towns, like Raton, good news traveled fast. Bad news moved even faster, only sometimes it is heard outside of the intended audience. Within the week, rumors were surfacing on the streets of Raton that Prohibition Agent Ray Sutton's time on Earth was limited.[45]

> **Authors' Perspective:** Hindsight would suggest that Sutton's physiognomy misled Campanella into underestimating the agent in the belief that he had the federal agent in his pocket. He certainly did not take Sutton seriously until he raided his personal property and arrested him. Then the bootlegger chief determined that he would never make the mistake of underestimating Sutton again. He may have taken great pleasure in the thought of a slow agonizing death for his nemesis.

9

Family, Leads and Plans

"Be careful in your line of work for some of those whom you believe to be your friends are not. It will not be your enemies who will seek to destroy you; it will be those whom you trusted too much at the wrong time. Someone who works with you or one who was formerly a coworker or involved in your line of business may do you great harm."—Denver spiritualist Mrs. Hartzell's warning to Union County Sheriff Ray Sutton, circa 1918, *Pioneer Living with Mema*

Dateline: Colorado and Northeastern New Mexico, August 1930

In Denver, Regional Administrator John F. Vivian assumed his position at the head of the line to receive whatever new data his field teams were developing on either of the two murder cases. He never ventured into the field to collect or assess the situation himself, but he put pressure on Senior Investigator John Richardson who was coordinating the Kearney field operations for daily updates. This meant that if anything went wrong in Vivian's eyes, he had someone to blame. He knew from previous action in the Denver office that Richardson would never throw himself on his own sword or anybody else's for the benefit of Vivian's reputation. Richardson was a competent and ideal person on whom he could count to assure that everything possible was being done by the Kearney Investigation Task Force.

Vivian was the bureau's man in charge of all regional prohibition operations and it was important for him to obtain, evaluate, maintain, and forward reports to Washington. He also kept United States Attorney Ralph L. Carr in the loop. Second, he had his own personal reasons to be first in line. The Kearney case was the region's priority investigation and one that could lead him to higher political office or open doors to other opportunities. To some of those watchers of all things political, it appeared as if he was keeping a running journal on the Kearney case and didn't want to miss anything. If Vivian had been doing so, he could and would not inform others. It just wasn't done in professional circles such as the one of which he was a part.

Unlike Vivian, Ralph L. Carr systematically read each report and memorandum on the investigation that came across his desk. His interest in the matter went beyond the nature of the crime and the public's continuing interests in the matter. Carr had instructed his staff to keep a vigilant watch on organized crime in Colorado, because of their endless expansion and hook-ups with other crime "syndicates" across the nation. Carr's well-placed confidential sources inside the Carlino criminal leadership circles attested to this reality.

Unknown to Carr, the Prohibition Bureau maintained a running collection process on data targeting the crime families and their state of unrest and a bit more. Vivian did not see fit to apprise Carr of any of these facts. Likewise, Carr hadn't shared with Vivian that he had an informant within Denver's criminal hierarchy.

The Kearney Investigation Task Force

The Kearney Investigation Task Force had begun to produce measurable investigative results with a continuing presence in the field and its increased numbers of arrests and seizures. Still, no one was able to directly identify the Carlinos as the killers of Kearney. True to the *muerta* code, no one was talking to authorities. The Carlino reputation for violence assured this state of silence.

In Raton, Ray Sutton spent the first of the week reviewing records seized from the John Campanella raid and conferring with the New Mexico's United States Attorney Hugh B. Woodward and Eighth Judicial District (Colfax and Taos Counties) Attorney Fred C. Stringfellow. It was a tedious job. Campanella had concealed his bootlegging activities rather well, but a handwritten notation caught Sutton's eye. On a single piece of paper, Sutton found scribbled, "Pueblo Club."

When Sutton broached the subject of the Pueblo Club with Fred Lambert, the veteran lawman told him it was a private gaming parlor in Taos operated by some local businessmen of nefarious reputation. One of these men was "Long John" Dunn, a gambler, rancher, and longtime Taos resident who hailed from Borger in the Texas Panhandle. Lambert had dealt with Dunn when he was a New Mexico Mounted Police officer working a kidnapping case in Taos County. Lambert also knew Mike Cunico and Joe McAllister had earlier roots in Taos County. Both men now had business association with John Campanella.[1]

Sutton may have wondered if these men had some financial interest in the Pueblo Club. Or maybe the club was part of their clientele and they used it as a distribution outlet. Either way, that locale was going to get some unwanted attention from District Attorney Stringfellow. Sutton and Stringfellow took on the task of coordinating the ground action with the Taos County sheriff's office and a few trusted personnel from Colfax County. By Monday, August 11, 1930, all arrangements had been made and the plan was executed the next day.

Ever alert for the latest investigative information, the *Raton Evening Gazette* announced the results of the Taos' Pueblo Club raid on Wednesday, August 13, 1930. The notice said four men were arrested during the raid and, after their preliminary hearing, were released on bond to appear in at the next session of the district court. Those arrested on special affidavits sworn out by Taos County Deputy Sheriff Malaquis Martinez were "Long John" Dunn of Taos; Bill Snyder, formerly of Raton; and Juan Lovato, formerly of Santa Fe. The fourth man was not named. Each man was charged with illegal gambling.[2]

9. *Family, Leads and Plans* 101

In a 1930 interview John Dunn said, "I invested everything I had in Taos County. I built a home, opened up four saloons, a gamblin' hall and a livery stable." After Dunn's death in 1953 a longtime friend recalled, "John Dunn was at his best behind a roulette wheel or Monte table where you never got more than was coming to you and if you didn't watch [out] it was less."[3]

Sutton arrived in Trinidad on Thursday, August 14, 1930, to share details of the Taos raid. A Kearney task force meeting was scheduled following every major arrest or seizure to assure that each team member had the intelligence derived from the last incident. Following a simple update, Sutton presented his plan to further debilitate the northeastern New Mexico bootlegging operations. Over the previous two weeks, Sutton had arrested the Wright brothers, Curley and Jimmy, at their still in the Moreno Valley about 12 miles from Agua Fria; arrested John Campanella in Cimarron; and honed his focus on the Cunico-Campanella-Pueblo Club connections in Taos.[4]

Sutton next scrutinized the actions of Joe McAllister and Al Shedoudy and looked into George Pobar's alleged association with John Campanella's bootleg operations in Colfax County. Shedoudy was believed to be the blunderbuss of the trio—the most likely to be persuaded to betray the group. Why he was described as such is unknown. Finally, Sutton outlined his plan to spend a few days visiting in the Raton area, letting a few select people know about "two stills out in the Dawson area" that interested him. After his presentation, Ray was asked to stay a few days in Trinidad to assist the task force on a raid.

The agents most likely had some comments concerning the recent directive from

Trinidad, Colorado, circa 1930 (courtesy Chuck and V.J. Hornung Western History Collection).

Washington that set a new standard for operating field searches or road blocks. When attempting to stop a car for inspection, all agents were required to post an official sign on the side of their vehicle clearly stating it was an automobile used by a prohibition agent. Citizens had complained they did not know that the men trying to stop them were official federal law enforcement personnel and not hijackers.[5]

Agents Richardson and Nance proceeded to outline upcoming task force action. This plan involved a raid of the premises and residences of the Dionisios and other Trinidad-based Black Hand Society representatives who had a business relationship with the Carlino crime family. The Dionisio crime family hated Dale F. Kearney. On the evening of July 4, 1930, Kearney and his wife dined at the Saddle Rock Café in Trinidad. While there, it appeared that one of the Dionisio family had "fingered" Kearney to his men.

Further, Agent Nance told the team he anticipated the arrest of Pete Carlino's brother-in-law, Joseph Riggio, who had worked as muscle for the Danna Brothers. Riggio's sister, Gennie, was married to Pete Carlino. The two opposing crime families, Danna and Carlino, had intermarried at some point between 1916 and 1923. Riggio and a few of his associates were currently operating near the town of Aguilar.[6]

Following the end of the task force meeting, Ray Sutton returned to his Trinidad hotel and telephoned Clayton. This day, Friday, August 15, 1930, was his wife's 56th birthday. It would be the second important family celebration he had missed within the past two weeks. News on the latest Trinidad raid appeared in a Raton newspaper that evening. The headline told the story: "Four Arrested In Kearney Murder Case." The names of those arrested included Joseph Riggio, Santos Alenci, Rosario Dionisio and

Prohibition Agent Howard Beacham with his roll-up roadblock sign. Beacham is standing in front of the New Mexico State School for the Blind on present-day Whitesands Boulevard in Alamogordo, circa 1930 (courtesy New Mexico State University Special Collections and Archives Howard S. Beacham Papers #0349).

R.V. Dionisio (the patriarch of the family). Neither the public nor the press was informed about the July 4th dinner incident at the Saddle Rock Café. The attorneys posted a $2,500 bond for each suspect to guarantee future appearances at the next session of the district court.[7]

When initially interrogated by task force team members, neither of the two Dionisio brothers would speak of any liquor violations or of anything remotely related to their Black Hand Society affiliations or the Kearney murder. The investigative team did get some raw intelligence, however, about a potential distilling operation in Colfax County. Ray Sutton noted two items for near-future action and investigation.

The Raton Plan

On Wednesday, August 20, 1930, Ray Sutton returned to Raton and initiated his plan of attack against the Campanella confederacy. The first item on his list was to pay a visit to Sheriff Al Davis. Sheriff Davis learned that working with federal agents was always easier when the agent or agents had prior local enforcement experience. And Sutton had that degree of experience and demeanor that kept him on Davis' "open access" list. Sutton understood a lot more about county officers' work than any of the other federal agents Davis had encountered (since Sutton had sat in the same chair in Union County). Davis understood how valuable Sutton was in their joint enforcement efforts. Sutton, like Davis, was a Republican who had been elected to office in a predominantly Democrat-populated county; therefore, he appeared to be always fighting an uphill battle with the Democrat-controlled county commissioners court for proper funding for his department.

Sheriff Davis sat behind a stack of budget reports while talking with Sutton who then told him of his current search for two stills out near Dawson. As the conversation continued, Sutton indicated that he had found information on a still operating in Raton and possibly another near Agua Fria in the Moreno Valley. He asked if he could count on him for some help in taking them down if he could verify their existence. Sheriff Davis agreed to the request whenever and wherever needed. During their discussion, Sutton had played his first strategic card. He hated that the "Raton Plan" included keeping his longtime friend in the dark even though he fully trusted the sheriff.

Sutton departed the sheriff's office and headed to the Seaberg Hotel. Grace McAlpin, the desk clerk, welcomed him back, as she did

Prohibition Agent Zaccheus Raymond "Ray" Sutton, circa 1930 (Ray Sutton's Official Personnel File).

on each of his visits, and turned to the large wooden message cabinet containing numerous mail or message slots. She retrieved a single phone message and handed it to Sutton. No name was given, but the agent knew that it was a response from Perry Caldwell whom he had contacted by phone earlier in the day. He checked his pocket watch, 10:00 a.m. He still had time to do some paperwork, mail off his daily reports to the task force and the state headquarters in Albuquerque. Maybe even get a bite to eat before heading out to check out the in-town still site tip.

As he sat at the small writing table in his hotel room, the phone rang. It was Caldwell. Ray suggested a meet, but Caldwell wasn't available. Instead Ray briefly described what he was looking for over the telephone: "Two stills over near Dawson." He asked Perry to see if he could come up with anything. Perry said he would check it out and get back to him in a few days. Ray told him that he'd be in and out of town working while staying at the Seaberg and asked Caldwell to keep checking back in case he missed his call. Caldwell had enthusiastically accepted the new assignment without any in-depth discussion.

Sutton reflected on Perry Caldwell's sudden spirit of cooperation. He filed that data away mentally to come back to later on. His gut was telling him that something was not quite right with the way he jumped in to assist him. Perry had been out of work on and off for the past month. Perhaps he was counting on a possible cash award to help him out in the event he was successful in his search.

On Sunday, August 24, 1930, Sutton conferred with agents John Richardson and W.E. Nance in Trinidad to update them on his "Raton Plan." He explained the pending action he and the Colfax County sheriff's office would be taking in Raton and Agua Fria. Sutton said that he would not be in need of any task force help since Sheriff Davis and his men had all the bases covered. He also mentioned that he had purposely let slip word of why he had returned to Raton every chance he had over the last few days: "I'm searching for two stills up near Dawson."

It seemed that no one had taken an interest, that is, until he talked to Perry Caldwell. Sutton looked at the two men who questioned Caldwell's motives and changed demeanor. Nance asked why Caldwell would do that unless he either suspected something was amiss or maybe he saw the writing on the wall as a result of the Campanella raid and arrest. Were there other events in the making that the team didn't know about? The team warned Sutton to be cautious.

Sutton's old Oklahoma lawman friend Chris Madsen was once asked to share some of his veteran wisdom for younger officers. He wrote some pointed advice:

> Many a well-planned raid has been made a failure because someone of the party had told his wife, a personal friend or a sweetheart of the dangerous work he had been selected for. And regardless of how much confidence one may have in his kinfolks and friends, and how anxious they may be to keep the secret, some word or some action may warn *the ever-watchful friends of the outlaws, who often have spies among the better people, and even in the offices of the officers.* [Emphasis added by the authors.][8]

One can wonder if Ray recalled Madsen's words as he showed a somber face to his colleagues. He reflected with them about an incident when he was sheriff in Union County during the Great War. He had visited a fortune teller's salon in south Denver and saw The Spiritualist who gave readings or "divined your future" from a deck of tarot cards.

9. *Family, Leads and Plans*   105

Prohibition raid in Raton, New Mexico. This is the official picture of the illegal liquor confiscated during the Raton raid. The car, identified by the Kansas license plate 84C-773, is Ray Sutton's government owned 1929 Pontiac coach. Note the car's wooden spoke wheel rims (courtesy New Mexico State University Special Collections and Archives Howard S. Beacham Papers # 0349).

Sutton recalled her warning: "Someone who works with you [...] may do you great harm." Following Ray's disappearance, the *Clayton News* reminded readers that he had often told friends that if he was ever killed it would be by the hand of a turncoat officer, not bootleggers.[9]

Sutton concluded his report by outlining the scheduled raids in Raton and the south end of the Moreno Valley. The meeting ended and Sutton returned to Raton to prepare for the raids. On Tuesday, August 26, 1930, Sutton, Sheriff Al Davis and Deputy William Ledoux, raided the residence of Sam Ullo at 1228 Cedar in Raton. Seized were one 30-gallon still and 200 gallons of mash. Sam Ullo appeared to be the same party or perhaps a relative of the Ullo family in and around Trinidad associated with the Carlino crime factions.

Ullo was arraigned before United States Commissioner Haines in Raton and pled guilty. The court "held [him] over for the Federal Grand Jury and released him on a $1,000 bond." On Wednesday, August 27, 1930, Sutton and Deputy Sheriff William Ledoux teamed up once more to conduct a wide area search for a possible still in the vicinity of Aqua Fria. The small trading center had a store operated by ethnic Italians. Curley Wright, a known bootlegger and Campanella contact, operated a small ranch in the area. The Sutton raid produced no illegal activity. On his return to Raton later that evening, Sutton figured the day's mileage to be 175 miles—a typical 15-hour workday duly recorded in his journal.[10]

Authors' Perspective: Colfax County Deputy Sheriff William Ledoux's brother, Julius Ledoux, had been the New Mexico Mounted Police officer assigned to northern New Mexico during the years 1919 and 1920. The mounted police were very good at their jobs. On Saturday, September 4, 1920, State Policeman Ledoux arrested "Big John" Campanella for selling whiskey. The case never went to trial because most of the commissions for the state rangers expired on New Year's Eve 1920 and the 1921 state legislature abolished the force a few months later. Campanella had been lucky that time because when his case was called for trial the judge released him on a technicality, no arresting officer was available to testify in the case against him.

The Convergence of Light and Darkness

Coincidentally, on Wednesday evening, August 27, 1930, "Big John" Campanella, Perry Caldwell, and Joe McAllister, as investigators would later learn, held a quiet meeting at McAllister's Raton home to further their conspiracy. On Thursday morning, while finalizing his reports on the Raton still seizure and the field investigation in Agua Fria, Sutton received a call from Caldwell saying that he had located the two stills that Ray had asked him to locate. They planned to meet at 2:00 p.m. "out near the Dawson Road."[11]

Ray Sutton and Joe Gilstrip, his longtime friend, ate lunch in the Seaberg Hotel dining room. They enjoyed the pot roast lunch special and planned a turkey hunt for Thanksgiving. Later, Gilstrip told a reporter that he had warned his friend about the street rumors he heard concerning Ray's safety and asked him to be extra careful. Sutton told Gilstrip, "If anybody ever gets me it will be a fellow officer or a former officer, not a bootlegger."[12]

10

You Shall Know the Truth ...

> "We are going to continue with the search, clues or no clues. We may stumble onto something anytime if we keep continuously on the job."—Charles Stearns, assistant regional director, Prohibition Region 18, *New Mexico State Tribune,* September 30, 1930

Eight years after Federal Prohibition Agent Ray Sutton disappeared, 17-year-old John George Pobar recounted to Colfax County law enforcement officers what he claimed to have witnessed on the afternoon of Thursday, August 28, 1930, at his family's dairy farm near the Koehler coal camp. Sheriff Barney Mitchell and District Attorney John Tittmann were dumbfounded by what the teenager related. Had they solved the mysterious disappearance of Ray Sutton? The narrative that follows is constructed from court records, contemporary newspaper accounts and participant interviews.[1]

A Tale of Death

Then-eight-year-old John Pobar approached the family's farmhouse after completing his assigned pasture chores. John was the ninth of 11 children of George and Margaret Pobar. The Pobar's leased a dairy farm a short distance east of the Koehler coal town properties in Coal Creek Valley. The property was owned by the St. Louis, Rocky Mountain and Pacific Company. The Koehler mine and company town had been established in 1906 and was closed in 1924. The mine reopened in 1936 only to close permanently and be dismantled in 1954. Today it is a ghost town closed to the public. Since 1910, the family had also worked a Moreno Valley homestead farm. None of the family discussed the father's sideline business of delivering bootleg booze.[2]

It was early evening, a few hours before sunset, as the boy neared his house. He had finished his field chores and hoped his mother would have supper ready. Young Pobar was surprised to see a number of unfamiliar vehicles parked near the storage barn. His family did not get many visitors, so being a curious soul, he quietly crept up near the barn siding where he could peer through one of the cracks.[3]

John Pobar's position was a few feet from the four men standing inside. He clearly saw his 53-year-old Austrian-born father, George Pobar, and some other men whom he recognized as friends of his father: John Campanella, Perry Caldwell, and another man he wasn't able to see clearly. The fourth man may have been Elias Albert Shedoudy.

The four men were standing in a semicircle around an older man with graying hair. The prisoner was slumped forward in a standing position. His head rested on his chest as his body was held upright by his outstretched arms over his head, while his tied hands hung from a rope attached to an overhead barn beam. What John Pobar could see of the man's face appeared bloodied, bruised and swollen. Blood stained the upper portions of the clothing the man was wearing. Two of the men had taken turns beating the victim with their fists before his body went limp. After a short time, the men spoke quietly between themselves and began motioning toward the cars parked to the rear of the barn. It appeared they were about to end their inquisition.

Young Pobar didn't want to get caught spying on his father, for he knew the wrath of an angered father. He had a terrible temper. Beatings were common when his father was displeased. On numerous occasions, little John had been on the receiving end of his father's violence; he referred to the punishment as "chastisement," but it was really unbridled rage and brutality. All of the Pobar children feared their father, for he was known far and wide for his authoritarian control over his family. Many persons over the years had observed George Pobar's behaviors on more than one occasion. It didn't matter where the family members were at the time, if George was displeased he would dispense his brand of parental reprimand to the fullest. John left the side of the barn and made his way unseen back towards the farmhouse.

The boy made his way to a point on the outskirts of the pasture to where he could watch the barn from afar. Soon he observed three men drag the tied-up, unconscious man out of the rear barn door to one of the parked cars, a black sedan, and load him into the rear seating compartment. John Campanella appeared to be giving the orders. Two of the men got in the sedan's front-seat compartment. The others loaded into another auto which then caravanned off the farm to the dirt road turning eastward. John grew up in this area and knew the shortcuts that paralleled the eastern road. He raced through the pathways, occasionally losing sight of the two cars. Finally, he reached a lookout point that gave him a fairly open view of the roadway. From this point John saw the two cars leave the dirt road and drive onto the flat terrain at the base of the surrounding low hills. They continued on into a small cut back in the hill and stopped.

John told investigators how he made his way closer to the site carefully and quietly. As he was straining to hear any conversation, he heard what sounded like a distant pop, not very loud, but definitely a pop with its faint echo coming up the arroyos. It sounded almost like a gunshot but not from a rifle. He then heard the cars' engines start and watched as the men drove away out of sight toward the Raton-Cimarron road. Young Pobar decided to wait and see what, if anything else, would occur. After an undetermined amount of time, he saw the headlamps of two cars approaching the arroyo site and its small stand of cottonwoods.

The black sedan was driven further into the arroyo and stopped. Then, the same four men John had seen at the farm pushed the sedan down a small incline where it came to rest wedged between two small cottonwood trees. While one man wiped the car's front interior, the others gathered dead tree limbs, logs, and brush they used to completely hide the car in a teepee formed structure. When they finished, they stood talking for a few moments with one man wiping his hands on a white cloth and discarding it on the ground. They all then entered the remaining car and drove off; as the headlights indicated, they were heading back toward the old dirt access road. John raced home hoping to get back before darkness overtook him or his father returned.

Days later when the boy and his siblings saw posse members in the area, searching the arroyos and surrounding foothills for a missing prohibition agent, John came to suspect what he had witnessed was this man's death. He recalled his father saying if any "revenooers" ever came on his place he'd shoot them and "they might fall into a well."[4]

John never mentioned what he had seen that August night in 1930 to his father or anyone else, at least not for almost a decade. His story came to light only after his father's body was found alongside the dirt road leading to the farm. It was then that John George Pobar revealed what he had seen that terrible night. He had to because he and his younger brother Joseph were arrested by Sheriff Mitchell and charged with the June 11, 1938, murder of their father.

By the time District Attorney John Tittmann presented the case to the district court jury, he had no solid evidence against young Pobar boys. Many people reported sympathy for the brothers since they had observed George Pobar's violent behavior toward his family on more than one occasion. The court dismissed the murder charges. Based on young John's troubled behavior, the judge declared him a delinquent and ordered his confinement at the New Mexico Industrial School for Boys, a juvenile detention and vocational training facility. It had been created by the territorial government and located at Springer since 1909. Joseph returned to the family farm.

Pobar was later transferred from the state school at Springer to Father Edward J. Flanagan's Boys Town in Omaha, Nebraska, for further rehabilitation. One day he told his priest-counselor about the Sutton incident. He never recanted his story.

John George Pobar had been born on January 20, 1922. When he became an adult in 1943 he was released from Boys Town and began a new chapter in his life. After some travel, he finally settled in Aurora, Colorado, and died there on September 14, 1998.[5]

Authors' Perspective: Twice John Pobar attempted to take Sheriff Mitchell and John Tittmann to the area from which he said he observed the final minutes of Ray Sutton's life. He failed at both attempts. After nine years John was unable to pinpoint the spot he described during his interrogations. It is possible that a flash flood, winds or vegetative growth had altered the site's appearance. Many asked themselves what would have been Pobar's motive to lie about witnessing a horrific event like a savage beating and a violent death?

Co-author Chuck Hornung has tried twice since 1971, when he was first guided to the site, to relocate where Sutton's car was discovered. He failed both times because his memory of the terrain and physical structure of the road and boundary fencing then did not match the current condition on the ground. These markers had changed over the decades.

John Pobar's story answers a number of questions about Sutton's final hours: the who, what, when, where and how, but lacks essential physical evidence for a court of law. The authors, however, believe it holds a ring of truth. In his 1888 novel *A Study in Scarlet*, Sir Arthur Conan Doyle had Sherlock Holmes, his consulting detective hero, make this observation, "It is a capital mistake to theorize before you have all the evidence. It biases the judgment." The authors agree. This is why we have begun this chapter with John Pobar's account of a day in August 1930.

Dateline: New Mexico and Colorado, Fall 1930–Winter 1931

The Labor Day weekend of 1930 was in full bloom across the nation with the usual parades, flags, rodeos, and picnics taking place in every town and city. According to federal crime reports on Monday, September 1, a tall, burly man with light sandy-colored hair walked up to the cashier counter of the Santa Fe Railroad's Harvey House (Fred Harvey Eating House) in Trinidad and requested the cashier to cash his government expense check. This was the same establishment where members of the Kearney Task Force normally stayed when they were in town. The cashier asked for identification, but all the man could produce was a masonic ring and lodge membership card. On the inside ring surface was "his" engraved name, "R. Sutton." The cashier looked at him and the masonic identification card bore the name "Ray Sutton." She took both items to the manager to obtain approval for the transaction. The man quickly scrawled "Ray Sutton" on the back of the check and the clerk paid him $152.35. He thanked her and left.[6]

Do We Have a Missing Agent?

A series of unusual events occurred in Trinidad, Raton and Clayton during the August week preceding the Labor Day holiday in 1930 and continued into the first week in September. These events went unnoticed by a number of people for whatever reason. In hindsight, one might suggest a lack of communication and coordination were at fault, but in the real-life situation each action didn't seem alarming at the time to any of the concerned parties.

The first person to notice something unusual was the manager of Hugo Seaberg's hotel in Raton. On Tuesday, September 2, Otto Jacobs observed that Ray Sutton had not checked out of his room and learned that none of his employees had seen him since the preceding Thursday. Normally Sutton gave Jacobs notice of his intentions to depart and always cleared his bill when leaving. This five-day absence appeared to be a change in Sutton's normal pattern of behavior, but Jacobs assumed Sutton would soon return since he also still had an open charge on his parking garage statement. He always paid this bill before leaving town for an extended period.[7]

In Trinidad, Officer Oscar Vandenberg had commented to his senior manager that Sutton had failed to meet him for a scheduled rendezvous to patrol the Raton Pass on the evening of August 28. The agent had always kept their appointments unless he had called to reschedule. The absence of any notice that he would be late or he had to call off the patrol troubled Vandenberg. He thought this behavior to be most irregular for Sutton and hoped he was not ill. He knew the agent suffered from heart problems because he had once witnessed a mild attack.[8]

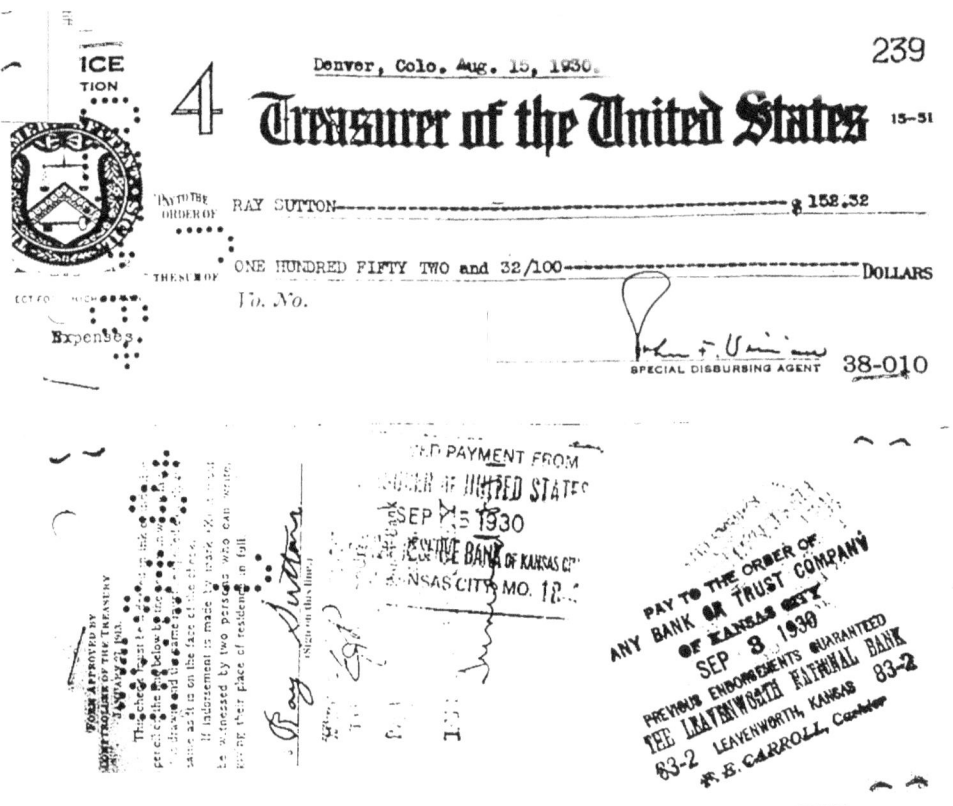

Ray Sutton's forged federal expense check (front/back). This government expense check was used as evidence against Perry Caldwell at his forgery trial in Pueblo, CO (Ray Sutton's Official Personnel File).

Members of the Kearney Investigation Task Force had noted Sutton's failure to attend their scheduled meeting in Trinidad on August 29. This was very unusual especially since he was to report on his latest meet with Perry Caldwell regarding the Campanella group. No one on the team had heard from him. Alarms should have been ringing loudly but no one seemed to hear. The meeting took place and a report was forwarded to Denver and Albuquerque.

Meanwhile, Charles Stearns was advised that no one in Albuquerque had heard from Sutton since the office had received his last report dated August 27 in Friday's mail. No more than 48 hours had ever passed without a contact by Sutton, either by report or by telephone. As a matter of record, he was known for always being punctual for his appointments and with his daily reports from the field. There were no known indicators that Sutton had been in harm's way, other than the normal state of being a federal prohibition agent working alone in the field. Yet once again alarm bells should have been ringing loudly but no one seemed to hear.

The seriousness of the situation would not become known until the afternoon of Thursday, September 4, when the clerk of the Federal District Court in Clayton telephoned the Albuquerque office to report that Agent Sutton had failed to appear in a case scheduled for trial. The clerk said that she had attempted to locate him by calling

The Seaberg Hotel, Raton, New Mexico, circa late 1940s. This hotel served as Ray Sutton's "Raton office." The facility underwent eight expansions between 1905 and 1928. When Sutton stayed at the hotel it contained 200 rooms, 100 of which contained private baths. The nightly room rate ran from $1 to $5. The hotel passed to new owners in 1938 and reopened as El Portal Hotel. In the 1950s Fred and Katie Lambert managed the hotel's coffee shop. The Raton sign is atop Goat Hill (courtesy Chuck and V.J. Hornung Western History Collection).

his home in Clayton but to no avail. The charges against the defendants had, therefore, been dismissed. The alarm bell was finally heard; something was amiss if Ray Sutton had failed at attend a court hearing.[9]

Thus began a series of excited and nervous inquiries by the Albuquerque Prohibition Bureau Office. A long-distance telephone call was made to Mrs. Sutton. Seldom did one or two days pass without Ray calling his wife to assure her of his well-being. She had not heard from him since before the Labor Day weekend. She told Stearns that the district court clerk had called her earlier also trying to locate her husband. She then asked if her husband was dead. Stearns replied that he did not believe so, but it seemed that Ray was missing. He told Maggie Sutton he would keep her informed of his progress in locating her husband.

The next long-distance call was made to the Colfax County sheriff's office. Sheriff Al Davis told the federal officer that he had no knowledge of Ray Sutton's present whereabouts. Stearns asked the sheriff to check with the hotel for any information they might have concerning his agent's movements. Davis queried the hotel desk clerk by phone to have Sutton's room checked, stating that he and his undersheriff George "Boots" Fletcher were on their way over to investigate.

Upon arriving at the Seaberg Hotel, Sheriff Davis and Undersheriff Fletcher learned that Sutton was not in his room. The lawmen found the room to be undisturbed and showed no evidence of a struggle or any violence. Sutton's work journal and papers, luggage and top coat were in the room; his wallet, pistol, and identification card and badge were missing. It was assumed he intended to return the same day. Davis immediately called Stearns and advised him that Sutton had not been seen by anyone at the hotel for three or four days and that Sutton's personal belongings were intact. Both Davis and Stearns realized the dire importance of the situation. Davis stated that he would begin organizing his men and a posse to conduct a major search and rescue effort in Colfax County beginning from the point near the Dawson Road turnoff where Undersheriff Fletcher had last observed him eight days earlier.

Deputy Administrator Stearns next telephoned Union County Sheriff A.W. "White" Tanner and asked if he had seen Sutton. The answer was negative. Suddenly, Charles Stearns had an epiphany: a second agent was missing or dead in a two-month period. What was happening in the Trinidad-Raton area? Stearns ordered an emergency meeting of his Albuquerque staff.[10]

> **Authors' Perspective:** It is a hard-rock dictum that the first 48 hours following the disappearance, kidnapping or murder of an individual is the most critical period of investigation. The chances of solving the crime or finding the victim are greater in the first hours and grow less so with each passing day. Clues are fresher, witness observations are more exact, and memories are less faulty. This is a general investigative Rule of Thumb in such cases and may be applied, for the most part, to all serious crimes. The format of organizing an investigation and search by management and law enforcement personnel in the field are fairly standard whether the key agencies have local, state, or federal jurisdiction.

The Area Search for Sutton Begins

At his emergency staff meeting, Stearns placed the state office on immediate alert and announced his pending travel to Raton to begin assisting and organizing an investigation into Sutton's whereabouts. He designated Agent Walter F. Hill to coordinate new leads and information as they were reported to headquarters. Hill would also direct the investigation as required, pending Stearns return to Albuquerque. The rest of the New Mexico field agents were notified of the situation and were instructed to heighten their security procedures and be available for quick action if needed in the search for Ray Sutton.

Agent Clarence U. Finley, a New Mexico agent who had been working the Kearney case in Colorado, was contacted and ordered to meet Stearns at Raton. Additionally, Agent James "Sidney" Huddleston, who had been covering Sutton's field territory while Sutton was assigned to the Kearney investigation, was requested to go to Clayton and serve as the liaison with Mrs. Sutton until her daughter arrived from Portales or her son from Denver.

Deputy Administrator Stearns developed a notification list: Regional Administrator Vivian, New Mexico's United States Attorney Hugh B. Woodward, Senior Investigator Agent James A. Richardson, and Agent William "Bill" Nance of the Kearney Investigation Task Force. He added the names and phone numbers for all concerned parties including Colfax County and Union County sheriffs' contact numbers. Stearns ordered up an immediate telegram setting forth the facts of Sutton's disappearance to be sent to the Region 10 Office in Denver, copying the federal district attorneys in both Denver (Carr) and Albuquerque (Woodward).

Later in Denver, Administrator John F. Vivian took Stearns' phone call concerning the facts around Sutton's disappearance. Stearns set forth the circumstances as known, saying that he would be en route to Raton on the next available train. The Task Force would be sending one or two of their men to Raton to assist in the investigation. Vivian was advised to expect a telephone call from Nance or Richardson, who would be providing a follow-up report on their ongoing activities involving Sutton's participation in the Task Force, as soon as practical.

Stearns told Vivian that Colfax County Sheriff Davis had begun organizing a search party even as they spoke. The Colfax County search plan was to fan out from the Dawson location where Sutton was last seen. Sterns recommended that Vivian prepare for the worst-case scenario: that Sutton had been murdered on or about August 28.

Vivian told Stearns that he would ask United States Attorney Carr to handle the notification of the United States Attorney General William Mitchell concerning the Sutton matter and that he would request approval and assistance to expand the federal investigation from southern Colorado into northeastern New Mexico. Carr received an immediate approval. Vivian would keep Director Woodcock informed of the search progress.

Meanwhile in Raton, Sheriff Davis telephoned 31-year-old Fred Conway Stringfellow, district attorney of New Mexico's Eighth Judicial District, to apprise him of Sutton's disappearance. Stringfellow promptly called his staff together and ordered them to prepare for a major investigation regarding Ray Sutton and his disappearance and possible murder. Those who would be assisting were reminded that the case would be handled on a strictly confidential basis with no discussions outside the office with the media or any other individuals, including family. Any information given out would be by him and him alone.

The district attorney would be receiving his first baptism by fire in working on a case of such magnitude—one that involved the kidnapping and probable murder of a federal agent. Stringfellow placed personal calls to Deputy Administrator Stearns and United States Attorney Woodward in Albuquerque to notify them of his activation of an investigation into Sutton's alleged disappearance. In both instances, preliminary agreements and guidelines on the roles of each agency were discussed and agreed upon. Colfax County had the investigative jurisdiction under the state authority of the district attorney and the sheriff's office. The Federal Prohibition Bureau would provide secondary search and investigative assistance as needed. Stringfellow wanted to be careful and correct in this new undertaking. He knew Ray Sutton personally, both as a friend and colleague, as well as one who was thorough and exact in his investigations.

Later, on Thursday afternoon, September 4, an early, hard, cold fall rainstorm arrived in the Raton area and settled in for the next three days making the field search intolerable. The rain should have been viewed as a bad omen, one that portends a bad outcome to any new endeavor undertaken in the midst of a storm.

Charles Stearns had worked through the day and late into Thursday evening assessing the depth of the crisis at hand and establishing a plan of operation. He had a late supper with his wife and took a short catnap. When the northbound Santa Fe passenger train pulled out of the Albuquerque depot at 3:10 on a predawn Friday morning, Stearns was onboard headed for Raton.

An Agents' Roundtable

Stearns held a Friday morning tactical meeting of the federal agents who had arrived in Raton, where a serious conflab ensued in Stearns' room at the Seaberg Hotel. Agents Nance and Richardson and other Colorado members of the Kearney Investigation Task Force team had come to help and share what information they had regarding Sutton's last plan of action in Colfax County. Two more agents would arrive from Albuquerque later in the day.

Agent Finley was designated as the on-scene federal coordinator in addition to his duties as an assigned member of the Kearney Task Force. Agent Huddleston left Clayton once Sutton's daughter Nello arrived at the family home. He connected with Finley prior to Stearns' arrival in Raton. The two agents reviewed the contents of Sutton's room at the Seaberg Hotel and established the initial field liaison with local authorities as events unfurled. They determined that Sutton's credentials and sidearm were missing and presumed in the possession of Sutton.

Sutton's green work journal containing his longhand field notes on his activities; information on completed, postponed, or pending transactions; and drafts of his latest daily reports, including those that Sutton had previously posted on August 28, were on the table. The ledger quickly became the centerpiece of the two agents' focus. About two-thirds of the way into Sutton's notebook, in an unused section, the men found a single name on a diagonal upward slant in the missing agent's handwriting. Sutton had written "James Perry Caldwell."[11]

When Caldwell's name was presented to the assembled group of investigators, Nance and Richardson took turns in describing the Sutton Plan that pertained to the use of Perry Caldwell by Sutton as a longtime confidential informant against the Campanella group. They reported that Sutton was to meet with Caldwell in the few days following their Trinidad meeting on August 24. The fact that Caldwell had a previous history as a prohibition agent concerned all the team members.

The agents found nothing in Sutton's notebook to indicate when the Sutton-Caldwell encounter had occurred or when Ray had written Caldwell's name in the journal. Even so, Caldwell and his bootlegging associates now rose to the top of the list as New Mexico suspects, until future investigation proved otherwise. The Caldwell lead needed to be checked out, immediately and quietly. An informal workup on him began to take shape. The investigators were to focus not only on his whereabouts currently, but they needed to determine what his activities had been and with whom he had been seen within the past several days. Agents Finley and Huddleston were assigned to undertake this mission. The meeting concluded.

The Search for Sutton Begins

Later Friday morning, Stearns conferred with Sheriff Davis and Undersheriff Fletcher. The men reviewed the strategic plan for the afternoon search-and-rescue effort and the continued plan for the next few days. They also discussed a contingency strategy for a recovery mission, should that option become operational.

That evening the *Raton Evening Gazette* published a special report on the search activities in place for finding Agent Sutton. The newspaper noted that Charles Stearns was in town and had informed the media that he believed Sutton was the victim of foul play. He indicated that additional federal officers would be sent into the area to help Sheriff Al Davis and his posse locate his missing agent.[12]

Reward!

For information leading to discovery of Ray Sutton or Car.

DESCRIPTION
Age—57 years.
Height—6 feet, 10 inches.
Weight—196 pounds.
Eyes and Hair—Gray.
When last seen was wearing large white cowboy hat; khaki trousers, and tan leather lumber jacket. Was driving a black 1929 Pontiac coach, with yellow wood wheels; Kansas license No. 84 C 773; Engine No. P641309.
Address:
FEDERAL PROHIBITION OFFICE
Albuquerque, New Mexico

The reward notice for information concerning Ray Sutton or his missing car. This postcard style notice was mailed to all law enforcement agencies in the Rocky Mountain region (courtesy the Raymond Ellsworth Sutton Family Archives).

Sutton had been missing for 192 hours cold and investigators knew at the outset that this case would be extremely difficult to solve even on the best of days. Now even the weather wasn't helping. Once the search had begun, rain continued to hamper ground efforts around Raton with a steady downpour turning country roads to mud, making routine and remote access difficult if not impossible. The open prairieland became soggy, hillsides turned into slippery slopes, and the usually dry streambeds gave way to impassable torrents. Experienced officers and trackers were appointed to lead individual search teams, who were ordered to follow a routine series of actions to methodically search all ground areas in and around remote cabins and barns, mining areas, active and abandoned coke ovens, orchards, and isolated roads. The extended rain made tracking extremely difficult for even the most skilled experts, as existing tire tracks or the foot prints of man could be washed away and forever lost.

With each succeeding day, search parties returned to the sheriff's office wet, tired, cold, hungry, and unsuccessful. The assigned search areas were marked off as they were completed, one by one, on the wall maps posted in the sheriff's command center. Lieutenants Cecil Bradbrick and Fred Junk flew a Colorado National Guard airplane on search patterns over the Raton Pass area. Sheriff Tanner from Union County, Sheriff Dan Cassidy from Mora County and a unit of the American Legion each provided manpower during the early search days. Later offers of assistance came from the Albuquerque Police Department, the Bernalillo County and Curry County sheriff's offices, and the United States Marshal's Office.[13]

On Monday evening, Stearns took a late train back to Albuquerque to handle urgent business at the office. He returned to Raton on Thursday. While in the Duke City he spoke with a reporter about the new horseback search of the hill country between the Dawson and Koehler coal camps. He was upbeat, saying, "We are hopeful that the horsemen may uncover something in that vicinity." The posse had the advantage of being higher with a better view of the area than a man on foot and much more mobile and able to cover a larger area quickly. The posse returned disheartened.[14]

The Sutton Family Arrived in Raton

Simultaneous to Administrator Stearns developing an understanding of the onsite scope of the local investigation, he arranged for Mrs. Sutton and her two adult children to come to Raton to pick up Ray's possessions from the hotel room. This was also an opportunity for Charles Stearns to informally visit with the Sutton family, before officially interviewing each of them.

Ray Sutton's son, Raymond George "Bud" Sutton, lived in Denver and his daughter, Nello, resided in Portales with her family. The children and their mother arrived in Raton on Monday afternoon September 8. Stearns and a contingency of agents were at the train station to meet Mrs. Sutton and accompany her and her adult children to the Seaberg Hotel. Mrs. Sutton reviewed the contents of her husband's belongings in the presence of Stearns and Finley. She was unable to determine if any specific items were missing since her husband had been on the road for several days before his last short visit home to retrieve fresh clothing. She could only acknowledge that the items in the room were his, nothing more.

Stearns spoke with the Sutton family privately while they were all together in the hotel room. He explained Ray's current assignment and his activities leading up to his disappearance. He concluded that in his opinion, Ray had been murdered. The room remained quiet as Mrs. Sutton stood and thanked Stearns for his kindness and honesty, as did the other family members. They were led to the outer lobby to register as the government's guests. Stearns had arranged rooms and meals for the family so they could stay overnight before returning home with Sutton's belongings on the morning train to Clayton.[15]

Paperwork

One of the reasons that Charles H. Stearns left Raton for a quick trip home to Albuquerque was to dictate a situation report on Ray Sutton's disappearance for Region Administrator John F. Vivian. The missive was forwarded to Denver via carrier for next-day delivery. The text follows:

Dear Mr. Vivian:

You are advised that Federal Prohibition Agent Ray Sutton, post of duty Clayton, N. Mex., has not supplied this office with a daily report for August 28 or any time since. On the morning of September 4, I tried to make contact with Agent Sutton by long distance telephone, without success. Sutton had been working at Raton, N. Mex., since August 22. During the afternoon of September 4, Sheriff Al Davis of Raton, N. Mex., advised me by telephone that his office had found Sutton's personal effects and portfolio of records, including his topcoat, in his room at the Hotel Seaberg,

Raton, N. M. He had not checked out and he had not been seen since August 28. After making the determination that Sutton was indeed missing, I departed that night for Raton, arriving there Friday noon, September 5.

Investigation revealed that the last seen of Agent Sutton was on August 28, about 2 p.m. when Deputy Sheriff Fletcher of Raton had passed Agent Sutton standing alone by his car, which was parked at the side of the road at a point about seven miles south of Raton, near the Dawson fork. Fletcher was of the opinion that Sutton was awaiting an appointment with some informer, and did not stop. We have since secured rather positive evidence that Sutton was seen at 5:30 p.m. on the same date, August 28, sitting in an unidentified car with an unidentified man, two miles south of Dawson, N. Mex., a coal mining camp about 30 miles from Raton.

With the assistance of Agent Finley from your office and Agent Dew and informer Moore of this office, I have conducted an investigation at Raton. I returned to this office today to set out some additional vouchers and reports, but will return to Raton tomorrow.

I believe that Agent Sutton has been murdered. We are on the trail of at least three suspects, and are taking the liberty of tapping certain telephone wires to assist us in getting some inside information. Numerous posses have been and are yet diligently searching the mountain and canyon country around Raton for any evidence of what might have happened. Sutton was using Govt. Pontiac coach, identification No. 3761, which has not yet been found.

I am placing a copy of this report in the hands of the [New Mexico] U.S. Attorney, Hugh B. Woodward, and will be pleased to receive from you any further suggestions as to how long to continue the search with the forces that I have, these men being known and not undercover.

I am of the opinion that if we do not arrive at more definite knowledge of Sutton's disappearance by September 15, it would be wise to withdraw our known investigators and have our Department send in some undercover well-trained sleuths.[16]

Stearns followed up on other outstanding cases his office was handling and took time to get an update from Agent Hill on his trial preparations. Clean clothes, a homecooked meal, a good night's rest and alone time with his family prepared Stearns for a return trip to Raton on Thursday.

Authors' Perspectives: There is no evidence that the "known investigators" to whom Administrator Stearns referred were ever withdrawn or that any special undercover "sleuths" were ever involved in the Ray Sutton investigation in Colfax County. Any further specifics as to the targets in the use of telephone taps and identities and continued involvement of "Agent Dew and informer Moore" remain unknown.

The authors have located no contemporary data to support the contention that someone had seen Sutton and another man sitting in a car around 5:30 p.m. on the day he disappeared. Perhaps the anonymous witness had seen Sutton and Caldwell in Sutton's car moments before Ray had been taken captive. The story told by John Pobar does suggest this possible scenario.

The Search Takes a Second Breath

The Albuquerque-based *New Mexico State Tribune* continued to update its statewide readership on the search for Ray Sutton. On Monday, September 8, 1930, they printed a United Press dispatch from Trinidad containing some disheartening information. Since the search conducted by a 100-man posse on Sunday uncovered no new leads, authorities now believed, due to the length of time elapsed since his disappearance, Sutton was dead and they were now searching for his corpse. New rewards were issued for the recovery of Sutton's body.

Charles Stearns was quoted as believing Sutton was captured and killed by rumrunners. He told an Albuquerque reporter, "I believe they would have believed they had a wildcat on their hands if they attempted to keep Ray Sutton alive." The article also divulged that Sutton had recently seized several stills in the Raton area and "he was assisted by an 'undercover' man who lived in Raton. A belief was expressed in some quarters that the undercover man, working with the rumrunners, had aided in leading Sutton to his death."[17]

Authors' Perspectives: With the revelation from Trinidad that made known "an undercover man who lived in Raton had assisted Sutton," it appears that someone—either on the Kearney investigation management team, a member of Stearns' team of agents, or Colfax County authorities—had commented out of turn. Nowhere else in any of the vast assortment of media reports did the authors find contemporary reference to the assistance of such an undercover operative who lived in Raton. No further media reference to this statement has been discovered except in official investigation reports. The reader may recall that both Joe McAllister and Albert Shedoudy, Campanella gang members, lived in Raton. Perry Caldwell was so often seen in Raton that some people may have also believed he lived in the city.

Fading Hope

The *Raton Evening Gazette* of Wednesday, September 10, 1930, headlined the following update: "Officers Still In The Dark As To Whereabouts Of Sutton." The subheading read, "24 Legion Men Join Posse." The main story focus was that the numerous posses were still seeking tangible clues during their ground searches and Colorado National Guard airplanes continued to fly search patterns. The newspaper carried a front-page photograph of Ray Sutton with a physical description of the agent.

Sutton was reported last seen in his black Pontiac four-door coach with yellow wheels and trimmed with a yellow stripe about the body and window sills. The vehicle carried an eight-cylinder engine with the manufacturer number 10641300. The vehicle carried a 1930 Kansas license plate numbered 84 C 773. The federal government gave Sutton's car identification number: 3761.[18]

The local newspapers continued their coverage of the search efforts and provided any additional information they learned about the simultaneous criminal investigations now underway. The following headline samples describe the search progress as the tale unfolds:

September 11, "Officers Continue Search for Ray Sutton: Rumors of Discovery of Agent False," *Raton Evening Gazette*; "Continue to Hunt Sutton Without Clues," *New Mexico State Tribune*; "Sutton Search Swinging Around Dawson Area," *New Mexico State Tribune*; "Search for Sutton Intensified," *Clayton News*; "Hope for Sutton Given Up," *Union County Leader*.

September 12, "No Trace of Ray Sutton Found Yet," *Raton Evening Gazette*.

September 13, "Sutton Search Futile as Posse Continues Hunt in Maxwell-Cimarron Area," *Raton Evening Gazette*; "Raton Scouts Aid in Sutton Search," *Clayton News*; "No Trace Yet of Missing Federal Agent," *Roy Record*.

September 14 [This date was a Sunday and no local newspapers were published.]

September 15, "Posse Works Moreno Valley in Sutton Hunt," *Raton Evening Gazette.*

September 16, "Sutton Search Continues with Posse Still Out," *Raton Evening Gazette.*

September 17, [No published report this date as the story was becoming "old news."]

September 18, "Manhunt Goes On, Hunt for Slayer is Being Pushed in NM & CO," *Raton Evening Gazette*; "Search for Sutton Given Up as Hopeless," *Clayton News.*

September 19 [Statewide evening newspaper coverage came alive on this Friday.]

Friday is known in the news media business as "Dump the Trash Day" because most people are focused not on breaking news stories but on the upcoming weekend and what they are going to do for fun and relaxation. Government agencies and businesses normally take advantage of this lack of concern and use this day to release or "dump" unfavorable information they do not want the public to closely examine.

Friday, September 19, 1930, was not a usual slow news day in New Mexico or Colorado. A major break in the Ray Sutton disappearance mystery headlined the front page of most newspapers and was presented as a leading story on local radio news broadcasts.

11

The Forged Check—
A Funeral—An Arrest

"Learn to get in touch with the silence within yourself, and know that everything in life has purpose. There are no mistakes, no coincidences, all events are blessings given to us to learn from."—Elisabeth Kübler-Ross, Swiss-American psychiatrist, a pioneer in near-death studies

Dateline: New Mexico & Colorado, September 10–October 31, 1930

On Wednesday, September 10, 1930, an administrative clerk at the Bureau of Prohibition's office in Albuquerque rushed into Agent Walter Hill's office. She handed him a cancelled government expense check in the amount of $152.32 issued to Ray Sutton that had been cashed four days after Sutton's disappearance. The check was redeemed at the Harvey Eating House contiguous to the Cardenas Hotel in Trinidad. Hill requested the office clerk to find out when the expense check had been issued and the date when and the location where it had been sent to Sutton.

Next, Hill placed a telephone call to the Colfax County sheriff's office in an attempt to locate Deputy Administrator Stearns. He was unavailable. Hill left a message for him to contact the Albuquerque office as soon as possible. While awaiting the return call, Hill obtained what additional check data the office clerk had located. Knowing that Stearns would require multiple copies of the forged check to launch this new investigation, Hill directed an office agent to have Sutton's check photocopied at a local photography studio. Each action Hill had undertaken would be recorded in his memorandum of the incident.

By 1:30 p.m. Hill had the memorandum at the ready. Stearns directed him to arrange a meeting with New Mexico's United States Attorney Hugh Woodward for the following morning in Albuquerque to discuss the check matter and, secondly, prepare a telegram for Denver setting forth the facts to date. Once the two offices reached an agreed upon course of action, Denver would be notified. As Hill had anticipated, Stearns ordered copies of the check to be completed and in the office by his return.

Stearns next placed a telephone call to John Vivian, advising him of the returned check and the particulars on the time and place where it had been cashed, along with the actions he would be taking, and the fact that the case would be turned over to the Colorado investigative task force leader, Investigator John Richardson, who would assume investigative responsibility for the check-cashing incident.

Stearns reminded Vivian that Sutton was known to carry considerable sums of money—from $100 to $200—and usually carried his expense checks for two to three weeks before he cashed them. Ray also carried two $20 dollar gold pieces bearing an open "A" scratched on the face of each coin. Stearns concluded his update saying that he had met with the Sutton family in Raton earlier in the week and that the search for Ray's car and/or body continued in northern New Mexico.[1]

On Friday, September 12, Agent C.U. Finley and Investigator John Richardson were on the arrival platform awaiting Deputy Administrator Stearns' return to Raton. Once settled at the Seaberg Hotel, Stearns and his agents discussed the course of action to be taken in this new investigation. The local authorities were not to be included in the check-cashing case until such time as their support or input became necessary. Plans were made to obtain bureau ID photographs of Perry Caldwell, a subject of continuing interest, and Sutton, as well a few other unrelated subjects in the event the Trinidad hotel employees remembered the check-cashing incident and the person who was given the money.

Agent Finley told the team he had located Perry Caldwell. Stearns suggested that he be interviewed away from the sheriff's office or the hotel. Agents Finley and Sid Huddleston were assigned to handle the questioning. As the day progressed, Stearns noted that the sheriff's ground searches were moving away concentrically from the original search area in which Sutton was last seen. This was a natural progression of events when conducting area searches—ever widening the search circle. Even though the search was being conducted systematically, Stearns offered a suggestion. On his trips out in the field, he had observed the ruggedness of the landscape in the hills that were situated west of Raton and in and around Cimarron. The bad weather had only made the situation worse. Since the search parties were moving out and away why not task the local ranch owners and their people to do periodic follow-up searches? Stearns suggested that Sheriff Davis ask the owners of the larger ranches in the area to have one or more of their hands search the multitude of arroyos and canyons on their properties for Sutton and his car. Should the ranchers offer any hesitation to assist, there was always the incentive of the $750 in reward money for the finders of the body or vehicle. Sheriff Davis agreed with the recommendation.

Agents Finley and Huddleston arrived at the Harvey Eating House in Trinidad around noon. On entering the lobby, they sought out the manager's office, knocked on the door, entered, and identified themselves. Finley offered the check copy for the manager's perusal. He looked at both the payee and endorsement sides noting that the back of the check was initialed beneath the endorser name as was the custom whenever the House honored such payment. Further, on the endorsement side of the check below the initials was the secondary payee, the hotel's stamped endorsement that remained partially unreadable. He identified Miss Stuttmann, the cashier, as the one completing the transaction. The manager called her in and the agents continued questioning her on her remembrance of this particular transaction.

Stuttmann recalled the incident, gave a description of the man, and stated that the only identification the man offered was his masonic identification card and his ring which bore his name engraved on its inside surfaces. The description of the suspect favored that of James Perry Caldwell as opposed to Ray Sutton. The check passer had been in his late-thirties, of a large burly stature, and light-colored almost blondish hair. His eyes may have been brown. He spoke clearly and displayed a friendly demeanor. The agents asked if she would recognize him again and she said yes.

Since the federal agents had not received the requested photographs of both Caldwell and Sutton, a new appointment was scheduled to view a series of photographs. Each agreed to make themselves available the following day and offered their complete assistance. The federal agents returned to Raton for a meeting with Deputy Administrator Stearns to discuss the results of their investigation.

The requested photographs were to arrive on the Sunday morning train the following day. If Caldwell could be identified as the check passer, the Denver headquarters was prepared to seek subpoenas and warrants for the arrest of Perry Caldwell and a search of his residence, along with data from former worksites that could assist in a handwriting analysis comparison of the name appearing on the forged check.[2]

The Sutton Family Grieves

Updates on the investigation continued to be reported by the *Raton Evening Gazette*. On Friday of the first week following the initial discovery of Ray Sutton's disappearance, the areawide newspaper reported:

NO TRACE OF RAY SUTTON FOUND YET
Posse Continues Search for Missing Officer Started Last Friday.
Rumors Keep Men Busy.
The officers have [nothing to work on and are putting forth their best efforts] to find some clue which will give them the key. The disappearance of Sutton remains a mystery, and if he was the victim of foul play, it would appear as if the persons who dispatched him had accomplished a perfect crime. Sutton and his car seem to have been swallowed up as no trace of either has been found.[3]

The Sutton family believed what Charles Stearns had told them in confidence: Ray was dead. On September 12, Maggie Sutton and her two children, Raymond George "Bud" and Nello, prepared to depart the Sutton home for the Clayton Cemetery, a short distance due east of downtown. The family drove slowly eastward arriving at the main parking area by the entrance to the cemetery. The Masonic section of the cemetery was located just inside the main entrance on the left side of the road and the Sutton family plot was just a few rows from the entrance. Standing near the Sutton plot was the family minister from the Clayton Methodist Church. A small temporary metal plaque bearing the inscription "Ray Sutton, 1873–1930" was already in place. Later, a more fitting marble headstone would be installed; it contained the Masonic emblem. Two spaces from Ray's marker was a marble headstone bearing the name of their daughter: "Hazel Sutton, 1905–1919." The space between the two markers was reserved for Maggie who would join them 25 years later. Young Ray would complete the family grouping decades later.

The minister reminded the family of a verse from Deuteronomy, "The eternal God is your refuge, and underneath are the everlasting arms." Later he added a few simple words about "the mysteries of life, the goodness of the departed, the love shared by the family, and the promise of eternal life together in the hereafter." The family conducted this tribute to their husband and father quietly and without fanfare. It was now over.[4]

The Net Closes Around Perry Caldwell

On Sunday morning, September 14, a special overnight courier package arrived at Raton's Seaberg Hotel for Deputy Administrator Stearns. It contained five photographs, one each of Caldwell and Sutton, and three others of persons unknown to Stearns. Agent Finley was dispatched to pick up the packet. The contents were confirmed by Stearns and given to Agents Finley and Huddleston who immediately set out for Trinidad.

Shortly before noon, Agents Finley and Huddleston again contacted both hotel witnesses and showed them a series of pictures. The manager could not be certain if he recognized anyone, but Miss Stuttmann immediately pointed to the photograph of James Perry Caldwell as the man for whom she cashed the check. She was absolute in her identification. Then something Stuttmann said refreshed the manager's memory. He, too, then identified Perry Caldwell. Neither of the two witnesses could add anything more to their previous day's comments. Written statements were taken and signed in the presence of the two agents before they departed.

Finley dialed the private number at the Colfax County sheriff's office and was immediately connected to Stearns. Once the information was relayed, Stearns ordered the men back to Raton to complete the necessary paperwork for submission to the concerned federal attorneys. A series of preliminary phone calls were directed to Regional Director John F. Vivian and to United States Attorneys Ralph L. Carr at Denver and Hugh B. Woodward at Albuquerque. The attorneys would coordinate their efforts once the necessary reports were delivered to them. Within two hours of the agents' return, all necessary reporting had been reduced to writing, including the letters of transmittal to the federal attorneys.

Politics

Once more, John F. Vivian was disturbed at home on a Sunday by an unexpected telephone call from the field. Stearns alerted him to the positive identification of Caldwell as the person who cashed Sutton's check. Stearns suggested to Vivian that no information be given to the media until the final reports had been delivered to the respective offices of the United States attorneys. He further requested that because of the positive identification received, he would be ordering the immediate arrest of Perry Caldwell whenever and wherever he may be found. Once that was completed, the necessary search warrants and subpoenas for the Caldwell home and subpoenas for his past and current worksites were to be served to obtain any handwriting samples that may be contained in any of them.

Vivian would have advised Stearns to hold off on any arrest until he had conferred with United States Attorney Carr for further direction. Stearns was ordered to contact United States Attorney Woodward in Albuquerque immediately by phone and request him to speak with Carr to develop a plan of action on these new issues. Of course, Agents Nance and Richardson had kept him apprised routinely of the two investigative matters on a daily basis. As was his political nature, resisting temptation to get his name in the media had never been one of Vivian's strong points. Before search warrants were issued or served, Vivian released notice of a pending action to be taken on the Sutton investigation.

Vivian made another call following his notification to Carr; this one to the home of the Denver Assistant Administrator Isaac S.T. Gregg. He sought his advice on how to proceed from an operational point of view. Gregg was a longtime trusted political ally and the one man who would fall on his own sword should the need arise to protect Vivian. Gregg suggested that a photocopy of Sutton's forged paycheck be obtained for handwriting expert Roland C. Goddard, the United States Secret Service Agent in Denver, to officially and scientifically determine if the endorsement on the forged check could be linked to samples of Perry Caldwell's handwriting.

Within a few days both Goddard and Gregg met to compare the signature on the check and recently obtained copies of weigh sheets from one of Perry's past mining job. Their conclusion: the endorsement had been made by Perry Caldwell. Vivian had concurred with Stearns initially that this singular act remained the probable key to the solution of Sutton's disappearance. According to Stearns, that's where the emphasis should be placed, the finding of Sutton or his remains and, of course, the identities of those responsible for his disappearance and probable murder. With this break in the case, he recalled that his earlier September report recommended a course of action to Vivian to place "skilled undercover sleuths" in the field. Now, this suggestion would no longer be a consideration by either of the two men.

By mid–October, the government was moving quickly on this case. Assistant Administrator Gregg attempted to bypass Stearns and Vivian's stated course of action by unilaterally directing Agent Finley to take Caldwell into custody at once and hold him awaiting the arrival of a deputy United States Marshal who would have possession of the Caldwell arrest warrant. Finley passed on this information to Stearns. There was no information available on the logic of Gregg's directed action, whether he had been ordered by Vivian to direct this action or if he had decided to act independently to claim his "15 minutes" of managerial fame. He was another of those political managers with no prior law enforcement background. In this instance, until a warrant has been issued, the United States Attorney called the play—not the Bureau of Prohibition in Denver.[5]

Colfax County Officials

On Saturday, October 18, 1930, with a deputy United States Marshal in attendance and the federal warrant in hand, Charles Stearns held a meeting with Colfax County Sheriff Al Davis, Undersheriff Boots Fletcher, and Eighth Judicial District Attorney Fred

Stringfellow. He notified them that federal agents had been quietly conducting an investigation of Caldwell without their knowledge. Proof that Caldwell had forged and passed Ray Sutton's expense check had been established positively and an arrest warrant and several federal search warrants had been issued. Stearns explained the necessity of maintaining secrecy on this issue, so as not to disrupt the ongoing countywide body/car search and other investigative efforts.

The Colfax County officials didn't express any degree of surprise about the federal government's action. They didn't need to ask why they were not apprised of this earlier. They understood both the jurisdictional and investigative issues involved. What the feds were saying to the county officials is that they now had a possible direct connection to the disappearance of Ray Sutton. If that were the case, the county officials would need to speak with Caldwell at the earliest opportunity. The assembled men were invited to participate in the forthcoming arrest and searches that were scheduled to take place within the hour.

> **Authors' Perspectives**: During National Prohibition, local authorities were routinely not included in federal investigations until such time as a courtesy invitation of support was extended. Federal investigations frequently encountered some degree of corruption among local law enforcement personnel. Sometimes complete exclusion of local and/or state investigative personnel occurred when prior incidents of corruption were known to exist. In Raton and Trinidad, corruption appeared to be isolated to a few lower-ranking personnel.

The Hammer Hits Perry Caldwell

Federal warrants were served on James Perry Caldwell on October 18, 1930, at his home in Cimarron. Family members present included Perry, his wife Jessie, and their three children. Stearns informed Perry that he was charged with the utterance (passing) and forgery of a $152.32 federal government check in the name of Ray Sutton passed at the Harvey House in Trinidad, Colorado, on September 1, 1930.

Agent Finley and two others began a detailed search of the home. A large desk in the house's parlor area yielded financial documents for the period mid–August to mid–September 1930. The team was searching specifically for anything from Trinidad or Raton in the way of irregular expenditures or earnings that may have happened immediately preceding and following Ray Sutton's August disappearance.

In the pocket of a man's pair of trousers hanging in the bedroom clothes closet, Agent Finley discovered a $20 gold coin bearing the "open A" mark used by Sutton, four $20 paper bills, and five $10 paper bills, a total of $130 of currency. Perry Caldwell would later admit the trousers found by the officers were his, but he had no explanation on how he obtained the coin or the paper money. During the search, Finley found a Masonic ring and a Masonic lodge identification card bearing Ray Sutton's engraved name in the dresser located in the same bedroom with the trousers.

Finley and Stearns reached the same conclusion. This discovery could prove to be the *prima facie* evidence against Caldwell on not only the forgery charge, but of even greater importance, Sutton's disappearance and suspected murder.

Caldwell had paid off two overdue miscellaneous bills and a $40 repair bill for his car. A variety of receipts showing payments made to other vendors within the designated time frame were also bagged. Charles Stearns questioned Caldwell about the things the officers had found in his bedroom, especially Sutton's Masonic property. Caldwell gave no answer, this was not his best day and he knew it.

Once the search was completed, Perry Caldwell was removed from his Cimarron residence and transported by a caravan of government vehicles to Trinidad where he was booked as a federal prisoner at the Las Animas County, Colorado, jail. Following Caldwell's booking into the Las Animas County jail as a federal prisoner, Agents Nance, Richardson, and Finley returned to Raton.

At the county jail facility, defense attorney Robert Morrow had arrived from Raton having been engaged by persons unknown on Caldwell's behalf. Caldwell was given specific instructions not to talk to anyone except his attorney. Robert Morrow's brother, a Democrat, represented Colfax County in the New Mexico State Senate.

> **Authors' Perspective:** When federal authorities discovered Sutton's Masonic identification card, ring and a $20 gold coin bearing Sutton's brand in Perry Caldwell's home, they established a *prima facie* case indicating a probable participation in Agent Sutton's disappearance. Caldwell's paying off of his overdue bills shortly after Sutton's disappearance added to the federal officers' case. A singular problem still confronted the federal prosecutors. They had to prove to a jury that Caldwell was involved in the Sutton mystery and Perry was not talking.

The Evidence Is Examined

All of the confiscated documents and artifacts taken from Caldwell's home—along with a photostatic copy of Sutton's expense check and a sample of Sutton's true signature—were marked as evidence. At the request of Administrator Vivian and U.S. Attorney Carr, United States Secret Service Agent Roland C. Goddard and Assistant Prohibition Administrator Gregg were scheduled to repeat their analyses of all collected documents pertinent to establishing the identity of the endorser of Sutton's expense check. Once completed, the two men determined without question that the endorsement had been written by James Perry Caldwell.

The bi-state investigative group was convinced of Caldwell's direct involvement in the Sutton disappearance and probable murder, as well as the forgery of the missing agent's government check. Ray Sutton's latest enforcement efforts in Colfax County centered on the John Campanella cabal and its interface with the Colorado crime syndicate. Stearns' team saw this specific inquiry as the probable key to Sutton's disappearance. They had no doubts, especially since Perry Caldwell had been identified as one of Sutton's current informants against Campanella.

Yet, there remained too many unknowns and possibly too few skilled investigators at hand to obtain the needed proof to indict the Campanella cabal in its entirety. With Perry Caldwell's arrest, the roadway was clear to federal investigators and prosecutors with respect to Caldwell alone: prosecute and convict, then use that conviction as a means to leverage his cooperation against others. It was a simple plan, but difficult to execute.

Perry Caldwell's Second Arrest

Based on the developed facts of the Caldwell investigation that included the finding of Sutton's personal property at Caldwell's home, United States Attorney Carr formally issued a new arrest warrant for Caldwell on October 19 which incorporated the more recent and specific facts supporting the government's "reasonable cause" for the arrest. Caldwell was served with the new warrant while in custody at Trinidad. Again, the order not to talk to anyone was received by Caldwell and he obeyed the directive.

On Sunday, October 19, 1930, the Denver and Trinidad newspapers published Ralph Carr's latest press release concerning Perry Caldwell's arrest, arraignment, and scheduled court date. In part the notice said:

> Ralph Carr, United States District Attorney forwarded a warrant today to Trinidad for the arrest of Perry Caldwell who is being held in jail at Trinidad. [...] This startling disclosure followed closely on the heels of an announcement made yesterday by John F. Vivian, regional director, that an arrest would be made in the next twenty-four hours. [...] Vivian today stated that handwriting experts had identified the signature as being a forged one, and declared that it was the signature of Caldwell and not Sutton. Vivian turned the whole matter over to Carr who will conduct the case investigation from now on.

On Monday, October 20, 1930, the *Trinidad Chronicle-News* announced that a "$15,000 Bond Is Demanded For Caldwell." The article reported that Caldwell was committed to the Las Animas County jail in default of bond by Lewis Worker, deputy U.S. Marshal, after the accused's arraignment before U.S. Commissioner James E. Kane at Trinidad. Caldwell, now charged with forgery, demanded a preliminary hearing which was set for Thursday, October 23.

On October 23, the Trinidad media reported: "Perry Caldwell Bound Over To U.S. Court; Accused Man Pleads Not Guilty to Charges; At Trinidad Hearing; Bond Fixed At $15000; Government Resists Efforts Made To Force It To Uncover Its Hand." In Ray Sutton's hometown the banner headline for the *Clayton News*, October 25, 1930, was, "Forger Of Sutton's Name To Expense Check Being Held As Murder Suspect."[6]

The Search for Ray Sutton's Car

In blazing headlines, the *Raton Evening Gazette* masthead of Monday, October 20, 1930, proclaimed "Sutton's Car Found Near Koehler." The $1,150 reward offered for finding the missing car had produced no result. James Lail, the 60-year-old range foreman for the massive Charles Springer Land and Cattle Company (CS Ranch), allowed his cowboys to search for Sutton's car while they rode the range. According to the newspaper, on Saturday, October 18, 1930, CS Ranch hand Rafael Zamora made the discovery of his life.[7]

While searching the foothills and arroyos just north of the Raton-Cimarron road, a few miles northeast of Cimarron, Zamora had urged his mount forward into one of the many arroyo openings between jutting fingers of the foothills as they met the plains. He pushed in further entering a dense cottonwood stand mixed in with the shrub and pinion tree covered area. A one-time staple of the Native Americans who frequented

Rafael Zamora at the site where he located Ray Sutton's missing car. Note that the car's back license tag is missing. Agents identified it as Sutton's vehicle via the engine number P641309 (courtesy the Raymond Ellsworth Sutton Family Archives).

this area decades before, these old pinion trees used to produce seasonal crops of pinion nuts. The cottonwoods were of more recent vintage signaling the presence of underground water.

The site was roughly 200 yards from the county road. Zamora was uncertain of the ownership of this particular location since the WS Ranch and the CS Ranch had contiguous land boundaries in this area. In fact, the arroyo hideaway site was on leased lands used by George Pobar for a dairy farm. About 30 feet into the arroyo, Zamora noticed an irregular shaped pile of old, dead pinion trees and brush stacked in a Native American "teepee" fashion against a stand of cottonwoods. Zamora dismounted and slowly made his way through the dead brush to the edge of the pile, removing some of it as he moved forward. He saw a small portion of a dirt-covered metal body and then the form of a car window.

In his interview with authorities Zamora described how he continued removing the brush, and the side of the object took shape: a dirty black automobile. Wiping away some of the surface dirt on the rear-door window, he was able to see inside and saw what he believed to be large dried blood-stained splotches on the floor carpeting and rear seat. He was unable to further identify the make of the car or its contents because of the volume of debris stacked on and around the car. Zamora knew he had found something important. Leaving everything as he discovered it, he raced back to the ranch headquarters to report the discovery.

Agent Finley, Sheriff Davis, and their men responded within the hour. Zamora returned to the highway near the car site to direct the authorities when they arrived. All available personnel and idle search party teams that could be contacted rushed to the site. As additional manpower arrived, the removal of brush and dead limbs yielded

Telegram notifying Washington that Ray Sutton's car had been found (Ray Sutton's Official Personnel File).

Sutton's missing 1929 Pontiac. A preliminary search confirmed that the car did not contain Sutton's body. A more in-depth processing of the car's interior would have to await the arrival of senior investigators. It had been 51 days since Sutton went missing. Union County Sheriff A.W. Tanner and five of his men, including fingerprint expert Deputy J.L. Pounds, joined the investigation team the next day.

Even before the media was officially notified, information about this new break in the case spread like wildfire throughout Colfax County. Raton's radio station KGFL (now called KRTN AM/FM) interrupted scheduled programing to announce the discovery of Sutton's car. Shortly after the broadcast, nearby area towns emptied as people raced to the location site—curiosity seekers mostly, but others were intent on finding Sutton's remains and claiming the reward. One or more guards were posted to keep the gathering crowds from destroying the crime scene and any remaining evidence yet undiscovered in the immediate area. At its peak, an estimated 800 persons made their way to the discovery site.

Following the arrival of Deputy Administrator Stearns and the District Attorney Stringfellow, requested fingerprint experts searched the vehicle for any possible prints inside or outside. Union County Deputy Sheriff J.L. Pounds had arrived on Sunday and began the inside search. J.P. Clements, from the state prison at Santa Fe, joined Pounds on Monday. Their initial processing yielded two fingerprints, according to unpublicized reports—one of which bore a horizontal-cut scar across the print surface, suggesting an old knife blade cut of the finger. This was a fairly common type of scar but the loca-

Gathered at site of Sutton's hidden car from left to right, Rafael Zamora, the cowboy who discovered Agent Sutton's black 1929 Pontiac Sudan, Colfax County Undersheriff G. R. "Boots" Fletcher, an unidentified man, J. P. Clements, fingerprint expert from the New Mexico State Penitentiary, and Union County Deputy Sheriff J. L. Pound (courtesy the Raymond Ellsworth Sutton Family Archives).

tion and dimensions of it on the finger could yield a positive identification of the party leaving the print, should he be encountered at a later date.

Identifying the owner of the print itself, however, would be problematic. Local fingerprint repository files were essentially non-existent during this era. A subsequent check of the single print file maintained within the federal fingerprint base under development by the Bureau of Investigation in Washington would prove negative.

Additional clues were developed. On close inspection, the vehicle's gas tank revealed it to be relatively full, indicating that the car had not been driven very far beyond the distance Sutton drove from Raton to the point where it was found, assuming the tank was full when he departed. Another item: a dirty, wadded-up, and discarded man's handkerchief containing what appeared to be a large amount of dried blood, as if it had been used to wipe someone's hands, had been found on the ground near the car. Also found inside Sutton's car was a dried bloody area on rear floor carpeting. This piece of carpet was removed in preparation of sending it to the Denver police lab to confirm the blood type and its possible match to that of Ray Sutton. None of Sutton's weapons or other gear were found in or near the automobile.

On completion of the primary search, evidentiary photos were taken of the car and its immediate surroundings as requested by one of the onsite lead officials. A makeshift effort to replace some of the tree limbs and bushes on the car was completed to illustrate and replicate, in part, the conditions existing when Zamora found the car.

Authors' Perspective: With all of the foot traffic and "sightseers" effectively destroying the locale around Sutton's automobile, the initial investigation of the area evolved into a "photo festival" rather than a protected crime scene. The usefulness of the evidence collected at the site fell into a questioned state. Due to the open access of the area by numerous local and visiting officials, the site became unduly contaminated over a two-day period to a point that it may have reached a state of inadmissibility. Preliminary pictures were taken for potential visual evidential purposes, although the majority were for "public relations and political references" to identify the officers and politicians who were present or those who came later to gawk and be seen.

Sutton's car remained at the discovery site for the better part of two days before being moved to a garage in Raton where a more in-depth examination occurred. On the secondary inspection, an expended .38 Special-caliber casing was found hidden in a seat crevice where it joined the back portion of the rear passenger compartment. The casing and other collected evidence were placed in District Attorney Stringfellow's case file. No information regarding the shell casing, the handkerchief, or fingerprint evidence was ever released to the media. From family members, investigators learned that neither Ray Sutton nor anyone else were known to have ridden in the rear seat of his two-door coach. Sutton didn't allow it. Authorities discussed several theories concerning the large quantity of blood in the backseat area. One scenario suggested that once a conscious or unconscious Sutton was placed in the car by his kidnappers, he was shot.

It was assumed, but never proven, that the .38 caliber shell casing found in Ray Sutton's car apparently fell between Sutton's body and the rear-seat back cushion where it finally slipped down into the seat crevice out of sight and had been missed by the killers when the body was removed. A unique problem comes to mind that questions the caliber of the casing found. Anyone who has handled firearms knows that a discharged cartridge casing must be manually removed from a revolver's cylinder, unlike an automatic weapon which ejects the spent cartridge casing as it loads a new cartridge. A .380 caliber shell used in an automatic pistol is of different design and measurement than a .38 caliber cartridge used by another type of revolver. Perhaps the cartridge casing found in Sutton's car had been discarded at an earlier time rather than during the circumstances surrounding his kidnapping. The authors' have been unable to locate any conclusive evidence to support the use of a .38 caliber firearm or any other weapon to kill Ray Sutton.

"Agent E.L. Burne"

The reporting of Perry Caldwell's arrest and removal to Trinidad had been overshadowed by the discovery of Ray Sutton's vehicle on the same day. One week later, on October 30, 1930, the *Raton Evening Gazette* briefly noted another development in the Sutton investigation: "A Second Arrest In Sutton Case Made In Denver."[8]

Denver federal investigators arrested E.L. Burne—alias E.L. Beirne and known in Denver as Harold G. Gibbs—on charges of "Impersonating an officer," based upon a warrant issued by Dudley Cornell, New Mexico's Assistant United States Attorney. This man, claiming to be a Washington, D.C., police officer on vacation in Raton, had been at the site of Ray Sutton's hidden car during the gathering of evidence. It was his glib talk that induced authorities to allow him to assist in the collection of evidence.

Burne had introduced himself to Agent Finley and proceeded to spin a clever tale of his past police work. Finley's incident report states that he first met the man at a Republican Party fundraiser in Raton featuring Congressman Arthur Free as the speaker. The congressman told Finley that he knew Burne to be an officer with the Metro Police, so Finley trusted him.

The "faux officer" persuaded Finley to allow him to deliver the blood-stained floor carpet found in Sutton's car to the Denver lab. He exclaimed that since he was already going to Denver to get some things he had left there, he could deliver the rug and save the federal officer a long trip. Agent Finley agreed to the offer and gave Burne the rug to deliver to the Denver facility at the regional office. The rug was delivered on time.

It was a few days after Burne left Raton that Agent Finley discovered that Burne had skipped town, owing the Swastika Hotel $58 for his room bill and an additional $15 cash he had swindled from the desk clerk as a "loan." It was discovered that he had an arrest record in Seattle, Washington; Santa Barbara, California; and in the nation's capital. Each arrest was for impersonating an officer.

On November 20, 1930, the *Raton Evening Gazette* reported that following the Burne debacle, certain administrative and procedural administrative actions took place within the region. These new actions included a blanket of secrecy being placed over all aspects of the Sutton investigation. Two purposes were achieved: first, any new information released by federal authorities would be controlled by the regional office and, second, John Vivian would control what information and in what form it would be released, subject to the approval of United States Attorney Ralph Carr.[9]

> **Authors' Perspective:** The release of crime scene evidence or any evidence to non-law enforcement personnel involved with transportation of that evidence destroys the admissibility of that evidence in any court of law. The car floor rug incident compromised that portion of the Sutton investigation, as well as did the replacing of brush and debris for a photo opportunity. However, a good defense attorney might be able to make a case that Agent Finley had commissioned Burne as a single purpose "temporary agent" representing Finley to deliver the rug sample since he did in fact complete that requested mission. District Attorney Fred Stringfellow should have had some private words on the subject with his federal counterparts over this particular incident but the authors have located no record of such a meeting.

The Kearney and Sutton Survivors Had to Move on with Their Lives

Dale Kearney had been a young man with a new family, working at an entry level government salary. What life insurance, if any, payable to his beneficiary at this stage of his career wouldn't go very far to sustain them. Quietly, some behind-the-scenes events were set in place. We don't know who arranged it or how it came about, but in mid–October 1930, President Herbert Hoover authorized a postal clerk's position at the Denver Post Office for Mrs. Frances Kearney. Her appointment waived all Civil Service examinations and she was placed at the head of the list over personnel who were awaiting a federal nomination. She accepted the post. Regional Administrator Vivian had once been the postmaster at the Denver suburb of Golden. It is unknown what part, if any, he may have played in this employment opportunity.[10]

Meanwhile, the well-being of Maggie Mae Sutton in Clayton was beginning to play out as well. On October 22, 1930, insurance broker H.G. McFadden of Clayton, wrote a letter to federal Judge H.A. Kiker of Raton concerning the Ray Sutton matter. McFadden, the District Manager for the Kansas City Life Insurance Company, stated that his company had a policy on Ray Sutton and that Mrs. Sutton had filed a claim for payment. The letter writer advised Judge Kiker that he was writing at the request of Mrs. Sutton, and the judge helped in obtaining some affidavits in support of Mrs. Sutton's claim. By the end of October, Judge Kiker had forwarded three affidavits, one each from: himself, Undersheriff G.R. "Boots" Fletcher, and Seaberg Hotel desk clerk Grace McAlpin. Each explained what they knew about Sutton's activities leading up to his disappearance.[11]

Henry Kiker had known Ray Sutton since before the Great War when he represented him in a real estate matter concerning the failure of a property owner to provide a clear title deed to property Sutton had purchased in Raton. At that time, Sutton may have been shopping for a site to expand the Des Moines State Bank into Colfax County. In the end, the real estate matter fell through and Sutton received a refund of the monies paid. As a practicing attorney in Raton, Kiker would later become Colfax County district attorney before his appointment to the federal bench in the years preceding Fred Stringfellow's election to his former prosecution office.[12]

The insurance company home office continued to defer its payment to Mrs. Sutton by requiring her to wait the legal standard of seven years to substantiate a death claim without an insured's physical body being found. The insurance company advised Mrs. Sutton that she could file this claim following the seven-year waiting period. However, something must have happened to change the Kansas City Life Insurance Company's corporate mind because the front page of the *Clayton News*, December 4, 1930, headlined, "Sutton's Insurance Has Been Paid to Widow."

The federal government's action to pay Mrs. Sutton money owed to her husband was a different story. In 1930, the Justice Department regulations contained no method on how to pay a salary or expense claim without the signed copies of the proper forms; disappeared or dead agents do not sign field reports. To add to the injustice, according to Sutton's official personnel file, the Albuquerque office of the Bureau of Prohibition had lost or misplaced Mrs. Sutton's written request for payment of government funds due to her on behalf of her husband missing in action. Five years passed with no attempt to right the *status quo*.

On August 20, 1935, one week short of five years following Ray Sutton's disappearance, President Franklin D. Roosevelt signed a Special Act of Congress authorizing the payments of Ray Sutton's last month of salary as a prohibition agent at $92.25 and his final expense check amounting to $152.32. The Congress also approved the full refund of the small amount that Ray Sutton had paid into his government retirement fund. Mrs. Sutton received a government check for $245.27.[13]

DOJ's Bureau of Investigation Reviews the Kearney Case

Around December 1, 1930, United States Attorney Ralph Carr held a meeting with Denver-based Special Agent in Charge William Larson of the Bureau of Investigation (BI) of the United States Department of Justice. No public mention of the Jack Dionisio interrogation in mid–September 1930 had yet been made by U.S. Attorney Carr. The subject had fled the area following the Kearney murder. He had been the one to "finger" Dale Kearney at the restaurant in Trinidad some 36 hours before Dale's murder. Dionisio had been wanted for questioning and had been arrested in Colorado Springs on bootlegging charges. Subsequently, four federal agents were accused of conducting a "third degree interrogation" of Dionisio over a four-day period. This came to the public's attention when a *Denver Post* reporter commented about Prohibition Agent Dierks past violence that included a state charge of murder being filed in late 1931. He had served early on in the opening portions of the Kearney investigation as a Special Employee. Dierks was named in the interrogation of Dionisio.[14] A full discussion of the incident appears in Chapter 12.

It is unclear who initiated the Carr-BI meeting. Perhaps it was the BI which sought to expand its public image by increasing a level of public exposure in the widely publicized Kearney-Sutton murder cases. Federal law at this juncture still gave the BI no jurisdiction to take charge of the murder investigation, but if the Bureau was specifically requested by United States Attorney Ralph Carr to do so, it would certainly be offered the opportunity to intercede on his behalf under special circumstances in which other violations of federal law may have occurred. On the other hand, Carr may have wanted merely to test the quality of the work of the Prohibition forces by requesting a preliminary overview of the Kearney case as seen through the Bureau's eyes.

On December 10, Carr met once more with Special Agent in Charge Larson to make his final decision as to whether a separate investigation apart from the ongoing Bureau of Prohibition's cases would be feasible. According to Larson, Carr had stated an interest in possibly using the BI to check out any "angles of this investigation" that may have been overlooked by Prohibition investigators. At a third meeting, on December 23, Carr told Larson that the Bureau of Prohibition's agents seemed to be handling the case adequately and recommended the termination of their preliminary investigation of the Kearney-Sutton cases.

Authors' Perspective: In July 1908, Attorney General Charles Bonaparte had established in the Department of Justice a Bureau of Investigation (BI), under his personal direction, to function as field investigators for the Justice Department's United States Attorneys. Initially, the bureau operated under a chief investigator who supervised the day-to-day administration. These federal officers had no authority to make arrests or carry sidearms; a deputy United States Marshal handled the arrests while the sidearm issue remained unaddressed for several years. In contrast, from the beginning, a Prohibition agent possessed both arrest powers and the right to be armed.

The Investigation Continues

Meanwhile, Carr's office remained active in following through on the forgery case against Perry Caldwell. On Wednesday, December 10, 1930, the office obtained a "true bill" from the federal grand jury sitting at Denver, charging Caldwell with "forgery and passing United States obligation." The government continued to hold Caldwell at the Las Animas County jail pending his transfer to the Federal Circuit Court in Pueblo to stand trial on Thursday, January 15, 1931.[15]

By now, almost four months had passed since Ray Sutton had gone missing. District Attorney Fred Stringfellow continued to monitor his office security practices concerning the Sutton investigation. He didn't want any leaks taking place from his office; however, such was not to be the case. It was reported to him privately that one of the county clerks had violated his order to keep all matters pertaining to the Sutton case confidential. It had been reported that she had revealed certain investigative data to an unidentified third party who in turn notified Stringfellow. Once her misdeed had been discovered, she was placed in a position that precluded any further access to the Sutton files. Stringfellow immediately notified Administrator Stearns.[16]

Stearns determined that no federal data had been compromised. He placed telephone calls to Finley and the other involved agents in both New Mexico and Colorado. Arrangements were made to use the Union County Sheriff's Office as a repository for all further Sutton leads in northeastern New Mexico in lieu of Colfax County.

The Carlino Brothers

On Thursday, January 8, 1931, federal agents were on the move. The target was a Carlino still located 50 or more miles northwest of Denver in Gilpin County. The Denver Office had received information from an anonymous source that a still was being operated in a deserted shack just outside of Rollinsville, an extremely small mountain village with a population under 200 persons.

A quick field investigation had yielded the discovery of the site. Federal agents and local deputy sheriffs arrested two men: 17-year-old Bruno Mauro of Pueblo and Joe Farraro, alias Giuseppe Catalino, of both Pueblo and Denver. The two men were known to be members of the Carlino gang. At the time of arrest, Mauro claimed that he was 19 years of age in an attempt to mask his real identity. At the booking station, he identified himself as one Frank Asti of Hastings, Colorado. Both Mauro and Farraro were released on bail and ordered for trial in nearby Central City on April 20; however, unforeseen life-changing events would occur before their trials would ever come about.

On site, the federal agents seized an estimated 270 gallons of mash, 85 gallons of finished whiskey, and two revolvers. Needless to say, this was one of the largest scores in the past few years and a devastating financial blow to the Carlino brothers. At $20 per gallon wholesale cost, the loss ranged between $5,400 and $10,800 at an anticipated wholesale price—not to mention the site, the equipment, and the supplies. United States Attorney Carr scheduled another meet with his undercover source who reported that he had significant, new information to report.

The Wickersham Commission

Other significant events were occurring in Washington, D.C. The findings of President Herbert Hoover's Special Commission to study the impact of Prohibition on America were being prepared for release. On Monday, May 20, 1929, former United States Attorney General, George Woodward Wickersham, had been appointed by President Hoover to head the 11-member panel to begin a national study to identify the causes of criminal activity and make recommendations to modify or support the current public policy regarding National Prohibition. As initial supporters of the Prohibition Act, Hoover's Commission members had clearly been informed of an approaching tidal wave of discontent led by The National Movement Against Prohibition with its call for a "return to normalcy" state of being. The momentum of the slogan was gaining ever increasing popular public support that called for an end to National Prohibition.

As part of its proposed study, the Commission was instructed to determine the extent of the public's evasion of the Prohibition laws and its impact on the nation as a whole. During the Act's nine-year lifespan to 1929, the Rule of Law, the Law of the Land, appeared to be providing fuel to the growth of organized crime across the nation, rather than curtailing "demon rum" and its negative societal impact as had been promised. No one doubted this.

On Wednesday, January 7, 1931, the National Commission on Law Observance and Enforcement released its final report. The primary author of the report was August Vollmer, a nationally known authority on criminal justice and law enforcement operations. The findings clearly and thoroughly documented the widespread public evasion of the Prohibition laws nationally and the inevitable negative impact these actions had on American society. The majority of Commission members agreed that Prohibition law should be curtailed or modified toward that end.

Yet, in its political wisdom the Commission recommended continuation of Prohibition with a more aggressive and extensive enforcement effort to be implemented in an attempt to gain a state of national compliance with the existing federal Prohibition laws already in effect. Police authorities were severely chastised for their overall failure to enforce all laws of violence influenced by organized criminal activities stemming from their illicit bootlegging enterprises. And ever true to the tenets of the political tiger, the report became a contradiction of recommendations, one in which America would have its cake and eat it too. President Hoover wrote that the Commission's "investigations failed to prove of any great use so far as prohibition was concerned, although it made recommendations for other legal reforms that were of lasting value."[17]

The 1931 publication received wide dissemination, especially in the halls of the Department of Justice in Washington. The head of the Department's Bureau of Investigation, John Edgar Hoover, was especially interested in the subject matter. His organization had no designated authority to enforce the Prohibition laws, but he would have more to say about the report and the Prohibition Bureau in his private discussions with his senior staff, however. A few years down the line, his views would have the opportunity to become much more expressive and openly unguarded in a series of official discussions.[18]

The Caldwell Forgery and Passing Trial

Meanwhile, Denver, Trinidad, and Raton authorities were focused on the trial of James Perry Caldwell. Promptly at 9:00 a.m. on Thursday, January 15, 1931, Federal District Judge J. Foster Symes took the bench in Pueblo's Federal Court House. It was the 15th day of the court's spring term and the courtroom was filled to capacity as the case of "The United States of America vs. James Perry Caldwell—3817" was called to order.[19] It was highly unusual for a forgery and passing case to command this much attention, but then Symes knew that this trial had significance far beyond that violation and could lead to Caldwell's involvement in a far greater crime. Judge Symes was one of the honest federal judges on the bench, intimately knowledgeable with the issues of federal prohibition enforcement efforts and those criminal characters at the dark center of the liquor business.

At the opening of the Court, the bailiff announced the taking of the bench and issued a call to order. Judge Symes acknowledged the presence of both the defendant and the government and their respective counsels in attendance: Assistant United States Attorney Charles E. Works, Esquire, for the prosecution and Henry Hunter, Esquire, for the defense. Both parties were prepared for trial. The bailiff brought in the panel of potential jurors for *voir dire* questioning by the attorneys. By noon, 12 jurors, all men, had been selected and impaneled. Later events, however, would suggest that the prosecution team should have done a better job of vetting the jury candidates and in prepping the defense witnesses for their testimony. Hindsight would also suggest that United States District Attorney Ralph Carr and his team were overconfident.

The prosecution's opening remarks set the tone of the trial, presenting the facts of the case: the issuance of the expense check to Sutton based on submitted claims for expenses in the field; the facts as known of Sutton's disappearance; the subsequent return of the check to the Albuquerque Bureau of Prohibition office after the date of Sutton's disappearance; the discovery of the forged signature; the statements of witnesses to be presented identifying James Perry Caldwell as the forger and passer of the check at the Santa Fe Railroad Harvey House in Trinidad, Colorado, on September 1, 1930; the service of the federal search warrants at Caldwell's home and work sites and the results thereof including the finding of Sutton's Masonic ring and identification card along with an open "A" inscribed $20 gold piece in Caldwell's bedroom; confirmation that the signature on the forged check was not that of Agent Sutton by Mrs. Sutton; two separate official handwriting experts identifying the signature on the check as being written by Caldwell; and the subsequent arrest and arraignment of Caldwell. The prosecution rested its case.

Next, the defense presented their introductory outline of events and denial of all charges. Although Perry Caldwell would not take the stand to testify in his own defense, through his attorney he continued to deny all charges. On the second day, the defense countered the prosecution's case by presenting the testimony of Jessie Caldwell. She testified that her husband had been at home the entire Labor Day weekend. She said she remembered the events because it was a holiday weekend and the family picnicked together that afternoon into the evening hours on Monday.

The defense's cross-examination of the Harvey House witnesses destroyed the prosecution's contentions. Although Perry Caldwell had been positively identified in September 1930, the witnesses were now, four months later, unable to identify him as being the man who cashed Sutton's check. On reexamination of the hotel witnesses, the prosecution was unable to elicit a change in their new testimonies as made under questioning from the defense lawyer.

The court dismissed the charge of passing a forged check due to lack of evidence. The check forgery was to be determined by the jury. By late Friday afternoon, January 16, 1931, the jury was ready for deliberation. Judge Symes instructed them that if a verdict is reached, "a sealed verdict may be given to allow jurors to go home over the weekend." The jury rendered a sealed verdict to the judge later that evening. Judge Symes adjourned court and called the next session for Monday morning, January 19.

On Monday morning, the jury foreman read their sealed verdict to the court and later that day the *Raton Evening Gazette* headlined, "Caldwell Jury Acquits Him Of Forgery Charge."[20] Caldwell was a free man and the prosecution and investigators were dumbfounded. Supervising Agents William Nance and John Richardson lost no time in reporting the results of the Caldwell trial to the Denver and Albuquerque offices. They made certain that the sheriffs of Colfax and Union Counties were also apprised even though their representatives were present during the entire trial.

During the follow-up polling, some jurors said since the principal witnesses failed to identify Perry Caldwell as the man who cashed the check the court dismissed that charge, so they doubted the other charge also. It was that simple. Furthermore, certain jurors were not impressed with the handwriting comparison charts created by the prosecution and felt that the defense attorney created doubt as to the level of accuracy and technical experience of the prosecution's handwriting experts.

On the advice of counsel, Caldwell would not talk to any law enforcement bodies or their representatives under any circumstances following his release. On January 26, 1931, Perry Caldwell celebrated his 42nd birthday as a free man, but at what price?

The federal government had planned on an assured conviction of Caldwell with the resulting sentencing phase to be used as a lynchpin to lever his cooperation to tell exactly what had happened to Ray Sutton. The prosecution believed their case had been well constructed and documented, so the only conclusion for their failure had to be someone got to a few of the jury members and the witnesses from Trinidad's Harvey House.

The United States Attorney and the Prohibition agents weren't stupid about the way crime groups played the court game, especially in Denver and Pueblo. It wouldn't be the first time that criminal bribes and threats had yielded a "not guilty" verdict. One or two jurors, or even an entire jury, and selected witnesses could always be bribed or intimidated. Agents from the Kearney Task Force were already working to identify the circumstances of the Caldwell jury verdict.

The Caldwell trial had been held in Pueblo, the acknowledged center of Colorado's organized crime factions under the tutelage of the Carlino and Blanda crime families. The Carlino brothers had a history of jury tampering in this courthouse via bribery or intimidation as recently as November 1926. They used both methods in that instance while they were stalking and murdering the Danna brothers.[21]

It was common street knowledge in Pueblo that the Carlino brothers utilized many ways to persuade juries or witnesses to bend to their will. Arrangements could be contracted for a fee or a "favor" to help anyone who could afford the brothers' service, even if the person on trial was an outsider from New Mexico, and they guaranteed their promised results. The investigators also knew that without someone coming forward, they would never be able to prove their suspicions much less make a case for bribery or intimidation. Within a few weeks, the federal agents had an answer to what had happened in Pueblo. According to reliable but unidentified sources, $25,000 had been paid to the jury for the not guilty verdict. Due to a lack of proof or sworn testimony no one was ever prosecuted for jury tampering.

Authors' Perspective: During the four months of James Perry Caldwell's legal troubles the *Springer Tribune* published only two small mentions on inside pages. Neither notice said he grew up in the community or that members of his family still lived in the area.

Police Wiretapping

The telegraph had been a method of communication in the United States since the 1840s and the telephone joined the mix in 1876. By the late 1920s the telephone was found in many homes and businesses across the country. The wireless mobile telephone had been developed in the late 1880s by a Murray, Kentucky, farmer named Nathan B. Stubblefield—but was not commercially viable until the microchip was developed decades later.[22]

Big city police departments began tapping telephone lines in the 1890s. The technology was relatively simple. The telephone company identified the suspect's line at their switchboard and the police had the company place a "tap," a splitter line attached to the suspect's phone line, for someone to listen to and/or record conversations. It took nearly four decades before the United States Supreme Court addressed this practice. During the 1928 high court session it ruled on *Olmstead vs United States*. Roy Olmstead was a Seattle bootlegger caught by a wiretap who appealed his conviction. Congress had made wiretapping illegal during the Great War because it was "ungentlemanly" to spy on spies. In a 5 to 4 vote the Supreme Court settled the issue saying wiretapping by law enforcement agencies did not violate a person's rights under the Fourth Amendment provision against improper search and seizure so long as the police had not trespassed on the suspect's property. The court's majority opinion was written by former president, now chief justice, William Howard Taft. Justice Louis Brandis wrote the minority opinion.[23]

The village of Cimarron, New Mexico, had initialed private telephone service in the late 1890s when the Maxwell Land Grant Company installed a local company line with a long-distance connection to Raton and Springer. When the Old Town and New Town sections incorporated in 1910, the new joint town council authorized a public subscription telephone exchange for the community. The Cimarron telephone directory for 1930 listed John Campanella as a subscriber to a private and business line.

In the past decades it had been the practice of federal agencies to avoid the use of wiretapping criminal suspects. Amos W.W. Woodcock had no such problem and told his dry agents to use wiretapping and catch bootleggers. William Mitchell, President Hoover's attorney general, agreed with Woodcock's directive but requested an approval authorization of such a written request by the bureau chief with his personal approval and that of the assistant attorney general.[24]

In the early 1950s, Charles H. Stearns, now retired from federal service, told his Albuquerque newspaper friend Howard Bryan that his agents had wiretapped the telephones of key bootleggers in Colfax County during the early days of the search for Sutton, but he had a shortage of agents to staff the "tap" and take notes so the effort was sporadic. On another occasion Stearns told Bryan that one of his agents had caught John Campanella talking to a "Wop" at a payphone in Raton. This was after the agents had arrested Campanella and he was out of jail on bond awaiting his trial. The Italian's voice was unknown to the agent. The conversation concerned Campanella needing more money "to take care of his toothache." Stearns and his agents were uncertain as to what Cimarron's bootleg king meant by "his toothache." It seemed the short-isolated conversation contained no useful data and it was not until after the jury acquitted James Perry Caldwell at his trial that federal agents picked up gossip about a jury payoff. Had Campanella and his friend used "toothache" as a code to discuss jury tampering? Is it possible that the agent who eavesdropped on Campanella's "toothache" conversation had heard the voice of Big John's mystery financial investor or his go-between? At this late date, historians must consider the wiretap conversation a closed door—an opportunity lost to history.[25]

> **Authors' Prospective:** During one of their Sutton conversations, Howard Bryan told author Hornung about the wiretap effort during the Kearney-Sutton murder investigations. Bryan said that he never used the information in his newspaper column due to the potential social implications behind the ethnic slur (Wop) used toward New Mexico's large Italian population. The 1970s was the Watergate Era and wiretaps and hidden taped conversations by government officials was a divisive topic for a columnist of a family-friendly local history newspaper feature.
>
> Bryan had not asked Stearns if the wiretaps had been recorded. It is doubtful that a small-town operation like Cimarron would have justified the expense of wiretap recordings. In 1930, the cost of the recording machine and the blank steel recording wire would have been substantial. The technology was relatively new and there were only a few minutes of recording space on the steel wire spool. If one was not very careful the recording wire could bend or break making it useless. Wax disk recorders were very bulky, expensive, and required skill to use. Magnetic plastic tape was decades in the future and a few more decades before being in common use.

The Confrontation of Federal Chiefs

On Friday, January 23, 1931, Colorado's United States Attorney Ralph Carr and his principal deputies; New Mexico's United States Attorney Hugh B. Woodward; Prohibition Regional Administrator John Vivian; Deputy Administrator Charles Stearns; and Agents Clarence U. Finley, William E. Nance, and John Richardson gathered in Carr's conference room. Details of this confrontational gathering moved at lightning speed throughout Region 10.

Carr opened the gathering by announcing to the attendees that they were invited to discuss the status of both the Kearney and Sutton investigations in light of the not guilty verdict. Carr advised that he was looking for a solution to the continuing crime problems. He wasn't interested in "managerial achievements" and recent statistics on arrests, seizures, closed speakeasies, and fines paid. He asked if any Bureau of Prohibition informants or anyone else had provided any information leading him to the killers of the two slain agents. Carr then unloaded his big surprise announcement of the pending organized crime meeting reported by his confidential source. He questioned the group about the Carlino-Roma meeting earlier in the month. He then apprised the group that the meeting had taken place two weeks prior and had centered on a call by the Carlinos for a confab of major bootleggers. The big crime conference would take place the next evening.

The Wheat Ridge Crime Family Conference

Saturday, January 24, 1931, was a day of extreme activity for the entire Denver office and the Kearney Task Force membership. All available men were in the field to help monitor the Wheat Ridge conference. The meeting site was determined to be a roadhouse located in the 6600 block of West 38th Avenue. Denver Police Department Chief of Detectives Albert T. Clark received an anonymous call the day before concerning the crime boss meeting and had been trying to confirm the veracity of the information. He called the Bureau of Prohibition. Chief Clark had wanted to enlist the federal officers in the planning of the raid but later decided that it was politically important that his department handle the meeting by themselves. The department's internal politics necessitated that he did so.

The federal government honored Clark's request with the assurance that any information obtained would be provided to the Bureau once the operation was completed. On the day of the scheduled meeting, Clark and a select number of his handpicked men were lodged in a lookout position with several others staked out nearby, out of sight and ready to respond once the roadhouse was full. Several individuals were immediately identified as they approached the entrance to the roadhouse. When the attendees closed the front doors from the inside, the raiding party began a 15-minute countdown.

At the designated time, a signal was given and the police department's 13-man raiding party, all armed with .45 caliber Thompson submachine guns, hit the location taking down the outside and inside lookouts with a minimum of effort. The strike force quickly took command of the meeting and its near 30 attendees.[26]

Arrested were Pete and Sam Carlino along with 27 other crime figures. The police knew that a number of the arrestees resided in Pueblo and other Colorado communities although each gave the police different local Denver addresses during the booking procedures. Unfortunately, the raid had interrupted the meeting before any agreement or compromise to the Carlino Plan had been reached among the crime organizations. The timing of the raid may have resulted in the police being blamed later for igniting a new gang war, one that both the public and most of the crime families did not want.

Joe Roma did not attend the meeting. It was only speculation, but some believed

11. The Forged Check—A Funeral—An Arrest 143

at the time that Roma was quietly using his own Denver bootlegging families to make his move on the Carlinos and their statewide operations. Roma was responsible for the decision to make certain there would be no booze whatsoever at the facility. The attendees needed no further alcohol possession charges filed against them. Roma would have need of them to be out on the streets preparing for the upcoming war with the Carlinos, not sitting in some local jail.[27]

Five days after the Wheat Ridge conference, the *Raton Evening Gazette* published a follow-up story from the Denver Associated Press: "Seek To Export 29 Bootleggers Held By Denver." Following a recap of the Saturday raid by the Denver police, the article told readers that the Colorado crime families held a second meeting on Monday. Three days after this second meeting, Detective Chief A.T. Clark's men arrested six more would-be bootlegger confederates. A total of 35 men had Denver police add new charges to their criminal records. The story ended saying, "They are planning to proceed with an organization that would bring together Denver and Southern CO liquor interests."[28]

12

The Jack Dionisio Matter

"So many affidavits, so studiously and artfully penned, to be safely sworn in one sense and read in another, are an aggravation."—Lord Mansfield, [Rex v. Beardmore 1759] *The Dictionary of Legal Quotations* 1904

Dateline: Colorado, September 1930–1932

The entire Kearney investigation changed on the morning of September 11, 1930, when Prohibition Agent Willard E. Lukens received a telephone call from Colorado Springs. El Paso County Sheriff Robert E. Jackson told Lukens that he and Detective Robert Wraith had arrested Jack Dionisio with a load of alcohol. Jackson had been made aware early on that federal agents were trying to locate Dionisio for questioning in the Kearney murder case. During the course of his conversation with Lukens, Sheriff Jackson suggested that federal agents "adopt" (assume investigative jurisdiction) the case as a federal bootlegging case.

Federal investigators jumped at the chance to interrogate Dionisio about his actions at the Saddle Rock Café in Trinidad in relation to Kearney and his wife on July 4. Thus, what appeared to be a routine alcohol possession, sale and distribution matter morphed into a major accusation of police barbarism, torture, and maltreatment of a prisoner. In this pre-Miranda Rights era some journalists referred to these style allegations as the "third degree" form of police questioning.

Washington responded to the September 30 charges in great detail in a series of internal investigations of those concerned in the matter. The *Denver Post* had published an article exposing an alleged coverup of misconduct in the Dionisio matter. The newspaper allegations initially targeted Prohibition Agent Henry Dierks in a series of stories concerning his history of past violence and alleged corruption, stemming from state charges being sought against him.[1]

Up to this time the media had been unaware of Dionisio's arrest or the internal probe. Why did it take 14 months for the federal government to allow public release of its investigation? It appears that the United States Attorney's Office at Denver had attempted to bury the matter.

Two changes were effective by December 31, 1931. Regional Administrator John

F. Vivian had resigned from office under pressure from another matter and Agent Dierks had been administratively terminated from the service on November 30, 1931. The actions against Dierks were pending conclusion of legal concerns surrounding jurisdictional authority over the filing of murder charges against him by the state of Colorado. The state claimed jurisdiction to try the federal agent while the federal government contended that the death of a civilian occurred while Dierks, a federal agent, was taking official action and, therefore, it had jurisdiction.

In retrospect, circumstances suggest that this matter was poorly handled. United States Attorney Ralph L. Carr and Dionisio's defense attorney, Sperry S. Packard, had reached an agreement to keep the Dionisio allegations of brutality private, sometime after the release of Dionisio from his initial arrest. Carr maintained that he did not want to try this case for fear that it would harm the Bureau of Prohibition activities in Colorado. According to the news article, Carr claimed he had no authority over the prohibition agents. The Dionisios were known to have had strong criminal connections in Pueblo and Trinidad that were closely allied with the Carlino crime family. Carr and his in-house undercover agent were both from that area of Colorado. Was this misstatement a slip-up by Carr, that he or his undercover investigator may have had a degree of involvement with various organized crime subjects in Denver, Pueblo and Trinidad?[2]

Based on the *Denver Post* article of November 26, 1931, and others concerning both the activities of Dierks and Vivian, officials in Washington, D.C., called for three special investigations of the facts of the alleged brutality before closing the matter with a letter of reprimand to Agent Lukens in early 1933. The factors behind Administrator Vivian's departure will be discussed in a later chapter.

> **Authors Perspective:** Early in 1931, the Wickersham Commission's final report was released and recommended that federal law enforcement officers no longer be allowed to use the "third degree" to coerce a criminal confession. The commission defined "third degree" treatment as "the employment of methods which inflicted suffering, physical or mental, upon a person in order to obtain information about a crime." Certain methods mentioned in the report included physical brutality, protracted questioning, threats and intimidation, lack of sleep, and refusal to allow legal counsel for the suspect during their police questioning.
>
> The importance of the various affidavits that follow can be found in the information, true or false, that is contained within the body of each document. They all include some environmental conditions existing during the period of the investigation, including investigative techniques and lines of questioning or reporting used during this period. They are published here for the first time.

Allegations from Affidavit of Jack Dionisio

Among the erroneous charges proclaimed in the "Statement of S.S. Packard" to U.S. Attorney Carr were the following allegations concerning Jack Dionisio's alleged mistreatment. Packard claimed Dionisio's affidavit had been transcribed by Miss Evelyn Brown, his secretary, on Sunday, September 21, 1930, at the county jail in Colorado Springs. Dionisio's alleged complaints were summarized as follow:

1. Agents cursed Dionisio in a most vile and grossly insulting manner;
2. Took him by the shoulders, shoved him away, and at the same time applied him with interrogatories as to who killed Agent Kearney;
3. Took him from the jail for several hours at night, during which time they dared and threatened him to try and escape;
4. Compelled him to remove his shoes, coat and shirt stating that they were looking for gun marks on his shoulders (shoulder holster marks);
5. Compared his shoes to prints drawn from the Kearney crime scene;
6. Dierks placed a pistol on the table in the cell and asked Dionisio if he wanted to fight him, to which the reply was negative;
7. Endeavored to have him sign some kind of a paper but he refused to do so without consulting his attorney;
8. Advised Dionisio that he did not have to sign as they "intended to take him for a ride and asked if there were any words he desired to send to his wife";
9. Dionisio believed the agents were endeavoring to manufacture some excuse to kill him;
10. Both Agents Dierks and Lukens were the ones to have been solely responsible for the mistreatment claims;
11. Had placed an Italian by the name of "Nitto" (Undercover "Special Agent Vacarrelli of the Chicago" office) in his cell at one point;
12. Both Lukens and Dierks slapped his face, slugged him with their fists, kicked him in the calf of his leg, grabbed his hair jerking his head from side to side—all the time plying him with questions in reference to the killing of Kearney;
13. The treatment continued at various times from the evening of September 18 until Saturday morning, September 20 but does not include interviews by Lukens and Dierks on September 10 and 11;
14. He was given no food or water, advised by the agents that water and soup brought to the cell had been poisoned, and they refused him calls of nature.
15. Forced him to take a two-hour cold shower resulting in his passing out and falling. Further he was given no chance to sleep resulting in his falling from loss of strength;
16. A rope was tied around his neck and when he was pulled up from his chair he would be struck in the stomach repeatedly;
17. Only Dierks and Lukens maltreated him. Agents Nance and Knowlton, the other two federal interrogators, did not strike or harm him in anyway.

The Statement of Defense Attorney Sperry S. Packard

On Tuesday, May 12, 1932, Defense Attorney Sperry S. Packard provided a signed statement to Prohibition Bureau Special Inspector Moyer concerning his view of the matter of Jack Dionisio's treatment while incarcerated at Colorado Springs. This document does not meet the requirements of a legal affidavit. It was signed by Packard, but it was not dated and witnessed so therefore it was inadmissible as testimony in a court of law. The document would have been viewed by the court only as a reference source to refresh the memory of the attorney. Packard's statement follows:

> As I recall now, without carefully re-checking back the date, I was first called to see Jack Dionisio on the afternoon of Sunday, September 21, 1930. At that time Miss Evelyn Brown, my Secretary[,] took his statement about the complaint of his treatment by officers Nance and Dierck [sic-Dierks, here and all hereafter] at Colorado Springs, during the week of September 14th to the 20th, 1930; he was very exhausted at the time and I took him into another room and he showed me his right abdomen, marks which appeared at that time as black and blue. He stated that his scalp was very tender and that he could not stand to have his head touched. He stated that he was going to be taken by some of his relatives back to Trinidad and I did not have an opportunity to see him after that for a short time or until the date of the affidavit which he signed at Trinidad. I was requested to make an investigation and in as much as the matter appeared on the face of the charge to constitute most unusual and vicious treatment of the prisoner I did not hesitate to proceed with the investigation as the telling of the story by Jack Dionisio in his own words at the time, of the various kinds of abuse given him, made me feel that it was a matter that should not be permitted under America's law [...]
>
> Subsequent to that time I proceeded to Colorado Springs and made an investigation there and the affidavit of the trusties were prepared, through Mr. Thomas I. Purcell. I found a reticence on the part of the officers to making any written statement, but they stated that they would tell the exact facts if there were a Government investigation where they would be protected. They knew about the fact of spree mis-treatment according to their statement but most of the action had occurred during their absence on the evening of the 15th or 16th of September, 1930, and later that week; that as to the trip during the night by the sheriff checking up with the jailor, and the jailor stated that they and Jack had not returned to the jail until about two a. m. [sic]. I found that they were investigating in reference to the killing of the Prohibition Agent Kearney and that they were under the impression that Jack Dionisio was connected with or knew something about the killing. They had therefore made inquiry of Rosario Dionisio and I have given to Special Investigator Ralph N. Moyer a copy of the statement signed by Nance and Diercks with the signature of Rosario Dionisio by mark. I know that he is unable to write.
>
> Upon my return to Pueblo, I was informed by an officer here that Nance [sic-Lukens] and Diercks and Newsbaum [sic-Knowlton] with some other officer, whose name I did not know, but later found was Lukens, had a top prisoner in Colorado Springs, in connection with the Kearney case, and had given him "the works" and rough-housed him in an endeavor to procure a confession. I found Jack Dionisio repeatedly referred to at Colorado Springs as the "wop prisoner." The reports were also received that the cook at the jail and some trusties knew in part about the action of the officers Diercks and Nance [sic-Lukens]. According to the information I received at that time, the only active part that Newsbaum [sic-Knowlton] and Lukens [sic-Nance] took was to question him and keep him awake by shaking him and slapping his face or having his face slapped, by one of the other of them with a cold towel.
>
> I made careful inquiry of Jack Dionisio and his relatives as to any matter that they might have concerning the whereabouts of Jack at the time of the killing of Agent Kearney, and among others I have furnished an affidavit of Philip Dazzo, a relative who is employed by the Missouri Pacific Railway Company of Kansas City, and was out here on a visit and traveling with Jack on a trip to El Paso, Texas, during that time, and I also procured a copy of the check that Jack Dionisio gave to a hotel at El Paso, Texas, on that trip.
>
> I also inquired as to the reputation of Jack Dionisio and found that Jack had been engaged in bootlegging on a small scale but he had no reputation for being a gunman or using a gun at that time, and so far as I could find, he was never arrested prior to his arrest in Colorado Springs. He had been employed as a salesman [sic] by his father-in-law, R. Dionisio. I have given a picture to the Agent [Moyer] of the mercantile house of R. Dionisio and also of Jack Dionisio's home.
>
> I found a copy of the newspaper report of the abusive treatment as it appeared in the paper at that time. When I saw Jack Dionisio, I requested that he be examined by a doctor as soon as he got back to Trinidad, and I have furnished Special Inspector Moyer a statement of Dr. Ben Beshar [sic] at that time.

After making the investigation I submitted the matter to Mr. Ralph L. Carr, United States Attorney at Denver, and showed him the affidavit of Jack Dionisio and informed him that the officers of Colorado Springs had made the statement that they did not want to put in writing, but that they would tell the full facts insofar as they knew them, if an investigation was made, and that they had expressed themselves as being very indignant over what they felt was a mistreatment of a prisoner in their jail. We had to make an agreement with Sheriff Jackson that we would not bring any suit against him as custodian, as he was fearful of the reaction on account of the fact that he would be running for office shortly again. Mr. Carr stated that he had investigated the matter and that he did not want to have this come out as it might seriously affect the Prohibition Enforcement in Colorado, with which I agreed, and told him I would leave the entire matter in his hands to handle, and invited the fullest investigation, and if there was any additional information that wished or any aid in any investigation that I would cooperate.

I procured the additional affidavit from the two trusties in the jail who had been called in by the officers who had isolated or arranged for the isolation of Jack Dionisio in the jail at Colorado Springs. I satisfied myself from the investigation and from the reports that I secured that there was no question about the fact that there had been the greatest possible brutality shown toward the prisoner.

It must be remembered in connection with this case that there was at that time an intense search being made by the representatives of the Government to locate the killer of Agent Kearney. The feeling was very intense throughout the entire region over that matter and it created a feeling that such killing constituted a challenge to law enforcement in this area. There had been intensive search into all of the so-called Southern Colorado Gang according to the reports I received, in the hope of locating this killer, and when Jack Dionisio was arrested it was believed by the officers that they had located the weakest one of a so-called bootlegging gang and that he could be forced to either confess to or give information about the killing of Kearney. With this back-ground and the intense anxiety of the officers to solve the Kearney killing, and with their belief that this man could either clear it up or furnish information, it is easy to understand why the action against this young man of about twenty-four years of age occurred.

After some time, Mr. Carr informed me that he had had an investigation made by an inspector or went whose name I recall was Baldisari [sic—Baldesareli] and that he had investigated Jack Dionisio and all of his family, and had found that they were not and could not possibly have been guilty of the Kearney killing. I satisfied myself to that fact and even stated to Mr. Carr, that if in my investigation I found that these parties or any of them were connected with that killing that I would not hesitate to disclose that fact to the Government, as I did not believe that an attorney had the right to cover up investigations in reference to a murder. But my investigation positively showed, at least to my satisfaction, that he had nothing whatsoever to do with it and knew nothing about it, nor did he know who might have committed it.

Mr. Thomas I. Purcell, of Colorado Springs, had seen Jack Dionisio and had an examination of him by some doctor whose name I do not at this time recall. I had the information at that time and assumed that this matter was entirely closed, but did not agree to keep the affidavits or statements which I have today furnished to Special Inspector Moyer.

Mr. Carr informed me sometime after I had given him the charge of the actions of Agents Diercks and Nance [sic—Lukens] against Dionisio, that he was satisfied that a wrong had been done Jack Dionisio, but I do not know what additional investigation he had made.

Although I was employed by Jack Dionisio and his family to make the investigation, I was interested only to the extent of the fact that I believed that such treatment should never be permitted any prisoner, and stood ready and have stood ready to furnish the Government and its representative any information that I could procure or furnish them with sources of information to investigate.

I have also given to Special Inspector Moyer, a copy of the letter of Thomas I. Purcell, to me, dated October 9, 1930.

If this matter of the investigation is kept confidential, I believe a statement can be procured from a number of these officers, although they would prefer to make the statement without putting it in writing. I received statements from a number of officers at that time who declined to write the statement out, from which corroborating evidence of the facts of the abusive treatment of Jack Dionisio appeared.

The condition of Jack Dionisio when I saw him was such that that fact alone established to my mind that he had suffered intensely and that he had undergone some kind of punishment. He could barely walk and he could hardly sit up and complained of severe pains in his abdomen where the bruises showed.

I believe that the additional names and the information given Special Inspector Moyer will enable him to get the corroborating facts, even [though these] matters [occurred] practically two years ago. The difficulty that he may meet is in the fact that there were no notations made by the officers of anyone excepting only the affidavits and matters in writing that have been furnished him, plus an additional copy of the report that I believe he can procure from Thomas I. Purcell, attorney, at Colorado Springs.

/s/ Sperry S. Packard, Pueblo, Colorado, May 12, 1932.

Affidavit of Prohibition Agent Willard E. Lukens

In this six-page affidavit, given incidental to the internal investigations by special inspectors, Agent Willard E. Lukens provided a view of the actions taken during the initial stages of the Kearney investigation unknown to the general public. On Monday, January 11, 1932, Agent Lukens attested to Federal Prohibition Agent Ida Richman the following:

I, W.E. Lukens, being a duly appointed Prohibition Investigator in the 10th Prohibition District, and being first duly sworn, make the following statement regarding the questioning of Giachomo, alias Jack Dionisio, in the County jail at Colorado Springs, Colorado, with reference to this knowledge of the murder of Agent Dale F. Kearney at Aquilar, Colorado, on July 6, 1930.

During the latter part of the month of August 1930 and the entire month of September 1930, [Lukens] was assigned to assist Agents W.E. Nance, Henry Dierks, W.H. Trimble, and S.A. Bonney in investigating violations of the National Prohibition Act in Southern Colorado as well as hunting for clues in the murder of Agent Dale F. Kearney at Aquilar on July 6, 1930.

While making these investigations, efforts were made at various times to locate Giachomo Dionisio, alias Jack Dionisio, alias Jack Dennis, for questioning in the Kearney murder case. [The feds] were unable to find him and were informed through confidential sources that Dionisio had gone to El Paso, Texas, where he was waiting for information from Trinidad and staying there in order that he could get into Old Mexico at a moment's notice if necessary. We made every effort to locate him at Trinidad by watching his residence at 1616 Arizona Street and through connections with confidential informers, but he was not to be found.

During our investigations, we secured evidence that on the night of July 5, 1930, when Agent Kearney had left Trinidad and gone to Aguilar, Colorado, where he was murdered from ambush, a maroon colored Chevrolet [sedan] had followed him from Trinidad to Aguilar. This automobile was traced to Robert V. Dionisio who is Jack Dionisio's brother and who also resides in Trinidad. We learned further that the tires used on this Chevrolet Sedan—all new Firestone tires—had been taken off and replaced by old ones just after the murder of Agent Kearney. We secured evidence that Jack Dionisio was in the Saddlerock Café at Trinidad, Colorado, with a party of other Italians when Agent Kearney and his wife entered, and when Agent and Mrs. Kearney left the café, Jack Dionisio stood up in his booth and pointed out Agent Kearney to the other Italians who were strangers. This incident [...] indicated that Jack Dionisio had pointed out Agent Kearney to the men who would do the killing.

Agents Dierks and Lukens went to Colorado Springs, arriving there at about noon on September 11, 1930. [They] made the usual investigation regarding the automobile, labeled samples of the 14 gallons of alcohol seized in the automobile and took statements from both the sheriff and Detective Wraith regarding the seizure and arrest.

That evening, at about 8:30 or 9:00 p.m. [they] went to the Sheriff's office and found that Jack Dionisio had been brought from the County Jail to this office. [Agents] Dierks and [Lukens] and

Sheriff Jackson questioned Dionisio regarding the violation, took his history sheet and attempted to secure information from him as to the source of the alcohol supply. Dionisio was warned at this time that anything he might say could be used against him, but that [they] would like to ask him a few questions about the load of alcohol with which he was arrested. Dionisio speaks very broken English and it was rather difficult to understand him, but he informed us that he had come to the United States in November 1922 from Sicily, that he was not a citizen, and during the time he had been in this country he was only able to account for five months in which he had had legal employment.

Dionisio told us in reply to our questions, that he had loaded up the alcohol near Pueblo, Colorado, receiving it from a man named Loui, who was driving a Chevrolet Coupe with a Kansas license. Dionisio stated that he had paid $7.00 a gallon for this alcohol and that he expected to get $10.00 for it in Colorado Springs. We had information that he had sold one gallon and had received $10.00 for it, and Dionisio admitted in reply to our questions that he had started with fifteen gallons, and this accounts for the fourteen gallons of alcohol which were seized.

Dionisio readily admitted the violations, and appeared to be afraid that [they] were going to ask him about something else. After questioning him about the alcohol transportation for a period of about two and a half or three hours, we started to question him as to his whereabouts on July 1st, 2d, 3d, 4th, 5th, and 6th of the same year, 1930. It could easily be seen that Dionisio placed himself on guard and was very careful of what he told us. We talked to him for some time before we mentioned the murder of Agent Kearney and spoke in an ordinary tone of voice. There were no threats or promises of any kind, nor was he abused in any manner. We talked to him until about 2:00 a.m. On September 18th, when [we] left and returned to Pueblo, Colorado. Sheriff Jackson stated that he would hold Dionisio until he heard from us.

On September 13, 1930, Agent Dierks and I went to the Police Station at Colorado Springs, Colorado, where with Chief of Police Hugh D. Harper, we questioned three men whom the Police had arrested there. These men were James Vinci, Russell Cacio, and Robert J. Dionisio, Jr. At the time he was arrested, Robert J. Dionisio, Jr., reached for a .32–20 Smith & Wesson pistol, and the officers were on the verge of shooting him. We questioned these men regarding their intentions when they came to Colorado Springs, and they denied having come there for the purpose of finding Jack Dionisio although everything indicated that they had, not knowing that he was in jail. At this time, James Vinci stated that he understood that Jack Dionisio had gone to Old Mexico about two months before, which would make it about the time of the murder of Agent Kearney.

On September 18, 1930, [Lukens] was instructed to assist Special Agents [Albro O.] Knowlton and [Daniel G.] Vaccarelli from the [Bureau of Prohibition] Chicago office in their investigation of the Kearney case, and to go with them and Agents Dierks and Nance to Colorado Springs. [His] daily report for that date shows that [they] arrived at Colorado Springs at 9:30 p.m. [They] met Sheriff Jackson and after a conference with him went to the County jail. [Lukens] received [his] instructions from Special Agents Knowlston [sic] and Vaccarelli [Vacarrelli] and endeavored to follow their orders.

Vaccarelli informed us that while he was in jail with Dionisio—a plan having been put into effect in which Vaccarelli was held in jail as a rum-runner and gangster from Chicago—Dionisio would pretend to be sick when he heard anyone coming and jump into bed and appear to be very ill. It was the opinion of these Special Agents that if we would question Dionisio for a period of time, that he would tell us about the others who were involved in the murder of Agent Kearney in order to hold himself. I understood that he had already made certain confessions to Special Agent Vaccarelli that he was connected with the murder, and it was from this that they believed he would tell us all the facts. It was nearly 11:00 p.m. when we started to question Dionisio, and during a part of this time, Agent Nance and Special Agent Knowlton talked to him.

On September 19, 1930, Jack Dionisio was questioned from midnight until 11:00 a.m. On the next day, and Agent Dierks and I participated in this questioning part of the time. We left the jail and did not return until 6:00 p.m. on this date when we again questioned Dionisio until 12 midnight when we stopped and Agents Nance and Knowlton talked to him until 6:00 a.m. on the morning of September 20, 1930. Dionisio was not questioned after this time by any of us.

The total time spent by all of us around the jail covered a period of about thirty-one hours. During this time, we did not talk to or question Dionisio continuously. On the afternoon of September

19th, Agent Bonney brought Mrs. Dale Kearney to Colorado Springs to identify Jack Dionisio as the man who had pointed Agent Kearney out in the Saddlerock Café. [...] This occupied some time although [Lukens did] not know how long as [he] was not in that part of the jail when this identification took place. Agent Nance told [him] that they had let Dionisio sleep for two or three hours during the time we were talking to him, and while [Lukens was] not certain just when this occurred, [he believed] Agent Nance stated that it was during the night of September 19th.

On or about the night of September 18th, Sheriff Jackson informed us that he had received information from a very reliable source—in fact, the same source that he had learned about Dionisio's transportation of alcohol—the friends of Dionisio were going to let him out of jail that night, two dressed and posing as Prohibition Agents with a prisoner; that they would come in very late at night—about 1:30 a.m.—and that when they got into the jail, they would hold up the night jailor and free Dionisio. The report was to the effect that these men were afraid Jack Dionisio would talk about the murder of Agent Kearney. Inasmuch as Dionisio was still in the custody of Sheriff Jackson and he was responsible for him, Sheriff Jackson asked us to assist him in guarding the jail that night. Just after dark, we went with Sheriff Jackson and secured three or four shotguns which were loaded with buck-shot and we all remained around the jail that night. Sheriff Jackson, however, took his automobile and went home to throw off suspicion the jail was being guarded, and that he might be reached if anyone tried to locate him.

On the evening of September 19th, the jail being crowded, Agent Dierks and I took Dionisio from the jail to the Sheriff's office at the suggestion of Sheriff Jackson. The Sheriff's office is located several blocks from the jail. [Lukens was] not certain of the time when this occurred, as [he] made no record of it. Later that night, or the next morning, [he] returned Dionisio to the County jail, going directly from the office to the jail in the same manner as [they] had brought him there.

During the earlier part of the evening on September 19th, when Agent Dierks and [Lukens] were talking to Dionisio, he stated that he was not feeling very well. We knew that he had pretended to be sick when Special Agent Vaccarelli was in jail with him, and therefore believed that he was shamming again. Either Agent Dierks or [Lukens] suggested that he might take a shower bath as there was one in the room in which [they] were questioning him. There was such an offensive odor about Dionisio that it was difficult to remain in the same room with him, and at [their] suggestion, Dionisio took a bath and returned and put on his clothes. When [Lukens] asked him if he did not feel better after the bath, he stated that he felt very much better.

Our questions to Dionisio were chiefly as to his whereabouts after the murder of Agent Kearney, why he had gone to El Paso, Texas, shortly thereafter; regarding his cousins Robert J. Dionisio and R.V. Dionisio and their whereabouts after the murder; the maroon colored Chevrolet automobile and the changing of the tires on this car just after the murder; what his connections were with John Boccaccio, Mayor of Aguilar, Colorado, who had left Aguilar a few hours after the killing of Agent Kearney and gone in the direction of Old Mexico; what he knew of the activities of his uncle, Rosario Dionisio, who owns a store in Trinidad, [...] handled liquor, and reported to be the head of the Italian black-handers in Trinidad; regarding his connection with John Cha wanted for a gang killing at Trinidad at that time and who fled the country; why a number of bootleggers and reported black-handers had held meeting in the basement of his Uncle Rosario Dionisio's store after the murder of Agent Kearney, and that he [Jack Dionisio] was also seen leaving these meetings; and also regarding his connection with the Mantelli brothers who were killed in gang warfare and had two plants blown up by dynamite and fire. In this connection, [Luken desires] to call your attention to an explosion and fire which occurred at the store and home of Rosario Dionisio on December 31, 1931, which was similar in a great many respects to the dynamiting [sic] of the Pete Carlino home at Denver, Colorado, on March 16, 1931. Pete Carlino and his brother Sam Carlino were the heads of a liquor ring in southern Colorado with headquarters at Trinidad, and they have since both been killed by gangsters.

When asked Jack Dionisio if he expected to be an American citizen and when he said that he did, we appealed to him from this angle, telling him that if he expected to be worthy of being an American citizen, he should assist us at this time in clearing up this brutal murder of an officer of the United States Government.

We talked to him about his mother who he told us lived in Sicily and was quite old, and she would feel if she knew that he was accused or suspected of murdering a Government officer. At one time, when we felt that Dionisio wanted to confess, we asked him if he wanted to see a Priest and that if he did, we would get any one he wanted, and also reminded him that Agent Kearney had been of the same religious faith as himself.

At first, Dionisio denied very vehemently that he had been in the Saddlerock Café and had pointed out Agent Kearney to some strange Italians, but he later told us that he had been there and had stood up in his booth to see something, but that it was not to point out Agent Kearney or show him to these men. He also admitted having followed Agent Kearney out onto the sidewalk, but denied that it was for the purpose of getting the license number and description of his automobile.

We questioned Dionisio about his connections with a number of Italians who are known bootleggers and gangsters at Pueblo, Aguilar, and Trinidad, Colorado. [Lukens did not have their names at the time of his affidavit and declared] [...] we had a long list of suspects—violators and others—who may have been involved in the Kearney murder.

As to the bath which Dionisio took it was at our suggestion that he took it, but no force of any kind was used, and he bathed himself. Food was brought to him by the jailor at different times when [Lukens] was there. Dionisio refused to take any food even when we urged him to eat some food, and there were no threats or suggestions of poison in the food, as reported in the press. Dionisio was allowed to go to the lavatory at any time he desired, and he was permitted to go whenever he made the request which he did on several occasions.

The clothes which Agent Kearney had worn at the time he was murdered were brought to Colorado Springs and shown to Dionisio, and the bullet holes and marks on the shoes were shown to him. We questioned him regarding his knowledge of the clothes Agent Kearney had been wearing when he was in the Saddlerock Café and at the time he was murdered. These clothes were procured from the Coroner at Trinidad [...] but [Lukens] did not know who got them or who returned them.

On several different occasions, Sheriff Jackson came into the room where [the agents] were questioning Dionisio and could see and hear what was going on. At no time during [their] stay at the jail were there any threats made to Dionisio nor was abused in any way. I did not, and I saw no one else strike or mistreat Dionisio nor do I know of any of the agents abusing him. During the time we were at the jail, to my knowledge the actual time we questioned Dionisio was about twenty-four hours. We first started questioning him at about 11:00 p.m. on September 18, 1930, and there were several intervals during the time from 9:30 p.m. until 6:00 a.m. on September 20th when we left.

On the morning of September 20th, we left the jail and had our breakfast, returning to the jail at about 8:00 a.m. When we were informed by the jailor that Dionisio was sick and that he had called a doctor who was then in the cell with Dionisio. Agents Nance, Knowlton, and I went into the cell, but as there was very little room there, [Lukens] went out while Agents Nance and Knowlton remained with the doctor in the cell. When the doctor [...] came out of the cell, I asked him if Dionisio was ill and what his condition was, and doctor replied that he believed Dionisio was trying to fool us—that his temperature and pulse were normal, and that he did not see anything wrong with him other than that he might be tired. The other agents stated that the doctor had given Dionisio a very thorough examination to ascertain if there was anything wrong with him.

During the period between September 11th and September 18th, the Sheriff informed us that friends and Dionisio's attorney were allowed to see him at the jail, and some of his relatives were there and had left some fruit for him. Sheriff Jackson will also be able to advise you of the name and address of the doctor who was called by the jailor.

We were informed about a week or ten days afterwards, that Dionisio had been in an automobile wreck and had broken his leg. We were unable to locate him and learned of the accident when making inquiry as to whether or not he had jumped his bond.

I have read the foregoing six pages of this affidavit, and the facts as stated therein are the truth to the best of my knowledge and belief.

/s/ W.E. Lukens

Lukens disclosed new information on the status of the investigation in September 1930, as well as potential targets in other areas of investigation developed later in Pueblo, Aguilar, and Trinidad. Other media research resources failed to note any such incidents.[3]

Summary Results:
Three Special Internal Investigations

Documents buried in the aging administrative files of a long-dead federal agency were discovered by co-author Lee Charlton during his search of the National Archives. These reports detail an internal quest by the agency's management to discover the methods used by agents to gather evidence to build a case for trial. They also provided impetus for the agency to protect the public image of the Prohibition enforcement agents who zealously pursued their suspects.[4]

In Washington, D.C., A.W.W. Woodcock, the director of the Bureau of Prohibition, ordered his Special Inspection Division to conduct an investigation of the allegations concerning the handling of the Jack Dionisio matter. P.A. Shirley completed his report on December 30, 1931. Woodcock found his findings to be incomplete and ordered a second investigation.

Ralph N. Moyer concluded his inquiry on July 21, 1932, but it would not be the final word. This report was also considered incomplete according to the director. Woodcock felt it to be biased in favor of the defense attorney Packard's revelations. In one of Packard's statements he noted a discussion he allegedly had with United States Attorney Ralph L. Carr wherein Carr told him his undercover man "Baldesareli" found that Dionisio and members of his family "were not and could not possibly have been guilty of the Kearney killing."

Lawrence L. "Baldy" Baldesareli had served as Carr's confidential undercover penetration into the Carlino crime family. According to Lukens, Special Agent Vacarrelli (also Vaccarelli) of the Chicago office had also served as one of Carr's special undercover operators imported to handle the Kearney investigation. Packard's document seems to indicate that in this instance the Bureau of Prohibition had been informed of Carr's penchant for outside undercover agent personnel.

A third review was commissioned and Sam H. Scott finished his task on September 22, 1932. Howard T. Jones, the acting director of Prohibition, accepted this report. Jones incorporated the results of the two previous investigations along with Scott's new data to justify that the probe be closed on November 30, 1932.

The three inquiry reports, with their mixed conclusions, are summarized below:

Inspector Perry A. Shirley's Findings: There is little, if any, evidence to support the charge that he was mistreated in any way, and it is my opinion that the complaint was made for the purpose of beclouding the issues and of saving himself from a charge of transportation of intoxicating liquors. His reputation as a violator of the liquor laws and as a gun-man is well known. He has been in the United States for about nine years and there is no record of his ever having been employed in any legitimate enterprise. From the evidence obtained during the investigation of the Dale Kearney killing it would appear that he was probably involved in that murder. It is, therefore, my opinion that this complaint should not be seriously considered. RECOMMENDATION: It is recommended that this case be closed and that no further action thereon be taken.

Further, UNDISPUTED FACTS: [...] After being questioned for upwards of forty hours, [Jack] Dionisio was released on bond [...] EVIDENCE TENDING TO PROVE CHARGES: Jack Dionisio is now a fugitive from justice and a direct statement could, therefore, not be obtained (February 3, 1932). His attorney, Sperry Packard, of Pueblo, Colorado, was engaged in some extensive state litigation during the time of this investigation and could not be contacted. However, the matter was discussed with United States Attorney Ralph Carr at Denver, Colorado, with whom the original complaint was filed by Dionisio's attorney. Mr. Carr stated that Packard did not express an opinion as to whether or not the charges made by his client were true [...][5]

Inspector Ralph N. Moyers' Findings: By this time Dierks had been separated from the service. Investigator Lukens was guilty of using severe "third degree" methods regarding the [investigation into the] killing of Agent Kearney. A letter of charges should be addressed to Investigator W.E. Lukens, charging him with the mistreatment of this prisoner and also with untruthfulness in his statements with reference thereto, and proper steps should be taken to remove him from the service, and it is so recommended.[6]

Inspector Sam H. Scott's Findings: [...] Lukens stated, in response to a specific question [by Inspector Scott], that Special Agent Daniel R. Vacarrelli seemed to be in charge of the investigation of the Kearney murder. He said that Vacarrelli was confined [undercover] in the same cell with Dionisio, under the guise of a fellow-prisoner; and that when Vacarelli was released, he stated that Dionisio was about ready to confess. Lukens stated Vacarelli directed for Dionisio to be questioned without rest or sleep; and predicted a confession of his participation in the Kearney killing would be obtained. Lukens asserted this was the reason Dionisio was questioned for a 30-hour period. Mr. Lukens further stated the officers offered to get a priest [of the same denomination as Dionisio] believing that Dionisio might more readily confess to the priest than to the officers [...]

There is some evidence tending to show that Attorney Sperry Packard was not averse to using the alleged inhumane treatment of Dionisio in the interest of his client in the liquor case. It appears he represented to United States District Attorney Ralph L. Carr at Denver that it would be unwise and poor policy for the Government to go to trial in the Dionisio case, in view of the alleged brutal treatment accorded Dionisio. Mr. Carr informed me on one occasion that there seemed to be sufficient grounds for the report of ill-treatment of Dionisio, to make it inadvisable to proceed against him. *The result is, Dionisio has never been tried on the liquor charges.* [Emphasis added.]

It is believed that Mr. Carr obtained most of his information regarding the treatment accorded Dionisio from Attorney Packard, although he may have conferred with one or two of the officers involved. Mention of these facts is made to show the possibility that the treatment accorded Dionisio may have been and probably was exaggerated for a purpose. That is, by Dionisio [...]

[It] seems safe to conclude that Jack Dionisio was not beaten and abused in the brutal and inhumane manner claimed by him. If he was, it appears the [two examining doctors at the jail] and the various other witnesses would have discovered more evidence of it when they examined and observed him on September 20, immediately following such alleged brutal treatment.

RECOMMENDATION: It is believed that any disciplinary measures that may be authorized as a result of this and previous investigations of this case, should be predicated upon the questionable treatment resulting from keeping Dionisio awake for such a long period, and frightening him; and not upon the theory he was brutally and inhumanely beaten. Accordingly, such recommendation is made. It is believed the evidence warrants the conclusion Dionisio was not beaten and abused in the cruel and inhumane way claimed by him, else more evidence of such treatment would have been discovered.[7]

On December 9, 1932, Howard T. Jones, acting director of Prohibition, dictated a letter to Prohibition Investigator Willard E. Lukens, noting in part:

The evidence obtained [surrounding the investigation of one Jack Dionisio] indicates that [he] was mistreated and deprived of sleep for a long period of time. Such acts on the part of Prohibition Investigators indicate a lack of intelligence and discretion and will not be countenanced by this Bureau. [...]

I am considering, however, that you and your fellow officers were endeavoring to obtain information concerning the murder of a fellow officer and realize that you probably were pushing this investigation quite vigorously. In view of the fact that your record since that time has been good I am going to close the matter without disciplining you further.[8]

United States Attorney Carr informed both the media and the Justice Department inspectors that in his discussions with defense attorney Packard the lawyer may have been trying to determine what information the federal government had suggesting a possible involvement of Jack Dionisio in the Kearney murder investigation. Carr stated that he did not support the abuse of federal suspects by the government's enforcement officers. Meanwhile, the investigating agents continually failed to locate anyone who would share their knowledge of the murder.

Authors' Perspective: Dale Kearney's death appeared to fit the hallmark of an isolated hit—one specifically ordered to serve as a warning to all other federal investigators to back off their enforcement activities. Further, it became highly probable that outside shooters, or the secretive Black Hand Society, may have been commissioned or self-appointed to "rub out" Agent Kearney. One must remember that Italian/Sicilian bootleggers were in control of the "black-handers" in Trinidad and elsewhere in southern Colorado. The organization in Trinidad was headed by the Dionisio crime family, a component of the Carlino Brothers' southern Colorado operations. If Kearney's murder was to serve as a local or regional threat to federal government agencies, a method that usually worked on the local police departments, the gangs totally underestimated the resolve of the investigative forces of the federal government in Prohibition Region 10.

It is interesting to note that defense attorney Packard also practiced water rights law parallel to those efforts that Carr would follow when he became governor. Carr established his national reputation in this field incidental to his gubernatorial position and later entry in to national Republican politics. Further, Sperry S. Packard of Colorado was the father of David "Dave" Packard, an electrical engineer and cofounder of the multifaceted Hewlett-Packard electronic enterprise, first established in 1939 in Palo Alto, California.[9]

Postscript: Henry Dierks

Because of pending state litigation, no affidavit was ever obtained from Henry Dierks concerning his alleged involvement as a co-interrogator alongside Agent Lukens in the questioning of Jack Dionisio at Colorado Springs. United States Attorney Carr never filed charges against Dionisio relative to the Colorado Springs bootlegging violation. Neither were any federal prosecutorial charges filed against any of the accused federal agents involved in this matter.

Dierks was placed on administrative leave without pay on November 30, 1931, due to a death he caused during a prohibition raid in Englewood, Colorado, on November 7. Milford G. Smith was killed by a blow on the head from Dierks' gun during a scuffle. A resulting *Denver Post* article reported Dierks' history of violence while operating under his position of federal authority, as well as other historical incidents that the media had uncovered. Colorado officials vied with the federal district attorney in a legal fight concerning jurisdiction to charge Dierks with murder. Homicide is a state crime, but the federal officials pleaded that they held authority to try him in federal court since the death had occurred from injuries sustained while Dierks was lawfully acting in accordance with federal law.[10]

On June 30, 1933, Dierks resigned from the Bureau of Prohibition "to enter private practice." The Dierks case would not be resolved until 1935 when the state finally held its trial with Dierks being found guilty and sentenced to state prison.

13

Valentines—Gangster War—New Plans

"Stick to what you know is right. Make crooks fear you. Don't be afraid of anything.
 Keep your eyes open and your conscience clean. Keep your badge bright and clean. Think of that badge as the outward symbol of your honor."—address to the officers of the Philadelphia Police Department, Brigadier General Smedley D. Butler, USMC (Retired), Director of Public Safety, Philadelphia, 1924

Dateline: Northeastern New Mexico and Southern Colorado, February 14–April 13, 1931

On Saint Valentine's Day, Saturday, February 14, 1931, Deputy Regional Administrator Charles H. Stearns prepared to address a Raton raiding team. The pending action would be the first major attack against the bootleggers since Perry Caldwell's release. Fifteen men were present and ready to shut down all known operations in Colfax County. Closure notices and search warrants had been obtained in advance. Shortly after the announcement of Caldwell's not guilty verdict, federal strategies were discussed at the highest regional levels and prepared for implementation.

Each of the three-man strike teams was organized according to their assignment and proceeded to their destinations. The raid results were posted in Monday's issue of the *Raton Evening Gazette*. The newspaper told how Charles Stearns led 15 Prohibition agents, aided by Colfax County Sheriff Al Davis and Chief Deputy Boots Fletcher, in raiding a dozen "booze joints" in Raton. The raider teams made exhaustive searches of Raton's pool halls, soft drink parlors and hotel lounges. The agents confiscated 500 gallons of liquor and passed out 25 "Valentines" in the form of summons to Santa Fe for the next session of the federal district court. All of the defendants earned either single or multiple complaints of possession and sale of alcohol and/or maintaining an establishment of public nuisance. After the mass raid, New Mexico's federal attorney ordered the officers to padlock all 12 locations raided.

Ray C. Hanna, federal commissioner for Colfax County, was quoted preceding the body of the article saying, "The spirit of Ray Sutton is abroad and his ghost is hovering over every bootlegger in Raton and will continue to do so until not another one is left in town."[1]

Meanwhile in Colorado

In Colorado, it appeared that neither the Los Animas County Sheriff's Office nor the Kearney Task Force had been successful in any of their efforts to develop new leads on the Kearney case. Their investigative efforts continued but none proved of value. *Omertà*, the Sicilian code of silence, remained in full force on the streets.

Since the takedown of suspects by Denver Police at the bootlegger convention in January 1931, the Carlino brothers appeared to be walking on eggs, every step was a cautious one. The big meeting, and the one that occurred the following Monday evening, two days after the January 24 raid, yielded a total rejection of the Carlino Plan. Pete and Sam had erred in estimating their powers to persuade. All crime families within the state had reassessed their relationships to them and began preparing for a gang war.

On Wednesday, February 18, 1931, Pete Carlino, while standing on the sidewalk in downtown Denver reportedly awaiting a scheduled meeting with unknown parties, heard the sound of a high-powered vehicle turn the street corner and come roaring down the street in his direction. As the car approached, unknown gunmen began blasting away from behind the car window curtains. Diving for cover while instinctively rolling on the sidewalk to a spot behind a nearby streetlamp post, Pete Carlino survived unharmed. He told police he had not seen any of the shooters' faces. When the media heard of this incident, they confirmed that once again the Carlinos were at war.[2] Or was this a concocted story, another scam by and for Pete Carlino to grab some headlines?

No one on the outside of the gang seemed to care about Pete Carlino's predicament other than Joe Roma. A secret plan had been set in motion early on with his infiltration of the Carlino crime family and their allied associations. Ignacio Vaccaro, one of the Carlino nephews, would later be identified by Denver police as having received 12 cash payments from the Roma factions during this time period. Vaccaro reportedly disappeared two days prior to this attempted hit on Pete Carlino.[3] His abandoned car was found over 20 miles east of Colorado Springs; neither he nor his body ever turned up. The Denver police chalked him up as being an early victim of the new crime family war.

> **Authors' Perspective:** Joe Roma maintained a set of the old country's traditional rules of organized crime; some would refer to these as "Roma's Personal Principles." Number One: Open defiance of authority and leadership cannot and will not be tolerated! Number Two: Opposition forces will be eliminated on their refusal to honor and obey any beneficial offer. The Carlinos were challenging the acknowledged crime leader in Colorado and, therefore, they had to be punished immediately lest others will also rise up. Joe Roma viewed the situation very coldly; he considered himself to be Colorado's crime boss—all others were mere contenders.

A Fire Bombing and a Few "Rats"

The *Evening Herald* of Decatur, Illinois, a newspaper published several hundred miles to the east of Denver, picked up the March 17, 1931, *Denver Post* story: "Denver Rum King's Home Destroyed By Rival's Bomb."

The press chalked up the bombing of Pete Carlino's home as part of the warfare between rival bootleggers, but the Denver police didn't think so. To them, it appeared to be an inside job based on their recovery of several gasoline cans found in the basement.[4] Within 24 hours after the bombing, Denver police named the suspected bombers as the Carlino brothers and three of their followers. No mention was made of the other man who had been present, the one that was always with Sam. With respect to the arson fire, it was learned that the United States Attorney's office had been the source of the information concerning the identity of the bombers. The media were told that confidential information had been received outlining the nature of the crime and roles of the arson perpetrators as subsequent investigative data supported. The specific source, or sources, of that information remained unidentified to all investigative authorities.

On Saturday, March 21, 1931, five days after the explosion, the Carlino gang members were in the wind. Each was either traveling or in hiding at their safehouse. Immediately following the blast, Pete Carlino quietly left the city in an effort to gain an army of "soldiers" to fight the Roma factions. Sam was left in charge during his absence.

That same evening, a dark sedan parked on a residential street in northwest Denver drew the attention of a beat police officer. As he approached the vehicle, he noticed the interior was hidden from view by drawn privacy curtains. He saw the vehicle rock or lurch as if it was occupied. A cursory investigation yielded the persons of Sam Carlino and his bodyguard, Lawrence L. "Baldy" Baldesareli.[5] Inside the car within the reach of the two men was what one detective later claimed to be a small arsenal of weapons. Baldesareli was found to be carrying a concealed weapon. Both men were placed under arrest and transported to police headquarters where they were questioned about the weapons, the fire at Pete Carlino's home and his current whereabouts, as well as the current locations of the remainder of the wanted arson suspects. No viable information was forthcoming from either man. Baldy Baldesareli claimed no knowledge of any crimes when questioned. He was charged with carrying a concealed weapon and paid a $25 fine at his immediate arraignment and was released.

Sam Carlino, on the other hand, was charged with arson and other assorted offenses and scheduled for trial on April 11. As a condition of his release on bond, the court ordered that he turn over all firearms in his possession, including those from his home and any business or office from which he was known to frequent or conduct business matters. His personal safety now depended on the mercy of his bodyguards and the protection that they alone could provide. The other conspirators had been located in the interim and all four subjects had been booked and released on bond pending a trial date.

Following their release on bond, these Carlino associates held a series of private discussions without the presence of Baldy Baldesareli. In the crime world, the bodyguard was routinely charged with the same offenses as his boss. They, boss and bodyguard, were inseparable in their criminal undertakings with the bodyguards doing the actual dirty work. The police and the prosecution knew this simple fact. So did the criminals.

Each gang routinely monitored their competition, always looking for unusual activities or behaviors that would suggest the placement of a "government rat." The entrenched crime family has its own intelligence collection methods. If there is a leak within one of them, then all of the other crime families in or near Denver would hear about it. Word of such penetration came routinely in spite of personal hostilities or alliances that competing gangs maintained with each other. The criminal communities could not and would not tolerate the presence of a "rat." They couldn't ignore the possibility of being infiltrated by police informants or government agents. Such a situation warranted unilateral action to be taken against the impacted gang.

The gangs' leaderships would have logically surmised that if there wasn't someone on the inside, how did the cops know who was involved in the arson of Pete Carlino's home so quickly? It became a simple exercise of analysis based on available facts. Declaring the identity of all members of the arson team within 24 hours was not a common feat for which the corrupted Denver police detectives were known. Their criminal investigative skills were not that effective. The Carlino gang members decided that Baldy Baldesareli had to be the leak; all fingers pointed to him. On the morning of the arson trial, Sam Carlino's attorney placed a motion for continuance before the court based on the fact that Sam had taken ill and would not be able to attend the day's proceedings. Sam had not notified Baldesareli of this change of plans even though the three other defendants knew and were already at the courthouse awaiting the court to convene. They, thus, had their alibis.

Later, investigation would determine that Baldesareli followed his general travel route and pattern of behavior with respect to picking up and transporting Sam Carlino from his home to the courthouse; he proceeded through the hotel lobby through the front doors and began his walk to the nearby garage. Two unidentified shooters fired multiple shotgun blasts at him from an old Ford sedan parked near the hotel entrance. Baldesarelli was hit in his left arm. The shooters continued their volleys as their target ran back into the hotel to a position of safety. The car rapidly departed the area.[6] Baldesarelli received temporary first aid to his wounds pending the arrival of an ambulance and the police. He directed the hotel manager to notify his "immediate superior" about the shooting. The man for whom Baldesarelli secretly worked was United States Attorney Ralph Carr!

It is unknown if it was the Carlino gang or the Roma gang that correctly surmised that Baldesareli was a snitch or an undercover agent. To them, it didn't matter that much either way because the elimination of an insider threat was a cost of doing business—nothing more, nothing less. Once the facts were made known to the responding officers, the police assumed the obvious and went directly to the courthouse where the three gangsters were calmly waiting for their case to be called. Carlino's men were arrested in the courtroom. Sam Carlino was picked up at his home.

All were charged initially with the attempted homicide of Baldesareli; however, the state lacked the evidence to file criminal charges. Their arrests did nothing more than get them off the street and provide the police another opportunity to talk to them.

James Colletti subsequently replaced Baldesareli as Sam Carlino's personal bodyguard. As one of the Carlino gang members working out of Pueblo, Colletti assumed his new job in all seriousness. He was the brother of arrested arsonist Daniel Colletti. Within a period of days fate would step in once more and Sam Carlino would neither be tried nor convicted of arson or any other crimes in the state of Colorado.

On Thursday morning May 7, 1931, James Colletti and Sam Carlino were attacked and shot in Sam's Denver home.[7] The May 9 issue of the *Denver Post* headlined: "Denver Gang War Flaring Anew As Bootlegger Slain; Youth Identified as Gun Killer by Victims." The article reported:

> The gang war over control of Denver's liquor traffic flared again when Sam Carlino, 41-year-old North Denver bootlegger, was shot to death in his home and Joe Colletti, 39, of Pueblo was seriously wounded. Mrs. Josephine Carlino, the slain man's widow, named Bruno Mauro, 17, of Pueblo as the killer. Colletti, who was taken to a hospital, also told investigators he and Carlino were shot by Mauro [...]
>
> Carlino's brother Pete is known to federal and state dry agents as the former head of southern Colorado's bootleggers. Pete's whereabouts were unknown to Colorado officers. He was ordered to leave the state several months ago after his arrest during what Denver authorities said was a "bootleggers" convention [...]
>
> Pete Carlino's home in North Denver was bombed several weeks ago. Officers at first believed the bombing to be the work of a rival faction but L.L. Baldesarelli, a federal undercover agent who had gained the confidence of the Carlino gang and who was serving as Sam Carlino's personal bodyguard, revealed the arson plot as one to collect insurance. Baldesarelli became the victim of an attempted drive by persons unknown and was wounded in the arm but survived. His true identity as an investigator of the United States Attorney became known and he became one of the state's chief witnesses in the conspiracy trial growing out of the bombing of the Pete Carlino home.[8]

Authors' Perspective: It would take the Denver police several months and several investigations involving informant operatives to identify and charge the three alleged associates of the Carlinoes (Daniel Colletti, Joseph Ferraro, and Joseph Petrolia) with attempted murder for the failed drive-by shooting of Pete Carlino in mid–February 1931. Within two years, these men would also be positively identified as being in the employ of Joe Roma at the time of the offense while still in the service of the Carlino brothers. Joe Roma's infiltration of the gang appeared complete. What had been considered by some to be a staged attempted murder had now been confirmed to be a legitimate elimination effort that went sour.

Dateline: Northeastern New Mexico, Early Winter 1931, Espousal Rejection

James Perry Caldwell spent more than 123 days in federal custody before being released.[9] His family survived without him thanks to the efforts of Jessie Caldwell's family, namely her sister Catherine, who came to help her for extended periods. Occasionally, Caldwell's sisters came by to check on Jessie and Robert Carl, age 13; Perry, Jr., age 11; and Dorothea, age 10. Jessie Caldwell had already closed her mind to her husband's extracurricular evening activities outside the home; going out "on business," he would always say. As long as there was food on the table and the bills paid, she gave little attention until events swept down and upturned her whole world.

She had read the newspaper stories and heard the rumors about Ray Sutton's disappearance and knew that her husband had been a colleague of Sutton in the past. However, she had not been aware of their actual relationship. When the warrants were served on Perry at their home, she first learned that he had some of Ray Sutton's personal property. Perry Caldwell never talked to his wife about what exactly happened or how Sutton's items came into his possession. And she never asked or probed the depths of his relationships with other lawmen or lodge brothers or, for that matter, anyone else. Since he left the government service, Perry rarely discussed the type of work he did other than he had been a prohibition agent. Following Caldwell's arrest in September 1930, Jessie thought a lot about their relationship, his activities, and where it all had led them. During her husband's trial, she had supported his alibi, testifying he had been at home over the Labor Day weekend. In fact, she couldn't recall exactly when he had been home that fateful weekend. Now, she wasn't certain that she did the right thing in court. From all appearances, Jessie was suffering a mental breakdown.

Authors' Perspective: According to an interview conducted by D. Ray Blakeley of the Union County Historical Society by Perry's nephew, Johnny Caldwell, the son of Berlin Caldwell, all of Caldwell's attorney fees were paid by his family members. Berlin had to sell off a number of cattle and a portion of his property near Springer. Johnny Caldwell also stated that the family believed that his uncle had not been involved in Ray Sutton's disappearance and murder; subsequent investigative facts prove otherwise.

Johnny Caldwell also claimed that after being cleared in federal court, James Perry Caldwell was employed by the Colfax County Cattle Grower's Association to put a stop to rustling in northcentral New Mexico. It would appear that the Caldwell family had exerted some local influence with that organization based on its membership and the family-owned cattle ranch in Springer. The authors have been unable to confirm this period of employment from independent sources.[10]

Jessie Caldwell's Health

Catherine Blanchard, Jessie Caldwell's sister, knew the Caldwell brothers and family very well. Early in 1923, she had married Perry's younger brother Walter, the New Mexico boxing champion—and philanderer. Their marriage had terminated within three years. Catherine was unaware that Jessie had come to believe her husband had been involved in the Sutton disappearance until, in a rare moment of rationality, Jessie expressed her fears that Perry would do her harm to silence her.[11]

Over the next several weeks following his release from jail, Perry Caldwell focused his efforts on finding a reasonable solution to Jessie's behavioral issues. The first item of business was to get Jessie out of Cimarron. Catherine took her home to Albuquerque. Perry managed to have his sisters move his three children to their homes until he could find a more acceptable solution. One of his sisters lived in Cimarron, another in Springer.

Perry next located a doctor who encouraged Jessie to allow an examination by a psychiatrist friend from the state mental hospital. Following a series of brief interviews by staff personnel, Jessie Caldwell was admitted for a 30-day period of observation and evaluation. Another health evaluation hearing followed the first 30-day period. Jessie's condition had fluctuated over her stay, but she gave indications of a positive response to treatment. She was to continue her treatment until such time that she be deemed "rational" once more to the extent that she could function normally in the community.

It is unclear if Jessie Caldwell ever told hospital staff why she feared her husband. Inasmuch as medical and psychiatric records are sealed we may never know for certain. Caldwell concurred with the new commitment and signed the necessary papers. Jessie had no say in the matter. Her response to questions put forth by the psychiatrist was silence. Her sister, Catherine, had nothing to contribute to her defense. This was a matter between husband and wife, and in Catherine's view, if ever stated, was of secondary importance to the prescribed treatment program. Later statements made to investigators by Jessie Caldwell made it clear that, at the time of her admission to the asylum, she hated and feared her husband and wanted no further relationship with him. She felt safe at the hospital and as long as she stayed in treatment, she would be free of him. In a sick way, this was a win-win solution for them both. She would be out of Campanella's reach and safe due to her mental state. He would be free of the fear that Jessie would bring him down if she talked to authorities. The children would not understand the situation at first, but they would be safe and Jessie knew her family would take care of them. In the end, Perry Caldwell accomplished what he had sought.

Investigative facts suggest that Perry Caldwell appears to have created a scenario to explain Jessie's absences, should he have received any inquiries from distant friends or his new neighbors in Albuquerque, but the possibility of an unexpected encounter would always remain problematic. He didn't worry about the old neighbors in Cimarron; they would believe the couple had left the area like so many other financially troubled families during these hard times. This move would be just another casualty of the Great Depression. Rumors circulated the James Perry Caldwell family had relocated to New Orleans where he had found new employment. This bit of misinformation was a logical move on Perry Caldwell's part to stay out of the media limelight—if out of sight, then, out of the minds of Colfax County residents.

Authors' Perspective: Once federal authorities learned that Perry Caldwell had relocated to Albuquerque, he became a continuing subject of interest to federal officers in that city. They determined that he had rented a room in a boarding house, a more permanent residence would come later. Deputy Administrator Charles Stearns and a few of his agents made it their personal missions to maintain an awareness of Perry Caldwell's activities. In this instance, their missions persevered for decades beyond their transfers or retirement from government service. The long arm of the law extends great distances and lawmen have long and unforgiving memories when intentional harm has been directed toward one of their own.

Years later former Prohibition Agent C.U. Finley, now retired, told a reporter, "If the death of Agent Kearney and the disappearance of Agent Sutton were not followed up and the perpetrators of the two crimes vigorously prosecuted, agents in this part of the country will simply become the prey of the moonshiners whenever it is necessary to avoid the penitentiary."[12]

14.

Star Power Visitors—Cornucopia—Vivian's Dismissal

> "And while the crime is still written down in the books as unsolved, men who were friends of Sutton and there were many, have not given up hope and someday expect to mete out justice to those who committed New Mexico's most notorious crime in recent years."—*Raton Daily Range*, August 28, 1931

Dateline: Northeastern New Mexico, September 19, 1930–December 31, 1931

On Friday, September 19, 1930, the headline of Albuquerque's *New Mexico State Tribune* notified its readers: "Sutton Case Suspect Jailed at Trinidad." The newspaper reported the arrest of Perry Caldwell, but it also told readers that United Artist movie star Douglas Fairbanks and two movie producer friends arrived in the Duke City. The men were headed to Raton for a short vacation at the hunting club facilities at the 350,000-acre Bartlett Estate at Vermejo Park. It was turkey-hunting season. After lunch at the Franciscan Hotel in Albuquerque, Fairbanks and his companions were passengers on the 1:50 p.m. Mid-Continental Airlines flight to Raton.

Raton Mayor A.R. Streicher's and other citizens' attentions were temporarily distracted from the search for a missing prohibition agent by a Hollywood star's arrival in the Gate City. After the usual celebrity greetings, and the action star's interview over Raton's radio station KGFL to promote his new movie project, a private car took the Hollywood guests to the hunting ranch. A week later, the action star was back at work and his New Mexico hunting trip had become a minor footnote to his career.

While the biggest local news in homes and coffee shops in Raton, Clayton, Trinidad, Cimarron and Taos concerned the fate of Prohibition Agent Ray Sutton, other events were not forgotten during the second week of September. New Mexico Governor Richard C. Dillon headed the state delegation to Raton's annual Frontier Day of '49, celebrating when the American military marched over Raton Pass and captured New Mexico during the Mexican War, while Major G.W. "Pawnee Bill" Lillie provided entertainment from his Wild West show. Joseph Tondre, New Mexico's United States Marshal, was also in Raton for the celebration, as well as to check on the Sutton investigation.

Even as the police investigation continued in high gear, the local mood was growing that Sutton had been killed. The first public pronouncement came from Ray's hometown when the weekly *Union County Leader* on September 11 headlined, "Hope For Sutton Given Up." A week later, the *Clayton News* agreed saying, "Search For Sutton Given Up As Hopeless." In short order today became tomorrow, tomorrow became a new week, a new week became a month, and then it was a new year, 1931.[1]

The Reward Fund

Back on September 9, 1930, within a week of Sutton's disappearance, District Attorney Stringfellow started a reward fund to encourage volunteers to help with the search. The DA's $200 reward was quickly matched by local police officers. A few days later, Agent Finley reignited the Sutton search effort when he added an additional $100 to the growing reward pool for finding Sutton and/or his car. The Union County Commissioners' Court pledged $100 and the United States Marshal's office staff in Albuquerque pitched in $50, as did other groups, to make the reward pool reach a total of $1,150. A separate $400 fund had been established for the arrest and conviction of those who had committed the crimes against the federal agent.

Joe Roma Visits Raton

No one seemed to notice the date or time that the small entourage of men and a single woman arrived at Raton's Santa Fe Railroad Depot. They had detrained from the southbound passenger train from Denver on or about Monday, April 13, 1931. Unfortunately, neither local nor federal law enforcement circles were aware that Joe Roma, Denver's crime boss, and the lovely Nettie Greco, his fiancée, were visiting Raton. According to crime historians Alt and Wells, Joe and Nettie were to marry on Tuesday, April 14, 1931, during their trip to Raton.[2]

The search for the remains of Ray Sutton and the identities of his killers continued in Colfax County. The latest round of major winter weather conditions had dissipated, but now the searchers were confronted with heavy April showers. Eight months had passed since Sutton's disappearance. The probability of developing any further clues in the field had long ago reduced the number of search volunteers, reward or no reward. The shared perception within the community had become one in which many believed that any continuing efforts to find him alive or his remains would be fruitless.

In spite of these parameters, the sheriff's office had been successful in sending out two teams per day to scour the hills and arroyos in the vicinity of Cimarron. Sheriff Davis maintained that all search efforts would continue as top priority items in spite of the weather. In reality, the sheriff's search efforts were limited to individual random private hunting parties who were tasked to keep their eyes open for anything that they thought would be of help to the sheriff.

Authors' Perspective: It remains a question as to why northern New Mexico was chosen as the locale for Roma's wedding. One might speculate that Colorado's gang war had made the Denver environment unfavorable for such a happy occasion. Holding any wedding in Denver for a well-known criminal personality would have placed too many wedding guests in a single location during a time of raging gang warfare. The whole of the crowd would have been at risk to unfriendly forces. Pete Carlino was still out there and no one knew where. The purpose of this trip did allow Roma a legitimate reason to be outside of Denver in the event he had wished to establish an alibi for events that were already in the making. How long and where he stayed in northeastern New Mexico, and with whom, remains unsubstantiated.

As Colorado's new crime boss, Joe Roma would have sought to solidify his bootlegging connections with his longtime New Mexico counterparts. Sources in Pueblo, Colorado, reported that Roma and his party had visited Pueblo on such a mission immediately prior to continuing southward to New Mexico. In Raton, unpublicized arrangements would have been made to meet with both John Campanella and his financial support to seek and assure stability for Roma's new bootlegging enterprise. Both organizations understood the way "business" should be conducted: professionally, without any appearances of grandeur or forced empowerment. These two factions were truly a new breed of skilled businessmen, the kind that some would say were entrepreneurial in their approach. Joe Roma saw himself sitting in the "catbird seat" for the present at least.

Evidence would come to light in 1932 that Roma and Big John Campanella shared a common supplier of bootlegging equipment and supplies, the Jacob Zerobnick Bottling Company in Denver. For six years the Bureau of Prohibition had tried to penetrate the bottling works operations without success. In March 1932, Prohibition Investigator W.E. Lukens was assigned to the case. A brief discussion of the case is discussed later in this tome.

Search Action at Koehler Lake

On Friday, April 17, 1931, the *Raton Daily Range* reported: "Search for Sutton Pushed; Lake Koehler Goes Down Slowly as Hunt Goes On; Hope to Find Solution of Mysterious Crime in Shallow Waters of Lake; Four-Inch Drain Pipe Used by Prohibition; Agents to Empty Big Pond." The day before the *Evening Gazette*, now under new ownership, had returned its original masthead, *Raton Daily Range*, used since January 21, 1887.

On April 23, 1931, headlines of the *Raton Daily Range* told the tale about the search efforts at Koehler Lake: "Rain Likely to Fill Up Koehler Lake; Water Up"; "Using Pump for Draining Water" on April 28; "Renew Work of Draining at Koehler" on May 7; "Expect Lake to be Empty Within Week" on May 15; "Propose to Drain Koehler on Sat." on May 22; and "Dragging of Lake Proves Futile Task" on May 26, 1931.

The Koehler Lake project proved to be a dead-end, but the ground searches continued. Deputy Administrator Stearns informed the general public: "In our search for the remains of Ray Sutton, we have drained one small lake and are now engaged in draining the largest. The work is slow and we're constantly fighting the rains, as you know. We haven't found any information or clues to identify where Sutton's remains may be deposited. We'll be conducting our program to fully drain the lakes until that action proves to be of no value."

Authors' Perspectives: There were some influential Ratonians, never identified publicly, who were concerned that Sheriff Al Davis was being too helpful to the federal authorities in efforts to locate the missing Sutton. The negative public relations impact of the numerous search teams, the recent bootlegger arrests, along with the closing of several "rum joints" was stifling the local illicit economy. Raton's business communities were raising economic concerns to the city fathers and the power brokers who quietly influenced political decision-making behind the public veil.

Since the search for the missing federal agent, the resulting money flow decline was being attributed to the presence of so many law enforcement personnel in the area. The drinking public was becoming very nervous they would lose their source of pleasure and the local basis for the town's most lucrative tourist attraction. Raton's leadership continued to hold the town's annual pioneer days celebration and parade while the search for Sutton proceeded in the background.

As Joe Roma continued to work from the shadows in Denver, so did John Campanella's money interests persevere in New Mexico. However, unlike his Colorado counterparts, John's silent financial backer held a degree of respectability and was quietly putting pressure on most, if not all, of the local officials through his coterie of third-party sycophants.

Sheriff Al Davis' Troubles

The *Raton Daily Range* on April 16, 1931, reported on just such a political countermove: "Sheriff Davis Charged With Assault As Result Old Fuss; Attorney General To Push Prosecution Of Local Peace Officer With Silver City Judge Likely To Sit In Case; Julius Lodine Complaining." The article explains the political undertone.

> Charges of assault have been lodged against Sheriff Al Davis of Colfax County and a preliminary hearing will probably be held in district court here on May 14, according to information learned today. The charge is the outcome of an altercation Sheriff Davis had with a man named Julius Lodine here several days after the November election, in which the sheriff is alleged to have pulled a gun on Lodine, after the latter had made a move to draw a pistol on the peace officer [...]
>
> [New Mexico] Attorney General [Ernest K.] Neumann, with his assistant Quincy Adams, have made two mysterious visits in connection with the case and it was learned today that they intend to handle the prosecution, in place of Fred Stringfellow, district attorney here. District Judge H.A. Kiker will not sit in the trial and Judge George Hay of Silver City has been asked to preside. According to the sheriff, Lodine became quarrelsome when questioned about his activities during the election and struck Davis after some words had passed between them. Davis then asserts that he struck back, after which Lodine reached back in his pocket, as if he were going to pull a gun [...]
>
> The sheriff then pulled his own gun and held Lodine at bay. Shortly after, Abe Hixenbaugh came up and told the sheriff he would take care of Lodine. Davis then got into his car and drove away, after which Lodine was searched but no gun was said to have been found on his person. A warrant, charging assault with a deadly weapon, was served on Sheriff Davis recently and he was allowed to go about his duties on his own recognizance.
>
> Sheriff Davis, who was the only republican elected to a county office during the last election, stated today that he believed the prosecution was the work of his political enemies.[3]

On Thursday, May 22, 1931, Sheriff Davis' trial began. That evening the *Raton Daily Range* reported on the quick trial, explaining the jury had been selected on Wednesday. First, Julius Lodine claimed he and Sheriff Davis got into an argument over the recent election and Sheriff Davis struck him twice and then pulled a gun on him. On cross-examination, Lodine denied reaching toward his rear pocket. Mrs. Lodine corroborated her husband's story. Witnesses J.P. Carlisle and H.R. Martinez agreed with Lodine's tale. Next, Dr. M.F. Smith testified to a conversation held with Lodine after the argument and said that Lodine told him, "We were going to push the prosecution in an effort to get Davis out of office."

Abe Hixenbaugh, then a Special Santa Fe Railroad Detective, followed Dr. Smith on the stand and related what he saw of the alleged incident. The popular, former multi-term sheriff told the district court he saw Lodine reach for his hip pocket gun before Davis drew his revolver. Hixenbaugh said he was the first person to arrive on the scene, before all the other witnesses who had testified, and he broke up the quarrel between Lodine and Davis. The jury rendered a not guilty verdict later that afternoon.[4]

Seemingly unruffled by this experience, Sheriff Al Davis returned to his duties forearmed with a determination to continue his efforts to locate the remains of his friend. He now understood how far some local power brokers were willing to go to stop the Sutton investigation.

> **Authors' Perspective:** Abe Hixenbaugh encouraged his friend Sheriff Davis to keep up the good fight. Abe, also a Republican, had served as Colfax County's last sheriff under the territorial system and the first under the new state government. Chuck Hornung's research uncovered that as a young girl Nona Neff, Hixenbaugh's wife, and her immediate family had lived next door to Deputy United States Marshal Wyatt Earp and his wife, Mattie, in Tombstone, Arizona Territory. Andy Neff, her father, would later become a mining partner with Wyatt, as well as serve as a special deputy town marshal at Tombstone under Wyatt's brother Virgil. Wyatt Earp often helped the young Nona do her homework after school and hosted her and her friends to ice cream at the local confectionary. After leaving Tombstone, Andy Neff settled in the Raton area. In late 1884, he tried to help recruit Wyatt Earp to serve as chief deputy or undersheriff under John Hixenbaugh, the newly elected Colfax County sheriff, Abe's older brother. Earp and his wife visited Colfax County to inspect the area but declined the offer in favor of mining and real estate investment in southern California. He and his wife later returned to the county to spend a Christmas with their friends Henry and Mary Lambert at their St. James Hotel in Cimarron.[5]

The Search for Sutton Continued

On Friday, May 29, 1931, the *Roy Record* of Union County told readers that Koehler Lake had finally been drained, but Sutton's body was not found. An editorial comment ended the story, "The Sutton case has proven to be one of the most baffling in the criminal history of the Southwest. Officers have failed to make any material headway in the solution of the mystery."[6]

Meanwhile, the *Union County Leader* reported that in a series of raids, Sheriff Tom Gillespie and deputies Oldham and Dodds discovered and seized a 150-gallon still they found in the area known as the "Brakes." This was a locale situated along the

Dry Cimarron River in the northern part of Union County. Thirty-three barrels of mash, nine sacks of sugar, ten gallons of liquor, and camping equipment and other paraphernalia were seized and destroyed. No arrests were made. A second smaller operation was confiscated at the Brite residence in the southeastern part of Clayton. Four arrests were made and a small amount of beer and a quantity of whiskey was destroyed.

On Thursday, May 21, 1931, William McDonald, a booze runner from village of Optimo in Mora County, died in an automobile accident in Colfax County on the road south of Springer. His car reportedly turned over on the eastern approach to the Taylor Springs bridge. Investigation by the Colfax County sheriff's office determined that he had been on his way to Texas with a load of several gallons of whisky in the car. Just whom McDonald represented or worked for could not be determined. He had once been a rancher in the area. The significance of William McDonald's death is that it gave evidence of a New Mexico southbound transportation route being used by at least one local bootlegger. This had not been substantiated previously.

The Tuesday, May 26, 1931, edition of *The Norwalk* (Connecticut) *Hour* carried a frontpage headline, "Body Perhaps That of Missing Agent." The article explained that hikers on Johnson Mesa north of Raton discovered the decomposed body of a man. The forensic evidence, however, shattered all hope that the remains were of Ray Sutton. The agent's son could not positively identify the remains, and his father's dental records supported the son's conclusion. Unknown to most people, Ray Sutton wore upper and lower false teeth. The *Roy Record*, June 4, 1931, identified the body as the remains of R.J. Holden, an early settler in the area.[7]

In spite of all of these continuing search efforts, no workable leads were found that were useful to move the Sutton case forward. Lawmen, however, were not yet ready to give up the hunt.

The Carlino-Roma Conflict Reaches a Climax

Back in Colorado, since the death of Sam Carlino, Joe Roma continued to revel over his complete control of the liquor business in Pueblo and the remaining areas to the South. It had been six weeks or more since Sam's death. Pete Carlino let it be known that he would "get Roma and wipe out his entire gang, regardless of the manpower and costs involved." Joe Roma wasn't too concerned about Pete's threat to even the score.

Authors' Perspective: If there is one thing that is worse than bad luck, it's having no luck at all. Pete Carlino found himself in the latter category. The Carlino name as a former crime family leader in the state no longer held standing with the eastern criminal communities, if it indeed had any such ranking before. It must have become clear to Roma, and finally to Pete as well, that there would be no out-of-town legions rushing to Colorado to aid them. Another of Carlino's dreams had died. Within a few weeks' time following their arrests, Pete's former soldiers, the "arsonists," were all tried and convicted and sentenced to prison.

Carlino never knew that a federal undercover agent had infiltrated his organization; he had to learn this bit of information from media reports about Lawrence L. "Baldy" Baldesareli. Carlino should have had no doubt that once he returned home, he would be "toast"—either from Roma or from Baldesareli testimony.

Elsewhere, his previously allied colleagues had scattered and formed new criminal gang alliances, or they were already victims of the latest Roma-Carlino warfare. Pete was completely alone. He had no known financial resources available to him due to seizure of his stills by authorities. Without merchandise to sell, he lacked cashflow for upfront money to "would-be soldiers" from back east. Besides, the eastern gangs had their own internal structures to maintain. Colorado was viewed as a nice place to visit when one of them wanted to "cool off," but it wasn't a place where they were interested in dying. Besides, by virtue of his own national network involving the Black Hand Society, Roma could hold off most any imported mercenaries should they come forward. He also had the Smaldone brothers in his band of enforcement associates readily available to counter such moves against his organization or affiliated crime families operating in other parts of the state. Carlino was effectively checkmated and had run out of time to be considered a potential "all-Colorado crime boss."

Unbeknownst to Carlino, who had yet to resurface from his trips to the East, Joe Roma and three of his close associates made a long overdue trip to New York. They held a series of meetings with unnamed crime families in an effort to short-circuit any connections that Pete may have established. As the new power in Colorado, they were received and acknowledged by those they visited. The men were very pleased to find that Carlino had failed to gain any eastern backing. Once the Denver police discovered Roma's period of travels, they questioned him but gave only a vague explanation for the trip: his "boys" had never been east before so he gave them a tour.

The Inside Man

Lawrence L. "Baldy" Baldesareli is known in Denver gangland history as the "inside man." Federal records are unclear as to whether anyone at the Prohibition Bureau sought to question Carr's special undercover man about the Kearney murder case. It appears that United States Attorney Carr would have been the one to respond to such inquiries in lieu of any direct questioning of Baldesareli. There is, however, no apparent indication that any such individualized request was ever formulated. Logic would suggest that Baldesareli should have had some insights into the murder since he had served as the personal bodyguard for Sam Carlino before he was forced to break his cover. Surely something had been said or overheard about Kearney during that time, yet there are no government reports that such information had been gathered. According to defense attorney Sperry S. Packard's statement concerning alleged mistreatment of bootlegger Jack Dionisio at Colorado Springs County jail in September 1930, Carr told him of Baldesareli and certain of his findings concerning the Dionisio family. Then in mid–November 1931, the *Denver Post* included similar information about Baldy Baldesareli.

Carr had offered nothing to support the involvement of the Carlinos with the Kearney murder. Neither would he suggest any involvement of the Jack Dionisio family. It appears that if the federal attorney knew the complete story, why had Carr failed to pass this information on to the federal investigators in the Kearney murder case? Why did they have to learn this from outside sources? Or did they already know from their personal contacts within the Department of Justice or outside agencies? The record is unclear and silent on this issue.

Authors' Perspective: As noted elsewhere, Ralph Carr was responsible for requesting undercover agents from other regions to assist with the Kearney-Sutton investigations. Prohibition Special Agents Daniel R. Vaccarelli and Albro O. Knowlton, from the Chicago Office, were sent to work on the probe. Vaccarelli was placed in charge of the Kearney investigation. The media was not privileged to this information, which would explain why the two undercover agents were never named in press articles. The terms of Vaccarelli's assignment in this capacity remains unknown to the authors. It is to be noted that Carr admitted using undercover agents in 1931 but refused to offer details during a media discussion following the Jack Dionisio incident. It appears that Vaccarelli and Knowlton may have been the "proven undercover agents" brought in to the region to augment local agents as first suggested by New Mexico's Charles H. Stearns following Sutton's initial disappearance.[8]

Senior investigative team members knew that Baldesareli's information concerning the internal operations of the Denver underworld had helped put in jail at least three of the arsonists of Pete Carlino's home and had served as the basis for the outstanding arrest warrant on the still-traveling Pete Carlino. Yet no one ever discussed or revealed in any government documents when or how Baldesareli had been recruited by Carr. The Bureau of Prohibition learned independently that the informant had been from the Trinidad area and was acquainted with the Carlino family, who also had once lived in the community.

Perhaps there are additional facts waiting to be discovered concerning United States Attorney Carr and his range of underworld contacts. It is possible that, had knowledgeable investigators interviewed Baldesareli, he might have indicated the degree of suspected high-level organizational corruption and paranoia that existed within the Denver Region's Department of Justice during this period. No such interview appeared to have happened. For whatever the reason, Baldesareli quickly disappeared into a special witness protection program. Contemporary rumors alleged that bootleggers had targeted him to be killed.

Along with his seemingly "new" friendship with Clyde Smaldone in the late 1930s, a question comes to mind relative to Carr's 1930 placement of Baldesareli within the Carlino crime family. Did Carr have a prior relationship with Roma and Smaldone? Were the Smaldone elements always calling the shots in the matter of Carr's role as the United States attorney? Was Baldesarelli, in reality, used as a spy by Carr for the Roma and/or Smaldone crime family operating through Carr? Did Baldesareli know the truth?

The authors were unable to locate further information pertaining to Baldesareli. His Bureau of Prohibition Official Personnel File was unattainable from the National Archives. It had been retained for unknown reasons by the Department of Treasury. No reason is noted for not forwarding the OPF to the National Archives and Records Center at St. Louis, Missouri, to be retained among the listings of former personnel working for the Bureau of Prohibition in 1930. The name Baldesareli appears in the center's indices; however, his file was not found among the official personnel records of the Departments of the Treasury or Justice.

Pete Carlino's Last Arrest

In late June 1931, the Denver police and local authorities arrested Pete Carlino at the Pueblo area farm of Charles Guardomondo, one of Carlino's relatives. He had recently returned to the area when news "leaked out" about his whereabouts. There had been some speculation that he had personally alerted Denver authorities before the Roma forces had a chance to "put him on the spot." If that argument had been valid, Carlino surmised correctly that the "law" offered him a safer passage to town than the alternate transportation option that the Roma legions could provide.

The *Pueblo Chieftain* reported the capture of Pete Carlino with the headline: "Noted Colorado Gangster Taken Into Custody." He had been wanted since February and was captured in the Pueblo area, trapped in a farmhouse. The mob boss meekly surrendered to the officers. The *Raton Daily Range* told readers, "Many Months Of Hard, Tedious Work Behind Gangster's Fall." Meanwhile, north in the Big Sky Country, the *Helena Daily Independent* headlined, "Reputed Big Liquor Dealer In The Toils." Pete Carlino had been the Rocky Mountain news sensation on Friday, June 19, 1931.[9]

On June 23, 1931, an ironic turn of events occurred. On that Tuesday the visitor's log of the Denver City County jail listed Joe Roma as visitor of Pete Carlino. Later that same day, Roma posted a $5,000 bail bond for Carlino's release. Had the two opponents finally acknowledged the fact that a gang war was not good for business? Had they finally sealed an agreement to work together and move on? These questions remain unanswered, but events would suggest the answers within the next few months.[10]

The Kearney Case: Solved?

By June 1, 1931, federal efforts to find anyone who could or would supply any meaningful information about Kearney's death were clearly unsuccessful. Media interest in the case had waned considerably by this time, a mere month short of the one-year anniversary of his death. The story had become old news to the point where reporting, if any at all, had declined to an occasional few lines of reference buried in separate crime articles on the inside pages of newspapers.

On September 13, 1931, a much larger story played out. Pete Carlino's partially decomposed body was found 22 miles southwest of Pueblo near the Siloam Road Bridge on the outskirts of Wetmore. It had been just three months since his arrest on arson charges. Allegedly, a large diamond ring on his finger, along with a number of addressed envelopes and letters found in the corpse's clothing, were used to identify the body. The face was unrecognizable and the top of his head was missing.[11]

The *Raton Daily Range* of Tuesday, September 15, 1931, unknowingly reported the most important story yet that would impact the Kearney murder investigation. This incident seemingly served to administratively close the investigation. The article headlined, "Use Poison Bullets To Kill Carlino–Body of Gangster, Badly Decayed–Found Along Road Near Pueblo." A medical examination of Carlino's body revealed that the flesh surrounding the bullet wounds was badly discolored and a poisonous infection had set in. The poison bullets accounted for the decomposed condition of the head and face. Discovery of Pete Carlino's automobile near Penrose convinced police his slayers trailed him from his cousin's ranch home. No one was ever arrested for the killing.[12]

Authors' Perspective: It is unclear why Pete Carlino's fingerprints were not on file to provide a comparative analysis to that of the deceased. There is, however, a possible explanation for the missing card. Since 1924, the Department of Justice's Bureau of Investigation fingerprint identification section was initiated and commenced collecting fingerprints for a new nationwide fingerprint classification center in Washington, D.C. The contents of the ambitious collection numbered just over one million cards by 1931, due mostly from fingerprint cards and information exchanges being made between the United States and Canada. The collection contained all the cards from the federal penitentiary at Fort Leavenworth, Kansas.

The "smart money" defense attorneys knew that the Justice Department's fledgling fingerprint record program would have limitations, but its future value as an aid to law enforcement would be endless. These lawyers frequently obtained court orders precluding the fingerprinting of their clientele by law enforcement; therefore, not all arrestees were fingerprinted. At the time, local, state, and federal law enforcement agencies had no set policy to follow requiring uniform fingerprinting of all arrested persons. This could explain why there were no comparison prints of Pete Carlino available at the Denver Police Department, the last known agency to have arrested him.

Whenever questions were directed to Joe Roma by local authorities or the media about the bootlegging war and the death of Pete Carlino, Roma would deny having any knowledge on the subject, stating that he was at a loss to understand who would kill Carlino. His death passed the mantle of "unquestioned boss" of crime (throughout the state of Colorado) upon Joe Roma and his very able band of criminal cohorts. The Carlino-brother murders remain officially unsolved.

The Raids Continue

In Union County, the combined federal and local law enforcement personnel reemphasized their efforts as the first-year anniversary of Ray Sutton's disappearance drew near. An increase in the number of stills seized suggested no letup of activities on the part of the bootleggers' creative energies, nor of the imaginative efforts of the officers to combat them.

Clayton's weekly *Union County Leader* of Thursday, August 20, 1931, took note of a recent seizure: "Agents Uncover $2000 Hooch Plant–2 Big Stills In Weekend Raid." The story told how on Saturday, August 15, Union County Sheriff Tom Gillespie, Deputy Sheriffs Luther Oldham, I.T. Dodds, and Prohibition Agents Sidney Huddleston of Clayton and William Randolph from Texline, Texas, had raided a still on the FDW Ranch north of Clayton in the Corrumpa badlands.

Frederick D. Wight had established the headquarters for his sprawling FDW Ranch at the headwaters of Corrumpa Creek, on the eastern slopes of Sierra Grande in the 1890s. By the early 20th century a small settlement was founded on the site. The community once had a store, school/church, and a post office. The mail service moved to Des Moines in 1919. The school's basketball team competed in numerous area championship games before it closed in mid-century. Today the community of Corrumpa is a home for ghosts, but the land is still cattle country.

When the posse seized Wight's still, two men fled to a waiting horse and bounded down the Corrumpa Creek canyon among the rocks. The pursuing deputies were in automobiles and had to go around the route taken by the fugitives and eventually lost the bootleggers.

The contents of the raid site were inventoried and then destroyed. The still's construct involved 60 feet of 1½ inch copper coil and a 300-gallon cooling tank for the coil. Fifty-five gallons of made liquor was discovered along with 1,250 gallons of mash; 50 large barrels; 800 pounds of sugar; a complete camping outfit including a tent; one heavy thresher pump with a 50-foot 2" diameter hose that was used to pump water from a well on the creek; three 50-foot garden hoses; a complete five-burner, two-tank gasoline heater for the still; five lanterns; six five-gallon gasoline cans; 11 five-gallon wooden kegs; and other items (including 100 gallons of gasoline).[13]

The August 20 issue of Clayton's weekly newspaper also reported details of a previous seizure near Guy, New Mexico, on August 13, 1931. In the 1930s, Guy was still a ranching supply center located about 37 miles northwest of Clayton, but today nothing remains of the settlement. When the still was discovered by federal agent Sid Huddleston and Deputy Sheriffs Luther Oldham and I.T. Dodds, they arrested D.W. Latkins and George Thomas as suspected bootleggers. Both men were arraigned at Clayton and held for arraignment before the federal grand jury at Santa Fe. The officers seized 110 gallons of liquor and 1,000 gallons of mash.

On August 27, 1931, the *Union County Leader* reported on a third raid in the county that month. On this occasion officers seized two extra-large stills in eastern Union County near the Oklahoma State line. This was in the same general area where in late 1929 local authorities had seized the largest still ever discovered in northeastern New Mexico. The Clayton newspaper summarized the adventure in its headline: "Sheriff Force Take Two Stills–Union & Cimarron County OK Sheriff Stage A Big Raid–Cimarron, OK Sheriff Identifies East Union County And West, OK County As 'Home of The Bootleggers.'" A supply source was broken and the "boots" lost thousands of dollars' worth of equipment and product.[14]

Within a week of the New Mexico-Oklahoma border raid, an army of federal and local law enforcement officers laid siege to Pueblo County, Colorado. Without public fanfare, the federal government had entered another stage of stepped up investigations to gather intelligence on the activities of Pueblo's crime gangs. Similar coordinated efforts were already underway in New Mexico.

The *Raton Daily Range* of September 15, 1931, published the following report: "Pueblo Bootleg Joints Raided–31 Dry Agents Concentrate On Cleaning Up City Before Fair." Within a day and a half, 31 federal agents accompanied by Pueblo police made 21 arrests as part of a cleanup of alleged bootleg establishments. The arrests were based upon evidence of possession and sale of liquor previously acquired by the officers. The city sought to obtain a crime-free environment during the scheduled operation of the Colorado State Fair which was to begin the following week.[15]

On August 28, 1931, the *Raton Daily Range* chronicled a seemingly final story on the first-year anniversary of Sutton's disappearance with the headline, "One Year Ago

Today Ray Sutton Disappeared From Raton And Whereabouts Still A Mystery." It would be one of the last such news items published incidental to the investigation for a number of months. As with the Dale Kearney murder investigation, with no major breaks in the case, the event lacked sufficient "front page" attention. In media terms the Sutton case had become old news. The article concluded with the hope that the crime would be solved. In the field, however, local investigators dismissed the media's lack of interest with disdain and persevered in the seemingly hopeless task before them.[16]

New Leadership in Washington, D.C., and Denver

Between August 31 and December 31, 1931, a quiet series of administrative investigations took place in Denver and Washington. The Denver office of the United States attorney, under the leadership of Ralph L. Carr, had ignited a spark that caused a whirlwind of subtle, yet capricious undermining of Regional Administrator John Vivian.

It was the responsibility of the United States attorney to oversee the regional operations of those agencies serving under the Department of Justice umbrella in his juris-

Director of Prohibition Amos W. W. Woodcock (left) conferring with the new Acting Regional Administrator I.S.T. Gregg (right) (courtesy Chuck and V.J. Hornung Western History Collection).

diction. If he suspected wrong direction or mismanagement, it was his duty to bring these issues to the attorney general's attention of any suspected operational breakdown in regional operations. It, then, became the duty of the attorney general or designee to contact the head of the offending bureau—in this case Director Amos W.W. Woodcock. The director made a surprise visit to Denver to confront John F. Vivian. On Wednesday, December 2, 1931, Woodcock accepted Vivian's written resignation and appointed Assistant Regional Director Isaac S.T. Gregg to serve as the acting regional director for Region 10 pending the selection and arrival of a permanent office head.[17]

Vivian had not seen the hammer coming. Civil court rulings on non-prohibition-related lawsuits indicated that Vivian had failed to file required legal reports with the courts as to the fiscal management and care of various trust accounts. In one case, Vivian had commingled $3,000 belonging to a confined mentally disturbed relative with his own personal funds. The court commented that if such action was taken against an infirm and mentally challenged relative, what could be expected of Vivian in his dealings with non-family members?[18]

Subsequently, the court determined that Vivian had accumulated more than $75,000 in personal debt. Further investigation uncovered tales of how Vivian had "borrowed" monies from as many as four of his agents and was in the process of completing a "loan" of $4,000 to $5,000 following his seemingly *quid pro quo* endorsement of Henry Dierks as a full-time Prohibition agent. Under these circumstances, his personal intervention in obtaining an appointment to public office for another was in violation of the Civil Service Commission Act, and as such served as a cause for dismissal from duty of all parties involved.[19]

Simultaneous to the notice of Vivian's resignation was the administrative termination from active duty of Henry Dierks. Dierks, who had been working out of the Pueblo office at the time of the Kearney murder and had been part of the initial response team to Aguilar when Kearney had been murdered. Since then, he had been promoted from Special Employee-Informant to Prohibition agent and assigned to Englewood, Colorado.

According to court records, while he was investigating a lead at an Englewood, Colorado, outdoor sandwich stand, Dierks observed 21-year-old Milford G. Smith take a small bottle of wine from his pocket and place it atop a table. Smith was preparing to eat lunch. Dierks attempted to confiscate the bottle and Smith sought to save his drink from a possible thief. No evidence was given to suggest that Dierks identified himself as an officer. A scuffle ensued and Dierks struck Smith over the head with his handgun. Smith was arrested and taken to jail where he died the next day from the head injury.

Director Woodcock believed Dierks had acted like a "stupid and brutal peace officer" and steps were taken to dismiss the officer from active federal service. First, Dierks was placed on administrative leave pending resolution of jurisdictional matters regarding state charges against Dierks. He maintained that he had been a federal officer acting in his official capacity when the death occurred and therefore the federal government retained the right to adjudge him in federal court. Regardless, the state claimed jurisdiction and charged him with murder.

Coincidentally, Dierks and another agent were also targeted in response to a newspaper article appearing in the same general period for past investigative behaviors when they masqueraded as active duty military personnel to affect an investigation. A small article appeared inside the *Steamboat Pilot* (Steamboat Springs, Colorado) issue of December 18, 1931: "Dry Agents Must Not Play Soldier." The article suggests the use of undercover prohibition agents in army uniform, masquerading as active duty military men, may have been the lynchpin that helped to cinch the end of Vivian's career. Even though Director Woodcock had extended service as a senior officer in the Maryland National Guard and frowned on a real or imagined denigration of the military uniform, it was fatuous fiscal dishonesty and lack of personal integrity that caused Vivian's firing.

The New Regional Administrator

Recently appointed Seattle Regional Administrator Carl Jackson, as the former deputy regional administrator of Wyoming serving under Vivian, replaced Vivian as the Region 10 Administrator of the Bureau of Prohibition. His first official act was to order, at the direction of the national director, the discontinuance of military disguises by undercover agents in the field. He also ruled that operatives must not drink liquor to obtain evidence (a common practice in the field to determine the type of liquor being served during an onsite investigation). Neither were field agents to use their pistols as clubs, but solely for the purpose of self-defense.[20]

> **Authors' Perspective:** It should be remembered that the Bureau of Prohibition's transfer to the United States Department of Justice meant the prohibition agents now served the attorney general of the United States. "Main Justice" was an entrenched partisan bureaucracy that operated in manners far beyond the understanding of the general public. The Bureau of Prohibition had entered into a well-established legal bureaucracy with its own breed of political sycophants, traditions and idiosyncrasies. Some historians would also add and their own system of corruption. Most of the new arrivals failed to fully comprehend the sophisticated and highly structured inner workings of Main Justice. Few bureau employees had any contact beyond the local office interfacings with this agency regarding violations of the National Prohibition Act.
>
> In Washington, overall managerial liaison and responsibility of prohibition enforcement remained with Director Amos W.W. Woodcock. He would continue to implement operational policies, but now it would be under the overall direction and approval of the attorney general. Local bureau managers knew Woodcock could not be everywhere, so they continued their practice of quietly gathering external support from their "political godfathers" within their state's congressional delegations. They knew these men would run political interference for them when necessary. John F. Vivian had always survived under this system. In the end, it failed him.

Part III
The Trail Markers Grow Dim

"Never fear shadows.
They simply mean there's a light shining somewhere nearby."
—Ruth E. Renkel, author and poet

15

Reassignments

"We trained hard [...] but it seems that every time we were beginning to form up into teams we would be reorganized. I was to learn later in life that we tend to meet any new situation by reorganization; and a wonderful method it can be for creating the illusion of progress while producing confusion, inefficiency, and demoralization."—Petronius Arbiter, Greek Navy, 210 BCE

Dateline: Northeastern New Mexico and Southern Colorado, January and February 1932

Once John F. Vivian was unceremoniously removed from office, the new regional administrator lost little time in restructuring the New Mexico operation. Prohibition Agent Clarence Ulysses Finley, assigned to Colfax and Union Counties, was ordered to report to Albuquerque for a staff meeting on Wednesday, January 6, 1932.

On Tuesday, January 5, 1932, Finley boarded the early morning train to Albuquerque. While en route from Raton, he reviewed his case notes for the past few months in preparation for a discussion to plan future actions. Finley, on orders from Albuquerque, had been keeping a low field profile in the state since his negative encounter with bootlegger Lee H. "Shorty" Bilk during a raid in Las Vegas. He had been in Colorado working on the Kearney murder case rather than in New Mexico working on Sutton's disappearance.

The Bilk-Finley Dustup

Agent Finley had launched a series of enforcement raids in New Mexico's San Miguel County on Friday, July 10, 1931. One target was Bilk's Tea House in the town of Las Vegas. The after-action report notes that once the premises were secured and customers were being questioned, Finley approached the counter where Bilk kept his cash register, a two-drawer model with each requiring a different register key combination to open. Bilk's loud commentaries on what he thought of the Prohibition agent's actions may have caused Finley to become a bit rattled as he attempted to open the register.

Eventually, the correct key combinations worked; one drawer held about $500 in cash and the other a handgun. The report is unclear whether or not the cash and weapon were seized as would have generally been authorized in the search warrant. The presumption is that a seizure occurred and the hearing judge had to determine the dispose of the items seized. A monkey wrench was thrown into the usual procedure.

"Dry Agent Accused Of $500 Theft" was the headline for the *Raton Daily Range* report of the raid on July 16, 1931. Highlights of the Las Vegas dispatch were simple. Lee H. "Shorty" Bilk charged Finley with taking $500 and a pistol from the double-drawer register in his place during a raid. San Miguel County Deputy Sheriff Tomas Segura arrested Finley and brought him to a preliminary hearing where he was granted bail by the court with the approval of District Attorney T.V. Truder. Las Vegas City Police Chief Henry Cifre and New Mexico's United States Commissioner W.G. Ogle posted the necessary bond and Finley was released to appear at trial when called by the district judge.

Finley was exonerated on all charges by the district court when his case was finally heard. However, because his story had appeared in newsprint, the public appeared inclined to accept the tale spun by Shorty Bilk as truth. Unfortunately, the erroneous reputation of the "bad apple" federal prohibition officers continued to impact the federal law enforcement agency.[1]

Federal Agents Hold a Summit

Deputy Administrator Stearns called the New Mexico staff meeting to order with all eight of his prohibition agents in attendance. Agent Finley was acknowledged for his efforts in the Ray Sutton case. The new Regional Administrator Carl Jackson and Stearns had agreed that a change in personnel and operational supervision were needed in the Sutton investigation, thus a series of personnel changes were to become effective immediately.

Agent Finley would be transferred permanently to Colorado where he followed up on old leads in the Kearney case along with a routine case load. Agent Sid Huddleston received acknowledgment for his support work in northeastern New Mexico. Recently retransferred from his Las Cruces duty station, newly appointed "Special Agent" Walter L. Hill became the lead Sutton case investigator. The meeting included a presentation from Special Agent Hill on the status of the Sutton case. A press release was issued concerning the Albuquerque meeting.

Agent Finley stopped in Raton on his way to his new assignment in Colorado and was visited with a reporter from the *Raton Daily Range*. The interview was published on Thursday, January 14, 1932, and the headline told his story: "Dry Agent Is Moved Over To Denver; C.U. Finley, Special Prober On Sutton Case, Removed To Headquarters." Most of the community took a deep yawn and continued their daily lives.[2]

A New Year and the Raids Continue

The Kearney Task Force investigators in southern Colorado persisted in seeking the killers of Agent Kearney and lost no time in continuing to take action during the post-New Year's holiday season. Inasmuch as the Carlino Brothers were no longer viable, remnants of their defunct criminal associates remained operational. These persons became the new law enforcement targets. Among the listed parties were the Riggio and Ullo crime family members.

Once more the *Raton Daily Range* helped historians by republishing a story from Trinidad's newspaper. On Tuesday, January 19, 1932, the newspaper's readers saw this headline: "Dry Agents Swoop Down On Trinidad–Make Large Hauls In Biggest Raid In Years–10 Arrested." The article recounted how the coordinated raids netted seven men and three women prisoners during the afternoon and evening hours of Saturday, January 16. A squad of Prohibition agents from Pueblo targeted the communities of Trinidad, Jansen, Sopris, and Starkville, confiscating two automobiles used as load cars, some barroom fixtures and a considerable quantity of beer, wine, whiskey and mash.[3]

It was further reported that the government undercover men had been in the Trinidad area on numerous occasions scouting the locations during the weeks preceding the raid. The federal agents booked their prisoners into the Las Animas County jail and placed the confiscated items in the custody of the authorities at the courthouse. The agents returned to Pueblo and the bootlegger cases moved to the prosecutor's office and the federal court system.

Authors' Perspective: One of the seven men arrested in the January 16, 1932, raid was Sam Ullo of Starkville, Colorado. The authors are uncertain if he was the same Sam Ullo arrested in Raton, New Mexico, by Ray Sutton on August 26, 1930, two days before his disappearance. When you connect the dots—the Raton still operator using the name Sam Ullo had been identified from leads developed by Sutton while assisting the Kearney Task Force with an early August 1930 raid near Trinidad—it is highly probable the two men were one and the same man.

The Reorganized Sutton Investigation Team Takes the Field

By mid–January 1932, Special Agent W.L. Hill had contacted local law enforcement authorities in Colfax and Union Counties and briefed them on the federal government's new line of action in support of the Sutton case investigation. He discussed the new regional structure and its purpose from the federal perspective. The basics of the investigation were to remain the same; however, all *federal* case documentation would be moved to the Union County sheriff's office from Raton in view of the possible Colfax County security breach within the district attorney's office. Raton would remain as the operational and jurisdictional search center. A new multi-pronged investigative campaign was inaugurated.

Eighteen months had passed since Ray Sutton's disappearance and a new media campaign was proposed to reignite awareness of the investigation. Colfax County District Attorney Fred C. Stringfellow issued a press notice to regional and national media that all the previously offered rewards remained in effect and asked for citizens' information. Additionally, the federal government printed and mailed a new reward notice to all law enforcement agencies and departments in the country.

In a second prong of attack, Hill launched a newly developed program to "track" local crime figures in order to learn their operations—what they're doing and when they're doing it. He ordered new surveillance and intelligence gathering operations to begin in earnest but done so as to preclude the target's attention. Hill's instructions were explicit, if the tracking is blown in any way, the tracker was to terminate the surveillance immediately and discontinue his observation efforts. He specified that if a surveillance is blown, the officer is to document where and when it began and ended. A new effort may be taken up later in that same area in hopes that the subject would continue to follow his same route. All surveillance and intelligence efforts might be followed up by a detailed incident report for proper record keeping and later review for additional leads.

Further, any publicity on the seizures of stills in the counties were to be minimized; but evidence, such as the stills themselves, were to be brought to town during the daytime, out in the open, for everyone to see. The target subjects, if they were not arrested onsite, were to remain under observation prior to and after any seizure in order to see what they do once they know they've lost another still or load. Agent Hill stressed the need for all the agencies to work together if the mission was to be accomplished.

Under Hill's plan, the first raid came quickly. In the third week of January 1932, the *Raton Daily Range* recorded the incident with a simple low-key notice: "A large still big enough to make approximately 500 gallons of liquor was brought to Raton recently by Prohibition Agent Sid Huddleston from near Wagon Mound. The still was uncovered by the dry agent at Shoemaker [in Mora County] and brought here." Wagon Mound had been established in the mid–1830s by the Mexican government as a custom checkpoint along the Santa Fe Trail. They collected fees for imported whisky shipped from St. Louis to *La Villa Real de la Santa Fe de San Francisco de Asis*.[4]

The Hunt Intensified

Meanwhile, the federal effort to locate the whereabouts of the bootleggers continued. The major focus was centered on finding the Elias Albert "Al" Shedoudy family of Raton and the Wright brothers from Colfax County's Moreno Valley region.

Joe McAllister, the Raton slaughterhouse owner, became the first *bona fide* John Campanella gang member targeted by law enforcement during the 1932 Sutton investigation reboot. In the beginning days of the new surveillance program, the data collected on McAllister indicated that he spent a great deal of time with Campanella and appeared to be less concerned about concealing his movements and activities than did Campanella.

> **Authors' Perspective:** It was determined that officials in Colfax and Union Counties still maintained Sutton investigative files among their historic records on into the 1970s and beyond. Within these remaining documents no information was located explaining why neither Joe McAllister nor John Campanella received an in-depth interview by federal agents or local authorities prior to mid–1932. Hindsight would suggest this oversight was a tremendous misstep on the part of investigators.
>
> Federal records suggest but are unclear as to whether McAllister or Campanella

were targets of any federal telephone intercepts. These investigative records indicated that early in the search for the killers of Kearney and Sutton, Deputy Administrator Stearns had recommended telephone intercepts in his original plan to Regional Administrator John Vivian—another misstep due to the manpower-intensive requirements such an operation would have required. Remember, such types of investigative techniques were in their infancies in the 1920s and 1930s. Rules were made, tried, used or rejected, and adjudged by the various courts almost in a catch-as-catch-can situation until the mid–1930s.

Affidavit of Joe McAllister

On Sunday morning July 10, 1932, federal agents intercepted and detained Joe McAllister while he drove southbound from Raton toward Springer. Rather than conduct his interview in Colfax County, Hill and his immediate team chose to transport him to their Des Moines "sub-office" some 82 miles to the East in Union County. This way, any chance that his detention would be noticed by his cohorts and reported to Joe Campanella would be minimized.

The interview between Hill and McAllister began shortly after noon and lasted only a few hours before the butcher broke down and gave the investigating team a signed statement pertaining to the Sutton kidnapping and murder. McAllister made it clear that he was not involved in any murder. Special Agent Hill took Joe McAllister's signed, handwritten statement and had it typed in affidavit format. The original was signed by McAllister and Hill before witness. A few carbon copies were also produced for select distribution.[5]

The verbatim text of Joe McAllister's affidavit, dated July 10, 1932, follows:

Before me the undersigned authority for taking affidavits of this character personally appeared Joe McAllister, who after being duly sworn deposes and says, that he is a citizen of Colfax County, Raton, New Mexico, and in regard to the murder of Prohibition Agent Ray Sutton has the following to say.

That just after July 22 1930 at which time John Campanela [sic] was arrested, he came to me and suggested that I assist him in killing Ray Sutton, I refused to have anything to do with this idea, Campanela then said that he had been giving Perry Caldwell money to pay Sutton with and [he] should not have been arrested, that he was going to kill both Caldwell and Sutton if he had to go to prison.

A short time before Campanela went to Albuquerque to Federal Court, he and Perry Caldwell met at my house in Raton, Caldwell agreed to assist Campanela in getting Sutton out alone, and to do this Caldwell suggested to Campanela that he be friendly with Sutton and offer to give him information regarding location of stills in Colfax County, also at this meeting there was much talk as to what they would do with the body.

Campanela talked to Caldwell again at my house on Aug. 27, 1930 and told Calweel he had tried three time [sic] to get Sutton out in the vicinity of Cimarron, but that each time he would bring others with him and he did not want to do the job when others were with him, Caldwell then told him he would bring him out near Cimarron and they could do as [they] liked with him.

Sutton was murdered by Campanela and three other wops on the night of Aug. 28. Campanela has told me this several times since then, he also told me that they buried the body near Cimarron and a place where it never could be found, he said that Caldwell assisted them in disposing of the body, he also told me that Caldwell took a Government check from the body together with a ring and some other money including a $20. gold piece.

Campanela also told me that he had spent a large sum of money assisting Caldwell in getting out of trouble at the time they had him charged with forgery on the check (sic), also that he had to furnish the money to fix the Jury with a [sic] Pueblo.

Campanela also told me that if Caldwell had not been arrested for cashing the check and the fact that they found the $20. gold piece on Caldwell that they would have "Got Him" [Campanella] for the murder of Ray Sutton.

/s/ Joe McAllister
W.L. Hill, Special Agent

Upon completion of his interrogation and his signing of the affidavit, Joe McAllister was returned to the vicinity of where he had been picked up and released from custody pending further investigation of his statements. At this point, McAllister's affidavit was nothing more than his allegations. It was a document that required verification through supporting evidence and/or additional testimony from others.

The McAllister affidavit was highly confidential, thus only a few copies were made and these were well protected from any disclosure outside the offices of those concerned. Joe McAllister most surely would not have wanted any part of his cooperative statement made public. To do so would have resulted in deadly consequences. The authorities held a hammer over McAllister's head and he never knew when it might be lowered. Once he broke, he had no other choice but to cooperate fully with the federal officers.

Authors' Perspective: The methods used by the federal agents in 1932 should not be judged in light of the methods employed today. The present-day law enforcement requirement to inform a person of their constitutional rights, including having an attorney at any questioning, while in police custody was decades in the future. The Supreme Court ruling *Miranda v Arizona* was issued in 1966 and is known today as "Miranda rights" notification. McAllister had these rights, but officers were not required to remind him of these civil rights in 1932.

Other Leads and Locating Curley Wright

The British statesman Winston Churchill said, "Success is walking from failure to failure with no loss of enthusiasm." This statement seems to be the motto of the agents working the Kearney-Sutton cases as they followed up all leads, even if they came from as far away as Arkansas and Washington State.

Records indicate that Raton officers interviewed an unidentified woman and her two young sons while seeking a man named Allan Lostrah who had lived in the Raton area during the time Ray Sutton disappeared. He had been employed as a "header" in the winter sheep camps in the surrounding mountains. Lostrah was finally tracked down in Walla Walla and held on a warrant issued by Colfax County. The officers questioning provided no useful assistance, but the search does exemplify the local determination to find Ray Sutton. Local and state authorities received many such leads during the active investigation surrounding the Sutton disappearance. Most such tips, however, proved to be hearsay not based on fact and of little or no value to move the case forward.

Meanwhile in Clayton, a letter dated September 8, 1932, was received by Union County Sheriff Gillespie from a G.P. Hathcock stating that he had his "hand on a man in Baxter County [Arkansas] who helped bury Ray Sutton and wanted to know how much the reward was if the body was recovered." It appeared that the new national mailing to law enforcement agencies concerning a $400 posted reward for Sutton's body had generated a response.

Union County Sheriff Tom Gillespie immediately answered the letter saying, "Please do not let this man get away if you think that he has the information." He received no answer to his letter. It was presumed that the Mr. Hathcock was a law enforcement officer, but no one knew for certain. Special Agent Hill was alerted to the inquiry and subsequently contacted Sheriff Jim Martin in Mountain Home, Arkansas. Following their long-distance telephone conversation, a follow-up letter dated September 22, 1932, was sent to Sheriff Martin confirming the details of Hill's request for assistance.

In later communications, it was learned that Hathcock was a farmer and had overheard a field hand say that his friend Curley Wright had helped to bury the body of a "revenuer" killed in New Mexico. Hathcock could not recall the name of the day laborer he had overheard talking.

Meanwhile, William Leonard "Curley" Wright was located living with his family in Tucumcari, New Mexico. A tracking team composed of federal agents out of Albuquerque, along with a number of personnel from Colfax and Union Counties, implemented their plan of attack. In a short time, Curley was arrested on bootlegging charges, transported to Union County, and while so incarcerated was interrogated on November 20 about the Sutton matter by both Stearns and Hill. As with Joe McAllister, Curley Wright would deny any involvement with the Ray Sutton case. His signed and witnessed affidavit is quoted below:

> Before me, the undersigned authority for taking statements of this character, personally appeared this day William Leonard [Curley] Wright, who after being duly sworn deposes and says, that he is a citizen of Tucumcari, Quay County, New Mexico and residing there with his family at this time.
>
> That I purchased a ranch in Moreno Valley near Agua Fria, New Mexico in the year 1930, and harvested a crop from said ranch during the month of August and September, that during the month of September 1930. I read in the newspapers and also heard from conversation with different people that Prohibition Agent Ray Sutton had disappeared, at the time I heard this report I lived in Taos, New Mexico.
>
> That sometime about June 1930 I had a still in the Moreno Valley which was located about 12 miles from Aqua Fria, when John Campanela [sic], my brother Jimmy Wright, or Cuppy Wallace who was there at the still, said [,] "This is John Campanela." Subsequent to my meeting him we had a conversation in general at which time he stated he did not know there was a "distilling outfit" in the Valley. Also that during this conversation he discussed with me the current prices of whiskey about the country, he stayed at the still a short time and left, since that time I have seen Campanela on a number of occasions and talked to him on at least one other occasion. That shortly after June 9th [sic], 1930 at which time the still, above mentioned, was seized by [unreadable] officers, Campanela came to my ranch and ask my son where I was at, also asked him if he knew anything about any corrals. Soon after Campanella was at my ranch. I met him on the highway at which time he ask [sic] me if I knew anything about those barrels that was [sic] in that Dugout [sic], or ask [sic] me if I knew what had happened to them, I told him I did not know anything about them, that I had not been back up there since the still was caught.
>
> That I have never sold or purchased any whiskey from John Campanela, or any other business [sic] in any manner. That I always heard from talk in general that he was able to get $20. per gal for his whiskey, same being of extra high grade. The insinuations were that Campanela rated very high with officials and was protected to some extent.
>
> Sometime in November 1930 I was in Dawson, New Mexico for a load of coal, while there under

the chute with a truck the man who was running the chute remarked that Ray Sutton's car had been found the neght [sic] before, in back of the Kaler [Koehler] coke ovens, covered in brush.

Affiant further says that he does not know E.A. Shedudy [Shedoudy], but has heard from general talk that he was in the whiskey business in the vicinity of Raton and Springer, New Mexico, during the year 1930. That I am well acquainted with Mike Cunico who lives at Taos, New Mexico.

That the day before Thanksgiving day 1929 I was on my way from Amarilla [Amarillo], Texas to Taos, New Mexico, when I was held up in Raton waiting for car repairs. On this occasion I was at a place in Raton, N.M. where liquor was served by some women, several were in my party, and I met Joe McAllister on this occasion, he was at the place above mentioned. I had heard much of him in Taos where he at one time lived and also had heard from general talk that he was considered a rather large liquor operator in Raton, New Mexico.

That I have never been in the State of Arkansas, therefore have not had any trouble of any kind there. That I have never told anyone that I assisted in the burial of Prohibition Agent Ray Sutton, furthermore that I do not have any idea as to who murdered Agent Sutton, one of the straightest officers that I have ever known, although he was friendly with me I always felt that he would catch me as he did all others if he could.

I have had the opportunity of reading this two-page statement and was afforded the opportunity of making any correction I desired and find that it is all true to the best of my knowledge and belief.

Wright's affidavit was reviewed, dated, witnessed, and signed by all the participants. Special Agent Hill sent off a second letter, dated November 20, 1932, to Sheriff Jim Martin at Mountain Home, Arkansas, seeking follow-up information.

Dear Sir:

I wish to thank you for your recent assistance in regard to the investigation being made into the death of Prohibition Agent Ray Sutton, and wish to ask another favor of you regarding same.

We have Curley Wright in custody on another charge and have questioned him at length regarding his connection with the "Mob" that we believe murdered Agent Sutton, he seemingly has told a truthful story of the whole affair, but makes a complete denial of having anything to do with same.

Now if you possible [sic] can immediately ascertain from Mr. Hathcock [the] name of the party that was working down there in that vicinity, [unreadable] who is supposed to have stated that Curley Wright had assisted in the burial of Agent Sutton, it would give us another lead, as we could therefore learn if he [the party there] ever knew or had been with Curley Wright.

Thinking [sic] you in advance for this information.

The response, if any, from Sheriff Martin has not been located. However, it is possible that the unidentified man known to Hathcock had no factual knowledge on the whereabouts of Sutton's remains. Apparently, the "unknown party" in Arkansas who claimed to know Curley Wright and his alleged involvement in the burial of Sutton was nothing more than a personal creation by the unknown person or the sheriff himself.[6]

Authors' Perspectives: The authors have not located any evidence to indicate that the federal government made an offer of immunity or any other agreement with Curley Wright concerning his continued assistance after National Prohibition was repealed. The outcome of his 1932 arrest is unknown. Curley Wright disappeared into the shadows of history.

The End of Joe Roma

On Saturday, February 18, 1933, the Denver Police Department responded to a small residence located at 3504 Vallejo Street within the heart of Denver's Italian district. Shortly after midday, several persons had entered the home of Joe Roma and shot him. Investigators concluded that Roma's killers were positioned on either side of him while he sat in his favorite overstuffed chair. One of the shooters sat on a piano stool next to the piano on Roma's right and the other in a chair across from him. The two gunmen unleashed a volley of .38 and .45 caliber rounds killing him instantly, with six rounds to the head and one to the body. He was 37 years old.[7]

The prime suspects, Clyde and Eugene (alias "Checkers") Smaldone, Louis Brandisi, and Jim Spinelli, were known associates and strong-arm confederates of Roma. Subsequently, Spinelli, Brandisi, and Eugene Smaldone admitted to police investigators they had visited the deceased on the morning preceding his death. They claimed that their visit had been nothing more than a social call on the "Little Caesar" and that their visit had been coincidental to the murder.[8] They contended that when they departed Roma's home they all had gone to a movie and later ate chili at a local diner. Each denied any knowledge of the killing until they learned of the death later in the evening.[9] The Denver police could not break their alibi. Roma's murder remains unsolved.

The mantle of "boss" in Pueblo passed to Charley Blanda, a member of the mafia crime syndicate. Blanda was considered the first true syndicate boss of Colorado. Under Blanda the crime family's gambling operations grew and the syndicate began to move into other regions encompassing parts of Wyoming and Idaho and became involved in a large-scale nationally known "layoff" pool for bookmakers. Blanda also maintained his criminal ties to the Chicago Outfit and the crime families of Madison, St. Louis, Kansas City and Los Angeles. He died in 1969.[10]

The Smaldones, firmly entrenched in Denver's mob scene, worked closely with the Pueblo crime families and subsequently enlisted Blanda as an ally in dividing Colorado, with Blanda assuming control of the southern section while the Smaldones ruled the northern territories.[11]

The End of Federal Prohibition

The accelerating decline of the national economy enhanced the political impact of the depression and brought a new national administration into power. The voters denied President Herbert Hoover a second term thus ending a 12-year period of Republican political control of the executive branch, ushering in a new progressive Democratic administration. Former New York Governor Franklin Delano Roosevelt (FDR) assumed his duties on Saturday, March 4, 1933. He quickly set forth a series of major economic and organizational reforms under the authority of Presidential Executive Order 6166 which in turn paved the way for a deathblow to the Bureau of Prohibition.

The beginning of the end happened on Saturday, June 10, 1933; on day 98 of his reign as president of the United States, Roosevelt issued Presidential Executive Order 6166 entitled, "Organization of Executive Office." The Bureau of Prohibition was split into two functions. The component concerned with the granting of permits and taxation remained in the Treasury Department as part of the Division of Internal Revenue. The criminal investigative and enforcement agents remained in the Bureau of Prohibition, and effective August 10, 1933, along with J. Edgar Hoover's Bureau of Investigation, composed the newly established "Division of Investigation" within the Department of Justice.[12]

Taps for the Dry Agents

Although it was not provided for as part of the National Prohibition Act in 1919, a federal prohibition enforcement unit was established in 1920 within the Internal Revenue Service of the Department of the Treasury administratively. Over time the Prohibition enforcement unit evolved from its original designation within Treasury's Bureau of Internal Revenue to become a separate bureau within the Department of Justice, Division of Investigation. On December 5, 1933, four months following this organizational shift ordered by President Roosevelt's Executive Order 6166, ratification of the Twenty-First Constitutional Amendment repealed the Eighteenth Amendment and brought National Prohibition to an end. The results were devastating to the personnel of the prohibition enforcement bureau.

By mid–1934, the final restructuring within the Justice Department's Division of Investigation led to a complete phase-out of the prohibition enforcement personnel. A reassigned investigative component had been newly charged with the responsibility to maintain oversight on alcohol tax collection and enforcement efforts as part of the new Alcohol Tax Unit of the Bureau of Internal Revenue. Any open Prohibition enforcement cases were closed or transferred to the succeeding agencies.[13]

> **Authors' Perspective:** Following the sudden abolishment to the Prohibition Bureau, Mrs. Ray Sutton found herself without any contact as to the disposition of her husband's murder investigation. In a state of anxiety, she offered a personal $500 cash reward to anyone providing her with information leading to the identification and recovery of her husband's body. She promised to ask no questions. It was 1934 and she wanted closure and to properly bury her husband. Sadly, no one came forward to claim her reward.

16

Conspiracy of Silence

"You can't go back and make a new start, but you can start right now and make a brand-new ending."—James R. Sherman, *Rejection*, 1982

Dateline: Colorado and New Mexico, 1935–Present

Following the end of Prohibition, the federal investigation of Ray Sutton's murder remained open and appears to have been headed by the Bureau of Internal Revenue Service. It remained in the limbo, sometimes active, other times inactive as late as 1963 when the Albuquerque FBI office interjected an inquiry into the case. Certain key suspects were still living at the time. On the other hand, the federal investigation of the Kearney matter had been closed administratively when all known or suspected principals were either deceased or unidentifiable. Exactly when Colorado's Las Animas County sheriff's office and New Mexico's Colfax County sheriff's office terminated their investigations is unknown.

Capitalizing on the earlier successes of Prohibition Special Agent Walter L. Hill and his efforts in obtaining signed affidavits from two associated crime subjects, the local enforcement authorities continued to plod on in the murder investigation of Ray Sutton. Eventually, the old federal cases faded away and began their fall to the "cold case" graveyard. Pressures from various local and federal political power centers slowly morphed into the new maxim: "What was in the past, leave in the past!"

New Mexico local and federal officers rejected this dictum. They were determined in their mission as they silently observed old suspects and sought out new information they hoped would provide verifiable cause to facilitate the prosecution of former members of the John Campanella crime organization. As with most states, New Mexico has no statutes of limitations for murder. The Colfax County sheriff's office kept the Sutton case active for several years until other issues and events became higher priorities.

Sutton's surviving colleagues, Charles H. Stearns, Clarence U. Finley, Walter L. Hill, and others, believed that if justice was to be achieved for their friend they must keep the investigation active, even if it was on their own time. The known and suspected "persons of interest" and their associates had to believe that they could not get away with murdering a federal agent. Those persons needed to keep looking over their shoulders and listening for the federal drum beat signaling their final resolution and takedown.

1936: The Devil's Wash Basin Search

The last major search in New Mexico for Ray Sutton's remains occurred in early April 1936. Clyde Tingley, New Mexico's popular two-term Democrat governor, received a written tip through an unnamed informant who claimed knowledge of where Ray Sutton's body may have been deposited. The governor directed Chief Ely J. House of the recently formed New Mexico State Police to verify or refute the information. The letter indicated that the informant had personally observed bootleggers dispose of a body, covered in a tarpaulin and wrapped with barbed wire, that he believed to be that of Sutton. The incident took place at a remote rock quarry lake called Devil's Wash

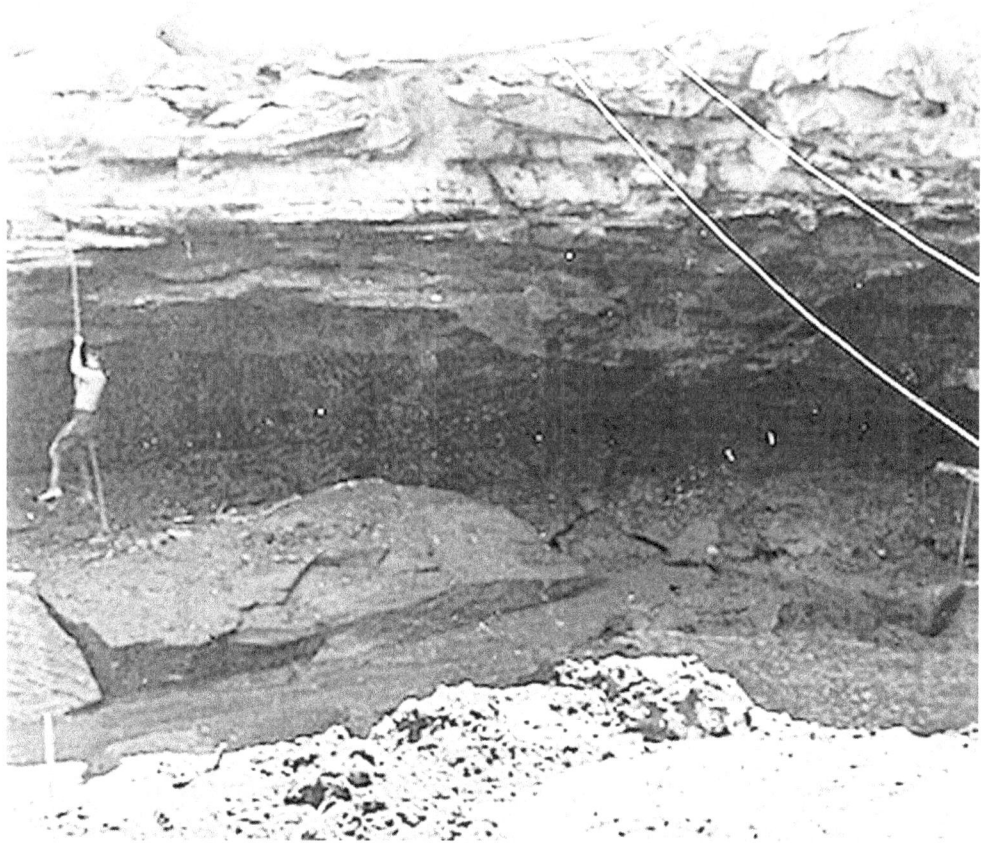

Searching Devil's Wash Basin near Des Moines, New Mexico. A New Mexico state policeman, searching for Ray Sutton's body, is rappelling down the cliff to reach the bottom of this remote water pit (courtesy the Historical Law Enforcement Archives of Sergeant Ronald Taylor, New Mexico State Police, retired, Historian of the NMSP).

Basin located in Union County near the New Mexico-Colorado border northwest of Des Moines. The informant also reported he had seen the remnants of an old discarded still in the basin.

Access to the lake was extremely difficult. The majority of the search team and equipment had to be lowered over 100 feet by rope and pulley in order to set up a viable pumping operation to drain the body of water. The searchers used small rowboats to navigate the lake until the water level allowed waist deep wading. A small tractor and winch were used to manipulate a large wedge to move several feet of mud to facilitate explorations once the lake had been sufficiently drained. The effort continued for several weeks.

As with the numerous ground searches and the draining Koehler Lake in Colfax County during 1930 and 1931, the results of the Devil's Wash Basin search proved negative for Sutton's remains. Even though human bones were discovered at the site, the medical examiner determined the relics belonged to two different individuals. Small lengths of barbed wire were also found in or near the drained lakebed, as were the remains of a still that littered the basin floor.

Chief House provided details of the state police investigation to a reporter and the story was published in the *Santa Fe New Mexican* on Saturday, April 23, 1936. The headline read: "Mystery Death In 1930 Is Laid To Liquor Gang–Bootleggers Raised $1,000 to Kill Federal Agent." The Associated Press report said, in part,

> A bootlegging gang which raised a $1,000 "Murder fund" was blamed tonight for the disappearance six years ago of a Federal prohibition agent as New Mexico state police abandoned a search which yielded the bones of two human beings. Chief E.J. House, Jr., of the State constabulary, revealed for the first time his reconstruction of a crime which may never have a sequel in court—the slaying of Agent Ray Sutton.
>
> Lack of *corpus delicti*, Chief House declared, is the vital circumstance which may forever keep from justice the men he believed conspired to do away with an officer who was "too conscientious in duty." The "Devil's Washbasin," an isolated little pool in the northeast corner of New Mexico, yielded slender evidence—three foot bones, a kneecap, some hand bones, and a vertebra. Because they cannot be identified more conclusively, the bones will never stand as evidence in a courtroom, but Chief House felt certain they were those of Sutton and another man, possibly a resident of the area who disappeared about 1927.
>
> "We had our net spread," said House. "We were ready to arrest the several men who contributed to a pot to pay the killers of Ray Sutton, along with the remaining one of the actual killers alive today." He pieced together, from reliable informants, a story of how bootleggers in the sparsely settled region raised a fund of $1,000 as a reward for Sutton's death. The prohibition agent [...] never was seen again. His blood-stained car was found later in a hidden box canyon. His last paycheck was cashed in Colorado over an apparently forged signature. Chief House was informed three men did the actual killing and that two of them are dead.[1]

Authors' Perspective: The results of the New Mexico State Police mission were given to Governor Tingley, but the report is not contained in his public papers in the New Mexico State Records Center and Archives in Santa Fe. The state police case files for that era are still classified. The authors were unable to confirm Chief House's assertion concerning a $1,000 assassin's fund or the data concerning the involvement of three unidentified men involved in the murder as accurate information. In the matter of the human bones found, these new mysteries remain unsolved. The alleged informant who submitted a letter stating the former data about the alleged crime was never identified publicly.

1939: The Murder of Bootlegger George Pobar

The body of George Pobar was discovered alongside a country road near his dairy farm. The one-time bootlegger had been one of the principal suspects in the disappearance of Ray Sutton after the agent's car was found on his leased property. Pobar's family believed that federal "revenuers" killed him because he wouldn't tell the officers anything about the Sutton murder. The "boots" had reason to be concerned that George Pobar, while in a fit of anger or even revenge against his colleagues, might tell what he knew about the murder and the whole area bootlegging operation. He was a loose cannon from time to time.

In the wake of the Pobar murder, agents of the new federal Alcohol Tax Unit opened an investigation into the circumstances surrounding Sutton's death, as well as that of George Pobar's murder, since both cases appeared to be linked. As with the earlier case, so with the new ones, both investigations hit stone walls. The Pobar murder remains officially unsolved.

1931–1962: James Perry and Agnes Jessica "Jessie" Blanchard Caldwell

According to Johnny Caldwell, Perry Caldwell's nephew, the expense of his uncle's defense severely strained his father's (Berlin Caldwell) financial resources. According to the nephew, the trial did not seem to have injured Perry financially. It appears that the nephew had no direct personal knowledge of Perry's finances or activities during his lifetime.

Following his trial, Perry Caldwell is known to have returned to Cimarron. At some point, he may have been hired by a cattle growers' association in Springer to put a stop to rustling in the area. No one knows how successful he was since the records of the group no longer survive, although family members in later years claimed many of these rustlers were brought to justice. Colfax County court records do not support this claim. It is factual to claim that at least 21 human remains were found by hikers during the Sutton investigation ground searches. Rumors wrongly suggested these deaths were the work of Perry Caldwell while employed by the cattlemen. Contemporary scientific testing determined that a vast majority of these remains were from frontier travelers and other unrecorded deaths in the late 1800s.

Although some claim they saw him periodically in Springer and Cimarron, Caldwell's permanent whereabouts cannot be established firmly until 1935. During these years Perry held a "dark reputation" among the residents of Springer and unconfirmed rumors quickly spread that Caldwell made a sudden trip to an unknown location in South America upon hearing about the elder Pobar's murder. If true, the length of his stay remains unknown.[2]

The 1939 *Albuquerque City Directory*, and earlier editions, listed James P. and Agnes J. Caldwell, along with James P. Caldwell, Jr., residing at 421 South Edith Boulevard. This residence appeared to remain valid through 1953. Between 1943 and 1949, available information suggests Caldwell's occupation was as a mechanical engineer. He had provided the *Albuquerque City Directory* with false information that his wife was self-employed as a teacher at her non-existent School for Handicapped and Retarded Children. It is logical to assume that Perry would indicate to anyone who inquired as to Jessie's availability that the school took up a lot of her time because she was frequently coordinating her work with the state mental institution. This appeared to be nothing more than a ruse created by Perry Caldwell—nothing more than an elaborate scheme to hide her confinement as a patient at that very institution.

During the early 1950s, Perry Caldwell changed occupations twice: first, becoming an equipment operator and then a security patrol guard. He and his wife Jessie allegedly resided at their new home at 409 Eleventh Street, Northwest, in Albuquerque's Old Town district. Based upon knowledge of Caldwell's arrogance and bravado, the choosing of this house, in this particular neighborhood, seems more than accidental. The selection was more likely a direct "in-your-face" challenge to Charles H. Stearns. The former deputy regional administrator of the prohibition enforcement unit had lived at 500 Eleventh Street, Northwest, since 1925. His home was one block north of Perry Caldwell's new home.

Should anyone, former neighbors or friends "back home" care to know, it appeared that Perry and his wife had reconciled their earlier differences and were living together in Albuquerque. Occasionally their son James Perry and his wife Velma, whom he married while attending college in Albuquerque during the 1940s, lived with his father.

James P. Caldwell, Jr., became a civil engineer and would go on to a long career with the United States Army Corps of Engineers with assignments in Europe and Washington, D.C. The only Caldwell daughter, Dorothea, studied music in Paris and later taught school in Maryland. The work and education of Caldwell's second son, Robert Carl, is unknown.

1953–1960s: Newspaperman Howard Bryan Keeps the Sutton Case Alive

An *Albuquerque Tribune* reporter named Howard Bryan focused on the Ray Sutton murder in his new weekly historical column "Off the Beaten Path" on August 27, 1953. It was the 23rd anniversary of the incident that stirred emotions across New Mexico. Bryan had located Charles Stearns living in Old Town Albuquerque. The retired federal agent provided Bryan with firsthand knowledge of the case. Over the next two decades Bryan annually reminded his readers of the continuing Ray Sutton mystery.

Authors' Perspective: Hornung first met Bryan in 1968 in the Albuquerque public library's New Mexico History Room at the Edith Street branch when he was preparing an exhibit on Fred Lambert and the New Mexico Mounted Police. Both men were friends of Lambert and they too became friends. In July 2005, when the Western Outlaw-Lawmen History Association held their annual national Shootout (history conference) in Santa Fe, Howard and Chuck co-hosted the fieldtrip to Old Town, Las Vegas. Howard Thornton Bryan, Jr., died in September 2011 and is buried in the Santa Fe National Military Cemetery. He was 91 years old and had published seven books following his retirement as a daily newspaper columnist.

1962–1963: Jessie Caldwell Seeks to Redact Her 1931 Testimony

The truth about Jessie Caldwell's life between 1931 and the late summer of 1962 was hidden from public view, as a result of her husband's farcical manipulation of events for three decades. In the summer of 1962 an ailing Jessie Caldwell was "furloughed" from the New Mexico State Hospital to live with her sister in Albuquerque.

An unexpected spark of renewed interest in the Sutton case surfaced when the two elderly sisters, Agnes Jessie Caldwell and the former Katherine Blanchard Caldwell contacted the Federal Bureau of Investigation field office in Albuquerque, New Mexico. In late summer 1962, the women were interviewed and an active administrative file was opened regarding the possible killing of a federal agent. This was done because the FBI established that a federal agent had been murdered and the FBI had no active open investigation. Agents took the ladies seriously and they began to check their information.

Jessie Caldwell stated that she had been a defense witness in her husband's federal criminal trial at Pueblo, Colorado, in January 1931. She also claimed she had knowingly perjured herself to substantiate the alibi of her husband James Perry Caldwell, Sr. Jessie explained that she desired to recant her trial statements to correct the record. In response to questions from FBI agents, she maintained that the delay in recanting her testimony was due to her long-term hospitalization at the New Mexico State Hospital. She blamed her husband for her continued incarceration.

Jessie explained that following the Pueblo trial, she had suffered a nervous breakdown once she realized that her husband had been complicit in the disappearance and murder of Ray Sutton. With this knowledge, her mental state declined to a point that she had to move from Cimarron to her sister's home in Albuquerque to get away because she feared and no longer trusted her husband. Perry followed her to Albuquerque and subsequently arranged for her commitment.

Records show that Jessie Caldwell spent decades at the state hospital assigned to the Occupational Therapy Department's sewing room, mending garments and making wearing apparel for her fellow inmates. She also braided rugs, participated in drapery weaving, raw wool spinning and making pillow cases and patient restraint belts. Caldwell said that she and her husband were never divorced and they had never resided as man and wife from the time following their departure from Cimarron and her subsequent hospitalization in 1931.

Had Jessie Caldwell been an abused wife and took this opportunity to escape Perry's wrath? Had she been mentally aware and acquiesced to the hospitalization to gain some degree of protection from him? What did she really know about the Sutton case? The answers to these specific questions remain unanswered because Jessie Caldwell died unexpectedly in September 1962.

Authors' Perspective: By March 1963, the Sutton disappearance case had been in an "open" or "inactive" status for almost 33 years. Co-author Charlton, at the time an FBI Special Agent stationed in Dallas, was assigned to review the Sutton case files which at that time were located in the regional office of the Internal Revenue Service in Dallas. He found among the many documents Sutton's personal work ledger, the one left in his hotel room at the time of his disappearance containing the name of James Perry Caldwell. Multiple file boxes composed the collection and appeared to be complete at that time, but there were no assurances or means for Charlton to verify that proposition. The gist of the files linked Caldwell and Campanella among the key suspects alleging that Sutton had possibly "surveilled them to an unknown location and had been kidnapped by them or others and murdered." No definitive proof of guilt of any of the known suspects mentioned within the case files could be located.

Years later, Hornung had discovered confidential affidavits obtained from bootleggers Joe McAllister and William "Curley" Wright and other documents that had not been observed in Charlton's 1963 review. He assumed the McAllister and Wright documents were contained within the larger case file. Or had these affidavits been lost or misplaced in the official files? Or were they purposely made to disappear at some point over the previous decades? The authors cannot answer these questions. Both the FBI Dallas and FBI Albuquerque office files have long since been destroyed or warehoused in accordance with the Bureau's administrative procedures and unavailable to the public. The Albuquerque investigation was terminated shortly after the review report was received and no further action was taken after Jessie Caldwell's death. The authors did not learn of her demise until we were compiling research for this book. Her death at such an early juncture following her hospital release could be considered as another one of the many strange twists to this story.

1968–2005: Hornung's Investigations and Writings about Ray Sutton

Chuck Hornung first met Fred Lambert, the last survivor of the legendary New Mexico Territorial Mounted Police, in the summer of 1967. He began his initial investigation of the Sutton murder while he was researching and writing Lambert's biography. The former territorial/state ranger had served over half a century as a New Mexico peace officer. While reviewing old case documents, Chuck discovered a crime report on Sutton's disappearance so he expanded the scope of his research on the bootlegging era in Colfax County. He was able to locate and interview many first- and second-generation partisans in the Sutton case. Some of these individuals are discussed below:

James Perry Caldwell

Fred Lambert was born and raised in Cimarron and knew the major parties involved in the Sutton disappearance investigation. He knew the Caldwell family from his school days in Springer. When he served as Cimarron's town marshal, he had arrested a couple of the brothers who had been partying too hard at a saloon operated by John Campanella in the Mexican section located along the river dividing Old Town from the New Town section.

In the spring of 1968, Fred Lambert required surgery for an eye injury and recuperated at Hornung's home. During the recovery, Lambert arranged for Chuck to interview Perry Caldwell. The two men met in Old Town Albuquerque with one stipulation, no audio or film recording would be made. Caldwell, then 73 years old, was still a big powerful man with a natural smile. Decades later, Hornung recalled that evening.

> I didn't know about Mrs. [Jessie] Caldwell or the McAllister and Wright affidavits concerning Ray Sutton's murder when I met Perry Caldwell. If I had known these things we would have had a very different conversation. At the time I was primarily interested in Mr. Caldwell's recollections about the early 1900s development of new town Cimarron and the railroad building to the site. I knew his family had a history of local police work, so a secondary focus was his views concerning police methods in the Prohibition era. At the time, I was focused on material for my Lambert biography, not on Ray Sutton's murder or even Mr. Caldwell himself.
>
> As I recall that evening my first impression has not changed. I have no doubt that I played a few games of pool with a man of lethal nature. I looked into the old man's steel gray eyes and saw death. I believe Perry Caldwell was an obdurate criminal. He acted the part of a gentleman and answered my questions about Lambert and Cimarron very frankly. Then he changed the subject to "the elephant" in the room and became circumspect.
>
> Over the rest of the evening, in a third-person narrative, I learned his account of what happened to Federal Prohibition Agent Ray Sutton. I didn't know enough about the case then to ask pointed questions, but he explained his version of events pretty clearly. I had no idea why Mr. Caldwell felt I might be interested in a 40-year-old murder mystery. Even while talking and a few drinks, he still won a decisive match. When we finished the games, I owed Mr. Caldwell 20 bucks for the lessons in the fine art of pool. He finished his tale and smiled saying, "You know the truth, but you'll never be able to prove it." His remark was spoken almost as a challenge. I had just heard an old man's tale of yesteryear describing the events of a long ago murder I understood little about and now he was daring me to prove the truth of his tale.
>
> At that point I was not interested in proving anything concerning the Sutton murder case. However, I was cognizant enough to understand I could not prove anything without supporting evidence. Caldwell had planted the seed that caused me to look closer. At the time I was unaware that federal authorities still had a cold case file on Sutton's death.
>
> When we finished our conversation, we shook hands at the door and Mr. Caldwell said, "Sleep well tonight, because that dammed Sutton sure is." I believed him then and after all these years I still believe his tale. I never saw or talked to him again.

Caldwell told Hornung that Sutton's remains were buried under the newly paved Raton-Cimarron highway, a few miles northeast of the Colfax ghost town site toward the old Hoxie Junction. Caldwell maintained that each time he drove over the paved gravesite he would roll down his car window and spit out the window to show his contempt and disrespect of Agent Ray Sutton.

Caldwell, the last living suspect in the disappearance of Ray Sutton, had discussed a dark moment in his life with a young man he did not know. Why would Caldwell do this? Hindsight would suggest that Caldwell, an old man at the time of the interview, knew that he had nothing to fear since he had outlived all witnesses and he knew of no evidence that could prove his guilt. Four years after the Caldwell interview, Hornung located the McAllister and Wright affidavits and realized that Perry Caldwell had verified the events discussed in these 1932 documents. It was only after he began collaboration with Charlton that Hornung learned that Mrs. Caldwell recanted her alibi for her husband but died before the FBI conducted a brief re-examination of the case.

Mrs. Fred Stringfellow

Virginia Mae Payne Stringfellow of Brazil, Indiana, and Fred Conway Stringfellow of North Little Rock, Arkansas, had been born within a month of each other in the fall of 1898. They met, married and settled to raise three children in Raton. Stringfellow was an attorney and served as district attorney for the Eighth Judicial District (Colfax and Taos Counties) during the early stage of the Sutton murder investigation. Stringfellow and Ray Sutton had been friends. Hornung recalled Mrs. Stringfellow:

> Ranking high among the people I enjoyed interviewing during my investigation of the Ray Sutton murder was Mrs. Virginia Stringfellow. She was a gracious person and a true lady. She was a Hoosier gal having been born on a Southwestern Indiana farm and I was a Kentucky farm boy, so we had our rural country heritage in common. Her varied interests were amazing and I felt lucky that she liked and trusted me.
>
> I asked her if we might talk about what she recalled of her late husband's part in the investigation. Mrs. Stringfellow explained that her husband had been very frustrated by the case and the information he knew and the inability of law enforcement officers to provide the corroboration he needed to prosecute the case.
>
> She asked me about my biography of Fred Lambert. I told her that since Fred Lambert's death I had shelved working on the biography because I found it too hard to emotionally deal with at that time. She asked how I had become interested in the murder of Ray Sutton for my weekly historical column in the *Raton Daily Range*. I told her Lambert had helped me talk with Perry Caldwell a few years earlier and that some other Cimarron people last year (1970) who knew about the incident gave me information for my book.
>
> Mrs. Stringfellow told me her husband had preserved some documents key to his Sutton case and a small box of Ray's mementoes including a shell casing. She asked if I wished to see these things and I said yes. I freely admit feeling sadness as I examined these physical reminders that Agent Sutton had been a real person and not just a name attached to official reports.
>
> One of the key papers I found in Mr. Stringfellow's Sutton case file was a copy of a one-page affidavit given by suspected co-conspirator Joe McAllister to Special Agent W.L. Hill. If District Attorney Stringfellow ever presented the contents of McAllister's statement to a Colfax County Grand Jury no action was taken against the persons the turncoat bootlegger had accused of murder. I found the document intriguing. Admittedly the affidavit was not hard evidence but coupled with what I had learned from Perry Caldwell it made a strong *prima facie* case for murder. Mrs. Stringfellow allowed me to copy the document.
>
> Mrs. Stringfellow and I never discussed the Sutton case again after that visit. That day she suggested that I just let this story fade into history. She said that she had made the same request of her husband when his investigation had reached a stone wall and she felt the stress of that case helped to shorten his life. Her husband hadn't listened to her advice and she suspected that I would not also.
>
> Mrs. Stringfellow's request did, however, cause me to rethink some of the information I had uncovered, but lacked court admissible evidence to support. I had no intention of using it in the current story I had almost completed writing, because I needed to find out more about the affidavit before I would consider publishing it. Years later, I did use some of this information in updated articles for historical journals. Decades later more hidden secrets finally gave a clearer picture to the story I discovered in the early 1970s.

Sheriff J. Riley Hughes

A short time after finding the Sutton case file held by Mrs. Stringfellow, Hornung was in Clayton doing research at the courthouse. He also visited former Union County Sheriff J. Riley Hughes, a past president of the New Mexico Sheriffs' and Police Association, who allowed Hornung to review his Sutton investigation file and let him make thermal-fax copies of the contents of the file. There was one stipulation: Hornung could not publish any of the information in the file as long as any of the principals were still alive. These documents supplemented the ones in the Stringfellow file. Hornung honored Hughes' request.

The Wards

Zenas P. Ward and his wife Margaret of Cimarron provided information about the highway paving project being conducted between Cimarron and Raton during the fall of 1930. Ward was the state highway project manager who gave Caldwell a job on the project. The Wards were the classic Western storybook couple; he was the cowboy/deputy sheriff who married the school teacher. Margaret's family were early settlers of Cimarron and she wrote two books about her life on the New Mexico frontier. Zenas died on New Year's Eve in 1972 and Margaret passed in 1977. They are buried in Cimarron's Mountain View Cemetery.

James T. Lail

James T. Lail was the CS Ranch range foreman in 1930. He had married Mary Elizabeth Whiteman Gimson, a divorcee who was 14 years his junior, and they lived a happy life until his death in November 1960. She died in 1974. They are buried together in Cimarron's Mountain View Cemetery. Mary Lail recalled that her husband had asked his fence riders to keep a sharp eye for any signs of Sutton's body or missing car. Rafael Zamora, a CS cowboy, found the car. Mrs. Lail and Henry Grant, Zamora's friend, described the car's hiding site and later Hornung was able to visit the site to gain insight into how the car remained hidden for so long. The visit helped him to understand how John Pobar could have become confused in his attempt to locate the vantage point where he claimed to have witnessed men hiding Sutton's automobile.

Other Research

Over a six-month period in 1972, Hornung visited old still sites in Taos, Colfax, Mora, Harding, and Union Counties escorted by some of the region's "Old Timers." He also spent time with J.B. McNeil, former Harding County sheriff, who recalled Sutton and their adventures hunting moonshiners in the flatlands of the state's least-populated county. Ray Marty, former Las Animas County sheriff, talked about the dry agents in southern Colorado and the Ku Klux Klan. Joe Marchiondo, then a successful Raton businessman, recalled how the moonshiners hated Sutton's guts because he was a non-bribable officer. A middle-aged Joe Campanella, John's second oldest son, and Fred Lambert took Hornung on a lighthearted discussion about the Prohibition Era in Cimarron.[3]

Newspaper Series

When the three-part *Raton Daily Range* series on the Ray Sutton mystery was published in the fall of 1971, it became the major topic of conversation around the office water cooler/coffee pot on Monday mornings. Lively discussion also took place at senior citizen centers in the region as old journeys were relived. Long-forgotten shadows crossed the dinner table of many families as buried secrets came alive for new generations.

Hornung experienced a low-key, but direct, attempt by the two sons of Joseph

Thomas DiLisio, founder of a banking and department store enterprise in Colfax County, to terminate his research into the Sutton disappearance. He was asked "not to stir the caldron too hard" because some of the families who had been involved in those events four decades before were now respected pioneer families of their communities. It was suggested that if he continued, someone could get hurt as a result. It was unclear if the comment was meant in a general manner or that physical harm, damage to reputation, or family embarrassment could come the author's way. Hornung recalled those events for this work:

> I had known Charles DiLisio since I brought my family to live in Raton. I did my banking with him and he helped me to finance a new home on the north mesa. He enjoyed my weekly newspaper column about the area's history and we worked well together raising funds for the area's Boy Scout program and the annual Junior Miss Pageant, which my wife and I hosted. So, I was surprised by his unenthusiastic reaction to our Sutton story. He suggested that I let this story slide into history because four decades, a whole generation, had transpired and things were different now. I told him I had finished writing the series and that the series was intended as just an overview of the incident—not a full-blown exposé. The matter was dropped.
>
> Charles' younger brother, whom I barely knew, demand I drop the story. I was really confused. I didn't understand why he wanted me to side-line a 40-year-old incident in Raton's history—a colorful history filled with street gunfights, killing a town marshal, public lynchings and vigilante reprisals. The Sutton story was just another episode in the saga I had been recording for the paper's readers. By 1971, I had heard the old rumors that the bank was used by local "bootleggers" as a repository, but I had found nothing to directly connect the DiLisio family to these illegal Prohibition Era activities and sure did not suspect any association with the Sutton case. The DiLisio brothers had told me that I might find out who killed Sutton, but that I would never be able to prove it.
>
> After a frank discussion with Gene Wisner, the *Raton Daily Range*'s publisher and Ed Murray, the editor, it was decided the newspaper would not "stir the caldron" with further articles featuring more in-depth details after the three-part story ended. The newspaper series was published as I originally wrote it—a simple straightforward story with few in-depth details or analysis. An epilogue concluded the story.
>
> A few weeks after the Sutton newspaper series ended and a new one started I discovered the McAllister affidavit. At this point my professional career and family concerns took charge of my life and the Sutton project lay dormant for decades.

In 1991, Hornung updated his newspaper research and wrote an expanded account of the Sutton murder for the *Journal of the National Outlaw-Lawman History Association*. This was the first time the McAllister and Wright affidavits were mentioned in connection with the Sutton murder case. This NOLA treatise was followed by a paper presented at the 2005 annual conference of the Historical Society of New Mexico held in Clayton. The HSNM presentation included for the first time information about Chuck's meeting with "Mr. C" and other new data.[4]

At this point, Hornung placed his research notes in storage and moved on to other writing projects and a new career. Another decade would pass before the Sutton story once more took center stage in his life.

2001–2009: Raymond Ellsworth "Bud" Sutton

Raymond Ellsworth "Bud" Sutton, Ray Sutton's grandson, was located by Lee Charlton in 2001. Bud had served as an assistant United States attorney and had been the acting United States attorney in Las Vegas, Nevada, 1963–1964. Bud Sutton indicated that he had returned to private practice in 1964 from which he subsequently retired. Over the next three years, he provided family histories, copies of family photographs, and documents which were retrieved from a long-stored collection of his grandmother's belongings. A portion of the collection consisted of newspaper articles amassed over the years by family relatives of Maggie Mae Sutton who were still living in Oklahoma. Among these articles were Hornung's three-part newspaper series on the Sutton investigation. This newspaper series led Charlton to contact Hornung in 2013.

Raymond Ellsworth "Bud" Sutton died in 2015 without having read this manuscript. His wife has cooperated with the authors on this project.

17

The Final Trail Markers

"At what point does the past and the present merge to form a stage for the play to begin again with the players in different form to a same end."—B. Lee Charlton

The march of history continues to move forward as nearly nine decades have passed since the murders of Prohibition Agents Ray Sutton and Dale Kearney. Also, death has claimed the main protagonists in the two mysteries including many of those in the second and third generations. Bitter family feelings have faded with the wind. Any remaining investigation records are stored and contemporary newspapers lay yellowing in libraries and archives, while the turmoil they preserve is forgotten by present-day historians. Fact and legend have now become so intertwined that truth is hard to discover. As individual trails end, the historian's task becomes more arduous. This epilogue updates the authors' half-century of research and draws to a close our collective narrative. A few of the major guideposts follow:

The File Closes on Major Colorado Participants in the Kearney-Sutton Drama

Frances E. Brown Kearney

Mrs. Dale Kearney was 30 years old when she became a widow; she never remarried. She raised her two daughters with the help of her parents and she became a grandmother. Frances Kearney died on October 4, 1976, and was buried in the Mountain View Cemetery at Longmont, Colorado, along with her husband and her namesake baby girl who had died in August 1925.[1]

Regional Administrator John F. Vivian

A native of Phoenix Mine, Michigan, Vivian died in Golden, Colorado, in 1954 at age 90. He was buried next to his wife, Addie, in the Golden City Cemetery. For John, the Kearney and Sutton murder cases became symbols of personal failure and no one with John F. Vivian's ego would acknowledge such a loss.

In November 1938, John Charles Vivian, his son, was elected Colorado's lieutenant governor, second in leadership behind his father's political nemesis Ralph Lawrence Carr. In January 1943, Lieutenant Governor Vivian succeeded Carr to become Colorado's 30th state governor and was reelected and served until 1947. He was a World War I Marine Corps veteran. His brother Chauncey served as an editor of the *Denver Times* and the *Rocky Mountain News*. John Charles Vivian and his wife Maude are also buried in the Golden City Cemetery. He died in 1964.[2]

United States Attorney Ralph Lawrence Carr

In 1933, Franklin D. Roosevelt's new Democratic administration quickly moved to appoint a loyal Democrat to replace Carr as the head of Region 10's Office of the United States Attorney in Denver. Ralph Carr left office and immediately entered private law practice in the Greater Denver area and recharged his work as a freemason. Among his clientele was Clyde Smaldone, one of the successors to the Roma crime family.[3]

Carr had been born in Conejos County, Colorado, in December 1887, a hotbed for the Black Hand Society. He grew up in Antonito, the county seat, and was a good student and became a believer in Christian Science as a way of life. Carr served eight years as Conejos County attorney before he was appointed Colorado's United States attorney.

In 1937, Carr represented Clyde Smaldone and Charlie Stephens, a co-conspirator, in a case stemming from their theft of a cigarette truck, presumably with a load of tobacco products, and an undetermined quantity of popcorn. The defendants were tried before Judge Henry A. Hicks. Both were adjudged guilty on all charges and sentenced to the Colorado State Penitentiary at Canon City. As the defendant's attorney, Carr would maintain that the Hicks Court had run roughshod over the defendants and that they did not get a fair trial. Carr was cognizant of Smaldone's prior criminal background before he represented him.

In 1929, his office had prosecuted the Smaldone Brothers on prohibition violations and followed the activities of the many organized crime families during his tenure as the United States attorney. In 1938, Carr was elected governor of Colorado and served until January 12, 1943. As governor, Carr loudly pledged to the voters that he would break with the tradition of giving Christmas pardons to convicted criminals as had been practiced by his predecessors. However, near the end of his second gubernatorial term Carr commuted the sentence or pardoned 17 state criminals; seven of the total were rapists.

Governor Carr had been successful in balancing Colorado's state budget during his service as the Centennial State's chief executive and received national attention for these efforts. In 1942, his lieutenant governor, John Vivian, pushed him to run for the United States Senate against the Democratic incumbent and former Colorado governor, Edwin C. Johnson. He lost this bid.

Earlier others in Washington had pushed him as a candidate for vice president of the United States based on his economic successes in Colorado. Former president Herbert Hoover and others were looking for Republicans to voice opposition to President Roosevelt's New Deal programs. He began receiving speaking engagements all over the country preaching his message of fiscal responsibility. In June 1940 at the Republican National Convention in Philadelphia, Wendell Willkie of Indiana won the nomination over frontrunners Ohio senator Robert A. Taft, the son of the late president William Howard Taft; Thomas Dewey, a crime-fighting district attorney from New York; and Michigan senator Arthur Vandenberg. All three had courted the first-term Colorado governor's support before they ever arrived in Philadelphia.

Adam Schrager, author of *The Principled Politician: The Ralph Carr Story*, claims that Willkie and Carr discussed the vice presidency in the nominee's suite in the Benjamin Franklin Hotel. Willkie showed his common sense in this selection: he was based in the East while Carr was a western politician; both men were fiscal conservatives and believed government should be run as a business. Carr didn't accept the invitation. Instead, he chose to run again for governor. He won that race in 1940 by a margin of 55,000 votes. Willkie won the state of Colorado and more votes than any previous Republican candidate in a national election paired against FDR, but he still lost the national election.

On December 24, 1942, just 19 days before Carr's second gubernatorial term expired, he pardoned Clyde Smaldone and Charlie Stephens. They had served five years of their original sentence. Carr's reasoning for the pardons echoed his earlier claim that Judge Hicks had not given his former clients a fair trial. Based on Carr's action, a new question arises: How long had this Carr-Smaldone relationship existed?

Following the prison release of his former defendant and the end of his gubernatorial term of office, Carr and Smaldone maintained a friendship until their deaths. Both men would attend the wedding of Pueblo mobster Charlie Blanda's daughter. At the wedding, Carr and Smaldone arrived in the same car driven by Carr's chauffeur and were together throughout the wedding ceremony and reception. Carr had become, or possibly always had been, one of the many "friends" of mob boss Clyde Smaldone.

Ralph L. Carr left the governor's mansion on January 12, 1943, and retired from public service until 1950, when he once again received the Republican nomination for governor of Colorado. Carr died on September 22, 1950, before the general election. He and his wife are buried in Denver's Fairmont Cemetery. The couple's only child, Ralph, died in Albuquerque, New Mexico, in April 2005.[4]

The File Closes on Major New Mexico Participants in the Kearney-Sutton Drama

Maggie Mae Walton Sutton

The year 1930 had been one of sorrow for Maggie Sutton; she lost three family members. First, her mother died and then she lost her husband. According to her grandson Bud Sutton, Maggie lost her granddaughter, Rayma Jeanne Means, due to unknown causes, within six weeks of Ray's disappearance.

Following her husband's disappearance and presumed death, Mrs. Sutton remained in Clayton residing at the family's white clapboard home at 405 Oak Street. During her years as a widow, she worked as a seamstress at the J.C. Penney's store on Front Street, across from the historic Luna Theater, just a few blocks from her home. She devoted her spare time to the activities of the First Methodist Church, the Eastern Star (she was Worthy Matron at the time of her husband's death), the Twentieth Century Club, and housework and friends.

In her later years, Maggie lived with her daughter Nello and her grandchildren in Kingman, Arizona. A few months before her death, she returned to Clayton where she died at the Mayfield Rest Home on September 25, 1955, at the age of 81. It had been a long journey from her birthplace in Cedar County, Iowa. She is buried in Clayton.[5]

Raymond George "Bud" Sutton

Maggie and Ray's son died in 1980 at the age of 79 after a long illness and hospitalization at the Veterans Administration Hospital in Denver. He is buried in the family plot in Clayton, alongside his mother, his younger sister Hazel Ann, and his father's empty grave.[6]

Nello M. Sutton Means Gilman

Nello had two known children by her marriage to Raymond Webster Means: George Means and Rayma Jeanne Means. During World War II, at the age of 43, Nello served in the Women's Army Auxiliary Corps (WAAC), a 150,000-member all-women corps to supply additional resources needed in the military and industrial sectors during the world conflict. Her son, Ray, served as a first lieutenant navigator on B-29 bombers in World War II. Following her divorce from her dentist husband Raymond Means, Nello remarried and moved to Kingman, Arizona. Her ex-husband followed and opened a barber or beauty shop, having given up dentistry. She remarried and her fate and those of the surviving members of her family remain unknown to the authors.[7]

John Campanella

John Campanella died Monday, October 12, 1953, at Cimarron, New Mexico, ten days short of his 70th birthday and just six days following the death of his wife, Mary. Causes of their deaths are unknown. The couple were buried in Cimarron's Mountain View Cemetery and the joint gravesite is marked with a marble monument. He was born October 22, 1883, while his wife Mary was born February 2, 1893.[8]

Always a target of investigation as a result of the Joe McAllister and Curley Wright affidavits, Campanella was never brought to trial for his alleged involvement with the Sutton kidnapping and murder. Allegedly, Treasury Department special agents were present at the hospital the day he died, seeking to obtain a deathbed confession from John Campanella regarding his part in Ray Sutton's disappearance. It never happened.

Joseph Thomas "Giuseppe" DiLisio

"Mr. Raton" died in the community he loved on February 26, 1972, at the age of 83.[9] He had been born on March 19, 1885. His wife Cristina Pone had been born in Italy on December 21, 1890. She died on November 24, 1975. They are buried side by side in Mount Calvary, Raton's Roman Catholic cemetery.

Mr. DiLisio's son Charles F. DiLisio (b. 1912) died in January 1974 and son Joseph Thomas DiLisio, Jr., (b. 1920) died in 1986.[10]

James Perry Caldwell

Perry Caldwell lived out his days in the Old Town area of Albuquerque. He died of natural causes on November 15, 1973, after a few days in the hospital. He was 83 years old and was buried at the Fairview Cemetery in Albuquerque, not far from the graves of Mr. and Mrs. Charles Stearns.[11]

Agnes Jessica Blanchard Caldwell

A short time after being released from the state hospital, Jessie Caldwell died on September 26, 1962. The 72-year-old was survived by her estranged husband, three children, five grandchildren, and five brothers and three sisters. Following a Seventh-Day Adventist Church service, she was buried in Sunset Memorial Park in Albuquerque. Her grave in Section 13 is marked with a flat headstone.[12]

Joseph "Joe" McAllister

The future status of the Joe McAllister affidavit fell on the shoulders of the Colfax County district attorney following the end of National Prohibition. The decision to pursue McAllister as an immunized viable coconspirator would only be determined if and when a probable cause, with documented proof, could be factually determined. This never occurred. It is believed that he remained as the owner and operator of McAllister's Meat Packing until the operation closed. His end is unknown.

William Leonard "Curley" Wright

Curley Wright gave his deposition and was released from jail at Clayton. He got on a bus headed south to Roswell and disappeared into the shadows of history.

Rafael Zamora

And what of Rafael Zamora, the Charles Springer Cattle Company ranch hand that discovered the hiding place of Ray Sutton's missing vehicle near Cimarron? Between $500 and $700 in reward money had been posted for the discovery of Sutton's car, but no portion of this amount was paid to Zamora or anyone else. It is possible that Zamora never asked for the reward. He may have considered his discovery to be an act of a civic duty, while maintaining a personal sense of pride in his accomplishment. The Zamora family has a plot in Cimarron's Mountain View Cemetery.[13]

Charles H. Stearns

Stearns retired and lived out his life in the Old Town Albuquerque home he had purchased in 1925. He died in December 1958 at age 92 years and is buried with his wife Mary in Albuquerque's Fairview Memorial Park.[14]

Conclusion

> "In this world nothing can be said to be certain, except death and taxes"—Benjamin Franklin to Jean-Baptiste Leroy, November 13, 1789 letter

This book has set forth the authors' discoveries, made along their individual and joint journeys in seeking "the who, what, when, where, why, and how" of the murders of Prohibition Agents Dale F. Kearney and Ray Sutton in the summer of 1930. We began our efforts in the 1960s, taking different paths until 2013 when we joined forces. First, we reviewed our separate inquiries and discovered commonalities in data and opinions. We chose to renew our efforts to close all of the open leads we had generated. This work is the culmination of our efforts.

We discovered information that provided an interactive and complete picture of how and why the crimes occurred and how the official investigations failed to establish the proof of guilt of those responsible. In the end, all the investigators had accomplished was a series of unconfirmed allegations, suspicions and little proof. And in the finality of our efforts, the authors too are left seemingly with little more except a timetable of events, listings of persons involved and impacted by the deaths of the agents, and the realization that we, too, now hear the laughing taunts from the past: "You may find out who killed them, but you'll never be able to prove it." Based upon the data found in the real world, the authors must conclude the following:

First, the National Prohibition Crusade was based upon a false narrative: At the beginning of his nationwide pro-prohibition "dry" crusades in the early 1920s, the Rev. Billy Sunday stirred audiences with his optimistic predictions. "The reign of tears is over. [...] The slums will soon be a memory. We will turn our prisons into factories and our jails into storehouses and corncribs. Men will walk upright now, women will smile and children will laugh. Hell will be forever for rent."

For years prior to the passage of the National Prohibition Act, principal domestic multinational corporations contributed funding to finance the prohibition movement: they were seeking a state of full-time labor without worker absences and labor strife due to alcohol abuse. This goal followed the same logic proffered by most Protestant and Evangelical churches that sought to support family values by ridding the country of "evil demon rum." And by achieving this, all would benefit: spouses would become better husbands or wives, parents would become models of family pride and morality, and workers would bring greater prosperity to themselves and their employers. These idealists believed victims, now freed from the debilitating effects of alcohol, would be able to rise to a higher moral plane and become more productive citizens.

On hindsight, all of these aims were idealistic and Utopian in concept whether they were presented in terms based on free market economics, social programming, or religious doctrine. In the end, the nation did not grow stronger economically; wives and husbands continued to have their differences; parents still fought to instill pride and moral behavior in their children; and the greater prosperity, once pronounced as the end resolve of this "noble experiment," failed. These "Utopian believers" were wrong, not in their professed moral sense but in the manner in which they sought to reform all men and all women through legislative action.

Second, the Kearney and Sutton murders were interconnected crimes: The Ray Sutton kidnapping/murder followed on the heels of the July 6, 1930, ambush-murder of Prohibition Agent Dale F. Kearney. A single Sicilian crime family, the Carlino Brothers, controlled southern Colorado's bootlegging enterprise at the time. They had been targeted by Kearney for several weeks and he had hurt them financially through a series of large bootleg seizures that totaled tens of thousands of dollars in lost revenues to the gang. Sutton had been working on the Kearney murder case in both southern Colorado and northeastern New Mexico as part of a bi-state federal task force at the time of his disappearance.

Sutton's primary investigative attention focused on the John Campanella cabal, those whom Sutton had targeted due to their direct connections with various Italian and Sicilian crime families throughout Colorado, New Mexico, and the country at large. Like Kearney, Sutton had severely hurt the local boots from a financial standpoint. One of his last acts involved the reactivation of a known and former corrupt prohibition agent operating within Campanella's operation. James Perry Caldwell, the informant, was the same man identified separately by the authors. The commonality of the Kearney-Sutton cases rests upon their bootlegging links.

Third, the absence of proof: Since agents completed their original 1930s investigations, additional discoveries have supported various conspiratorial hypotheses put forth over the decades. Some of this evidence explains "how" a prohibition network operated in southeastern Colorado and northeastern New Mexico but does not answer all five of the remaining "W" questions.

The authors conclude that no one was ever charged or brought to trial for the murder of Dale Kearney or Ray Sutton because no one could provide verifiable evidence and/or substantiated proof of guilt against any of the suspected parties. With the exception of Joe McAllister, no witnesses would cooperate with authorities until decades later when James Perry Caldwell's estranged wife recanted her support of his alibi. She, however, died before any action could be taken. Unknowingly at the time, when James Perry Caldwell presented his version of the events, he confirmed portions of the McAllister affidavit as to what had occurred in the kidnapping and murder of Agent Sutton. We don't know if McAllister remained a cooperative co-defendant over an extended period; he definitely would remain identified as a principal and co-conspirator in the plot to kidnap and murder. No definitive evidence was ever found to connect any of the accused or suspected subjects (Campanella, McAllister, Caldwell, Shedoudy, Pobar, among others) to Sutton's disappearance and murder with the exception of Caldwell's possession of Sutton's Masonic identification and ring, and Perry wasn't about to cooperate with authorities.

In a strange twist of fate, Caldwell, the "last man standing," broke the code of silence and told his version of the those dark days in 1930–1931. He knew his tale could never be used in court without hard evidence for collaboration; he and his confederates had escaped justice. The prophetic words uttered by the DiLisio brothers and James Perry Caldwell have echoed across the decades: "You may know who killed Sutton, but you'll never be able to prove it."

The authors believe circumstantial "proof" of guilt is found in the statements and actions of those who sought to thwart the Kearney-Sutton investigations, as well as those who supported the investigations. The absence of proof remains in spite of any individual or public opinions or desire to adjudge the guilt or innocence of those suspected in the deaths of Sutton and Kearney.

Fourth, Prosecution in the Sutton murder case was lost with Perry Caldwell's acquittal at his Pueblo trial: With respect to the Sutton murder case, the single major investigative and prosecutorial initiative that may have delivered the cooperation of James Perry Caldwell was lost as a result of the "not guilty" verdict in his check forgery case. Combined criminal forces had successfully prevailed in that matter through their practices of intimidation and bribery of witnesses and jurors. No efforts were noted in the data reviewed as to anyone being charged criminally in the matter once it had been determined that members of the Pueblo jury had been bribed. It must be assumed that this was another instance of "an absence of verifiable proof." The "code of silence," *omertà*, remained supreme in its culture of persuasion.

Fifth, the National Prohibition law enforcement effort was corrupt and ineffective: The Bureau of Prohibition would never rid itself of its political hacks and corrupt investigators in spite of the early efforts of the agency's principal reorganizer, Assistant Secretary of the Treasury Lincoln C. Andrews. His fact-gathering had disclosed that the Prohibition Unit had experienced a turnover of more than 10,000 employees during the first five years of the agency's existence. This statistically equates to five complete turnovers of national staff personnel annually assuming 2,000 people were needed for normal enforcement operations each year.

This organizational disaster can be blamed on the practice of political patronage, appointments of sycophants and ward heelers rather than a professional police service to conduct the nation's law enforcement business. General Andrews' reconstruction efforts helped to correct a vast array of issues, but not all problem employees were eliminated over the life of National Prohibition.

From an economic perspective, the human factors represented within local and state business and community power structures were more interested in the short-term balancing of their bottom lines. Any continued efforts to quietly ignore the law or encourage others to discontinue any efforts at resolving selective crimes in the interest of community did nothing more than establish a cohesive program of self-protection of the livelihoods of those having the same entrepreneurial financial interests.

Additionally, a lack of quality police candidate selection and proper training impacted the effective operation of national prohibition law enforcement. There were some exceptional personnel serving honorably, however. These men and women continued to influence the practice of the personal ethics of the few to overcome temptation, corruption and cultural biases of the many.

We sometimes forget that various locales within the Rocky Mountain region were not too far removed from the era of the "Wild West" wherein each town maintained its own unique culture of community infrastructures and belief systems. Examples of these would be the communities of Cimarron-Raton-Clayton, New Mexico, and Aguilar-Trinidad-Pueblo, Colorado. It would take decades for these and other communities to change or morph into some form of mutual accommodation to effect a law abiding populace. Some did not succeed completely.

Sixth, Agents Kearney and Sutton contributed to their own deaths: In the Kearney investigation, we discovered that the alleged instigators of his death, the Carlino Brothers, were themselves subsequently caught up in the ensuing gangland violence and were dethroned without ceremony. Like Sutton, Kearney had made a series of tactical mistakes. Where Sutton failed to follow his own rule of independently verifying his informant's information before taking action, Kearney preferred to practice his own form of "lone wolf" enforcement techniques to the point of placing his physical safety in constant jeopardy. Both agents were guilty of breaches of investigative common sense. One brief lapse of precaution cost each man his life.

Seventh, the Vivian-Carr feud hampered cohesive team work: The breakdown in communications within and between the Region 10 leadership caused great stress within the enforcement arm and prosecution arm of the Prohibition effort in the Rocky Mountain west. The issues arising from managerial, political, or personal agendas led to problematic situations that precluded any meaningful solutions. Administrator John F. Vivian did nothing without considering his personal political ideology and self-aggrandizement. His every action orchestrated his focus on his personal image. United States Attorney Ralph L. Carr failed to include Administrator Vivian in his circle of confidants by not informing him of the undercover agent (L.L. Baldesareli) within the Carlino crime family at the height of the Kearney investigation. For example, Carr's wait-and-see attitude concerning the forwarding of information about the major meeting of crime families in Wheat Ridge, Colorado, negatively impacted the entire investigation.

Carr knowingly interjected a new and unnecessary form of political corruption embodied in his intentional power play to embarrass Vivian before his own men. His apparent reluctance to provide his informant to the Kearney Task Force investigators for interview during the course of the investigation and thereafter could be considered an intentional slight verging on interference with a criminal investigation or worse, a mere directed comeuppance and display of investigative superiority. We don't know Carr's rationale as to why the data were not shared. Perhaps Carr believed that since the federal government had no investigative jurisdiction in the murder case, he was not obligated to provide Baldesareli to the Kearney team. Or he might have considered his undercover man to be much too valuable to his own independent investigation of Colorado organized crime to unmask him for a lost cause.

Eighth, Congress failed the American people: Let's not forget the Congress of the United States and their great circus act of creating political stalemates aimed at curtailing any meaningful changes that would impact sycophants and special interest groups. National lawmakers passed grandiose Utopian-themed morality legislation while working behind the scenes to thwart all attempts to apply real changes when and where they were most desperately needed. Change was slow. The greater part of the public became too busy trying to survive in a totally strange and changing world. Public apathy grew toward anything political and personal regarding man's morality and alcohol.

Historian Herbert Asbury, in his eulogy to the Prohibition Era, wrote:

> It must be remembered [...] that the fourteen years from 1920 to 1934 were not only the era of unparalleled crime and corruption; they were also the era of the Big Lie. The "drys" lied to make prohibition look good; the "wets" lied to make it look bad; the government officials lied to make themselves look good and to frighten Congress into giving them more money to spend; and the politicians lied through force of habit.[1]

With the end of National Prohibition, Congress faced new national priorities directed toward resolving the Great Depression's social and economic issues: runaway unemployment, mass population movements, environmental droughts, national infrastructure development, affordable healthcare, rise of labor unions, banking and Wall Street recovery, along with new social programs for the needy.

Ninth, National Prohibition gave rise to organized crime: Efforts to corral organized crime waned while small gangs of bank-robbers, kidnappers, and hired killers made news headlines. Occasionally the deaths of key Prohibition Era mobsters and old "cold murder cases" garnered some public attention. In hindsight, we observed, as have others, that the decades of the 1920s and 1930s were the beginnings of syndicated crime in the United States and its orchestrated growth internationally. Organized crime factions quietly expanded their geographic territories, focusing on their new footholds in racketeering, narcotics, prostitution, and gaming enterprises, and infiltrating legitimate businesses and the professions. It would be decades before congressional hearings forced the Federal Bureau of Investigation to focus on the problem. The FBI leadership had denied what "the man on the street" knew as fact: organized crime was alive and well-entrenched in all facets of American society.

Tenth, history is the final judge: As other investigators have discovered in similar unresolved cases, we are left with many more questions at the end of our inquiry than when we began. The closed Kearney-Sutton cases are approaching the century mark as we close our narrative. It would seem that in the eyes of humanity, two perfect murders were committed in 1930. Everyone originally connected with the investigations has died—the suspects, the prosecutors, the investigators, the family members, friends and other contemporaries. Once more it has been proven that all crimes of murder are not solved.

If Perry Caldwell was telling the truth regarding the whereabouts of Sutton's body, buried under the then-new highway construction between the ghost towns of Colfax and Hoxie Junction, then perhaps new light could shine on this story and give some final closure to these sad events.

The Kearney and Sutton stories may continue to stir the interests of others, and if they do, perhaps their stories will develop new lives of their own. Perhaps a new investigator can use our discoveries and locate new ones. The anticipation of new clues and truths is exciting. Until then an "absence of proof" doesn't matter to the victims, they already know the truth.

Chapter Notes

Chapter 1

1. The assassination of Kearney is reconstructed from information contained in field reports in Official Personnel File of Dale F. Kearney, Bureau of Prohibition (hereinafter OPF-Kearney).

2. Within hours of Kearney's murder, John Boccaccio, the mayor of Aguilar, was in his car headed to Old Mexico. He quickly became a person of interest with knowledge of the killers' identities, Affidavit of Prohibition Investigator Willard E. Lukens, 11 January 1932, Bureau of Prohibition Records, National Archives. (hereinafter BPR).

3. OPF-Kearney; "Dale Kearney Ambushed and Killed by Unknown Gunman," *Trinidad Chronicle-News*, July 8, 1930; "Prohibition Officer Shot Down," *Raton Evening Gazette*, July 8, 1930.

4. "Dale Kearney Preferred to be Lone Wolf," *Trinidad Chronicle-News*, July 8, 1930.

5. Official Personnel File of Zaccheus Raymond Sutton, Bureau of Prohibition (hereinafter OPF-Sutton); "Murder of Kearney Is Being Probed, *Raton Evening Gazette*, July 8, 1930; "Government Begins War on Rum Gangs," *Raton Evening Gazette*, July 10, 1930; "Kearney Murder Still Remains Deep Mystery," *Trinidad Chronicle-News*, July 12, 1930; "Drive Planned on Gangs by Government," *Walsenburg Globe Journal*, July 16, 1930; "Drive Planned on Gangs by Government," *Raton Evening Gazette*, July 16, 1930; "Three Held in Slaying of U.S. Agent," *Pueblo Daily Chieftain*, July 16, 1930; "Nine Held As Suspects in Kearney Case," *Raton Evening Gazette*, July 31, 1930; and "Officers Continue Round Up of Alleged Rum Ring," *Raton Evening Gazette*, August 2, 1930.

6. Interview Notes: Chuck Hornung with Fred Lambert, Ray Sutton Research File, Chuck and V.J. Hornung Western History Collection (hereinafter Hornung Collection).

7. The Seaberg Hotel was the largest such facility in the state. The Swedish born Hugo Seaberg immigrated to America in 1888 and worked as a cowboy before studying law. By 1893, he had married and became wealthy as a lawyer-real estate mogul. His daughter Agnes was a vocalist at the Metropolitan Opera House in New York City.

8. *Ray Sutton Research Notebook (Misc.)*, Hornung Collection.

9. Extrapolation of handwritten notations dated August 25, 1930, in Agent Sutton's *Work Journal* found in his room at the Seaberg Hotel in Raton, BPR.

10. "Four Arrested in Kearney Murder Case," *Raton Evening Gazette,* August 15, 1930.

11. See Stephan Talty, *The Black Hand: The Epic War Between a Brilliant Detective and the Deadliest Secret Society in American History*, New York: Houghton Mifflin Harcourt, 2017, for a detailed look inside this organization.

12. Robert J. Torrez, "La Mano Negro: A Personal Search for the Black Hand in Tierra Amarilla," *La Cronica de Nuevo México,* April 2006, Santa Fe: New Mexico Historical Society.

13. Interview Notes: Chuck Hornung with Robert J. Torrez, Hornung Collection.

14. Interview Notes: Chuck Hornung with Mary Lail, Hornung Collection.

15. Dewey Tidwell, "Dawson: A Personal Recollection," *New Mexico Magazine*, June 1981; F. Stanley, *The Dawson New Mexico Story*, Pantex, TX, 1961.

16. "Mounted Police at Dawson," *Santa Fe New Mexican*, Oct. 29, 1913; "Removal of Bodies of 120 Is Underway," *Albuquerque Morning Journal*, Feb. 9, 1923; F. Stanley, *The Dawson Tragedies*, Pep, TX: Print Shop, 1965.

17. Sheriff G. R. Fletcher File, Hornung Collection.

Chapter 2

1. Jack S. Blocker, Jr., *Retreat from Reform: The Prohibition Movement in the United States 1890–1913*, Westport, CN: Greenwood Press, 1976.

2. "Prohibition Came 50 Years Ago; 'Noble Experiment' That Failed," *Albuquerque Journal*, January 16, 1970.

3. See Herbert Asbury, *The Great Illusion: An Informal History of Prohibition*, Greenwood, NY: Praeger and Stanley Baron, *Brewed in America: The History of Beer and Ale in the United States*, Boston: Little, Brown for a detailed examination of this topic.

4. See William Hogeland, *The Whiskey Rebellion: George Washington, Alexander Hamilton, and the Frontier Rebels Who Challenged America's Newfound Sovereignty*. New York: Scribner, 2006.

5. "History of Alcohol Prohibition," *National Commission on Marihuana and Drug Abuse* (The Shafer Report), Washington, D.C.: Government Printing Office, 1973.

6. Calvin D. Linton, *The Bicentennial Almanac: 1776–1976: 200 Years of America*, Nashville: Thomas

Nelson, 1975; Arthur M. Schlesinger, Jr. (Gen. Ed.), *The Almanac of American History, Revised and Updated Edition,* New York: Barnes & Noble Books, 2004.

7. See Jeremy Agnew's *Alcohol and Opium in the Old West: Use, Abuse, and Influence, 1840–1900,* Jefferson, NC: McFarland and Kristofer Allerfeldt's *Organized Crime in the United States, 1865–1941,* Jefferson, NC: McFarland, for a deeper examination of this timeline and the events discussed.

8. "U. S. Marshal's Sale of Property Condemned, to be Sold for Violation of Internal Revenue Laws, *Santa Fe Weekly Gazette,* February 20, 1869.

9. David J. McCullough, "Bone Dry? Prohibition New Mexico Style 1918–1933." *New Mexico Historical Review,* January 1988.

10. Lt. John Collier, NMMP research file, Hornung Collection.

11. Jack S. Blocker, Jr., *Retreat from* Reform; Herbert Asbury, *The Great Illusion.*

12. *Instructions for Special Officers and Deputies Assisting in Suppressing the Liquor Traffic Among Indians and the Principal Federal and State Laws Relating to the Liquor Traffic Among Indians,* United States Indian Service, Department of the Interior, Washington, D.C.: Government Printing Office, 1915, Lambert Papers/Hornung Collection. The published record of New Mexico's territorial session laws for 1876, 1897, 1903 and 1907 make interesting comparative examination as to the changing degree of intolerance granted the sellers of illegal liquor to Indians living in the territory, Hornung Collection.

13. In 1916, a Constitutional amendment bill was introduced in Congress designed to require a national referendum authorizing any declaration of war by the federal government. The proposed amendment also required that any man voting yes on the war measure also had to volunteer for military service. The bill failed in committee as did a similar bill in 1936. An 1893 amendment bill to abolish the United States military also failed in committee.

14. See Herbert Molloy Mason, Jr.'s *The Great Pursuit, Pershing's Expedition to Destroy Pancho Villa,* New York: Smithmark Publishers, 1995, for an in-depth study of this military exercise that provided a training field for American troops later involved in the European campaign of the Great War. Chuck Hornung's father road with Pershing into Mexico in 1916 and then followed him to France a year later. They both came home safe in 1919.

15. Barbara Tuchman's *The Zimmermann Telegram,* New York: Random House, 1958, is the premier study on the subject, while Dean Smith's article "The Zimmermann Telegram, 1917," in *American History Illustrated,* June 1978, is a simple straight forward presentation on the ramifications of the message.

16. See Arthur G. Daniells, *The World War: Its Relation to the Eastern Question and Armageddon,* Nashville, Southern Publishing Association, 1917, and Albert Bushnell Hart (Ed), *America at War: A Handbook of Patriotic Education References,* New York: National Security League, 1917, for contemporary reaction in America concerning the declaration of war and the effort to fund, equip, recruit, train and mobilize an overseas army.

17. James L. Stokesbury, *A Short History of World War I,* New York: HarperCollins, 1981.

18. See Chuck Hornung's books *The Thin Gray Line: The New Mexico Mounted Police,* Fort Worth: Western Heritage Press, 1971, and *New Mexico's Rangers: The Mounted Police,* Charleston, SC: Arcadia Publishing, 2010, for more information about the New Mexico Mounted Police company of 1918–1921.

19. Patricia Cadigan Armstrong, *A Portrait of Bronson Cutting Through His Papers, 1920–1927,* Albuquerque: University of New Mexico Press, 1959.

20. Annual *Report of the Superintendent of the State Department of Safety (Colorado Rangers) to the Governor;* relative Colorado state laws, and other records of the force, Colorado Rangers file, Hornung Collection.

21. John Maurice Clark, *The Costs of the World War to the American People,* New York: Augustus M. Kelley, 1931; Hugh Rockoff, *Until It's Over, Over There: The U.S. Economy in World War I,* Working Paper 10580, June 2004, National Bureau of Economic Research, Cambridge, MA.

22. *Final Report on the Enforcement of the Prohibition Laws of the United States, National Commission on Law Enforcement Observance and Enforcement* (The Wickersham Commission Report on Alcohol Prohibition), Washington, D.C.: Government Printing Office, 1931. The final report of the Wickersham Commission's hearings is the foundation to any study concerning National Prohibition and the enforcement effort to comply with the Volstead Act of 1919. "Section One—History, Part 2—History of Prohibition Enforcement Before the Bureau of Prohibition Act of 1927," covers this subject. In his *Memoirs* President Hoover wrote, "This body (The Wickersham Commission) made an exhaustive investigation of every phase of the problem."

President Wilson masked his administration's progressive leap into controlling countless aspects of the American citizen's way of life behind his patriotic cry to save food for the war effort through regulating what Americans could eat and drink. Wilson redefined the Constitution's limited role of the federal government's authority to invade a citizen's right to life, liberty and the pursuit of happiness. The irony of President Wilson's "save the food" cry is that the message fell on deaf ears 20 years later. During World War II, another progressive president and Congress encouraged the accelerated production of tobacco, beer and spirits while draft boards granted exemptions to brewery workers and farmers considering their jobs as essential to the war effort.

23. *Final Report* (The Wickersham Commission), "Section One—History, Part 1—The Eighteenth Amendment and the National Prohibition Act" provides a timeline for these two subjects.

24. Arthur M. Schlesinger, Jr., *The Almanac of American History, Revised and Updated Edition.*

25. For more information about presidential pets consult Brooke Janis and Roy Rowan, *First Dog: American Presidents and Their Best Friends,* Chapel Hill, NC: Algonquin, 2009; Jennifer B. Pickens, *Pets at the White House: 50 Years of Presidents and Their Pets,* Ashland, OH: Fife and Drum Press, 2012 and Julia Moberg, *Presidential Pets: The Weird, Wacky, Little, Big, Scary, Strange Animals That Have Lived in the White House,* Watertown, MA: Charlesbridge, 2016.

26. Herbert Hoover, *The Memoirs of Herbert Hoover 1920–1933: The Cabinet & The Presidency,* New York: The Macmillan Company, 1952.

27. *Testimony of Gen. Lincoln C. Andrews, Assistant Secretary in Charge of Customs, Coast Guard, and Prohibition, The National Prohibition Law Hearings Before* the Subcommittee *of the Committee on the Judiciary, United States Senate, Sixty-Ninth Congress, April 5 to 24, 1926,* Washington, D.C.: Government Printing Office, 1926.

28. Laurence F. Schmeckebier, *The Bureau of Prohibition: Its History, Activities and Organization,* The Brookings Institution, Washington, D.C.: The Lord Baltimore Press, 1929.

29. See Betty Alt and Sandra K. Wells, *Mountain Mafia: Organized Crime in the Rockies*, Nashville: Cold Tree, 2008, and *Ban the Booze: Prohibition in the Rockies,* Indianapolis: Dog Ear Publishing, 2013, for a wide-ranging view of the conditions in the Rock Mountain region.

30. "Vivian To Head Enlarged 'Dry Law' District," *Colorado Transcript* (Golden), July 3, 1930.

31. Lee J. Alston, Wayne A. Grove and David C. Wheelock, *Why Do Banks Fail? Evidence from the 1920s,* New York: Academic Press, 1994; Lee K. Davison, and Carlos D. Ramirez, "Local Banking Panics of the 1920s: Identification and Determination," *Journal of Monetary Economics*, V 66, 2014.

32. The song lyrics and joke are in the childhood scrapbook of coauthor Hornung's mother, Hornung Collection.

33. In the spring of 2016, astronomers discovered a nearby star in our galaxy with seven Earth-size planets in her orbit. These new worlds are believed to be able to sustain human life. In 2017, astronomers located the orbit of a true ninth planet of our sun, but the heavenly body is still traveling on the other side of the galaxy and has yet to be spotted in orbit. The search continues.

Chapter 3

1. Asbury, *The Great Illusion.*
2. "Temperance & Prohibition-Medicinal Alcohol," Rex D. Davis Historical File, ATF Reference Library and Archive. Internet accessed 2001.
3. Herbert Hoover, *The Memoirs of Herbert Hoover 1920–1933*; *Final Report on the Enforcement of the Prohibition Laws of the United States* (The Wickersham Commission Report on Alcohol Prohibition), National Commission on Law Enforcement Observance and Enforcement, Government Printing Office: Washington, D.C., 1931. The final report of the Wickersham Commission's investigation is the basic foundation to any study concerning National Prohibition and the enforcement effort to comply with the Volstead Act of 1919.
4. "Temperance & Prohibition-Medicinal Alcohol."
5. *The New York World*, September 17, 1927.
6. *The National Prohibition Law Hearings Before the Subcommittee of the Committee on the Judiciary, United States Senate, Sixty-Ninth Congress, April 5 to 24, 1926*, Government Printing Office: Washington, D.C., 1926. This subcommittee report contains a vast store of data concerning early enforcement of the National Prohibition law.
7. *Final Report* (The Wickersham Commission).
8. *Testimony of Gen. Lincoln C. Andrews.*

9. Mabel Walker Willebrandt, *The Inside of Prohibition*, Indianapolis, IN: Bobbs Merrill, 1929.
10. *Final Report* (The Wickersham Commission).

Chapter 4

1. See J. Anne Funderburg's *Bootleggers and Bear Barons of the Prohibition Era,* Jefferson, NC: McFarland, 2014, for a discussion concerning how cross border bootleg smuggling routes operated during the Prohibition Era.
2. "Officers Get a Big Still N.W. of Town," *Union County Leader*, August 1, 1929.
3. "671 Criminal Cases Tried During 1929," *Raton Evening Gazette*, July 16, 1930.
4. Mario Machi; Allan May, and Charlie Molino, "Denver, Colorado Crime Families," Internet accessed 2002; Jonathon Eig, *Get Capone*, New York: Simon & Schuster, 2010.
5. "The Atlantic City Conference," Internet accessed 2017.
6. Mario Machi; Allan May, and Charlie Molino, "Denver, Colorado Crime Families."
7. Interview: Chuck Hornung with Ray Marty, Hornung Collection; Robert Alan Goldberg, *Hooded Empire: The Ku Klux Klan in Colorado,* Chicago: University of Illinois Press, 1981.

Chapter 5

1. 1900 United States Census, Bodie, Delama Township, Humboldt County, Iowa; 1900 United States Census, Longmont, Boulder County, Colorado.
2. OPF-Kearney.
3. OPF-Kearney; 1930 United States Census, Trinidad, Las Animas County, Colorado.
4. See Morris F. Taylor's *Trinidad, Colorado Territory*, Trinidad: Trinidad State Junior College, 1966, and Robert K. DeArment, *Bat Masterson, The Man and the Legend,* Norman: University of Oklahoma Press, 1979, for a detailed examination of this period in Trinidad's frontier history. In 1969, Trinidad's unique character would take a walk on the wild side when gender-reassignment medical specialists began preforming surgeries that made the city the "Sex Change Capital of the World."
5. *Highways to the Sky: A Context and History of Colorado's Highway System for the Colorado Department of Transportation,* Littleton, CO: Associated Cultural Resources Experts, 2002.
6. Interview: Chuck Hornung with Ray Marty and J. Riley Hughes, Hornung Collection.
7. Alt and Wells, *Mountain Mafia*.
8. "Woodcock Accepts Post as Prohibition Enforcement Chief," *Baltimore Sun*, June 24, 1930; "The Man Who Becomes the Nation's Day Chief," *Salisbury Times*, June 24, 1930; "Woodcock Chosen Dry Bureau's Head," *Washington Post*, June 24, 1930; "New Dry Chief Faces a Difficult Task, *New York Times*, June 29, 1930.
9. Charles A. Fecher (ed.), *The Diary of H. L. Mencken*, New York: Alfred A. Knopf, 1989; "Mr. Woodcock's Promotion," *Baltimore Sun*, June 25, 1930; "Woodcock Chosen Dry Bureau's Head," *Washington Post*, June 24, 1930; "New Prohibition Head

Big Small Town Man, *Washington Post,* June 29, 1930; "Colonel Woodcock, Our New Dry Czar," *Literary Digest,* July 12, 1930.

10. Alt and Wells, *Mountain Mafia.*

11. John F. Vivian is discussed in detail in a later chapter.

12. Amos W. W. Woodcock, "Our Plan to Enforce Prohibition," National Broadcasting System radio address transcript, August 30, 1930, and *The Value of Law Observance,* Department of Justice, Washington, D.C.: Government Printing Office, 1930, Reprint, Honolulu: University Press of Hawaii, 2003.

13. Amos W. W. Woodcock, "The First Year of the Bureau of Prohibition Under the Department of Justice," Columbia Broadcasting System radio address transcript, July 7, 1931.

14. *Final Report* (The Wickersham Commission); Laurence F. Schmeckebier, *The Bureau of Prohibition: Its History, Activities and Organization,* The Brookings Institution, Washington, D.C., Baltimore: The Lord Baltimore Press, 1929.

15. OPF-Kearney.

16. Amos W.W. Woodcock, "The Problem of Prohibition," *Current History,* April 1931; "Aid of Education Leaders Asked in Prohibition Study," *Washington Post,* May 11, 1931; John S. Gregory, "M. Woodcock Sees America," *Outlook and Independent,* July 22, 1931.

17. OPF-Kearney.

18. See Kenneth W. Lucas, Sr., *History of Prohibition Badges* for a detailed review and photographs of the identification cards and badges used by state and federal Prohibition enforcement officers from 1919 to 1935.

19. Kearney's normal work habits and his final days are reconstructed from notes in his log book and information Fran Kearney provided the investigation team, OPF-Kearney; local newspaper stories following his death.

Chapter 6

1. Interview: Lee Charlton with Raymond Ellsworth Sutton, Charlton Collection; 1870 United States Census, Plattsville, Taylor County, Iowa. OPF-Sutton.

2. "Caldwell Family" by the Caldwell (Colwell) Family Heritage. An Internet genealogy document with family stories, records, and photos. Internet site is no longer listed, accessed in 2001.

3. Interview: Lee Charlton with Raymond Ellsworth Sutton, Charlton Collection; "Old Soldier Gone," *Fargo Reporter,* March 12, 1909; Fairmont-Fargo Cemetery Records.

4. See George H. Shirk, *Oklahoma Place Names,* Norman: University of Oklahoma Press, 1965, for detailed information concerning location naming in the state.

5. Interview: Lee Charlton with Raymond Ellsworth Sutton, Charlton Collection; Ray Sutton documents and scrapbook, Ray Sutton Family Archives.

6. See Homer Croy, *Trigger Marshal: The Story of Chris Madsen,* and Glenn Shirley, *Temple Houston: Lawyer With A Gun* for excellent biographies of these Oklahoma pioneers and lawmen.

7. Bob Ernest, "Prohibition Enforcement in Oklahoma," *Oklahombres Journal,* Spring 1994.

8. *Ellis County Commissioner's Proceedings, Book 1,* Ellis County Courthouse, Arnett, Oklahoma, page 309 noting the bonding of Ray Sutton as sheriff on January 9, 1911.

9. Listing of successive reelections of Ray Sutton in 1912 and 1914 with a handwritten notation "resigned 6/7/15," Sutton Family Archives; "Good News," *Clayton News,* April 24, 1915; *Union County Deed Book X,* P. 200.

10. Interview: Lee Charlton and Raymond Ellsworth Sutton, Charlton Collection. The Oklahoma Territory had five homestead land rushes for White settlers. These were: 1. First Land Run into the Oklahoma Territory, April 22, 1889; 2. Opening of the Iowa, Sac-Fox, Pottawatomie, and Shawnee Joint Reservation, September 22, 1891; 3. Opening of the Cheyenne and Arapaho Indian Reservation, April 19, 1892; 4. Opening of the Cherokee Outlet lands, September 16, 1893; 5. Opening of the Kickapoo Indian Reservation, May 3. 1895. Trivia: Tonto, the Indian friend of the fictional western hero The Lone Ranger, was the son of a Pottawatomie clan chief.

11. F. Stanley, *The Des Moines NM Story,* Pep TX, 1963; LaMoine Langston, *A History of Masonry in New Mexico, 1877–1977,* Roswell, NM: Hall-Poorbagh, 1977.

12. Interview: Chuck Hornung with C. E. Black, Hornung Collection.

13. "The Ellis County (OK) Boys, 1915–1922," Hornung Collection; Pearce S. Groves, Becky J. Barnett and Sandra J. Hansen (Eds.), *New Mexico Newspapers,* Albuquerque: University of New Mexico Press, 1975.

14. *Ray Sutton Research Notebook (Misc.),* Hornung Collection.

15. *Clayton News* editorial, November 9, 1918.

16. *Ray Sutton Research Notebook (Misc.),* Hornung Collection, "Clayton Rotary Club An Association of Nick Names," *Clayton News,* November 16, 1918; *Union County Deed Book X,* P. 431.

17. Interview: Chuck Hornung with C. E. Black and *Ray Sutton Research Notebook (Misc.),* Hornung Collection.

18. Henry Chase, "Memorable Visitors: Classic White House Encounters," *American Visions,* February–March 1995; William Loren Katz, *Eyewitness: The Negro in American History,* New York: Pitman Publishing Corporation, 1967.

19. Interview: Chuck Hornung with C. E. Black and *Ray Sutton Research Notebook (Misc.),* Hornung Collection.

20. Clara Toombs Harvey, *Not So Wild, The Old West,* Union County, New Mexico, Denver: Golden Bell Press, 1961.

21. Interview: Lee Charlton with Raymond Ellsworth Sutton, Charlton Collection; Myrtle Greenfield, *A History of Public Health in New Mexico,* Albuquerque: University of New Mexico Press, 1962; David Dray, *Frontier Medicine from the Atlantic to the Pacific, 1492–1941,* New York: Knopf, 2009.

22. Interview: Lee Charlton with Raymond Ellsworth Sutton, Charlton Collection.

23. "Sheriff is Charged with Attempting to Influence Witness," *Clayton News,* October 16, 1920.; *Santa Fe New Mexican,* October 14, 1920.

24. "Officers—Farmers and Stockman Bank of Clayton, 1920–1922," Hornung Collection.
25. Interview: Lee Charlton with Raymond Ellsworth Sutton, Charlton Collection; Ray Sutton documents and scrapbook, Ray Sutton Family Archives.
26. Cecilia Tafoya Cleveland, *New Mexico Blue Book 1943–44*, Santa Fe: Santa Fe Press, 1944.
27. OPF-Sutton.
28. Ray Sutton documents and scrapbook, Ray Sutton Family Archives; OPF-Sutton.
29. Woodcock said in a memo to President Hoover's secretary Walter H. Newton on September 27, 1930 that he was willing to bend the Civil Service rules so he could retain "agents of long standing, who, for some technical reason" could not pass the new government examination, President Herbert C. Hoover Papers, NA; OPF-Sutton.
30. Ray Sutton's day journal is part of his murder case file.

Chapter 7

1. OPF-Kearney.
2. Official Personnel File-John F. Vivian.
3. OPF-Vivian.
4. "Prohibition Chief Has Fine Record, A. W. W. Woodcock." *Raton Evening Gazette*, July 8, 1930.
5. OPF-Vivian.
6. *Testimony of Gen. Lincoln C. Andrews*.
7. OPF-Kearney.
8. "Government Begins War On Rum Gangs," *Raton Evening Gazette*, July 10, 1930.
9. OPF-William E. Nance.
10. OPF- Kearney.
11. OPF-Sutton.
12. Torrez, "La Mano Negro"; "Denver, Colorado Crime Families."

Chapter 8

1. F. Dean Sneed, *Las Animas County Ghost Towns and Mining Camps*, Private Printing, 2000; 1900 and 1920 United States Census, Aguilar, Las Animas County, Colorado.
2. Chuck Hornung, *Blood on the Land: The Colfax County War Chronicles, Book 1*, Robert Lee, TX: AD.C. Publishing, 2007; F. Stanley, *Raton Chronicle*, Denver: World Press, 1948; Jay T. Conway, *A Brief Community History of Raton, New Mexico, 1880–1930, Commemorating Her Fiftieth Birthday*, Raton: Gazette Print, 1930.
   In 1948, Raton's Roman Catholic parishioners had as their shepherd a priest named Stanley Francis Louis Crocchiola, known by all as Father Stanley. He was also a member of the Raton Historical Society and chaired the project to compile a history of the community in anticipation of the Gate City's 70th anniversary in 1950. One of the men who provided information for the project was Joe DiLisio, the city's leading ethnic banker and booster of all things good for the community. Local artist Joe Apache created a cover for the small paperback history depicting a bespectacled field mouse, resplendent with top hat and cane, reading a massive volume bearing the title *Raton Chronicle*. Father Stanley used material collected by early Raton historians Jay T. Conway and Kenneth Fordyce to gain an understanding of the people that settled Colfax County. The Conway and Fordyce papers are in the Raton history collection of the Arthur H. Johnson Memorial Library, Raton.
3. Dewey Tidwell, "Dawson: A Personal Recollection," *New Mexico Magazine*, June 1981; F. Stanley, *The Dawson New Mexico Story*, Pantex, TX, 1961.
4. Same paper mining script from the Blossburg Mercantile Company store are in the Hornung Collection.
5. Crandall Shiflett, *Coal Town Life, Work, and Culture in Company Towns of Southern Appalachia, 1880–1960*, Knoxville: University of Tennessee Press, 1995.
6. Tom Sharpe, "Remembering the Dawson Mining Disaster, 100 Years Later," *Santa Fe New Mexican*, October 19, 2013.
7. Interviews: Chuck Hornung with John Southwell, Charles DiLisio and Joe Marchiondo, Hornung Collection.
8. Interviews: Chuck Hornung with George Stump and Joe Russo, Hornung Collection.
9. Interviews: Chuck Hornung with Father Stanley and Nancy Robertson, Hornung Collection.
10. F. Stanley, *The Gardiner, New Mexico Story*, Pep, TX, 1965; Interviews: Chuck Hornung with John Southwell and Charles DiLisio, Hornung Collection.
11. Boyle, Liz DiLisio, "About Christina Pone DiLisio: Faith, Family DiLisio's Mainstay." https://www.geni.com/people/Elizabeth-Liz-DiLisio-Boyle/6000000006964665200. Accessed: November 26, 2014.
12. This topic section is based upon information contained in *The Ludlow Massacre: The Official U.S. Government Report of the Colorado Miners' Strike of 1913–1914*, U.S. Commission on Industrial Relations, Washington, D.C.; Government Printing Office, 1913; Zeese Papanikolas and Wallace Stegner, *Buried Unsung: Louis Tikas and the Ludlow Massacre*, Lincoln: University of Nebraska Press, 1991; "Prelude to the Massacre," The *Colorado Coalfield War 1913–1914*. Accessed: November 22, 2014; Boyle, Liz DiLisio, "About Christina Pone DiLisio: Faith, Family DiLisio's Mainstay."
13. Interviews: Chuck Hornung with Father Stanley, John Southwell and Joe Marchiondo, Hornung Collection.
14. Interviews: Chuck Hornung with John Southwell, Charles DiLisio and Joe Marchiondo, Hornung Collection.
15. Boyle, Liz DiLisio, "About Christina Pone DiLisio: Faith, Family DiLisio's Mainstay."
16. Interviews: Chuck Hornung with John Southwell, Charles DiLisio and Joe Marchiondo, Hornung Collection.
17. Lee J. Alston, Wayne A. Grove and David C. Wheelock, *Why Do Banks Fail? Evidence from the 1920s*, Academic Press, 1994.
18. Lee K. Davidson, and Carlos D. Ramirez, "Local Banking Panics of the 1920s: Identification and Determination," *Journal of Monetary Economics*, Vol. 66, 2014.
19. "Report on Raton Meeting of Bankers of Group 2," *Union County Leader*, July 29,1929; "Nation's

Bankers See Return of Good Times—Positive Projection," *Raton Evening Gazette*, September 4, 1930.
20. Wheelock, David C., "Regulation, Market Structure and the Bank Failures of the Great Depression," *Review of the Federal Reserve Bank-St. Louis*, March/April 1995.
21. *Statues of New Mexico Annotated 1915; New Mexico Blue Book 1943–1944*.
22. *New Mexico Blue Book 1919*.
23. Woodlan P. Saunders, New Mexico State Bank Examiner, "Report of Examination International State Bank, September 15, 1942," Corporation Archives, New Mexico State Records Center and Archives, Santa Fe.
24. Chuck Hornung, *The Thin Gray Line* and *New Mexico's Rangers: The Mounted Police*.
25. OPF-Sutton.
26. David W. Maurer in his *Kentucky Moonshine*, Lexington: University Press of Kentucky, 1974, draws upon the in-depth knowledge of Quinn Pearl as he describes techniques of manufacturing illegal spirits (moonshine), marketing the product, and evading the "revenooers." See also David J. McCullough's "Bone Dry? Prohibition New Mexico Style 1918–1933," *New Mexico Historical Review*, January 1988 for another view point.
27. OPF-Richardson; W.E. Lukens Master Report to Deputy Administrator Richardson, April 11, 1932.
28. Interview: Chuck Hornung with Margaret Ward, Hornung Collection.
29. OPF-James Perry Caldwell.
30. Caldwell (Colwell) Family Heritage Document. An internet genealogy document appearing as "Caldwell Family" with documentation and photos. Website no longer active. Accessed: 2001.
31. Jim Berry Pearson, *The Maxwell Land Grant*, Norman: University of Oklahoma Press, 1961; William A. Keleher, *Maxwell Land Grant, A New Mexico Item*, Santa Fe : The Rydal Press,1942; F. Stanley, *The Grant That Maxwell Bought*, Denver: World Press, 1952.
32. Caldwell (Colwell) Family Heritage Document.
33. Hornung, *The Thin Gray Line* and *New Mexico's Rangers: The Mounted Police*.
34. Caldwell (Colwell) Family Heritage Document; OPF-Caldwell.
35. "Kearney Murder Still Remains Deep Mystery," *Trinidad Chronicle-News*, July 12, 1930.
36. "Drive Planned on Gangs by Government," *Raton Evening Gazette*, July 16, 1930; "Drive Planned on Gangs by Government," *Walsenburg Globe Journal*, July 16, 1930.
37. One of the sources Sutton depended upon to use his "mail box" was Fred Lambert of Cimarron.
38. Interview: Chuck Hornung with Fred Lambert, Hornung Collection.
39. Fred Lambert Papers, Cattle and Sheep Sanitary Board Records, Hornung Collection.
40. Interview: Chuck Hornung with Joe Russo, Hornung Collection.
41. Brownlow Wilson, "Bootlegging," *Reminiscences of a Nautical Rancher*, Exposition Press: New York, 1971.
42. OPF-Kearney.
43. "Nine Suspects Held As Suspects In Kearney Case," *Raton Evening Gazette*, July 31, 1930.
44. Affidavit: Joe McAllister, July 10, 1932, Hornung Collection.
45. Interview: Chuck Hornung with Karl Laumbach, Hornung Collection.

Chapter 9

1. Interview: Chuck Hornung with Fred Lambert; Fred Lambert's Mounted Police casebook, Hornung Collection.
2. "Officers Raid Famed Pueblo Club at Taos," *Raton Evening Gazette*, August 13, 1930.
3. Max Evans, *Long John Dunn of Taos*, Los Angeles: Westmoreland Press, 1959.
4. "Officers Continue Round Up of Alleged Rum Ring," *Raton Evening Gazette*, August 2, 1930.
5. "Dry Agents' Auto Will Be Marked," *Raton Evening Gazette*, August 21, 1930. It would seem that agents in New Mexico had been using roadblock signs since 1928. The *Alamogordo News*, December 12, 1928, credited local federal Prohibition officer Howard S. Beacham with developing a banner, rolled like a scroll, that quickly established an identification for the men operating a roadblock.
6. Kearney Task Force case reports; Agent Sutton's *Work Journal*, BPR.
7. "Four Arrested in Kearney Murder Case," *Raton Evening Gazette*, August 15, 1930.
8. Diron Ahquist, "Chris Madsen's 1941 Interview," *Oklahombres Journal*, Fall 2000.
9. Thompson, *Pioneer Living with Mema*; "Forger of Sutton's Name to Expense Check Being Held As Murder Suspect," *Clayton News*, September 25, 1930.
10. *Ray Sutton Research Notebook (Misc.)*, Hornung Collection.
11. Affidavit: Joe McAllister, July 10, 1932, Hornung Collection.
12. Interview: Chuck Hornung with Karl Laumbach, Hornung Collection; "Forger of Sutton's Name to Expense Check Being Held As Murder Suspect," *Clayton News*, September 25, 1930.

Chapter 10

1. *Ray Sutton Research Notebook (Misc.)*, Hornung Collection; "Nine Year Old Slaying of U.S. Officer Solved," unidentified newspaper clipping, Ray Sutton Family Archives, Charlton Collection.
2. F. Stanley, *The Koehler New Mexico Story*, Pep, TX, 1964.
3. In his situation report to John Vivian on September 9, 1930, Charles Stearns says he had evidence that Sutton was seen sitting in a car with an unknown man at 5:30 in the countryside near Dawson.
4. Interview: Dan Vukelich, *Dallas Morning News* reporter, with John Tittmann, October 1992, Sutton File.
5. George Pobar File, Hornung Collection; Harold Honeyfield, *Families of Colfax County, New Mexico 1880–2004*, Davis, CA: Honeyfield Publishing, 2005.
6. OPF-Sutton.
7. "Federal Dry Agent Missing," *New Mexico State Tribune*, September 5, 1930.
8. "No Word Yet Concerning Ray Sutton," *Raton Evening Gazette*, September 6, 1930.
9. "Reports Cease," *New Mexico State Tribune*, September 6, 1930.

10. Situation Report: Charles Stearns to John Vivian, September 9, 1930.
11. Agent Sutton's *Work Journal*, BPR.
12. "Federal Prohibition Officer Ray Sutton Feared Victim Of Foul Play: Last Seen August 28," *Raton Evening Gazette*, September 5, 1930; "Union County Posts $500 Reward For Discovery Of Ray Sutton Or His Auto," *Raton Evening Gazette*, September 9, 1930; "Search For Sutton Intensified," *Clayton News*, September 11, 1930.
13. "No Word Yet Concerning Ray Sutton," *Raton Evening Gazette*, September 6, 1930; "Two States Mobilize Sutton Posse," *New Mexico State Tribune*, September 6, 1930; "No Clues Discovered," *Raton Evening Gazette*, September 8, 1930.
14. "Search Area Swing Around Dawson Area," *New Mexico State Tribune*, September 9, 1930.
15. "Volunteers Wanted for Sutton Posse," *Raton Evening Gazette*, September 8, 1930.
16. OPF-Sutton.
17. "Think Officer Lured on by Rum Runners," *New Mexico State Tribune*, September 8, 1930.
18. "Officers Still in the Dark as to Whereabouts of Sutton," *Raton Evening Gazette*, September 16, 1930; "Hope For Sutton Given Up," *Union County Leader*, September 11, 1930; "Search for Sutton Given Up As Hopeless," *Clayton News*, September 18, 1930.

Chapter 11

1. OPF-Sutton.
2. "Arrest Made in Sutton Case," *Raton Evening Gazette*, September 19, 1930; OPF-Sutton; Interview: Lee Charlton and Raymond Ellsworth Sutton, Charlton Collection.
3. "No Trace Of Ray Sutton Found Yet," *Raton Evening Gazette*, September 12, 1930.
4. *Bulletin*, Methodist Episcopal Church South, Clayton, NM, Hornung Collection.
5. OPF-Sutton.
6. "Sutton Case at Standstill During Day-Officers Question Caldwell but Decline to Give Results," *Raton Evening Gazette*, September 20, 1930; "Caldwell Will Be Arraigned Today," *Raton Evening Gazette*, September 22, 1930; "$15,000 Bond Is Demanded for Caldwell," *Raton Evening Gazette*, September 26, 1930; "Flash News!," *Raton Evening Gazette*, September 26, 1930; "Perry Caldwell Hearing to Be Held Thursday," *Raton Evening Gazette*, October 1, 1930; "Perry Caldwell Bound Over to U.S. Court," *Raton Evening Gazette*, October 3, 1930.
7. "Dry Agent's Car Found Hidden in Arroyo Near Raton Saturday," *Raton Evening Gazette*, October 23, 1930; "Searchers Passed Within 200 Yards of Sutton's Car," *Raton Evening Gazette*, October 22, 1930; "Sutton's Automobile Found Saturday," *The Roy Record*, October 25, 1930; "Nothing New in the Sutton Case," *The Roy Record*, October 25, 1930.
8. "Second Arrest in Sutton Case Made in Denver," *Raton Evening Gazette*, October 30, 1930.
9. "Secrecy Veils Investigation on Sutton Case," *Raton Evening Gazette*, November 20, 1930.
10. OPF-Vivian.
11. Letter: H. G. McFadden, Kansas City Life Insurance Co. to Judge Henry A. Kiker, October 22, 1930, Henry A. Kiker Papers, New Mexico State Records Center and Archives, Santa Fe; OPF-Sutton.
12. Case: "Ray Sutton v. Harry Lammon," Union County District Court, No. 3010, 1918, Henry A. Kiker Papers.
13. Ray Sutton Project File, Hornung Collection.
14. OPF-Kearney; OPF-Richardson; "Victim Says He Was Tied and Beaten," *Denver Post*, November 26, 1931.
15. "Perry Caldwell is Charged with Forgery in Sutton Case," *Raton Evening Gazette*, December 11, 1930.
16. Interview: Chuck Hornung with Virginia Stringfellow, Hornung Collection.
17. Hoover, *The Memoirs of Herbert Hoover 1920–1933*.
18. *Final Report (The Wickersham Commission)*.
19. "Pleas In The District Court of the United States for the District of Colorado Sitting at Pueblo," Defendant: James Perry Caldwell, Indictment and Jury members, January 15, 1931. https://www.atf.gov/content/about/our-history/fallen-agents/ray-sutton. Accessed: May 2015.
20. "U.S. Jury Acquits Perry Caldwell Forgery Charges," *Raton Evening Gazette*, January 22, 1931.
21. B. Lee Charlton Prohibition Archives Collection: Newspaper Articles and Publications.
22. Stubblefield's current-powered voice transmitter/receiver used airwaves, not copper wire, as a carrier system he called "Wireless Telephone." This system should not be confused with wireless telegraph of electric dot and dashes. The Stubblefield system worked with airplanes in flight, ships at sea, station to station telephones, and moving "horseless carriages." He used these same wireless transmission principles to develop a wide area voice messaging/entertainment broadcast system he called "Raddio." Nathan Bowman Stubblefield was granted United States and British Empire patents for his invention in 1907.
23. The Federal Communications Act of 1934 made it illegal for a private citizen to intercept another person's wire or wireless communications and divulge its contents. The Supreme Court revised this ruling in 1967 saying a person had the expected right of privacy and the police needed probable cause and a search warrant to execute a legal "tap" on a person's private conversations. The court ruling was incorporated into the Omnibus Crime Control and Safe Streets Act of 1968. The Wiretap Act of 1986 added private e-mail to the list of legal area for warrant approved searches.
24. Walter F. Murphy, *Wiretapping on Trial: A Case Study in the Judicial Process*, New York: Random House, 1965. J. Edgar Hoover, director of the Bureau of Investigation, forbid his men to use wiretapping as a surveillance tool in 1930 because he felt it was "unethical."
25. Interviews: Chuck Hornung with Howard Bryan, Hornung Collection; Situation Report: Charles Stearns to John Vivian, September 9, 1930.
26. Alt and Wells, *Mountain Mafia*; "Police Armed with Machine Guns Raid Bootleg Convention and Arrest 29 Men," *Denver Post*, January 25, 1931.
27. Dick Kreck, *Smaldone: The Untold Story of an American Crime Family*, Fulcrum: Golden, CO. 2009.
28. "Seek to Export 29 Bootleggers Held by Denver," *Raton Evening Gazette*, January 29, 1931.

Chapter 12

1. "(Agent)Accused of Torturing Colorado Springs (Man)," *Denver Post*, November 26, 1931; "Victim Says He Was Tied and Beaten," *Denver Post*, November 26, 1931; OPF—Lukens; OPF- Dierks.
2. OPF-Henry Dierks; OPF-Richardson; OPF-Lukens.
3. Incomplete newspaper excerpts regarding an internal investigation in connection with an alleged mistreatment of Jack Dionisio by W. E. Lukens and three others in OPF-Lukens; Affidavit of Jack Dionisio, marked: Exhibit A. Note: The document is unsigned, undated, not witnessed or signed by person receiving the statement, transcribing or originating the document, OPF-Lukens.
4. Personnel Investigation Cover Sheet, District 9, Case No. 760 re: Prohibition Agent Henry Dierks; Special Agent Albro O. Knowlton; Prohibition Investigator W. E. Lukens; and Special Agent William E. Nance, OPF-Lukens.
5. Perry A. Shirley, Special Inspector, *Summary Report to Director of Prohibition, Subject: W. E. Nance, Special Agent, Kansas City Division, Re: Mistreatment of Prisoner, February 3, 1932*; "Victim Says He Was Tied and Beaten," *Denver Post*, November 26, 1931; OPF-Lukens.
6. Ralph N. Moyer, Special Inspector, *Summary Report to Director of Prohibition, Re: Investigation of Charges That Special Agent W. E. Nance Mistreated a Prisoner*, August 29, 1932.
7. Sam H. Scott, Special Inspector, *Summary Investigation Report to Director of Prohibition, re: Inquiry Made at Direction of Chief, Special Inspection Division, Alleged Inhumane Treatment Accorded Jack Dionisio at Colorado Springs, CO*, October 24, 1932; OPF-Lukens.
8. Howard T. Jones, Acting Director of Prohibition, Letter to W. E. Lukens, December 9, 1932, OPF-Lukens.
9. Adam Schrager, *The Principled Politician: The Ralph Carr Story*, Golden, CO: Fulcrum Publishing, 2007.
10. Colorado v. Symes, Judge of the District Court of the United States for the District of Colorado, No. 19, Original. 286 U.S. 510 (1932). Rule to show cause issued March 21, 1932. Return to rule submitted April 11, 1932. Decided May 31, 1932.

Chapter 13

1. "Federal Prohibition Officers Raid 12 Raton Joints Saturday," *Raton Evening Gazette*, February 16, 1931.
2. Alt and Wells, *Mountain Mafia*; "Attempt to Murder Pete Carlino Fails," *Pueblo Chieftain*, February 19, 1931.
3. Kreck, *Smaldone*; *Gang Murders List*; "Ignacio Vaccaro, disappeared (presumed dead)," *Raton Evening Gazette*, February 15, 1931.
4. Alt and Wells, *Mountain Mafia*; "Carlino Faction May Have Set Off Blast, Police Say," *Denver Post*, March 18, 1931.
5. Alt and Wells, *Mountain Mafia*; "Police Jail Brother of Pete Carlino and seize Gang Weapons," *Denver Post*, March 21, 1931.
6. Alt and Wells, *Mountain Mafia*; "Federal Undercover Agent Shot by Denver Gangsters," *Denver Post*, April 11, 1931.
7. Alt and Wells, *Mountain Mafia*; "Sam Carlino Is Slain in Home," *Denver Post*, April 11, 1931.
8. "Denver Gang War Flaring Anew As Bootlegger Slain; Youth Identified as Gun Killer by Victims." *Denver Post*, May 9, 1931.
9. The information in this section was derived from statements made by Jessie Caldwell in 1962 during an interview with agents of the Federal Bureau of Investigation in Albuquerque, NM. At that time, she wished to redact her testimony given at her husband's January 1931 federal trial. She claimed that she had committed perjury.
10. B. Lee Charlton Research Notes 2000–2015, Interview: Lee Charlton with D. Ray Blakeley, Charlton Collection.
11. Caldwell (Colwell) Family Heritage.
12. Interview: Dan Vukelich, *Dallas Morning News* reporter, with John Tittmann, October 1992, Sutton File.

Chapter 14

1. "Hope for Sutton Given Up," *Union County Leader*, September 11, 1930; "Search for Sutton Given Up As Hopeless." *Clayton News*, September 18, 1930.
2. Alt, and Wells, *Mountain Mafia*.
3. "Sheriff Davis Charged with Assault As Result Old Fuss," *Raton Daily Range*, May 5, 1931.
4. "(Sheriff Al Davis) Trial Opens This Morning," *Raton Daily Range*, May 22, 1931.
5. Chuck Hornung, "Wyatt Earp's New Mexico Adventures," *Old West*, Summer 1999.
6. "Koehler Lake Drained; Sutton Not Found." *The Roy Record*, May 29, 1931.
7. "Mystery Body Found in Rock Grave off Pass Is R. J. Holden," *The Roy Record*, June 4, 1931; "Body Perhaps That of Missing Agent," *The Norwalk* (Connecticut) *Hour*, May 26, 1931.
8. Personnel Investigation Cover Sheet, District 9, Case No. 760 Re: Prohibition Agent Henry Dierks; Special Agent Albro O. Knowlton; Prohibition Investigator W. E. Lukens; and Special Agent William E. Nance, OPF-Lukens; OPF-Sutton.
9. "Reputed Big Liquor Dealer in the Toils (Pete Carlino)," *Helena* (MT) *Daily Independent*, June 19, 1931; "Noted Colorado Gangster Taken into Custody-Pete Carlino Wanted Since February," *Raton Daily Range*, June 19, 1931; "Many Months of Hard, Tedious Work Behind Gangster's Fall," *Raton Daily Range*, June 19, 1931.
10. Alt and Wells, *Mountain Mafia*; R. E. Lepley, "Carlino Freed on Bond Given by Joe Roma, His Former Enemy," *Denver Post*, June 19, 1931.
11. Alt and Wells, *Mountain Mafia*; "Pete Carlino is Found Murdered on Lonely Highway Near Pueblo," *Denver Post*, September 14, 1931; "Carlino's Body to be Sent to Denver. No Inquest Held," *Pueblo Chieftain*, September 15, 1931.
12. "Carlino Assassins Apparently Employed Poisonous Bullets," *Denver Post*, September 15, 1931.
13. "Agents Uncover $2,000 Hooch Plant, 2 Big Stills in Weekend Raid," *Union County Leader*, August 15, 1931.

14. "Sheriff's Force Take Two Stills, Union & Cimarron County OK Sheriff Stage a Big Raid," *Union County Leader*, August 27, 1931.
15. "Pueblo Bootleg Joints Raided," *Raton Daily Range*, August 27, 1931.
16. "One Year Ago Today Ray Sutton Disappeared from Raton and Whereabouts Is Still a Mystery," *Raton Daily Range*, August 28, 1931.
17. OPF of John F. Vivian.
18. OPF-Vivian; OPF-Dierks.
19. OPF-Dierks.
20. "Dry Agents Must Not Play Soldier," *Steamboat Pilot*, Steamboat Springs, CO, December 18, 1931.

Chapter 15

1. "Dry Agent Accused of $500 Theft," *Raton Daily Range*, July 16, 1931.
2. "Dry Agent Is Moved Over to Denver (C. U. Finley)," *Raton Daily Range*, January 7, 1932.
3. "Dry Agents Swoop Down on Trinidad," *Raton Daily Range*, January 19–20, 1932.
4. "500 Gallon Still Is Uncovered in Mora County," *Raton Daily Range*, January 22, 1932.
5. McAllister Affidavit copy, Hornung Collection. This copy is quoted here.
6. *Ray Sutton Research Notebook (Misc.)*, Hornung Collection.
7. Alt and Wells, *Mountain Mafia*; "Joe Roma Latest Victim of Colorado's Gang War," *Pueblo Chieftain*, February 19, 1933; "Frank Farley: 'Isolation of Roma House Prevents Anyone Seeing Arrival of His Slayers,'" *Denver Post*, February 19, 1933.
8. Kreck, *Smaldone*.
9. Alt and Wells, *Mountain Mafia*; Kreck, *Smaldone*.
10. Charles J. "Charlie" Blanda Biography. http://www.mafia.wiki/Charlie_Blanda. Accessed: November 16, 2017.
11. Kreck, *Smaldone*.
12. Schmeckebier, *The Bureau of Prohibition*.
13. "Prohibition Reorganization," *TIME Magazine*, August 3, 1925; Bureau of Prohibition Reorganization Act of 1927; Presidential Executive Order 6166, June 10, 1933.

Chapter 16

1. "Drain Lake in Search for Missing Agent," *Amarillo Daily News*, circa 1936; "Hidden Lake Searched by Officials for Verification of Agent's Death." *Associated Press*, Des Moines, NM. April 6, 1936.
2. Letter: Karl Laumbach to Chuck Hornung, 03 May 2005. Laumbach recalls his mother's recollections (92 years old in 2005) of her years in Springer and the Caldwell family, Hornung Collection.
3. Interviews: Chuck Hornung with J. B. McNeil, Ray Marty, Joe Marchiondo, Fred Lambert, and Joe Campanella, Hornung Collection.
4. Chuck Hornung, "The Mystery Death of Federal Prohibition Officer Ray Sutton," *Quarterly of the National Association and Center for Outlaw and Lawman History*, April 1991.

Chapter 17

1. Dale F. Kearney File, Hornung Collection,
2. John F. and John C. Vivian File, Hornung Collection.
3. Kreck, *Smaldone*.
4. Adam Schrager, *The Principled Politician: The Ralph Carr Story*, Golden, CO: Fulcrum Publishing, 2008.
5. "Rites For Mrs. Sutton Today," *Union County Leader*, September 29, 1955.
6. *Ray Sutton Research Notebook (Misc.)*, Hornung Collection.
7. Interview: Lee Charlton with Raymond Ellsworth Sutton and his wife, Charlton Collection.
8. Nancy Robertson (Ed), *Colfax County Roots: Cemetery and Probate Records*, Raton, NM: Friends of Raton Anthropology, 1980.
9. Chuck Hornung's youngest son was born in the hospital at Raton, New Mexico on the day "Mr. Raton" died. It was a cold rainy morning and it snowed that evening. The first installment of Hornung's three-part examination of Ray Sutton's disappearance was published on October 10, 1971, five months before Joseph DiLisio, Sr.'s death.
10. Robertson, *Colfax County Roots*.
11. Perry Caldwell obituary, Fairview Cemetery records.
12. Jessie Caldwell obituary, Sunset Memorial Cemetery records.
13. Robertson, *Colfax County Roots*; Interview: Chuck Hornung with Victor Grant, Hornung Collection.
14. Charles Stearns obituary, Fairmont Cemetery records; Interview: Chuck Hornung with Howard Bryan, Hornung Collection.

Conclusion

1. Herbert Asbury, *The Great Illusion: An Informal History of Prohibition*, Praeger Publishing: Greenwood, NY, 1968.

Bibliography

Primary Sources

Boyle, Liz DiLisio. "About Christina Pone Dilisio: Faith, Family Diliso's Mainstay." From *The Raton Range* [Family Genealogy.] http://www.geni.com/people/Elizabeth-Liz-DiLisio-Boyle/6000000006964665200. Accessed Nov 26, 2014.

Caldwell (Colwell) Family Heritage. A genealogy document with source data and family photos. Internet site is no longer active, accessed in 2001.

Cleveland, Cecilia Tafoya (Secretary of State). *New Mexico Blue Book 1943–1944*. Santa Fe: Santa Fe Press, 1944.

Daniells, Arthur G. *The World War: Its Relation to the Eastern Question and Armageddon*. Nashville, Southern Publishing Association, 1917.

Davis, Stephen B., Jr., and Merritt C. Mechem (compilers and annotators). *Statues of New Mexico Annotated 1915*. Denver: The W. H. Courtright Publishing Company, 1915.

"The Family of Tony Marchiondo." Research Document, Special Collections Library (genealogy and local history), Albuquerque, NM.

Fecher, Charles A. (Ed). *The Diary of H. L. Mencken*. New York: Alfred A. Knopf, 1989.

Final Report on the Enforcement of the Prohibition Laws of the United States. National Commission on Law Enforcement Observance and Enforcement (The Wickersham Commission Report on Alcohol Prohibition), Washington, D.C.: Government Printing Office, 1931.

Gregory, John S. "Mr. Woodcock Sees America." *Outlook and Independent*, July 22, 1931.

Hart, Albert Bushnell (Ed). *America at War: A Handbook of Patriotic Education References*. New York: National Security League, 1917.

Highways to the Sky: A Context and History of Colorado's Highway System for the Colorado Department of Transportation. Littleton, CO: Associated Cultural Resources Experts, 2002.

Hogg, J. "Interview with John Dunn, 1930." *El Crepusculo* section of *The Taos News* as quoted in Max Evans, *Long John Dunn of Taos*. Santa Fe, New Mexico: Clear Light Pub,1993.

The Ludlow Massacre: The Official U.S. Government Report on the Colorado Miner's Strike of 1913–1914, U.S. Commission on Industrial Relations. Washington, D.C.: Government Printing Office, 1915.

Lucero, Antonino J. (Secretary of State). *New Mexico Blue Book 1919*. Santa Fe: Santa Fe Press, 1919.

The National Prohibition Law Hearings Before the Subcommittee of the Committee on the Judiciary, United States Senate, Sixty-Ninth Congress, April 5 to 24, 1926. Washington, D.C.: Government Printing Office, 1926.

"Prohibition Reorganization." *TIME Magazine*, August 3, 1925.

Stathis, Stephen W. *Report for Congress: Federal Holidays, Evolution and Application, February 8, 1999*. Washington, D.C.: The Library of Congress, 1999.

Testimony of Gen. Lincoln C. Andrews, Assistant Secretary in Charge of Customs, Coast Guard, and Prohibition, the National Prohibition Law Hearings Before the Subcommittee of the Committee on the Judiciary, United States Senate, Sixty-Ninth Congress, April 5 to 24, 1926. Washington, D.C.: Government Printing Office, 1926.

Tidwell, Dewey. "Dawson: A Personal Recollection." *New Mexico Magazine*, June 1981.

Ward, Margaret. *Cimarron Saga*. Springer, NM: Springer Tribune Press, 1964.

———. *Cousins by the Dozens*. Springer, NM: Springer Tribune Press, 1965.

Wilson, Brownlow. *Reminiscences of a Nautical Rancher*. Exposition Press: New York, 1971.

Woodcock, Amos W. W. "The First Year of the Bureau of Prohibition Under the Department of Justice." Columbia Broadcasting System radio address transcript, July 7, 1931.

———. "Our Plan to Enforce Prohibition." National Broadcasting System radio address transcript, August 30, 1930.

———. "The Problem of Prohibition." *Current History*, April 1931.

———. *The Value of Law Observance*. Department of Justice, Washington, D.C.: Government Printing Office, 1930. Reprint, Honolulu: University Press of Hawaii, 2003.

Interviews Conducted by the Authors

B. Lee Charlton

Blakeley, D. Ray, director of research, Union County Historical Society, 2001–2005.

Darden, William H., former deputy district attorney, Colfax County, NM, 2004.

Fernandez, Leslie, deputy district attorney, Colfax County, NM, 2003.
Lemon, Herman, Ray Sutton's nephew, 2002.
Pappas, Mike, historian, Raton, NM, 2003.
Sutton, Raymond Ellsworth, Ray Sutton's grandson, Las Vegas, NV, 2001–2003.
Taylor, Sgt. Ron (NMSP), historian of New Mexico State Police, Las Cruces, NM, 2013–2015.
Weiland, Herman, Union County historian and researcher, 2002.
Wright, Lem L., Ray Sutton's nephew, 2002.

Chuck Hornung

Black, C. E., friend of Ray Sutton's children, Golden, CO, 1971.
Bryan, Howard, newspaperman-friend of Charles Stearns, Albuquerque, NM, 1968–2011.
Caldwell, James Perry, a suspect in the Sutton murder case, Albuquerque, NM, 1968.
DiLisio, Charles, banker-community leader, Raton, NM, 1970–1973.
Fornoff, Lois, childhood friend of Joe McAllister's kids in Raton, Albuquerque, NM, 1989–1991.
Grant, Victor, Colfax County historian-researcher, Cimarron, NM, 1967–1974.
Hughes, J. Riley, former sheriff of Union County, Clayton, NM, 1971.
Lail, Mary, wife of James T. Lail, foreman of the CS Ranch (1930), 1968–1971.
Lambert, Fred, veteran, lawman, historian, author, Cimarron, NM, 1967–1971.
Laumbach, Karl, family friend of Joe Gilstrap, Las Cruces, NM, 2005.
McNeil, J. B., former sheriff of Harding County, Roy, NM, 1971.
Marchiondo, Joe, son of Tony F. Marchiondo, Raton, NM, 1971.
Marty, Ray, former sheriff of Las Animas County, Trinidad, CO, 1971.
Money, Jim, friend of Ray Campanella's children, Cimarron, NM, 1967.
Robertson, Nancy, Colfax County historian, researcher, Raton, NM, 1968–1990.
Russo, Joe, old-time Cimarron businessman, Cimarron, NM, 1968–1972.
Southwell, John E., early Raton businessman and historian, Raton, NM, 1964–1971.
Stanley, F. (Stanley Francis Louis Crocchiola), priest, historian, Nazareth, TX, 1974–1978.
Stringfellow, Virginia, wife of District Attorney Fred Stringfellow, Raton, NM, 1971.
Stump, George, retired businessman, Cimarron, NM, 1968–1972.
Taylor, Sgt. Ron (NMSP), historian of New Mexico State Police, Las Cruces, NM, 2000–2015.
Torrez, Robert J., retired state historian and author, Farmington, NM, 2016.
Ward, Margaret, wife of Zenas P. Ward, road construction (1930), Cimarron, NM, 1964–1972.

Secondary Sources

Ade, George. *The Old-Time Saloon.* New York: Ray Long and Richard R. Smith, 1931.
Agnew, Jeremy. *Alcohol and Opium in the Old West: Use, Abuse, and Influence, 1840–1900.* Jefferson, NC: McFarland, 2014.
Ahquist, Diron. "Chris Madsen's 1941 Interview." *Oklahombres Journal,* Fall 2000.
Allerfeldt, Kristofer. *Organized Crime in the United States, 1865–1941.* Jefferson, NC: McFarland, 2018.
Alston, Lee J. Grove, and Wayne A. Wheelock. [qm]Why Do Banks Fail? Evidence from the 1920s." *Explorations in Economic History.* 31, no. 4 (1994): 409–431.
Alt, Betty and Sandra K. Wells. *Ban the Booze: Prohibition in the Rockies.* Indianapolis: Dog Ear Publishing, 2013.
_____. *Mountain Mafia: Organized Crime in the Rockies.* Nashville: Cold Tree, 2008.
Ames, Neil. "View from the Pass." *Raton Daily Range,* Raton, NM, June 17, 1975.
Armstrong, Patricia Cadigan. *A Portrait of Benson Cutting Through His Papers, 1910–1927.* Albuquerque: University of New Mexico Press, 1959.
Asbury, Herbert. *The Great Illusion: An Informal History of Prohibition.* Greenwood, NY: Praeger, 1968.
Baron, Stanley. *Brewed in America: The History of Beer and Ale in the United States.* Boston: Little, Brown, 1962.
Beck, Warren A., and Ynez D. Haase. *Historical Atlas of New Mexico.* Norman: University of Oklahoma Press, 1969.
Blocker, Jack S., Jr. *Retreat from Reform: The Prohibition Movement in the United States 1890–1913.* Westport, CN: Greenwood Press, 1976.
Branner, Anita. *The Wind That Swept Mexico.* Austin: University of Texas Press, 1971.
Chase, Henry. "Memorable Visitors: Classic White House Encounters." *American Visions,* February-March 1995.
Clark, John Maurice. *The Costs of the World War to the American People.* New York: Augustus M. Kelley, 1931.
Davison, Lee K., and Carlos D. Ramirez. "Local Banking Panics of the 1920s: Identification and Determination." *Journal of Monetary Economics,* V. 66, 2014.
DeArment, Robert K. *Bat Masterson, the Man and the Legend.* Norman: University of Oklahoma Press, 1979.
Deutsch, Sarah. *No Separate Refuge: Culture, Class, and Gender on an Anglo-Hispanic Frontier in the American Southwest 1880–1940.* New York: Oxford University Press, 1987.
Dray, David. *Frontier Medicine from the Atlantic to the Pacific, 1492–1941.* New York: Knopf, 2009.
Duis, Perry R. *The Saloon.* Urbana: University of Illinois Press, 1983.
Eig, Jonathon. *Get Capone.* New York: Simon & Schuster, 2010.
Ernest, Bob. "Prohibition Enforcement in Oklahoma." *Oklahombres Journal,* Spring 1994.
Evans, Max. *Long John Dunn of Taos.* Los Angeles: Westernlore Press, 1959.
Funderburg, J. Anne. *Bootleggers and Beer Barons of the Prohibition Era.* Jefferson, NC: McFarland, 2014.
Gentry, Curt. *J. Edgar Hoover: The Man and the Secrets.* New York: W.W. Norton & Company, 1991.
Goldberg, Robert Alan. *Hooded Empire: The Ku Klux Klan in Colorado.* Chicago: University of Illinois Press, 1981.

Grant, Blanch C. *When Old Trails Were News: The Story of Taos.* New York: The Press of the Pioneers, 1934.

Greenfield, Myrtle. *A History of Public Health in New Mexico.* Albuquerque: University of New Mexico Press, 1962.

Grove, Pearce S., Becky J. Barnett, and Sandra J. Hansen (Eds.). *New Mexico Newspapers.* Albuquerque: University of New Mexico Press, 1975.

Harvey, Clara Toombs. *Not So Wild, the Old West, Union County, New Mexico.* Denver: Golden Bell Press, 1961.

Haskins, Frederic J. "Prohibition," *The American Government Today.* Washington, D.C.: Self-published, 1911 (Revised 1923).

Hime, Robert V. *The American West: An Interpretive History—Second Edition.* Toronto: Little, Brown and Company, 1984.

"History of Alcohol Prohibition." *National Commission on Marihuana and Drug Abuse* (The Shafer Report). Washington, D.C.: Government Printing Office, 1973.

Hogeland, William. *The Whiskey Rebellion: George Washington, Alexander Hamilton, and the Frontier Rebels Who Challenged America's Newfound Sovereignty.* New York: Scribner's, 2006.

Honeyfield, Harold. *Families of Colfax County, New Mexico 1880–2004.* Davis, CA: Honeyfield Publishing, 2005.

Hoover, Herbert. *The Memoirs of Herbert Hoover, 1920–1933: The Cabinet & the Presidency.* New York: The Macmillan Company, 1952.

Hornung, Chuck. *Blood on the Land: The Colfax County War Chronicles.* Book 1. Robert Lee, TX: ADC Publishing, 2007.

_____. "Blood-Stained Sutton Auto Found Empty." *Raton Daily Range,* October 23, 1971.

_____. "Break Develops in Prohibition Officer's Case." *Raton Daily Range,* October 17, 1971.

_____. "The Death of Federal Prohibition Officer Ray Sutton." A presentation to the Historical Society of New Mexico, annual meeting, Clayton, 22 April 2005, unpublished.

_____. "The Mystery Death of Federal Prohibition Officer Ray Sutton," *Quarterly of the National Association and Center for Outlaw and Lawman History.* Vol. XV, April 1991.

_____. *New Mexico's Rangers: The Mounted Police.* Charleston, SC: Arcadia Publishing, 2010.

_____. "The Sutton Story: Some Afterthoughts." *Raton Daily Range,* November 4, 1971.

_____. *The Thin Gray Line: The New Mexico Mounted Police.* Fort Worth: Western Heritage Press, 1971.

_____. "Whatever Happened to Prohibition Officer Sutton? Disappeared Here" *Raton Daily Range,* October 10, 1971.

_____. "Wyatt Earp's New Mexico Adventures." *Old West,* Summer 1999.

Katz, William Loren. *Eyewitness: The Negro in American History.* New York: Pitman Publishing Corporation, 1967.

Kazin, Michael. *War Against War: The American Fight for Peace 1914–1918.* New York: Simon & Schuster, 2017.

Keleher, William A. *Maxwell Land Grant: A New Mexico Item.* Santa Fe : The Rydal Press, 1942.

Kessler, Ronald. *The Bureau: The Secret History of the FBI.* New York: St. Martin's, 2002.

Kreck, Dick. *SMALDONE: The Untold Story of an American Crime Family.* Golden, CO: Fulcrum, 2009.

Langston, LaMoine. *A History of Masonry in New Mexico, 1877–1977.* Roswell, NM: Hall-Poorbagh, 1977.

Linton, Calvin D. *The Bicentennial Almanac: 1776–1976: 200 Years of America.* Nashville: Thomas Nelson, 1975.

Lucas, Sr., Kenneth W. *History of Prohibition Badges.* Private: Private, 2015.

Luckingham, Bradford. *Epidemic in the Southwest 1918–1919.* El Paso: Texas Western Press, 1984.

McCullough, David J. "Bone Dry? Prohibition New Mexico Style 1918–1933." *New Mexico Historical Review,* January 1988.

McCutcheon, Marc. *The Writer's Guide to Everyday Life from Prohibition Through World War II.* Cincinnati, OH: Writer's Digest Books, 1995.

Mason, Jr., Herbert Molloy. *The Great Pursuit: Pershing's Expedition to Destroy Pancho Villa.* New York: Smithmark Publishers, 1995.

Maurer, David W., with the assistance of Quinn Pearl. *Kentucky Moonshine.* Lexington: University Press of Kentucky, 1974.

Metcalfe, Philip and Amy Ross. *Whispering Wires: The Tragic Tale of an American Bootlegger.* Portland, OR: Inkwater, 2007.

Murphy, Walter F. *Wiretapping on Trial: A Case Study in the Judicial Process.* New York: Random House, 1965.

Myers, Carol McClary. *Dawson: A Way of Life.* Private: Private, 1984.

Papanikolas, Zeese and Wallace Stegner. *Buried Unsung: Louis Tikas and the Ludlow Massacre.* Lincoln: University of Nebraska Press, 1991.

Pappas, Mike J. *Raton History Mystery and More.* Raton, NM: Coda Publications, 2003.

_____. "Foul Play Suspected in Sutton Case," *Raton Daily Range,* February 8, 1989.

_____. "Officer Vanishes in Prohibition Drama." *Raton Daily Range,* January 31, 1989.

_____. "Ray Sutton Case Remains Unsolved." *Raton Daily Range,* February 14, 1989.

Pearson, Jim Berry. *The Maxwell Land Grant.* Norman: University of Oklahoma Press, 1961.

Peck, Garrett. *Prohibition in Washington, D.C.: How Dry We Weren't.* Charleston: The History Press, 2011.

Popejoy, Tom L. "Analysis of the Causes of Bank Failures in New Mexico, 1920 to 1925." *The University of New Mexico Bulletin, October 1, 1931.* Albuquerque: University of New Mexico Press, 1931.

Rakocy, Bill. *Villa Raid, Columbus, New Mexico, March 9, 1916.* El Paso: Bravo Press, 1981.

Robertson, Nancy (Ed). *Colfax County Roots: Cemetery and Probate Records.* Raton, NM: Friends of Raton Anthropology, 1980.

Robinson, Margaret Blake. "The Saloon in an Illinois Coal-Mining Town." *Missionary Review,* Vol. 25, 1902.

Rockoff, Hugh. *Until It's Over, Over There: The U.S. Economy in World War I.* Working Paper 10580, June 2004, National Bureau of Economic Research, Cambridge, MA.

Schiflett, Crandall. *Coal Town Life, Work, and Culture in Company Towns of Southern Appalachia, 1880–1960.* Knoxville: University of Tennessee Press, 1995.

Schlesinger, Jr., Arthur M. (Gen Ed). *The Almanac of American History, Revised and Updated Edition.* New York: Barnes & Noble Books, 2004.

Schmeckebier, Laurence F. *The Bureau of Prohibition: Its History, Activities and Organization.* The Brookings Institution, Washington, D.C., Baltimore: The Lord Baltimore Press, 1929.

Schrager, Adam. *The Principled Politician: The Ralph Carr Story.* Golden, CO: Fulcrum Publishing, 2008.

Shirk, George H. *Oklahoma Place Names.* Norman: University of Oklahoma Press, 1965.

Smith, Dean. "The Zimmermann Telegram 1917." *American History Illustrated,* June 1978.

Smith, Toby. *Coal Town, the Life and Times of Dawson, New Mexico.* Santa Fe: Ancient City Press, 1993.

Sneed, F. Dean. *Las Animas County Ghost Towns and Mining Camps.* Private Printing, 2000.

Stanley, F. *The Clayton New Mexico Story.* White Deer, TX, 1960.

———. *The Dawson New Mexico Story.* Pantex, TX: 1961.

———. *The Dawson Tragedies.* Pep, TX: 1965.

———. *The Des Moines New Mexico Story.* Pep, TX, 1963.

———. *The Elizabethtown New Mexico Story.* Dumas, TX: 1961.

———. *The Gardiner New Mexico Story.* Pep, TX, 1965.

———. *The Grant That Maxwell Bought.* Denver: World Press, 1952.

———. *The Koehler New Mexico Story.* Pep, TX, 1964.

———. *One Half Mile from Heaven or the Cimarron Story.* Denver: World Press, 1949.

———. *Raton Chronicle.* Denver: World Press, 1948.

———. *The Springer New Mexico Story.* Pantex, TX: 1962.

Stokesbury, James L. *A Short History of World War I.* New York: HarperCollins, 1981.

Talbot, David. *Devil Dog: The Amazing True Story of the Man Who Saved America.* New York: Simon & Schuster, 2010.

Talty, Stephan. *The Black Hand: The Epic War Between a Brilliant Detective and the Deadliest Secret Society in American History.* New York: Houghton Mifflin Harcourt, 2017.

Taylor, Morris F. *Trinidad, Colorado Territory.* Trinidad: Trinidad State Junior College, 1966.

Thompson, Mrs. Harry (Goldieanne Guyer). *Pioneer Living with Mema.* Albuquerque: Publishers Press, 1971.

Thornton, Mark. "Alcohol Prohibition Was a Failure." *Policy Analysis,* No. 157, July 1991.

Time Capsule 1929: A History of the Year Condensed from the Pages of Time. Time Inc., New York, 1967.

Torrez, Robert J. "La Mano Negro: A Personal Search for the Black Hand in Tierra Amarilla." *La Cronica De Nuevo Mexico.* Santa Fe: New Mexico Historical Society, April 2006.

Townsend, David A. and Cliff McDonald. "Howard S. Beacham: Otero County's Eliot Ness." *Southern New Mexico Historical Review,* January 2000.

Tuchman, Barbara. *The Zimmermann Telegram.* New York: Random House, 1958.

Valentine, Douglas. *The Strength of the Wolf: The Secret History of America's War on Drugs.* New York: Verso/R.R. Donnelley & Sons, 2004.

Van Cise, Philip S., *Fighting the Underworld.* New York: Houghton Mifflin, 1936.

Vukelich, Dan. "Prohibition Agent's Disappearance Unsolved After 62 Years." *Dallas Morning News.* Dallas, TX, Oct 4, 1992, reprinted from the *Albuquerque Tribune.*

Waugh, Daniel. *Evans Rats: The Untold Story of the Prohibition Era Gang That Ruled St. Louis.* Nashville: Cumberland House, 2007.

West, Elliott. *The Saloon on the Rocky Mountain Mining Frontier.* Lincoln: University of Nebraska Press, 1979.

Wheelock, David C. "Regulation, Market Structure and the Bank Failures of the Great Depression." *Review of the Federal Reserve Bank-St. Louis,* March/April 1995.

Wither, George. *A Collection of Emblemes, Ancient and Moderne.* London: Private Printer, 1635.

Online Sources

Machi, Mario, Allan May and Charlie Molino. "Denver, Colorado (Crime Families)." http://glasgowcrew.tripod.com/bosslist.html. Site no longer available. Accessed: circa 2002.

Poholek, Catherine H. "Prohibition in the 1920s, Thirteen Years That Damaged America." wysisyg://bottom.138/http://www.geocities.com/athens/troy/4399/. Accessed: April 22, 2002.

"Temperance & Prohibition-Medicinal Alcohol." Rex D. Davis Historical File, ATF Reference Library and Archive. http://prohibition.history.ohio-state.edu/Medicinal_Alcohol.htm. Accessed: Dec 30, 2001.

"The World War Cycle." *The World War I / Prohibition Era in U.S. History (1910–1920).* wysiwyg://contnet.3/http??www.timepage.org/cyc/gen/ww1.html. Accessed: April 22, 2002.

Research Facilities

AMARILLO CATHOLIC DIOCESE MUSEUM AND ARCHIVES, AMARILLO, TX

F. Stanley (Stanley Francis Louis Crocchiola) Papers, research notebooks

ARTHUR H. JOHNSON MEMORIAL LIBRARY, RATON, NM

Jay T. Conway Papers
Kenneth Fordyce Papers (copy)
Raton Range (Evening Gazette) bound newspaper collection 1880–1980
Victor Grant Cimarron-Colfax County History Collection

Bibliography

CENTER FOR SOUTHWEST RESEARCH, UNIVERSITY OF NEW MEXICO, ALBUQUERQUE

New Mexico census data 1850–1940 (microfilm)
United States Marshal Records, New Mexico District, 1850–1950
W. A. Kelleher New Mexico Newspaper Collection (microfilm/bound)

COLFAX COUNTY, NM: COUNTY CLERK'S OFFICE, RATON

Colfax County Newspapers Collection (bound) 1869-present
Livestock Brand Book 1900–1930
Mortgage/Land Deed Records 1900–1930
Property Tax Records 1900–1930

NATIONAL ARCHIVES AND RECORDS CENTER, ST. LOUIS, MO

Bureau of the Census: Fourteenth Census of the United States, 1920, Clayton, Union County, New Mexico; Fifteenth Census of the United States, 1930, Clayton, Union County, New Mexico; Ray Sutton family.
National Commission on Law Enforcement Observance and Law Enforcement: *Final Report on the Enforcement of the Prohibition Laws of the United States* (The Wickersham Commission Report on Alcohol Prohibition). Government Printing Office: Washington, D.C., Jan 7, 1931.
World War I Selective Service System Draft Registration Cards. *1917–1918.*

NATIONAL PERSONNEL RECORDS CENTER, ST. LOUIS, MO

Official Personnel File (Bureau of Prohibition Agents and Officials): James Perry Caldwell, Dale F. Kearney, Zaccheus Raymond Sutton, John F. Vivian, Carl Jackson, Charles H. Stearns, John C. Richardson, Walter L. Hill, Clarence U. Finley, James Sidney Huddleston, Willard E. Lukens, William E. Nance, Henry Dierks and Isaac S. T. Gregg.

NEW MEXICO STATE RECORDS CENTER AND ARCHIVES, SANTA FE

Commission of Public Records: Henry A. Kiker Papers. "Ray Sutton V. Harry Lammon," District Court, Union County, Case No. 3010, 1918.
Corporation Archives : Saunders, Woodlan P., New Mexico State Bank Examiner. "Report of Examination International State Bank, September 15, 1942."
Newspaper Archives: Colfax and Union Counties newspaper archive microfiche, 1928–1932.
State Hospital Records: Information Document. "New Mexico State Hospital Records."

RIO GRANDE HISTORY HISTORICAL COLLECTION, NEW MEXICO STATE UNIVERSITY, LAS CRUCES

Frank Alpers Cimarron-Colfax County History Collection
Howard S. Beacham Scrapbook and Papers
New Mexico and Texas newspaper collection (microfilm)
Stock Growers' Association of New Mexico Records

SERRA RESEARCH CENTER, SAN DIEGO (CA) PUBLIC LIBRARY

Burran, James A. "Prohibition in New Mexico," *New Mexico Historical Review*, 48:2,1973.
Meyers, Lee. "An Experiment in Prohibition," *New Mexico Historical Review.*,40:4, 1965.

UNION COUNTY, NM: COUNTY CLERK'S OFFICE, CLAYTON

Mortgage/Land Deed Records
Property Tax Records
Union County Newspapers Collection (bound) 1893-present

Private Archives

B. LEE CHARLTON PROHIBITION ARCHIVES COLLECTION

Historical Newspaper Articles and Publications, author's internet/microfiche research
Ray Sutton Family Archives (copy)
Union County (NM) Historical Society communications with author

RAY SUTTON FAMILY ARCHIVES (RAYMOND ELLSWORTH SUTTON, LAS VEGAS, NV)

Marriage License of Ray Sutton and Maggie M. Walton before Magistrate Shannon McCray, Office of the County Judge, Woodward County, The Territory of Oklahoma, Aug 4, 1896.
Ray Sutton Family assorted historical documents and scrapbook clippings
Ray Sutton Family Photograph Collection
Zaccheus R. Sutton Homestead Claim, Filing No. 11032, Receipt No. 3519 for 158.56 Acres, August 6, 1906 at Woodward, OK and related documentation.

CHUCK AND V. J. HORNUNG WESTERN HISTORY COLLECTION

Brownlow Wilson autobiography (copy #162 of 200)
Cimarron-Colfax County History Collection (Old Timer interviews)
Colorado Rangers Collection
Fred Lambert Papers, Photographs and Archives
Joe McAllister Affidavit (copy)
New Mexico Blue Book 1919
New Mexico Blue Book 1943–1944
New Mexico Mounted Police Collection and Archives
New Mexico Statutes Annotated 1915
Ray Sutton Project File (research notes, documents and interview notes)
Ray Sutton's Union County Sheriff's Papers (copies)
W. L. Wright Affidavit (copy)

Newspapers and News Magazines

Colorado Newspapers
Daily Chieftain (Pueblo)
Denver Post
Colorado Transcript (Golden)
Longmont Daily Times-Ledger
Steamboat Pilot
Trinidad Chronicle-New
Walsenburg Globe Journal

New Mexico Newspapers
Albuquerque Evening Tribune
Albuquerque Morning Journal
Clayton News
Dawson News
Deming Graphic
Deming News
Des Moines Swastika
Gate City Sun (Raton)
Las Vegas Daily Optic
New Mexico State Tribune (Albuquerque)
Raton Daily Range
Raton Evening Gazette
Roy Record
Santa Fe New Mexican
Springer Tribune
Tucumcari American
Union County Leader (Clayton)

Oklahoma
Daily Oklahoman (Oklahoma City)
Fargo Reporter
Woodward Democrat
Woodward Dispatch
Woodward Jeffersonian
Woodward News
Woodward Star

Other Areas
Amarillo Daily News
Cedar Rapids Evening Gazette
Current History Magazine
Dallas Morning News
Decatur (IL) Evening Herald
Helena (MT) Daily Independent
Literary Digest Magazine
New York Times
Norwalk (CT) Hour
Outlook and Independent Magazine
Reno (NV) *Evening Gazette*
Salisbury (MD)*Times*
Washington Post

Index

Abernathy, B.F. 55
Abernathy, Mattie 55
Adams, Quincy 166
Agua Fria, NM 101, 103, 104, 106, 184
Alamosa, CO 93
Alamosa County, CO 71
Albuquerque, NM 55, 58, 68, 71, 94–95, 104, 111–115, 116–119, 121, 124–125, 134, 138–139, 141, 161–163, 178–179, 182, 188, 191–195, 202, 204–205, 213, 216, 220, 222–227
Alenci, Santos 102
Allied Powers 19–20
Alpine Rose Café, Aguilar, CO 7–8, 96–97
American Medical Association (AMA) 2
American Relief Administration (ARA) 25
Ammons, Elias M. 80
Andrews, Lincoln C. 27, 32–34, 64–65, 89, 209, 215, 217, 222
Anti-Saloon League (ASL) 17, 25, 63
Antonito, CO 95, 201
Apishapa River Valley, CO 73–74
Appalachian Mountains, CO 15, 217, 225
Arango Arambula, Jose Doroteo (alias Pancho Villa) 19–20, 214, 224
Arbiter, Petronius 178
Arcade Hotel, Aguilar, CO 7, 96–97
Arkansas 89, 183, 185, 195
Asbury, Herbert 211, 213–215, 221, 223
Atchison, Topeka, and Santa Fe Railroad 74, 89
Atlantic Monthly 6
Atlantic Ocean 20, 216, 223

Austria-Hungary Empire 19
Authors' Perspective 10, 13, 17, 28, 35, 38, 40, 64, 68, 71, 83, 87, 92, 98, 105, 109, 113, 127, 132–133, 135, 140, 145, 155, 157, 161, 164, 167–168, 170, 172, 176, 180–181, 183, 187, 190, 192–193, 209

Baca County, CO 43
Baldesareli, Lawrence L. "Baldy" 148, 153, 158–160, 169–170, 210
Bank of Des Moines, NM 54, 57, 134, 225
Barrick, H.W. 36–37
Bashoar, Dr. Ben 70
Beacham, Howard 59
Beaubien-Miranda (Maxwell) Mexican Land Grant 89, 140, 218, 224–225
Bernalillo County, NM 58, 116
Bilk, Lee H. "Shorty" 78–179
Black, C.E. 53–55, 216, 223
Black Hand Society (BHS) 10–11, 443, 49, 55, 72, 90, 102–103, 108, 119, 131, 151, 155, 169, 201, 213, 225
Black Lakes, NM 90
Blair, Henry 16
Blakeley, D. Ray 161, 220, 222
Blanchard, Catherine (also Katherine) 161
Blanda, Charlie (also Charley) 139, 186, 202, 221
Blossburg, NM 76, 78, 84–85, 217
Blue Bird Café, Aguilar, CO 97
Boccaccio, John 151
Boise City, OK 36
Bolton, Will E. "Billy" 52
Bonaparte, Charles 138
Bonney, S.A. 149, 151
Bootleggers 10, 29, 36, 38–41, 47, 65–66, 68, 70, 72, 74,

85, 88, 92, 95–96, 105, 141–143, 151, 155–156, 158, 160, 170, 181, 189–190, 198, 215, 219, 223
Borger, TX 100
Boston, MA 39, 56, 213, 223
Boulder County, CO 42, 215
Bowman, Mason T. 43, 219
Boyle, Liz DiLisio 217, 222
Bradbrick, Cecil 116
Brandis, Louis 140, 186
Brazil, IN 195
Brilliant, NM 76
Brookings Institute 26, 215
Brown, Evelyn 145, 147
Brown, Frances Elizabeth 10, 42, 49, 68, 71, 134, 200
Brown, John 50
Bureau of Alcohol Prohibition 23, 26, 32, 35, 43–44, 46, 48, 63, 109, 150, 187, 213–215, 222, 225, 226
Bureau of Alcohol, Tobacco, Tax, Explosives (BATFE) 23, 26, 43, 109, 215, 219, 225
Bureau of Investigation (BI) 13, 27, 131, 135, 172, 186, 219
Burne, E.L. (aliases E.L. Beirne and Harold G. Gibbs) 132–133
Butler, Civilian Deputy 36
Butler, Smedley D. 156

Cacio (Caccio), Russell 150
Caldwell, Agnes Jessica "Jessie" Blanchard 91, 126, 138, 160–162, 191–195, 204, 220–221
Caldwell, Berlin 91, 161, 191
Caldwell, Count 90
Caldwell, Dorothea 192
Caldwell, James M. 89
Caldwell, James Perry, Jr. 192
Caldwell, James Perry, Sr. 9–10, 50, 87–92, 106–107, 111, 115, 119, 122–128, 126–128,

132, 136, 138–141, 156, 160–163, 182, 191–196, 204, 208–209, 211, 219–221, 223, 226
Caldwell, Johnny 61, 191
Caldwell, Lee 91
Caldwell (née Brown), Martha Letitia 50
Caldwell, Matilda 91
Caldwell, Robert Carl 192
Caldwell, Walter 91
California 31, 39–40, 86, 91, 133, 155, 167
Campanella, Joe 197
Campanella, John 9–10, 13, 86–89, 92–96, 98, 100–101, 103–108, 119, 127, 140–141, 162, 165–166, 181–184, 188, 194, 197, 203, 208, 214, 216, 220–221, 223
Canon City, CO 97, 201
Capone, Alphonse "Scarface Al" 9, 36, 39, 215, 223
Caputa, Jim 97
Cardenas Hotel, Trinidad, CO 121
Carlino Brothers 9, 38–40, 43, 46, 70, 72, 88, 100, 102, 136, 139, 142–143, 145, 151, 153, 155–160, 165, 168–172, 180, 208, 210, 220
Carlino (née Riggio), Gennie 102
Carlino, Pete 39–40, 72, 102, 142, 151, 157–160, 165, 168–172, 220
Carlino, Sam 39–440, 43, 142, 151, 153, 157–160, 168–169, 171, 180, 208, 220
Carlisle, J.P. 167
Carlson, George Alfred 63
Carr, Ralph Lawrence 62–63, 65–67, 69, 71, 88, 95, 99, 100, 114, 117, 119, 122, 124–125, 127–128, 133, 135–136, 138, 141–142, 145–146, 148, 150, 153–155, 158–159, 168–170, 174, 201–202, 210, 220–221, 225
Carranza, Venustiano 20
Cassidy, Dan 116
Catskill, NM 78
Cattle King Hotel, Woodward, OK 52
Cedar County, IA 50, 203
Cha, John 151
Charles Springer Cattle Company (CS Ranch), Cimarron, NM 13, 128–129, 197, 204, 221–223
Charlton, B. Lee 153, 193–195, 199–200, 216–217, 219–222, 226

Chase, John 80, 216, 223
Chicago, IL 36, 39–40, 74, 146, 150, 153, 170, 186, 215, 223
Christo, Tony 97
Churchill, Sir Winston 183
Cimarron, NM 9, 11–12, 36, 54, 75, 85–86, 88, 92–95, 101, 108, 120, 122, 126–128, 140–141, 161–164, 167–168, 173, 182, 191, 193–197, 203–205, 210, 218, 222–223, 225–226
Civil Service Commission 27, 35, 46–47, 59, 134, 175, 217
Clark, Albert T. 142–143
Clark, Melvin K. 59
Clayton, NM 8, 36–37, 53–55, 57–58, 68, 71, 90, 102, 105, 110, 112–115, 117–120, 123, 128, 134, 163–164, 168, 172–173, 183, 196, 198, 202–204, 210, 216–220, 223–227
Clements, J.P. 130–131
Coal Creek Valley, NM 107
Colfax County, NM 8–13, 444, 75–76, 78, 84–86, 88–91, 93, 95, 100–101, 103–105, 107, 112–115, 118–119, 121, 124–27, 130–131, 134, 136, 139, 141, 156, 161–162, 164, 166–168, 178, 180, 184, 188, 190–191, 194–198, 204, 211, 217–218, 221–226
Colfax County (NM) Grand Jury 196
Colletti, Daniel 160
Colletti, James 160
Colletti, Joe 160
Collier, John 17, 214
Collier, Louise 17
Colorado 2, 6, 9–11, 22, 24, 28, 37–46, 53, 58, 62–69, 71–73, 75–76, 78–82, 86, 88–89, 91–95, 99, 101, 109–110, 114–116, 119, 121–122, 126–127, 135–136, 138–139, 141–153, 155–157, 160, 164–166, 168–169, 171, 173, 175–180, 186, 188, 190, 193, 197, 200–202, 208, 210, 214–215, 217, 219–223, 225–227
Colorado and Southern Railroad 53
Colorado Fuel & Iron Company (CF&I) 79–80
Colorado Highway Department 37, 443, 222
Colorado Mine Labor War 73, 79
Colorado Rangers 22, 214, 226
Colorado Springs County Jail 169

Colorado State Fair 173
Colorado State Penitentiary 201
Columbia Broadcasting System (CBS) 222
Columbus, NM 19–21, 224
Colwell (Caldwell) Family Heritage 218, 221–222
Commonwealth of Kentucky 24, 74, 140, 196, 218, 224
Commonwealth of Virginia 24
Conejos County, CO 95, 201
Constilla Creek, NM 90
Cornell, Dudley 132
Corrumpa Creek, NM 172–173
Costello, Frank 39
Cozzi, Charles 70
Cruz, Manuel 93
Cunico, Mike 100–101, 185
Curry County, NM 116
Cutting, Bronson 21, 214, 225

Dalitz, Morris Barney "Moe" 39
Dalton, Bill 51, 53
Danna Brothers 40, 70, 97, 102, 139
Davis, Al 10, 13, 103–105, 112–114, 116, 117, 122, 125, 129, 156, 164, 166–167, 215, 218, 220, 222–225
Davis, Elza 54, 57
Dawson, NM 9–13, 76–78, 84–85, 95, 101, 103–104, 106, 113–114, 117–119, 184, 213, 217, 219, 222, 224–225, 227
Deficiency Acts of 1929 and 1930 30–31
Delgado, Lorenzo 21
Dempsey, Jack 91
Denver Post 135, 144–145, 155, 158, 160, 169, 219–221, 227
Department of Justice (DOJ) 2, 227, 32, 34, 45–49, 66–67, 69, 136–137, 170, 172, 174, 176, 216, 222
Department of the Treasury 15–16, 23, 25–27, 32–34, 47–48, 59, 64, 89–90, 170, 186–187, 203, 209
Des Moines, NM 52–55, 189–190, 216, 221, 225, 227
Detroit, MI 39–40
Devil's Wash Basin, NM 189–190
Dew, Harold S. 59, 118
Dewey, Thomas 202
Dierks, Henry 70, 135, 144–147, 149–151, 154–155, 175, 220–221

Index

Dillon, Richard C. 163
DiLisio, Charles F. 198, 209, 223
DiLisio, Christina Pone 217
DiLisio, Giuseppe Tomas (aliases Joseph "Giuseppe" Thomas DiLisio, "Joe" DiLisio and "Mr. Raton") 78–80, 82–85, 204, 221
DiLisio, Joseph Thomas, Jr. 204, 209
Dionisio, Giachomo (aliases Jack Dionisio and Jack Dennis) 11, 49, 102–103, 135, 144–155, 169–170, 220
Dionisio, Robert J., Jr. 150
Dionisio, Robert V. 10, 149
Diulio, Martin 97
Dodds, I.T. 167, 172–173
Doolin, Bill 51, 53
Doran, Dr. James M. 32, 34
Dorsey, William D. 31
Dow, Neal 15
Dry Cimarron River, NM 168
Drys 17, 211
Duling, Elijah J. 8, 41, 68–71, 96–97
Dunn, "Long John" 100–101, 218, 222–223

Eagle Café, Aguilar, CO 7, 96–97
Eagle Nest Lake, NM 75
Earp, Virgil 167
Earp, Wyatt 5, 43, 74, 167, 220 224
Eighteenth Amendment 24–25, 33–34, 44, 187, 214
El Moro, CO 78
El Paso, TX 144, 147, 149, 151, 224
El Paso County, CO 144
Ellis County, OK 52–54, 216
Emerson, Ralph Waldo 1
Evening Herald 158, 227

Fairbanks, Douglas 163
Fairmont Cemetery, Denver, CO 202
Fairmont Cemetery, Fargo, OK 50, 216
Fairview Cemetery, Albuquerque, NM 221
Farmers and Stockmen Bank of Clayton, NM 57, 217
Farmington, NM 223
Farraro, Joe (alias Giuseppe Catalino) 136
Fawcett, Henry 7, 8, 96, 97
Federal Bureau of Investigation (FBI) 193, 211, 220
Federal Circuit Court—Clayton, NM 112

Federal Circuit Court—Pueblo, CO 43
Federal District Court—Santa Fe, NM 57
Federal Reserve Bank—St. Louis 218, 225
Ferraro, Joseph 160
Ferris, George 97
Fetrico (Petrico), John 97
Finley, Clarence Ulysses 59, 71, 95, 113–118, 122, 124–129, 133, 136, 141, 162, 164, 178–179, 188, 221, 226
First National Bank of Cimarron, NM 85
First National Bank of Raton, NM 85
Fletcher, George R. "Boots" 9, 13, 112, 116, 118, 126, 131, 134, 156, 213
Fornoff, Fred 18, 223
Fornoff, Lois 223
Franciscan Hotel, Albuquerque, NM 163
Frank, Glean 1
Franklin, Benjamin 73, 207
French, NM 82
Friedman, Milton 14

Garcia, V.A. 36
Gardiner, NM 76, 78, 82, 217, 225
Gardner, Theodore 78
Gillespie, Tom 167, 172, 183–184
Gilstrip, Joe 9, 106
Goddard, Roland C. 125, 127
Golden City Cemetery, Golden, CO 200–201
Golden, Jefferson County, CO 28, 63
Gonzales, Maria Cleofas 94
Gouthro, Marie 98
Grant, Henry 197
Great Depression 28, 34, 65, 162, 211, 218, 225
Greco, Nettie 164
Green Light Café, Aguilar, CO 8, 96–97
Gregg, Isaac S.T. 28, 125, 127, 174–175, 228
Guardomondo, Charles 171
Guy, NM 173

Hamilton, Alexander 15, 223, 224
Harding, Warren G. 25, 84
Harding County, NM 197, 223
Harp, Toke 95
Harper, Hugh D. 150
Harrison, Benjamin 50

Harrison Act 23
Hartzell, Mrs. 99
Harvey House (Fred Harvey Eating House) Trinidad, CO 67, 71, 110, 121–122, 126, 138–139
Haskell, Charles N. 53
Hasting Mine Explosion 74
Hatch, Carl 64
Hathcock, G.P. 183–185
Hay, George 166
Hayes, Rutherford B. 16
Haynes, Roy Asa 32, 34
Hicks, Henry A. 201–202
Hill, Walter L. 59, 113, 118, 119, 179–185, 188, 226
Historical Society of New Mexico 198, 217, 224–225
Hixenbaugh, Abe 166–167
Hobbs, NM 29
Hoboken, NJ 20
Holden, R.J. 168, 220
Holliday, John Henry "Doc" 43
Holmes, Sherlock 109
Home production 31, 65
Hoover, Abraham C. 93
Hoover, Herbert Clark 25, 30, 44, 50, 61, 66, 134, 137, 186, 214–215, 217, 219, 223, 224
Hoover, John Edgar 27, 64, 137, 219, 223
Hornung, Chuck 19, 21–22, 41, 45, 74–75, 94, 101, 109, 112, 141, 167, 174, 192, 194–199, 213, 214–221, 223–224, 226
House, Ely J., Jr. 189–190
Houston, Sam 51
Houston, Temple 51, 53
Huddleston, James Sidney "Sid" 113–115, 122, 124, 172, 179, 181, 226
Hudspeth, Andy H. 55
Hughes, J. Riley 13, 196, 215, 223
Hunter, Henry 138

Illinois 86
Independent bootleggers 39–40, 65, 87–88, 92, 97
Indian Territory (OK) 18–19, 50–52, 89–90, 93, 214, 216
Influenza pandemic of 1918 156
Internal Revenue Service (IRS) 16, 22–25, 27, 51, 186–188, 193, 214
International State Bank, Raton, NM 82, 218, 226
Ireland 19, 56
Italy 19, 78, 204

Index

Jackson, Carl 176, 179, 226
Jackson, Robert E. 144, 148, 150–152
Jacobs, Otto 93, 110–111
James, Jesse 34
Jansen, CO 180
Jefferson County, CO 28, 63, 215, 223
Jennings, Ed 52
Johnson, Edwin C. 201
Jones, Charles "Charlie" 96–97
Jones, Mrs. Charles 96–97
Jones, Howard T. 153–154, 220
Journal of Monetary Economics 83, 215, 217, 223
Journal of the National Outlaw-Lawman History Association 198
Juliano, Charles 69
Junk, Fred 116

Kansas City 147, 186, 220
Kansas City Life Insurance Company 134, 219
Kearney, Caroline 42
Kearney, Dale Francis 1–3, 6–10, 13–14, 25, 37–38, 42–45, 47–49, 62–71, 91–97, 99–103, 110–111, 113–115, 119, 133–135, 139, 141–141, 144, 146–155, 157, 162, 169–171, 174–175, 178–180, 182–183, 188, 200, 202, 207–211, 213, 215–221, 226
Kearney, Frances "Fran" Elizabeth Brown 10, 42, 48–49, 68, 71, 134, 200, 216
Kearney, Kathleen 42
Kearney Investigation Task Force 9–10, 30, 33, 62–63, 65–69, 71, 94, 96–97, 99–104, 110–111, 114–115, 122, 139, 142, 153, 157, 164–165, 179–180, 208, 210, 218
KGFL (KRTN AM/FM) Raton, NM 130, 163
Kiker, H.A. 134, 166, 219, 226
Kingman, AZ 203
Kiowa National Grasslands Reserves, NM 36–37
Knowlton, Albro O. 146–147, 150, 152, 70, 220
Koehler, NM 76, 78, 107, 117, 128, 165, 167, 185, 190, 218, 220, 225
Koehler Lake, NM 165, 167, 190, 220
Kramer, John F. 23, 30, 32
Ku Klux Klan (KKK) 10, 40–41, 197, 215, 223

Kübler-Ross, Elisabeth (Elizabeth) 121

Laddie Boy (dog) 28
Lail, James T. 128, 197, 223
Lail, Mary 197, 213, 223
Lambert, Fred 12, 93, 94–95, 100, 112, 167, 192, 194–197, 213–214, 218, 221, 223, 226
Lambert, Henry 167
Lambert, Katie 112
Lambert, Mary 167
Lansky, Meyer 39–40
Larrazolo, O.A. 21
Las Animas County, CO 6, 8, 40, 43–45, 66, 68, 70, 73, 91, 97, 127–128, 136, 157, 180, 188, 197, 215, 217, 223, 225
Las Vegas, NM 199, 223, 226
Latkins, D.W. 173
Lazeroff, Mike 8, 97
Leadville, CO 97
Ledoux, Julius 105–106
Ledoux, William 106
Leroy, Jean-Baptiste 207
Lile, James G. 7, 70
Lillie, Gordon "Pawnee Bill" 54, 163
Lindsey, William E. 21, 56
Literary Digest 28, 45, 216, 227
Live Stock Inspector 22, 52, 73, 82, 95, 226
Local Banking Panic of 1920s 84, 215, 217
Lodine, Julius 166–167
Longmont, CO 42, 200, 215, 227
Longmont Daily-Times Ledger 227
Lord Mansfield 144
Los Angeles, CA 186, 223
Lostrah, Allan 183
Louisiana 86
Lovato, Jose G. 35, 100
Love, John E. "Jack" 52
Luciano, Charles "Lucky" 39
Ludlow Massacre 22, 79, 81–82, 217, 222, 224
Lukens, Bob 42
Lukens, Willard E. 70–71, 88, 144–155, 165, 213, 218, 220, 226
Luna County, NM 91
Luna Theatre, Clayton, NM 203

Madison, WI 186
Madsen, Chris 52, 104, 216, 218, 223
Maine 15

Mantelli Brothers Gang 151
Marchiondo, Joe 82, 197, 217, 221, 223
Marchiondo, Tony F. 222, 223
Marijuana 35
Martin, Jim 184–185
Martinez, H.R. 167
Martinez, Malaquis 100
Marty, Ray 40–41, 197, 215, 221, 223
Masterson, James 43
Masterson, W.B. "Bat" 43, 215, 223
Matelko, John 97
Mauro, Bruno 136, 260
McAllister, Joe 98, 100, 101, 106, 119, 181–185, 194–196, 203–204, 208, 218, 221, 223, 226
McAllister Affidavit 182–185, 194–196, 198, 203–204, 218, 331, 226
McAlpin, Grace 9, 103, 134
McClenahan, E.H. 63
McCray, Shannon 52, 226
McDonald, William 168
McFadden, H.G. 134, 219
McGrath, Herbert 21
McGuffey's Reader 63
McIvar, Stephanie 91
McNeil, J.P. 197, 221, 223
Means, Rayma Jeanne 202–203
Means, Raymond George 52, 203
Means, Raymond Webster 203
Mellon, Andrew W. 33
Merino (Marino), James "Jimmy the Jew" 7–8, 96–97
Michigan 88, 200, 202
Mid-Continental Airlines 163
Miller, Daniel 17
Miranda vs. Arizona 144, 183
Mississippi 15, 24
Mississippi River 24
Mitchell, Barney 107, 109
Mitchell, William Dewitt 45, 63, 69, 114, 141
Moreno Valley, NM 95, 101, 103, 105, 107, 120, 181, 184
Morrow, Robert 127
Morton, Pauline Joy 34
Morton Salt Company 34
Mount Calvary Cemetery, Raton, NM 204
Mountain Home, AR 184–185
Mountain View Cemetery, Cimarron, NM 197, 203, 205
Mountain View Cemetery, Longmont, CO 42, 200

Mulhall, OK 51
Murray, KY 149

Nance, William E. "Bill" 46–47, 53, 68–71, 85, 88, 94–97, 102, 104, 113–115, 125, 127, 139, 141, 146–152, 154, 191, 198, 207, 217, 220, 226
Narcotics 211
Narcotics Division of the Internal Revenue Service 23
Nation Bank Holiday of 1933 84
National Agriculture Act of 1918 24
National Bank of New Mexico 85
National Broadcasting System (NBC) 216, 222
National Commission of Law Obedience and Enforcement 31, 33, 63, 137, 214–216, 219, 222, 226
National Flood Control Act of 1917 23
National Prohibition Act of 1919 10, 23, 25, 33, 87, 149, 176, 187, 207, 214
National Rifle Association (NRA) 75
Navajo Indian Reservation 28
Nazaro, Dominic 97
Neal, Robert L. 59
Neblett, Colin 57
Neff, Andy 167
Neff, Nona 167
New Mexico Cattle Sanitary Board 93
New Mexico Eighth Judicial District 100, 114, 125, 196
New Mexico Industrial School for Boys 109
New Mexico Mounted Police 21, 55, 86, 91, 100, 105, 192, 214, 224, 226
New Mexico Sheep Sanitary Board 93
New Mexico State Banking Department 84
New Mexico State Hospital 193, 204, 226
New Mexico State Records Center and Archives 85, 190, 218–219, 226
New York, NY 10, 32, 344, 3
Neumann, Ernest K. 9–40, 42, 44, 65, 82, 169, 186, 202, 213–216, 218–219, 222–225, 227
Niagara Falls Gazette 42
Nickoloff, Lewis 97
The Norwalk Hour 168, 220, 227

Official Personnel File 58, 67, 89, 103, 111, 130, 134, 170, 213, 215–223, 226
Ogle, W.G. 179
Oklahoma 36–37, 50–54, 58, 71, 89–90, 104, 173, 199, 215–216, 218, 223–227
Oldham, Luther 167, 172, 173
Oleta Township, OK 51
Olmstead vs United States 140
Optimo, NM 168
Organized Crime 14, 22, 39, 45, 62, 65, 67, 88, 99, 137, 139, 142, 145, 157, 201, 210–211, 215, 223
Original Package Act of 1890 16, 18
Ottoman Empire 19

Pacholl (Pacheel), Mike 98
Packard, David "Dave" 155
Packard, Sperry S. 145–146, 149, 153–155, 169
Penitentes (Brotherhood of Light) 156
Pericles 50
Pershing, John J. 20, 47, 214
Petrico (Fetrico), John 97
Petrolia, Joseph 160
Phelps-Dodge Corporation 76–77
Philmont Scout Ranch, Cimarron, NM 75
Phipps, Lawrence Cowle 62
Phoenix Mine, MI 200
Plains-Mountain Highway 43
Plattsville, Taylor County, Iowa 50, 216
Plum, Preston 16
Pluto 29
Pobar, George 101, 129, 191
Pobar, John George 107–110, 118, 197, 208, 218
Pobar, Joseph 109, 197
Pobar, Margaret 197, 218
Pone, Cristina 80, 217, 222
Pounds, J.L. 131
Pratt, John 17
Presidential Executive Order of 02 September 1917 23
Presidential Executive Order of 10 June 1933 186
Prohibition Reorganization Act of 1927 221
"prohis" 47
Pryor, J.L. 54
Pueblo Chieftain 171, 213, 220, 227
Pueblo, CO 43, 45, 46–49, 62, 68–69, 79–80, 93, 96–97, 100–101, 111, 136, 138–140, 14, 145, 147, 149–150, 152–153, 160, 165, 168, 171, 173, 175, 180, 183, 186, 193, 202, 209–210, 213, 218–221, 227
Pueblo Club 100–101, 218
Pueblo Olive Oil Company 39
Purcell, Thomas I. 147–149
Pure Food and Drug Act of 1906 118

Randolph, William 172
Raton, NM 8–13, 43–44, 54, 68, 74–76, 78, 82–85, 88–93, 98, 100–106, 108, 110–120, 122–124, 126–128, 130–134, 138–141, 143, 156–157, 163–168, 171, 173–174, 178–183, 185, 195–198, 204, 210, 213, 215, 217–227
Raton-Cimarron Road 9, 11–12, 554, 75, 85, 88, 92–93, 101, 108, 120, 122, 126–128, 140–141, 163–164, 167–168, 173, 182, 195–197, 204, 210, 212, 222–223, 225–226
Raton Coal & Coke Company 74, 78, 82
Raton Daily Range 163, 165–166, 171, 173, 179–181, 196–198, 220–221, 223–224
Raton Evening Gazette 10, 44, 84, 100, 116, 119–120, 123, 128, 132–133, 139, 143, 156, 213, 215, 217–220, 227
Raton (NM) Historical and Anthropology Society 217
Raton Pass 12, 43–44, 74, 89, 110, 116, 163
Rauzi, Modesto 83
Reed, Paul A. 31
Renkel, Ruth E. 177
Revenooers 30–31, 88, 184, 191
Rhode Island, RI 24
Richardson, John C. 9, 47, 62, 68, 96, 99, 102, 104, 113–115, 122, 125, 127, 139, 141, 218–220
Riggio, Joseph 102, 180
Riggio Carlino, Gennie 102
Rio Arriba County, NM 11, 21, 35
Rio Grande 11, 58, 165, 226
Roaring 20s 22, 74
Rockefeller, John D., Jr. 79, 81
Rocky Mountain Fuel & Iron Company 79
Rogers, Will 14
Roma, Giuseppe (alias Joseph [Joe] Roma) 40, 88, 142–143, 157–160, 164–166, 168–172, 185–186, 201, 204, 217, 220–221

Roosevelt, Eleanor 34
Roosevelt, Franklin Delano 26, 186, 202
Roosevelt, Theodore 18
Roosevelt County, NM 58
Roper, Daniel Calhoun 23
Roy, NM 223
Roy Record 119, 167–168, 219–220, 223, 227
Rudkus, Jurgis 18
Russia 18
Russo, Joe 93, 95, 217–218, 223

Saddle Rock Café, Aguilar, CO 49, 102–103, 144
St. James Hotel, Cimarron, NM 93–94, 167
St. Louis, MO 39, 84, 107, 170, 181, 186, 218, 225–226
Saint-Nazaire, FR 20
St. Vrain Creek, CO 42
San Bernardino, CA 40
San Miguel County, NM 17, 21, 58, 89, 178–179
Sangre de Cristo Mountain Range 69, 71, 76
Santa Fe New Mexican 21, 35, 77, 190, 213, 216–217, 227
Saunders, Woodlan P. 85, 218, 226
Scarino, Dan 49
Scarino, Joe 49
Schmeckebier, Laurence F. 26, 215–216, 221, 225
School for Handicapped and Retarded Children 192
Schrager, Adam 202, 220, 221, 225
Scott, Sam H. 153–154, 220
Seaberg Hotel, Raton, NM 9, 92–93, 103–104, 106, 110, 112–113, 116–117, 122, 124, 134, 213
Segura, Thomas 179
Sena, Apoliano A. 21
Shattuck, OK 52–53
Shedoudy, Elias Albert "Al" 101, 107, 181, 185, 208
Sherman, James R. 188
Shirley, P.A. 153, 220
Shoemaker, NM 181
Siegel, Benjamin "Bugsy" 39
Skelton, J.E. 55
Smaldone, Clyde 88, 169–170, 186, 201–202, 219–221, 224
Smaldone, Eugene "Checkers" 186
Smith, Melford G. 155, 175
Smith, M.F. 167
Smith, P.D. 70
Snyder, Bill 100

Sopris, CO 180
Spinelli, Jim 186
Springer, NM 82, 84–85, 88, 90–92, 109, 128, 140, 161, 168, 182, 185, 191, 194, 204, 221–222, 225, 227
Springer Tribune 140, 222, 225, 227
Starkville, CO 180
State Bank of Des Moines, NM 54, 82, 84–85, 134, 218, 226
Steamboat Pilot 176, 221, 227
Stearns, Charles H. 9, 59, 71, 94–95, 107, 111–119, 121–127, 130, 136, 141, 156, 162, 165, 170, 179, 182, 184, 188, 192, 205, 218–219, 221, 223, 226
Stearns, Mary 205
Stephens, Charlie 201–202
Stringfellow, Fred Conway 100, 114, 133–134, 136, 166, 180, 195–196, 223
Stringfellow, Virginia Mae Payne 196, 219, 223
Stubblefield, Nathan B. 140, 219
Stuttman, Miss 122–124
Sugarite, NM 76
Sunday, Rev. Billy 207
Sunset Memorial Park Cemetery, Albuquerque, NM 204, 221
Sutton, Hazel Ann 52, 54, 56–57, 123, 203
Sutton, Hiram 51
Sutton (née Walton), Maggie Mae 50–52, 57, 112–113, 123, 134, 199, 202–203, 226
Sutton, Nello Mae 51, 52, 54, 57, 115, 117, 123, 203
Sutton, Raymond Ellsworth "Bud" 51–52, 57, 116, 129, 131, 198–199, 216–217, 219, 221, 223, 226
Sutton, Raymond George "Bud" 57, 117, 123, 203
Sutton, Zaccheus Raymond "Ray" 1–3, 6–14, 38, 44, 50–60, 71, 92–96, 98–107, 109–136, 138–139, 141–142, 157, 161–168, 170, 172–174, 178–185, 187–199, 200, 202–204, 207–211, 213, 216–221, 223–224, 226
Symes, J. Foster 138–139, 220

Taft, Robert A. 202
Taft, William Howard 18, 63, 140
Tanner, A.W. "White" 36, 113, 116, 130

Taos, NM 21, 58, 68, 71, 84, 90, 95, 100–101, 163, 184–185, 196–197, 218, 222–224
Taylor, Frederick Winslow 33
Taylor, Ronald 189, 223
Thomas, George 173
Time 34, 221–222
Tittman, John 107, 109, 218, 220
Tondre, Joseph 163
Torrez, Robert J. 11, 213, 217, 223, 225
Trimble, W.H. 149
Trinidad, CO 6–11, 22, 39–41, 43–44, 46, 62, 66–68, 70–73, 78, 81, 91, 93, 95, 96–97, 101–102, 104–105, 110–111, 113, 115, 118, 121–122, 124, 126–128, 132, 135, 138–139, 144–145, 147, 149, 151–152, 155, 163, 170, 180, 210, 213, 216, 221, 223, 225, 227
Trinidad Chronicle-News 8, 62, 67, 91, 128, 213, 217–218, 225, 227
Trotter, William Monroe 56
Truder, T.V. 179
Tucumcari, NM 54, 76, 184, 227
Twenty-First Amendment 32, 34, 187

Ullo, Sam 10, 105, 180, 214
Union County, NM 38, 55–56, 84, 164, 167–168, 172–173, 215
Union County Leader 37, 119, 164, 167, 172–173, 215, 217, 219–221, 223, 227
Union County (NM) Historical Society 161, 217, 226
United Mine Workers of America (UMWA) 79–81
United States Bureau of Investigation 13, 27, 131, 135, 172, 186, 193, 211, 219–220
United States Coast Guard 26, 215, 222
United States Customs Service 26, 215, 222

Vacarelli (Vacarrelli, Vaccarelli), Daniel G. "Nitto" 150, 151, 153, 154, 170
Vaccaro, Ignacio 157, 220
Valdez, Alex 78
Valentino, Rudolph 39
Van Houton, NM 76, 78
Vandenberg, Arthur 202
Vandenberg, Oscar 44, 110, 202
Veterans Administration Hospital (Denver, CO) 203

Index

Victor-American Fuel Company (VAFC) 79, 223, 225
Vinci, James 150
Vivian, John Charles 63, 200–201, 221
Vivian, John F. 28, 46, 59, 62–69, 71, 95, 99, 113, 117, 121, 124, 128, 133, 141, 174–176, 178, 182, 200–201, 210, 217–219, 221, 226
Volstead, Andrew John 25–26, 30–31, 214–215
Volstead Act 25–26, 30–31, 214–215

Wagon Mound, NM 81
Walla Walla, WA 183
Walsenburg, CO 8, 22, 38, 68, 73–74, 81, 92, 213, 218, 227
Walton, Bertha A. 51
Walton, George, Jr. 52
Walton, George, Sr. 53
Ward, Margaret 88, 197, 223
Ward, Zenas P. 88, 197, 223
Washington, George 15, 213
Washington Post 44–45, 215–216, 227

Western Outlaw-Lawmen History Association 192
Wets 17, 211
Wheat Ridge Crime Conference 142–143, 210
Wheelock, David C. 84, 215, 217–218, 223, 225
Whiskey Act of March 1791 18
White Caps Hispanic Gang 72
Wickersham, George Woodward 31, 33, 63, 137, 145, 214–216, 219, 222, 226
Wight, Frederick D. 172–173
Willard, Jess 91
Willebrandt, Mabel Walker 34, 215
Williams, L.W. 69
Willkie, Wendell 202
Wilson, Woodrow 16, 19–20, 23–25, 55–56, 81, 95, 214, 218, 222, 226
Wisner, Gene 198
Women's Army Auxiliary Corps (WAAC) 203
Women's Christian Temperance Union (WCTU) 17
Woodcock, Amos Waller

Wright 44–47, 62–64, 67, 114, 140–141, 153, 174–176, 216–217, 222
Woodward, Hugh B. 100, 113, 118, 121, 124–125, 141
Woodward, OK 51, 226–227
Works, Charles E. 138
World War I 20–22, 25, 33, 42, 63, 104, 140, 201
Wraith, Robert 144, 149
Wright, "Cuppy" 101, 184
Wright, Jimmy 101, 184
Wright, William Leonard "Curley" 101, 105, 183–185, 194, 203, 204

Zamora, Rafael 128–129, 131, 197, 204–205
Zerobnick, Jacob 88, 165
Zimmerman, Arthur 20, 214, 225

www.ingramcontent.com/pod-product-compliance
Lightning Source LLC
Chambersburg PA
CBHW081551300426
44116CB00015B/2840